Words and Worlds

Words and Worlds

Modelling Verbal Descriptions of Situations

Lieven Verschaffel
University of Leuven

Brian Greer
Portland State University

Wim Van Dooren
University of Leuven

Swapna Mukhopadhyay
Portland State University

SENSE PUBLISHERS
ROTTERDAM/BOSTON/TAIPEI

A C.I.P. record for this book is available from the Library of Congress.

ISBN 978-90-8790-936-9 (paperback)
ISBN 978-90-8790-937-6 (hardback)
ISBN 978-90-8790-938-3 (e-book)

Published by: Sense Publishers,
P.O. Box 21858, 3001 AW
Rotterdam, The Netherlands
http://www.sensepublishers.com

Printed on acid-free paper

All Rights Reserved © 2009 Sense Publishers

No part of this work may be reproduced, stored in a retrieval system, or transmitted in any form or by any means, electronic, mechanical, photocopying, microfilming, recording or otherwise, without written permission from the Publisher, with the exception of any material supplied specifically for the purpose of being entered and executed on a computer system, for exclusive use by the purchaser of the work.

PREFACE

We would like to express our sincere thanks to all those who have contributed to the production of this book.

First of all, we would like to thank all the authors and discussants for agreeing so enthusiastically to contribute, for the exceptionally smooth cooperation during all stages of the production process, and for the high quality of their final products.

We also express our thanks to the editors and publishers of the Sense Publishers series "New Directions in Mathematics and Science Education" for accepting the book for publication in this series and for their encouragement and support during the whole production process.

Furthermore, we thank Mrs. Betty Vanden Bavière, Mrs. Karine Dens, and Mr. Erik Lenaerts for their editorial assistance in the preparation of the final book manuscript and in the correction of the galley proofs.

We are also indebted to the International Scientific Network on "Stimulating Critical and Flexible Thinking" of the Fund for Scientific Research-Flanders and to the Sponsor of the Grant GOA 2006/01 "Developing adaptive expertise in mathematics education" (Research Fund of the Katholieke Universiteit Leuven, Belgium) for their financial support during various stages of the production process of this book.

Finally, we thank all the students and teachers in many parts of the world who participated in the work reported here, and on whose behalf we are collectively striving to improve mathematics education.

Lieven Verschaffel
Brian Greer
Wim Van Dooren
Swapna Mukhopadhyay

CONTENTS

Preface   v

Introduction: Making Sense of Word Problems: Past, Present, and Future   xi
*Brian Greer, Lieven Verschaffel, Wim Van Dooren,
and Swapna Mukhopadhyay*

PART I: THEORETICAL PERSPECTIVES   1

1   Theory of Authentic Task Situations   3
    Torulf Palm

2   Genre, Simulacra, Impossible Exchange, and The Real: How Postmodern Theory Problematises Word Problems   21
    Susan Gerofsky

3   "I am not talking about reality": Word Problems and the Intricacies of Producing Legitimate Text   39
    Uwe Gellert and Eva Jablonka

Discussion I. On the Problematic of Word Problems – Language and the World we Inhabit   55
    Wolff-Michael Roth

PART II: SOCIOCULTURAL FACTORS   71

4   Word Problems: Footprints from the History of Mathematics   73
    Frank J. Swetz

5   Realistic Contexts, Mathematics Assessment, and Social Class: Lessons for Assessment Policy from an English Research Programme   93
    Barry Cooper and Tony Harries

6   Developing a Criticalmathematical Numeracy through *Real* Real-life Word Problems   111
    Marilyn Frankenstein

Discussion II. Can Mathematics Problems Help with the Inequities in the World?   131
    Jo Boaler

CONTENTS

PART III: PROBING STUDENTS' CONCEPTIONS   141

7   The Relationship Between Posing and Solving Division-with-remainder
    Problems among Flemish Upper Elementary School Children   143
    Lieven Verschaffel, Wim Van Dooren, Limin Chen, and Katrien Stessens

8   Realistic Problem Solving in China: Students' Performance, Interventions,
    and Learning Settings   161
    Ziqiang Xin

9   Learning to Model: Coordinating Natural Language and Mathematical
    Operations when Solving Word Problems   177
    Roger Säljö, Eva Riesbeck, and Jan Wyndhamn

10 The Issue of Reality in Word Problem Solving: Learning from Students'
    Justifications of "Unrealistic" Solutions to Real Wor(l)d Problems   195
    Noriyuki Inoue

Discussion III. Research Efforts On Probing Students' Conceptions
    in Mathematics and in Reality: Structuring Problems, Solving
    Problems, and Justifying Solutions   211
    Shuk-Kwan S. Leung

PART IV: PROBING TEACHERS' CONCEPTIONS   225

11 Teachers' Conceptions and Use of Mathematical Contextual Problems
    in Canada   227
    Olive Chapman

12 Analysis of the Realistic Nature of Word Problems in Upper Elementary
    Mathematics Education in Flanders   245
    Fien Depaepe, Erik De Corte, and Lieven Verschaffel

13 How and Why Secondary Mathematics Teachers Make (or Don't Make)
    Real-world Connections in Teaching   265
    Julie Gainsburg

Discussion IV. Teachers' Knowledge and Practices Regarding Contextual
    Problems and Real World Connections   283
    João Pedro da Ponte

PART V: CHANGING CLASSROOMS   295

14 Working Towards Teaching Realistic Mathematical Modelling
and Problem Posing in Italian Classrooms   297
Cinzia Bonotto

15 Stimulating Reflection on Word Problems by Means of Students'
Own Productions   315
Christoph Selter

16 Differing Conceptions of Problem Solving in Mathematics
Education, Science Education, and Professional Schools   333
Richard Lesh and Elizabeth Caylor

Discussion V. The Changing Realities of Classroom Mathematical
Problem Solving   351
Lyn D. English

BRIAN GREER, LIEVEN VERSCHAFFEL, WIM VAN DOOREN,
AND SWAPNA MUKHOPADHYAY

INTRODUCTION

Making Sense of Word Problems: Past, Present, and Future

PAST

In 1992, the first two editors attended a workshop on arithmetic at the Max-Planck Institute in Munich and began a conversation on word problems that has continued to this day. With our colleagues, we did a considerable amount of research and analysis about arithmetic, particularly on the conceptual fields of additive structures (e.g., Verschaffel & De Corte, 1993, 1997) and multiplicative structures (e.g., Greer, 1992). Much of that work was framed in terms of the situations for which the four basic arithmetic operations provide models (Greer, 1987; Verschaffel & De Corte, 1993, 1997). At the meeting in Munich, we were becoming aware of many compelling, and largely independent, observations with the common theme that they apparently showed students in mathematics classes abandoning their sense-making capabilities, and in particular, carrying out arithmetic calculations that did not make sense in relation to the situations described. Our reaction was to embark upon an extended investigation of the phenomenon, continued in this book.

Of course, these were not original ideas. For example, in *The Psychology of Arithmetic*, Thorndike (1922, pp. 100-101) listed a number of examples of what he termed "ambiguities and falsities", including the following (with his comment):

6. If a horse trots 10 miles in one hour how far will he travel in 9 hours?

7. If a girl can pick 3 quarts of berries in 1 hour how many quarts can she pick in 3 hours?

(These last two, with a teacher insisting on the 90 and 9, might well deprive a matter-of-fact boy [sic] of respect for arithmetic for weeks thereafter.)

Even earlier, the mathematician Charles Dodgson, better known by his pseudonym Lewis Carroll, composed an enlightening satire on typical "rule-of-three" problems, by analysing this example:

If 6 cats kill 6 rats in 6 minutes, how many will be needed to kill 100 rats in 50 minutes? (Fisher, 1975; and see discussion in Verschaffel, Greer, & De Corte [2000, pp. 132–134]).

In his analysis, humorously phrased yet making a very serious point, Dodgson takes a modelling perspective and shows how, in distinction from routine application of "rule-of-three" procedures, the answer to the question depends on the assumptions made (for similar points, see Säljö, 1991).

The most startling body of work was inspired by a letter satirising mathematics, from the novelist Gustave Flaubert, in which he wrote:

> Since you are now studying geometry and trigonometry, I will give you a problem: A ship sails the ocean. It left Boston with a cargo of wool. It grosses 200 tons. It is bound for Le Havre. The mainmast is broken, the cabin boy is on deck, there are 12 passengers aboard, the wind is blowing East-North-East, the clock points to a quarter past three in the afternoon. It is the month of May. How old is the captain? (Cited in Wells [1997, p. 234])

Research carried out in France and elsewhere used a simplified version:

> On a boat there are 20 sheep and 6 goats. How old is the captain?

and other questions of the same general nature. The findings, that many children would respond to such questions by, for example, adding the number of sheep and goats, became a *cause célèbre* in France (Baruk, 1985) and considerable further research has attempted to explicate the children's behaviour (e.g., Selter, 1994; this volume).

However, our interest focused on a distinctly different kind of case, where the question asked was not nonsensical in the style of "How old is the captain?" but, rather, students' responses were (to us) failing to make sense because of unthinkingly applying arithmetic operations suggested by the situation described, under the apparent assumption that the situation could be unproblematically mapped onto these operations. Thus, in Greer (1993) and Verschaffel, De Corte, and Lasure (1994), we gave students (respectively, 13-14 years old and 10-11 years old) pencil-and-paper tests consisting of matched pairs of word problems. In each pair, one problem (called a *standard* problem, or S-problem) was such that the application of an arithmetical operation was reasonable (in our judgment); the other problem (called a *problematic* problem, or P-problem) required consideration of more subtle aspects of the situation described.

For instance, in the study by Verschaffel et al. (1994) the following S-item and P-item were paired:

> Pete organised a birthday party for his tenth birthday. He invited 8 boy friends and 4 girl friends. How many friends did Pete invite for his birthday party?

> Carl has 5 friends and Georges has 6 friends. Carl and Georges decide to give a party together. They invite all their friends. All friends are present. How many friends are there at the party?

In Verschaffel et al. (1994) ten such pairs of items were used. Responses were categorised as "realistic" *either* if the answer given implied some awareness of the calculation not being straightforward *or* if a comment accompanying a straightforward, non-realistic answer implied such awareness. Results indicated that S-problems are overwhelmingly answered appropriately, whereas percentages of "realistic responses" (as defined above) are uniformly low (almost all in the range 5-20%).

Replications, using translations of essentially the same items (translated as necessary), have been carried out in many countries, including Belgium, China, Germany, Hungary, Japan, Northern Ireland, Switzerland, The Netherlands, and Venezuela (for an overview of these replication studies, see Verschaffel et al., 2000; see also Xin, this volume). The findings were strikingly consistent with the initial results obtained by Greer (1993) and Verschaffel et al. (1994), sometimes to the great surprise and chagrin of these other researchers who had anticipated that the "disastrous" picture of the Northern Irish and Flemish pupils would not apply to their students. While variations on the accompanying instructions have been used in the various replications, the minimal indication that P-problems might be indeed problematic has been a warning to this effect, and the respondents have been invited to comment on anything unusual they noticed about the item.

Besides replication work, other aspects were taken up by a number of collaborators, for example the contributors to a special issue of *Learning and Instruction* (Greer & Verschaffel, 1997). These perspectives included the nature of the task setting and how it is presented (Reusser & Stebler, 1997), teachers' conceptions and beliefs about word problems (Verschaffel, De Corte, & Borghart, 1997), and sociolinguistic analysis (Wyndhamn & Säljö, 1997). A related body of work was developed in another ongoing research program centred in Leuven, probing the phenomenon of inappropriately assuming linearity, a pattern that is found at all ages and across many branches of mathematics (De Bock, Verschaffel, & Janssens, 1998; Van Dooren, De Bock, Hessels, Janssens, & Verschaffel, 2005; Van Dooren & Greer, in press). Some of the P-problems developed by us and others, and others such as those from Thorndike (1922) cited earlier, illustrate the making of answers that apparently assume linearity in cases where it is not reasonable.

The interim culmination of this activity was the book *Making Sense of Word Problems* (Verschaffel et al., 2000). We began this book by summarising the many examples showing that children frequently manifest what looks, at first sight, to be "suspension of sense-making" when solving school word problems (Schoenfeld, 1991). At second sight, and in response to interviews of students by ourselves and others, we came to agree with Schoenfeld, who stated that:

> Taking the stance of the Western Rationalist trained in mathematics, I characterized student behavior ... as a violation of sense-making. As I have been admonished, however, such behavior is sense-making of the deepest kind. In the context of schooling, such behavior represents the construction of a set of behaviors that results in praise for good performance, minimal conflict, fitting in socially etc. What could be more sensible than that? (p. 340)

Accordingly, our attention in Part II of *Making Sense of Word Problems* turned to the nature of mathematical schooling, in general, and to the ways in which word problems are used, in particular. We analysed the effects of traditional mathematics education in this respect, and considered a number of design studies and innovative curricular projects in which attempts were made to use more realistic and challenging tasks in ways that would lead students to adopt a more appropriate modelling stance.

In Part III, we considered philosophical questions about the nature of mathematical modelling, the use of language in and with mathematics, the sociocultural contexts in which mathematical schooling takes place, and we proposed a reconceptualisation of word problems (to be more precise, those word problems that putatively describe real-world scenarios) as "exercises in mathematical modelling".

At the end of the book, we flagged numerous aspects of (genuine) mathematical modelling only partly addressed in the book, and others needing deeper analysis, many of which are developed further in the present volume, the assembly of which was prompted by our knowledge of many researchers sharing an interest in the curious genre that goes by the term "word problems" or "story problems".

PRESENT

In this volume, we have gathered together related work from many countries that extends the empirical investigations and philosophical analyses of earlier work. The book is divided into five parts, each with a reaction.

Part I: Theoretical Perspectives

The contributors to the first part develop further a central topic discussed in Verschaffel et al. (2000), namely characterisation of the form of reality that is supposedly evoked in word problems and how that can be modelled (and to what purpose). We may say that there are two aspects of modelling that are implicated. First is the mathematical modelling of aspects of our world, both physical and social, that is pervasive in modern life (Davis & Hersh, 1986; Gellert & Jablonka, 2007; Skovsmose, 2005). Second, there is the transformation of that activity into the particular activity system that is school (Lave, 1992), a process that goes by various names, such as "recontextualisation" (Bernstein, 1990; Gellert & Jablonka, this volume), "didactical transformation" (Chevallard, 1985), and "alchemy" (Popkewitz, 2004). A constant theme throughout the (first part of the) book, and from earlier work, is that the presentation of word problems as routine exercises in mapping descriptions of scenarios onto arithmetical operations is detrimental to the kind of critical understanding of modelling that is needed in contemporary society. Many traditional treatments of word problems in mathematics education have been based on rationalist/empiricist assumptions of the transparency of representations, of one-to-one matchings or mappings of language, numbers, and geometric figures onto learners' experiences of life – and vice versa.

In the first chapter, Palm's aim is to systematically analyse the features of school tasks that make them more or less authentic simulations of the corresponding "real" activities. His starting point is that many teachers, textbook writers, and assessment developers are indeed struggling with the development of more "realistic" mathematical school tasks that resemble "out-of-school" task situations. He asks the question: What are the features of more "authentic" word problems, and how do they affect students' word problem solving? After discussing the terminology that has been used in the research literature to describe the "realism" of word problems, he presents a comprehensive framework for what might constitute word problems that closely emulate out-of-school task situations and shows how that framework has been used to critically analyse teaching and testing materials. (For an example of such an application, see the chapter by Depaepe, De Corte & Verschaffel in Part III of this volume).

The other two chapters in this part ask profound philosophical questions about the nature of reality relative to descriptions, simulations, and models of it. In Chapter 2, Gerofsky provides a wide-ranging review, drawing on theorists such as Baudrillard, Lyotard, Lacan, Derrida, Zizek, Bakhtin, and McLuhan. She addresses powerful and profound notions of language, simulation, and knowledge in our contemporary techno-cultural environment. Such theorists of postmodernity trouble the sense of a transparent, self-evident reality and its representations in many ways. In particular, Gerofsky adopts this perspective to deconstruct common perceptions that word problems embody simple and transparent representations, simulations, and straightforward applications of mathematical knowledge (or can be so treated for the purposes of teaching mathematics).

Gellert and Jablonka discuss in Chapter 3 the relationships between "words and worlds", which are represented in mathematical word problems, in terms of relationships between "domains of practice". These relationships consist in the recontextualisation of out-of-school practices for didactical purposes, including an inescapable relocation and appropriation of the corresponding discourses by pedagogic discourse. The students in the mathematics classroom face these issues as the demands of recognising different forms of discourse and of producing legitimate text. After analysing illustrative examples of the dilemmas that students face when confronted with these types of task, they discuss categories of expression and content of word problems from the perspective of recontextualisation.

The reader will notice, not only in this first part but throughout the whole book a tension – constructive, we believe – between those authors who argue that the detrimental aspects of word problems as currently deployed can be identified and addressed, and those that argue that the endeavour is fundamentally flawed. Whatever the degree of change called for (and there is unanimity on the need for reform of practices around word problems worldwide) there is a corresponding responsibility to propose how the use of word problems in mathematics education – if they are to be retained in some form – could be improved.

In his overview of the three chapters, Roth digs deeper into issues of language, and the nature of the social interaction that takes place when a person, or group of people, are presented with a word problem as a task, whether in school or as part of an experiment. What are the implicit rules, the "didactical contract" in class between teacher and students, or the "experimental contract" between child and researcher? How does someone in this situation construe the nature and purpose of this particular kind of social interaction?

Indeed, by asking these questions, Roth's critique not only bears on the chapters of the first part but, in profound ways, foreshadows key aspects of the succeeding parts, as will be seen. In particular, from the perspective of cultural-historical activity theory, he argues that the analysis of what happens around word problems, and of mathematics education in general, must be treated within the activity system that is *schooling*, and in relation to its sociopolitical effects (see Varenne & McDermott, 1998). Several aspects of this argument are addressed in the next part.

Part II: Sociocultural Perspectives

Word problems are cultural artefacts. As a humorous, but revealing, illustration consider a cartoon by the American humorist Gary Larson. It depicts a man who is clearly in Hades as indicated by the devil and flames shown in the background. He is contemplating bookshelves laden with thick volumes with titles "The big book of word problems", "Word problems galore", and so on. The caption for the cartoon reads "Hell's Library".

In Verschaffel et al. (2000) we noted that word problems, as a genre, have been around for a very long time, and in many cultures. In Chapter 4, Swetz provides a great deal more detail on their history, showing that word problems appear to have always been a part of the mathematical teaching and learning process. From inscriptions on clay tablets, renderings on bamboo strips and papyrus sheets to the message of the printed page, such problems have historically been a source of mathematical communication, learning, and in many cases, student frustration. In this respect, they supply intellectual footprints of how mathematics was used and valued, but also insights into the social and economic climate of their times. His contribution surveys the construction and employ of word problems in an historical and societal context, thus providing part of what is needed for a cultural-historical perspective, as urged by Roth. Swetz's review also reminds us that academic mathematics and school mathematics emerged out of a rich diversity of mathematical practices, as particular kinds of mathematical practice (Lave, 1992).

Cooper and Harries (Chapter 5) take up an issue flagged in Verschaffel et al. (2000), namely the differential ways in which currently applied forms of assessment affect diverse students. Greer, Verschaffel, and Mukhopadhyay (2007, p. 96) suggested that:

> If a decision is made to mathematize situations and issues that connect with students' lived experience, then it brings a further commitment to respect the diversity of that experience across genders, classes, and ethnicity.

Following Bernstein (like Gellert & Jablonka), Cooper and his colleagues have conducted an extensive program of research on how social class and gender differences impact performance on standardised assessments. In the chapter here by Cooper and Harries, they employ one particular item from a national annual programme for testing mathematical achievement in the U.K. to illustrate some relations between social class, gender, and validity. The item deals with data about the traffic outside a school, and the key point is whether students attend to the data presented, or base responses on their knowledge of the world. Cooper and Harries draw on interviews with children as they demonstrate how easy it is to modify items so that validity interacts differently with such factors as social class and gender. A body of sociological analysis, including that of Bernstein and Bourdieu, indicates how the use of such contexts might introduce differential validity by social class into the testing process (as commented by Roth, this volume).

Frankenstein (Chapter 6) starts by addressing concerns about the current push to include real-life mathematics word problems in the curriculum, particularly the non-neutral "hidden curriculum" that results from particular selections of real-life data used to create contrived and/or context-narrow word problems. The focus of her chapter is a discussion of examples, in various categories, of what she terms *real* real-life math word problems that are studied in a broad enough context so that students can see how understanding numbers and doing calculations can illuminate meaning in real life. From this discussion, she goes on to develop guidelines on how to construct such problems and then generalises some key quantitative understandings that emerge and deepen through working on *real* real-life mathematics word problems. These understandings underlie the kinds of questions she argues that we need to ask in order to grapple with various economic, political, and social issues.

Boaler approaches the three chapters in this part through the question "Can mathematics problems help with the inequities in the world?". Current rhetoric emphasises equity *in* mathematics education, but is it possible to go beyond that and pursue equity *through* mathematics education by providing students with the tools to critique and act upon issues of importance in their lives, in their communities, and for humankind in general (Gutstein, 2006)?

Each of the three chapters, in different ways, bears on the question posed by Boaler. She illustrates how the plentiful examples from many cultures and times furnished by Swetz illuminate aspects of inequity in society, for example in relation to gender. Drawing on her own experience, Boaler cautions about the challenges and difficulties of following Freire's dictum that education is politics, since (p. 134) "such examples make many students and teachers extremely uncomfortable, if not angry". Frankenstein's point, however, is that the supposedly neutral curriculum is inherently political, and that her purpose is to expose that. Boaler has also contributed significantly to the domain of concern addressed by Cooper and Harries, in particular in relation to how female students are more likely to engage with aspects of reality when addressing contextualised questions (e.g., Boaler, 1994). While reminding us that equity can also be pursued through the ways in which classroom relationships and discourse are guided, she concludes that the authors in this part do indeed show ways in which mathematics education could contribute to a more equitable society.

Part III: Probing Students' Conceptions

In this part and the next, studies are reported that investigate how students and teachers, respectively, approach word problems. The methodologies used include not only pencil-and-paper tests, but go beyond these (as is essential for deeper understanding) to activities such as solving and posing problems in small groups and individual interviews.

Verschaffel, Van Dooren, Chen, and Stessens (Chapter 7) address the relationship between solving and posing realistic word problems, specifically problems involving division with remainder (DWR), i.e., where the appropriate "core calculation" is division of one positive number by another that does not divide exactly, and where the appropriate interpretation of the result of this calculation is an issue. One of the early observations that piqued our interest was reported by Davis (1989). In a lesson introducing division, students were given five balloons to be shared between two people One boy cut a balloon in half, leading to the question raised by Davis (1989, p. 144): "Was this boy really thinking about solving the actual problem ... or was he trying to accommodate himself to the ... culture of the American school?". This situation was adapted for matched S- and P-items in Greer (1993) (with slightly different versions in Verschaffel et al. [1994]):

If there are 14 pizzas for 4 children at a party, how should they be shared out?

If there are 14 balloons for 4 children at a party, how should they be shared out?

Among the P-items used in the study by Verschaffel et al. (1994) and its replications, this one has generally elicited a high percentage of realistic responses (50 to 80% "realistic reactions"), but in a fascinating twist, a Community College student gave the answer "4", but added *"the answer is really 4.5, but you can't have half a balloon"* (Greer, Verschaffel, & De Corte, 2002, p. 278, emphasis added).

In the study reported here by Verschaffel et al., Flemish students in grades 4–6 were given both problem-solving and problem-posing tasks relating to DWR problems. The quantitative and qualitative analyses of the results reveal that children from all age groups showed non-realistic perspectives in their problem-posing as well as in their problem-solving endeavours (with the results for problem posing being considerably weaker), that both the problem-solving and the problem-posing skills improved with pupils' age and mathematical ability level, and that there was a significant positive relationship between children's abilities to pose and solve realistic problems.

In Chapter 8, Xin addresses the question how Chinese students perform on P-items by reviewing and discussing the available research, especially his own research, on Chinese students' realistic problem solving and how it is influenced by prevailing and alternative instructional settings. His conclusion is that, like their Western counterparts, Chinese pupils generally do not take real-world considerations into account when responding to P-problems. He invokes the theoretical construct of "cognitive holding power", as developed by Stevenson and Evans (1994), who distinguish between settings possessing first and second order cognitive holding power. The former pushes students towards the direct acquisition and utilisation of procedures. In such an environment, students merely follow a teacher in learning how to accomplish specific tasks. Settings possessing second order cognitive holding power push a student into the utilisation of procedures that achieve more general purposes by operating on specific procedures to enable the interpretation of new situations, solving of problems, and learning of new skills. Such settings poses unfamiliar goals, and elicit the execution of second order procedures. On the basis of the research and his knowledge of Chinese mathematics education, Xin suggests that, in order to promote students' realistic problem solving, a series of measures should be taken, including supplementing P-problems in daily teaching and examinations, designing effective instructional approaches, and establishing learning settings with high second order cognitive holding power.

Whereas the first two chapters from Part III presented studies using pencil-and-paper tests, it is essential to probe further by interviewing, and otherwise interacting directly with, students, and the other two chapters in this part take this approach.

In the study by Säljö, Backlund, Riesbeck, and Wyndham (Chapter 9) the issue of realistic modelling has been investigated in the context of how upper elementary school pupils, working in groups of three, struggled to model a "realistic" word-problem about fair sharing in order to come up with an answer. The results show that the groups use different models, some of which are quite complex, but, in spite of this, their reasoning is not successful because they are hindered by the assumption that there is one mathematical model that can provide an exact numerical answer to the problem. It is argued that solving this kind of problem requires learning to reason at a meta-level about the situation and the mathematical model. It is interesting that this meta-level reasoning is conspicuously absent in the students' problem-solving activities, even among those who are very good at mathematics (as judged by the usual criteria). What this study points to is an alternative perspective on human knowing and skills in which the discursive nature of our knowledge is emphasised.

Inoue (Chapter 10) questions previous interpretations of students' responses as representing unrealistic answers to real wor(l)d problems with the assumption that the students had not seriously considered familiar aspects of reality. His study used interviews to afford the students the opportunity to provide justifications for responses on paper-and-pencil tasks that would be categorised as "non-realistic" by the criteria adopted in earlier studies. In contrast to a rather similar approach by Selter (1994, this volume), who worked with young children, Inoue interviewed university students. He suggests that examining a variety of "unrealistic" responses in mathematics classrooms could serve as an invaluable opportunity for us to discover effective ways of filling the gap between the theoretical and applied approaches to mathematical problem solving. According to Inoue, considering different justifications of the calculational answers and examining different sets of assumptions for solving word problems can provide rich opportunities for students to learn how to use their mathematical knowledge beyond school-based problem solving. This approach could help the students conceptualise word problem solving in terms of meaningful assumptions and conditions for modelling reality, rather than the assumptions imposed by textbooks, teachers, or other authority figures.

In her review of these four chapters, Leung stresses the limitations of ascertaining experiments that reveal and document failings in the mathematical performances of students (at least as viewed from the perspectives of the researchers). In general, she makes the point that students cannot be expected to do things spontaneously, such as problem posing, for which they have not been instructionally prepared (see Hatano, 1997, for similar comments). Thus, to interpret more fully how students behave, it is essential to have some knowledge of their instructional histories. As Leung points out, moreover, the nature of the interaction in all four studies was, to a greater or lesser extent, likely to cue the students towards playing the "word problem game" (De Corte & Verschaffel, 1985; Verschaffel et al., 2000). Consequently, there is a need for intervention studies, now often called design experiments, to study the effects of prolonged exposure to a different pedagogy (such as Leung's own work on classroom interventions to promote problem posing). Many such efforts were reviewed in Verschaffel et al. (2000), and others are reported in Part V of this book. Leung also suggests an enhancement of Polya's (1945) model of phases in problem solving to take account of points in the process at which realistic considerations might lead the solver to reconsider and backtrack to an earlier phase. She also argues that there are important differences between well-structured and ill-structured problems, a distinction that is very relevant to the distinction between S-problems and P-problems.

Part IV: Probing Teachers' Conceptions

Much research has examined the nature of word problems in published mathematical curricula and student responses to word problems as well as to more complex, authentic mathematical modelling problems. Less attention has been paid to how teachers think about and attempt to implement connections between school mathematics and the real world. Attention to teachers is of fundamental importance, however, because what teachers think and do essentially governs whether and how students will encounter real-world connections for the mathematics they learn in school. More generally, teachers are crucial in any attempt at innovation (Atweh, 2008). Moreover, as argued by Leung (this volume), a student's instructional history influences profoundly how she/he will respond.

It is generally agreed that characterising word problems as exercises in modelling, necessarily involving *flexible* as opposed to merely *routine expertise* (Hatano, 2003), requires heavy intellectual investment (Hatano, 1997). It is also generally accepted that trying to persuade teachers to change their practices radically carries major responsibilities for engaging them as partners in the process (Atweh, 2008). Consequently, extended studies of teachers engaged in such processes are essential.

According to Chapman (Chapter 11), there is little research available on experienced mathematics teachers and their conceptions and use of contextual problems in their teaching. Understanding the nature of teachers' conceptions and the relationship between these conceptions and their teaching could enhance our understanding of instruction and of the types of professional development that could help teachers to change or improve their thinking and use of contextual problems in their teaching. Chapman's research indicates that teachers may conceptualise contextual problems in terms of computation, text, object, experience, problem, and tool. She further suggests that a teacher may hold one of three contrasting philosophical positions, that she terms objectivist, utilitarian, and humanistic. On the basis of in-depth interviews, she suggests how these conceptualisations and philosophical positions, and other factors such as expertise and experience, may relate to teachers' pedagogical styles.

INTRODUCTION

Depaepe, De Corte, and Verschaffel present in Chapter 12 an in-depth analysis of the word problems in a textbook series that is widely used in Flanders. Moreover, based on a seven-month observation period they investigated which problems from the textbook were used by two teachers during that period and which self-generated problems they added. They used the theoretical framework proposed by Palm (2002; this volume). Overall, both textbook-developed and teacher-developed materials seem to simulate quite well a number of aspects that are assumed to be important in designing realistic tasks, but for other aspects of Palm's scheme, the results are considerably less positive.

In Chapter 13, Gainsburg reports on a study investigating mathematics teachers' decisions about real-world connections (RWCs) in their teaching – how they use connections, why, and the factors that influence that use. Building on a prior, exploratory, study (Gainsburg, 2008), Gainsburg's new study included responses of mathematics teachers to a questionnaire, observations of their lessons, and follow-up interviews. The findings are discussed in terms of frequency of classroom use of types of RWCs, teachers' reasons for use and non-use of RWCs (and resources supporting use), differentiation of use of RWCs across types of student or class, teacher beliefs about the pedagogical power of RWCs, and the impact of school and district contexts on use of RWCs. Her findings may inform future research and teacher-education efforts concerning real-world connections in mathematics teaching.

As Ponte points out in his overview of this part, the ways in which teachers do or do not incorporated RWCs in their teaching reflect, on the one hand, their beliefs, conceptions, knowledge, and "craft knowledge" and, on the other hand, the constraints under which they operate, in terms of curriculum, textbooks, assessment demands, school practices, and so on. Indeed, the factors influencing what a teacher does are situated in the classroom, the school, the educational system, and the culture at large (see Greer et al., 2002, p. 285).

Ponte notes that educators and researchers, under the broad mantle of constructivism, have urged fundamental changes in the role of the teacher, from deliverer of knowledge to facilitator of learning. The extent to which this has actually happened is both limited and highly variable (and this variation needs to be considered in any attempt to generalise findings).

Part V: Changing Classrooms

In order to change in the direction broadly agreed upon, necessary steps include engaging in the ideological argument, demonstrating results through exemplary initiatives, and systemic change. In Verschaffel et al. (2000), several systematic attempts to design and implement learning environments were described and, in this book in general, and this final part in particular, the authors make suggestions about what might be changed, and how.

Bonotto (Chapter 14) analyses a number of teaching experiments consisting of a series of classroom activities in upper elementary school, using suitable cultural artefacts, interactive teaching methods, and aiming to create and sustain new sociomathematical norms in order to create a substantially modified teaching/ learning environment. The focus is on fostering a mindful approach toward realistic mathematical modelling, problem solving, and also a problem-posing attitude. Based on results obtained in these teaching experiments, Bonotto argues that it is not only possible but also desirable, even at the primary school level, to introduce early on fundamental ideas about modelling, especially "emergent modelling". She also argues for modelling as a means of recognising the potential of mathematics as a critical tool to interpret and understand reality, the communities children live in, and society in general.

Chapter 15 by Selter is a theoretically founded description of several activities that he and his team developed in order to encourage students to reflect on (solving) word problems. It is the main goal of this approach to teaching to give children more responsibility and to see them as experts for their own learning. By constantly using their own productions, their reflection on word problems was encouraged in classroom discourse and small-group work – more and more independently from the teacher, and not always as expected. His experiences lead him to the conclusion that it is a realistic option to gradually give children freedom that they can use effectively, even if a difficult topic such as word problems has to be tackled – sometimes with surprising results. This approach exemplifies an idea suggested by Greer (2009) that, as well as talking about mathematics in classrooms in order to try to "enter the child's mind" (Ginsburg, 1997), educators and researchers should share with students what we know, or think we know, about the nature of learning and teaching mathematics. In the case of Selter, children become partners in problematising the genre of word problems.

The final chapter by Lesh and Caylor greatly enlarges the scope of the discussion, by placing the critique of word problems in the context of inquiry activities in science education, case studies and problem-based activities in professional schools that are heavy users of mathematics, science, and technology, and model-eliciting activities from Lesh's extensive research program. According to the authors, it is productive to try to tease out distinctions, not in order to criticise one type of activity compared with another, but to identify testable hypotheses that may advance thinking about each. They end their chapter by arguing that in both mathematics and science education, as well as in fields where mathematical thinking is used, a great deal more research and development will be needed to keep pace with changes that are taking place beyond schools and in modern learning sciences, and by providing a list of trends whose implications need to be investigated in research in mathematics and science education.

In her overview, English draws attention to the widespread calls for mathematical activities to be more relevant and meaningful. Likewise she points to the need for people to be able to engage with more complexity in terms of both interpersonal communication and co-operation and in relation to technological advances.

There has been considerable attention paid in cognitive psychology and mathematics education for many decades now to problem solving. English comments on the generally disappointing results in terms of building on Polya's analysis to improve students' problem solving. As she points out, there is a need to clarify the various relationships between "word problems", "problem solving", "problem posing", and "modelling". Indeed, as Jonassen (2004) commented, problems (ironically) are caused by the use of the word "problem" to mean different things. Along with Lesh and his colleagues (e.g., Lesh & Zawojewski, 2007), English (e.g., 2006, in press) has worked towards a more integrated approach that theoretically relates problem solving, in the tradition of Polya, with mathematical modelling, with heavy emphasis on ill-structured problems. One suggestion, prompted by such work, is that beyond routine and adaptive expertise, as characterised by Hatano (2003) there is need for an even more advanced form of expertise, namely "creative expertise" which is needed to pose and solve ill-defined problems within complex situations – and English proposes a long list of ways in which classroom experiences could support the development of such expertise.

FUTURE

Given the severe criticisms of standard school word problems, why do we think it is still important to study and analyse them, and devote this book to the topic? Perhaps the most important reason is that, as is generally the case, there is a large gap between the enlightened state of researchers and scholars (or at least what they take to be enlightened) and practice in actual classrooms, in textbooks, tests, and in public discourse. Further, the problematising of word problems does not rule out the possibility that their faults could be rectified and their virtues retained – throwing out the bathwater while keeping the baby, so to speak. In particular, many propose that the most effective reform is through assimilating word problems within an approach to mathematics education that puts major stress on modelling.

In any case, this book shows clearly how many issues are thrown up by looking at word problems in mathematics classrooms and the practices around them, but by no means exhausts the topic. We believe that word problems should continue to engage our interest and research, providing, as they do "a microcosm of theories of learning" (Lave, 1992, p. 74).

While this volume has extended and deepened many of the issues identified in our previous book, there are many others discussed or identified by the authors that remain to be fully developed. For example, one topic that has received limited attention is affect (Roth, this volume). At the end of *Making Sense of Word Problems*, Verschaffel et al. (2000, p. 181) stated that:

> The evidence laid out in the early chapters of this book affronts our conception of how children should come to regard mathematics and we are not alone in this reaction. Freudenthal (1991, p. 70) commented:

> Wouldn't it be worthwhile investigating whether and why this didactic breeds an anti-mathematical attitude and why the children's immunity against this mental deformation is so varied?

> It is arguable that the complex of practices in which word problems are embedded provides a prototypical example of what is wrong with mathematics education in general. The cost of continuing to teach mathematics, and word

problems in particular, according to current practices may be a population in which the majority of people remain alienated from mathematics.

As is implied in the last-but-one sentence of the above quotation, we take the view that the study of word problems has implications that go beyond word problems as such, and this view is reflected in many of the chapters. Hatano (1997) took a sceptical position about conventional word problems being useful for teaching the modelling perspective and argued that the P-problems used "are too trivial for students to recognise the significance of 'high-cost' modelling activity, which requires a great deal of time and effort to perform" (p. 384). Our response is that many important principles of modelling can be introduced through relatively simple word problems (see Usiskin, 2007), the most central being the realisation that it is important to consider whether a description of a scenario is appropriately, approximately, or inappropriately modelled by an arithmetic operation.

Indeed, in several chapters, this discussion goes even deeper, into how we experience and talk about what we call "reality". Which relates to further questions such as: How does the teaching of modelling in school mathematics relate to the modelling that takes place, increasingly, in our society? Could school mathematics be put to the task of better preparing people for life in a world that is complex and technological, and in which many aspects of our lives are mathematised and demathematised (Gellert & Jablonka, 2007; Skovsmose, 2005)?

Hatano is certainly right, in our view, to stress that teaching in this more complex way carries a heavy cost in terms of extra hard work for teachers, curriculum and textbook writers, and students (Verschaffel, 2002). The cost of not doing so is, potentially, to produce students that believe that mathematics has no connection with reality, but is an activity carried on solely within its own rules. Further, there is the potential of producing adults who are unable to evaluate critically the simplest of mathematical arguments about issues that are important, as argued by Frankenstein (1989; this volume). Skovsmose (2005, p. 140) suggests that, in a world where more and more aspects of our lives are controlled by hidden mathematical models, people may be divided into certain roles, that he labels constructors, operators, consumers, and "the disposable" and he asks (p. 143) "How could mathematics education counteract the tendency to establish groups as 'disposable'? How could mathematics education help to ensure citizenship (active and critical) for everybody?".

Making a distinction between "understanding by schema application" and "understanding through comprehension activity" (Hatano, 1996), Hatano (1997, p. 386) makes two suggestions for increasing the return for the high cost of comprehension activity:

> First, we can make a problem or its solution critically important for people's lives. Alternatively, we can establish a culture that enjoys and highly evaluates comprehension activity in the target domain.

Greer et al. (2002, p. 285) asserted that "while it is an appropriate starting point to take a classroom as the unit of analysis, form a wider perspective, students' and teachers' beliefs about word problems (as for mathematics in general) are embedded in the school setting, the educational system, and most broadly in society..." and later conjectured (p. 287) that the highly consistent results obtained in replications in many different countries of the original study by Verschaffel et al. (1994) could be attributed to homogeneity in practices of school mathematics, masking cultural differences in this context.

Hatano makes the (entirely reasonable, in our view) claim that the kind of teaching that we have been advocating "provides a majority of students with an opportunity for enduring modelling activity only after they have developed a social and intellectual atmosphere supporting it" (p. 386). That is precisely the point behind the design experiments reported in Verschaffel et al. (2000), and in the work of many of the authors represented in this book.

To summarise, there are a number of themes running through our collective work on this topic – past, present, and future – that apply, not just to the practices surrounding word problems, but to the teaching of mathematics in general:

- We assume that the child learning mathematics (or anything else) comes with an innate drive for sense-making that should not be violated, and believe that attention should be given in teaching mathematics to make connections with children's lived experience.
- Teachers of mathematics and others involved in managing this teaching – teachers of teachers, administrators, curriculum developers, test constructors – should not do so mindlessly, "because that is how it has always been done", rather need to reflect deeply about what they are doing, and why.
- In contrast to typical mathematics teaching in schools, that arguably constitutes a training in simplistic forms of thinking – word problems being an extremely potent case in point – an understanding of the very idea that mathematics can be used to model aspects of reality, and that this process is complex, and has many limitations and dangers, is essential to effective and responsible citizenship.

REFERENCES

Atweh, B. (2008, October). *Innovations supporting teachers for teachers supporting innovations* [Plenary talk]. International Conference on Science and Mathematics Education, Quezon City, The Philippines.

Baruk, S. (1985). *L'âge du capitaine. De l'erreur en mathématiques.* Paris: Seuil.

Bernstein, B. (1990). *Class, codes and control: Vol. 4. The structuring of pedagogic discourse.* London: Routledge.

Boaler, J. (1994). When do girls prefer football to fashion? An analysis of female underachievement in relation to "realistic" mathematics contexts. *British Educational Research Journal, 20,* 551–564.

Chevallard, G. (1985). *La transposition didactique.* Grenoble, France: La Pensée Sauvage.

Davis, P. J., & Hersh, R. (1986). *Descartes' dream: The world according to mathematics.* Sussex, U.K.: Harvester.

Davis, R. B. (1989). The culture of mathematics and the culture of schools. *Journal of Mathematical Behavior, 8,* 143–160.

De Bock, D., Verschaffel, L., & Janssens, D. (1998). Solving problems involving length and area of similar plane figures and the illusion of linearity: An inquiry into the difficulties of secondary school students. *Educational Studies in Mathematics, 35,* 65–83.

De Corte, E., & Verschaffel, L. (1985). Beginning first graders' initial representation of arithmetic word problems. *Journal of Mathematical Behavior, 4,* 3–21.

English, L. D. (2006). Mathematical modeling in the primary school: Children's construction of a consumer guide. *Educational Studies in Mathematics, 62,* 303–323.

English, L. D. (in press). Modeling with complex data in the primary school. In R. Lesh, P. L. Galbraith, C. R. Haines, & A. Hurford (Eds.), *Modeling students' mathematical modelling competencies: ICTMA 13.* New York: Springer.

Fisher, J. (Ed.). (1975). *The magic of Lewis Carroll.* London: Penguin.

Frankenstein, M. (1989). *Relearning mathematics: A different third R - radical math(s).* London: Free Association Books.

Freudenthal, H. (1991). *Revisiting mathematics education.* Dordrecht, The Netherlands: Kluwer.

Gainsburg, J. (2008). Real-world connections in secondary math teaching. *Journal of Mathematics Teacher Education, 11,* 199–219.

Gellert, U., & Jablonka, E. (Eds.). (2007). *Mathematisation and demathematisation: Social, philosophical and educational ramifications.* Rotterdam, The Netherlands: Sense Publishers.

Ginsburg, H. (1997). *Entering the child's mind.* Cambridge, U.K.: Cambridge University Press.

Greer, B. (1987). Understanding of arithmetical operations as models of situations. In J. Sloboda & D. Rogers (Eds.), *Cognitive processes in mathematics* (pp. 60–80). Oxford, U.K.: Oxford University Press.

Greer, B. (1992). Multiplication and division as models of situations. In D. A. Grouws (Ed.), *Handbook of research on mathematics education* (pp. 276–295). New York: Macmillan.

Greer, B. (1993). The modeling perspective on wor(l)d problems. *Journal of Mathematical Behavior, 12,* 239–250.

Greer, B. (2009). Helping children develop mathematically. *Human Development, 52,* 148–161.

Greer, B., & Verschaffel, L. (Eds.). (1997). Modelling reality in mathematics classrooms [Special issue]. *Learning and Instruction, 7* (4).

Greer, B., Verschaffel, L., & De Corte, E. (2002). The answer is really 4.5: Beliefs about word problems. In G. C. Leder, E. Pekhonen, & G. Törner (Eds.), *Beliefs: A hidden variable in mathematics education?* (pp. 272–291). Dordrecht, The Netherlands: Kluwer.

Greer, B., Verschaffel, L., & Mukhopadhyay, S. (2007). Modelling for life: Mathematics and children's experience. In W. Blum, P. L. Galbraith, H.-W. Henne, & M. Niss (Eds), *Modelling and applications in mathematics education (ICMI Study 14)* (pp. 89–98). New York: Springer.

Gutstein, E. (2006). *Reading and writing the world with mathematics: Toward a pedagogy for social justice.* New York: Routledge.

Hatano, G. (1996). A conception of knowledge acquisition and its implications for mathematics education. In L. P. Steffe, P. Nesher, P. Cobb, G. A. Goldin, & B. Greer (Eds.), *Theories of mathematical learning* (pp. 197–217). Mahwah, NJ: Erlbaum.

Hatano, G. (1997). Commentary: Cost and benefit of modelling activity. *Learning and Instruction, 7,* 383–387.

Hatano, G. (2003). Foreword. In A. J. Baroody & A. Dowker (Eds.), *The development of arithmetic concepts and skills: Constructing adaptive expertise* (pp. xi–xiii). Mahwah, NJ: Erlbaum.

Jonassen, D. H. (2004). *Learning to solve problems: An instructional design guide.* San Francisco: Pfeiffer.

Lave, J. (1992). Word problems: A microcosm of theories of learning. In P. Light & G. Butterworth (Eds.), *Context and cognition: Ways of learning and knowing* (pp. 74–92). New York: Harvester Wheatsheaf.

Lesh, R., & Zawojewski, J. (2007). Problem solving and modeling. In F. K. Lester, Jr. (Ed.), *Second handbook of research on mathematics teaching and learning* (pp. 763–804). Charlotte, NC: Information Age Publishing.

Palm, T. (2002). *The realism of mathematical school tasks. Features and consequences.* Unpublished doctoral dissertation, University of Umea, Sweden.

Polya, G. (1945). *How to solve it.* Princeton, NJ: Princeton University Press.

Popkewitz, T. (2004). The alchemy of the mathematics curriculum: Inscriptions and the fabrication of the child. *American Educational Research Journal, 41,* 3–34.

Reusser, K., & R. Stebler (1997). Every word problem has a solution: The suspension of reality and sense-making in the culture of school mathematics. *Learning and Instruction, 7,* 309–328.

Säljö, R. (1991). Learning and mediation: Fitting reality into a table. *Learning and Instruction, 1,* 261–273.

Schoenfeld, A. H. (1991). On mathematics as sense-making: An informal attack on the unfortunate divorce of formal and informal mathematics. In J. F. Voss, D. N. Perkins, & J. W. Segal (Eds.), *Informal reasoning and education* (pp. 311–343). Hillsdale, NJ: Erlbaum.

Selter, C. (1994). How old is the captain? *Strategies, 5*(1), 34–37.

Skovsmose, O. (2005). *Travelling through education: Uncertainty, mathematics, responsibility.* Rotterdam, The Netherlands: Sense Publishers.

Stevenson, J., & Evans, G. (1994). Conceptualisation and measurement of cognitive holding power. *Journal of Educational Measurement, 31,* 161–181.

Thorndike, E. L. (1922). *The psychology of arithmetic.* New York: Macmillan.

Usiskin, Z. (2007). The arithmetic operations as mathematical models. In W. Blum, P. L. Galbraith, H.-W. Henne, & M. Niss (Eds*.), Applications and modelling in mathematics education The 14th ICMI Study 14* (pp. 257–264). New York: Springer.

Van Dooren, W., De Bock, D., Hessels, A., Janssens, D., & Verschaffel, L. (2005). Not everything is proportional: Effects of age and problem type on propensities for overgeneralization. *Cognition and Instruction, 23,* 57–86.

Van Dooren, W., & Greer, B. (Eds.) (in press). Students' behaviour in linear and non-linear situations [Special issue]. *Mathematical Thinking and Learning.*

Varenne, H., & McDermott, R. (1998). *Successful failure: The school America builds.* Boulder, CO: Westview Press.

Verschaffel, L. (2002). Taking the modeling perspective seriously at the elementary school level: promises and pitfalls [Plenary lecture]. In A. Cockburn & E. Nardi (Eds.), *Proceedings of the 26th Annual Conference of the International Group for the Psychology of Mathematics Education: Vol. 1.* (pp. 64–82). Norwich, U.K.: University of East Anglia.

Verschaffel, L., & De Corte, E. (1993). A decade of research on word-problem solving in Leuven: Theoretical, methodological and practical outcomes. *Educational Psychology Review, 5,* 239–256.

Verschaffel, L. & De Corte, E. (1997). Word problems: A vehicle for promoting authentic mathematical understanding and problem solving in the primary school. In T. Nunes & P. Bryant (Eds.), *Learning and teaching mathematics: An international perspective* (pp. 69–97). Hove, East Sussex, U.K.: Psychology Press.

Verschaffel, L., De Corte, E., & Borghart, I. (1997). Pre-service teachers' conceptions and beliefs about the role of real-world knowledge in mathematical modelling of school word problems. *Learning and Instruction, 4,* 339–359.

Verschaffel, L., De Corte, E., & Lasure, S. (1994). Realistic considerations in mathematical modeling of school arithmetic word problems. *Learning and Instruction, 4,* 273–294.

Verschaffel, L., Greer, B., & De Corte, E. (2000). *Making sense of word problems.* Lisse, The Netherlands: Swets & Zeitlinger.

Wells, D. (1997). *The Penguin book of curious and interesting mathematics.* London: Penguin.

Wyndhamn, J., & R. Säljö (1997). Word problems and mathematical reasoning: A study of children's mastery of reference and meaning in textual realities. *Learning and Instruction, 7,* 361–382.

Brian Greer
Portland State University
U.S.A.

Lieven Verschaffel
Centre for Instructional Psychology and Technology

Katholieke Universiteit Leuven
Belgium

Wim Van Dooren
Centre for Instructional Psychology and Technology
Katholieke Universiteit Leuven
Belgium

Swapna Mukhopadhyay
Portland State University
U.S.A.

PART I: THEORETICAL PERSPECTIVES

TORULF PALM

1. THEORY OF AUTHENTIC TASK SITUATIONS

INTRODUCTION

This book is about word problems and how students interact with them. Word problems have been defined differently in different publications. Here I will use the definition provided by Verschaffel, Greer, and De Corte (2000) in the preface of their book. They define them as "textual descriptions of situations assumed to be comprehensible to the reader, within which mathematical questions can be contextualised". They also note that word problems "provide, in convenient form, a possible link between the abstractions of pure mathematics and its applications to real-world phenomena" (p. ix). This is a broad definition that includes pure mathematical tasks "dressed up" in a real-world context that for their solution merely require that the students "undress" these tasks and solve them. It also includes tasks requiring that students be involved in the full mathematical modelling cycle. The "situations" that are described may be of different kinds such as fairy tales, vocational practice, or everyday life. The latter two types can be further divided, which the framework of the OECD's International Programme for Student Assessment (PISA) does, into tasks with contexts that "have been chosen to make them look superficially like real-world problems" and tasks that someone "in an out-of-school setting is likely to be called upon to address" (OECD, 1999, p. 51).

In many countries, there are requests to link school mathematics more closely to the real world outside mathematics. Such requests are not new but have led to recent curricula and assessment reforms in several countries (Palm, 2005). There are several reasons for the inclusion of applications and modelling (including word problems) in mathematics education (for a review of the arguments presented in the literature on mathematics education, see Blum & Niss, 1991). The reasons include the possibilities of the use of applications and modelling to (1) facilitate the learning of necessary skills for being able to use (and critically examine the use of) mathematics outside the mathematics classroom, and (2) facilitate the development of an experience of school mathematics as useful and powerful for solving meaningful task situations in life outside the mathematics classroom. The latter could provide motivation for, and establish relevance of, mathematical studies as well as facilitate the development of a comprehensive picture of mathematics that includes applications and modelling. That students obtain such a picture of school mathematics is a goal expressed in different curriculum documents from professional organisations and national ministries (e.g., Finnish National Board of Education, 2004; NCTM, 2000, p. 279).

To attain the goals inherent in such reasons, many researchers have argued that "realistic" or "authentic" word problems be included in the set of word problems

L. Verschaffel et al. (eds.), Words and Worlds: Modelling Verbal Descriptions of Situations, 3–19.
© 2009 Sense Publishers. All rights reserved.

the students are given. Burton (1993) argues that: "[...] realistic problems are equally important to ensuring that learners perceive that mathematics does contribute to working at and resolving issues of living" (Burton, 1993, p. 12). Niss (1992) describes "an *authentic* extra-mathematical situation as one which is embedded in a true existing practice or subject area outside mathematics, and which deals with objects, phenomena, issues, or problems that are genuine to that area and are recognised as such by people working in it" (p. 353). PISA does not preclude the inclusion of virtual contexts but its authors emphasise the use of real-world problems with authentic contexts describing out-of-school settings and problems that someone in such settings would be called upon to address (OECD, 1999). Not marginalising such tasks may be important since, as Niss suggests, focusing only on "as if" situations, "leads to the perception that applications and modelling is a sort of game [...]. Furthermore, it leads to the perception that school mathematics is not powerful enough to treat authentic extra-mathematical situations and problems. And from there it takes only a small step to arrive at the perception that school mathematics is useless." (Niss, 1992, p. 354).

However, many researchers (and teachers and students) have argued that too many word problems are "pseudo-realistic" and require the students to think differently than in out-of-school task situations (e.g., Boaler, 1993; Nesher, 1980; Verschaffel et al., 2000). Verschaffel et al. argue that "Rather than functioning as realistic and authentic contexts inviting or even forcing pupils to use their common-sense knowledge and experience about the real world in the different stages of the process of solving mathematical application problems, school arithmetic word problem are perceived as artificial, puzzle-like tasks that are unrelated to the real world" (p. xv). Indeed, the general conclusion from a number of studies in the 80's and 90's is that students have a tendency not to make proper use of their real-world knowledge and to suspend the requirement that their solutions must make sense in relation to the out-of-school situation that is described in the task (for an overview see Verschaffel et al., 2000). In another line of research Cooper and his colleagues (see Cooper & Harries, this volume) observed that student solutions that *do* include "realistic" considerations sometimes include the task developers' intended specific realistic considerations, but sometimes they include general realistic considerations, which are not always accorded full credit in assessment tasks. They also showed that a major reason for this difference in the type of realistic considerations taken into account is a different interpretation of what the tasks demand and that the likeliness of each type of interpretation is dependent of social class.

Thus, in the literature, one can detect hopes for what "really real", authentic word problems could offer mathematics education, but at the same time a lot of critique that the available word problems do not live up to the characteristics that are argued would facilitate the attainment of important educational goals. Although there are publications that do give some evidence of positive effects of using more "authentic" word problems (e.g., Bonotto, 2004; Palm, 2008; Verschaffel & De Corte, 1997) the field lacks a firm body of convincing empirical evidence for the effects (in any direction) of the use of more "authentic" word problems. In addition, the terms used for the concordance between school word problems and the, possibly, "real-world" situations indicated by the textual descriptions are ill-defined. The meanings of terms like "really real", "realistic", and "authentic" tasks differ between authors, are sometimes vaguely defined, and are sometimes not clarified in a publication at all (Palm, 2002). There is also a lack of frameworks to guide research and synthesise research results, which may be one of the reasons for the lack of synthesised research results in this area.

In this chapter I will suggest a local theory of authentic task situations and a framework specifying one way of looking at the notion of authentic tasks. These developments may contribute to a theoretical base for the study of word problems that are "realistic", or "authentic", in the sense of concordant with the real-world situation that is indicated in the task. One purpose is to capture the idea of concordance between in- and out-of-school situations in a fine-grained operational framework that can be used to guide, structure, and synthesise research. In addition, it can support development and analysis of tasks as well as a discussion of the meaning of, and characteristics of, authentic tasks among both practitioners and researchers. I will also argue that sometimes it may be productive to view theory as a combination of a framework, a set of claims, and how they fit together. One reason for this is that the framework can sometimes be used for a number of different research issues other than those within one specific theory. Thus, such a focus on the components of the theory facilitates the possibilities to discuss the usefulness, validity, and necessary refinements of the theory as well as of the framework alone when the framework is used for other purposes than as a part of a specific theory. For example, the framework suggested in this chapter, specifying the notion of authentic tasks, may be used and judged for its usefulness and appropriateness as a part of the theory of authentic task situations with claims about student task-solving behaviour. But it can also, for example, be assessed for its appropriateness and value as support for teachers' and researchers' development of word problems with high concordance with real-world situations indicated by the task descriptions. Before the theory of authentic task situations and the framework describing authentic tasks are described I will briefly discuss theories and research frameworks in general.

THEORIES AND RESEARCH FRAMEWORKS

Although the role and use of theory in the discipline of mathematics education has grown considerably the last 30 years (Silver & Herbst, 2007), many leading researchers are now emphasising the importance of developing theories to advancing this field of inquiry (e.g., Lester, 2005; Niss, 2007; Silver & Herbst, 2007). Silver and Herbst (2007) observe that such theories can appear in many guises and at many levels, and identify at least three different types of theories: *grand theories* of mathematics education, *middle-range theories* that concern subfields of study, and *local theories* that help mediate specific connections among practices, research, and problems. Thus, theories include, for example, general philosophical theories, such as theories of learning, but also theories having the role of providing terminology and distinctions to research (Niss, 2007).

But, although theory is a key entity in developing research in mathematics education Niss (2007) notes that "it is neither clear what 'theory' is actually supposed to mean, nor what foundations theories have" (p. 1308). He suggests that:

A theory is a system of concepts and claims with certain properties, namely
- A theory consists of an *organised network of concepts* ... and *claims* about some extensive domain, or a class of domains, consisting of objects, processes, situations, and phenomena.
- In a theory, the *concepts are linked in a connected hierarchy* ...in which a certain set of concepts, taken to be basic, are used as building blocks in the formation of the other concepts.
- In a theory, the *claims are either* basic hypotheses, assumptions or axioms, taken as *fundamental* ...or statements obtained from the fundamental claims by means of *formal* ... or *material* ... *derivation* ... (p. 1308).

Lester (2005), not believing in a grand "theory of everything", suggests that:

...we should focus our efforts on using smaller, more focused theories and models of teaching, learning and development. This position is best accommodated by making use of conceptual frameworks to design and conduct our inquiry. I propose that we view the conceptual frameworks we adopt for our research as sources of ideas that we can appropriate and modify for our purposes as mathematics educators" (p. 460).

He describes a research framework as:

...a basic structure of the ideas (i.e. abstractions and relationships) that serve as the basis for a phenomenon that is to be investigated. These abstractions and the (assumed) interrelationships among them represent the relevant features of the phenomenon as determined by the research perspective that has been adopted. The abstractions and interrelationships are then used as the basis and justification for all aspects of the research (p. 458).

Eisenhart (1991) differentiates between three types of research frameworks: theoretical, practical, and conceptual. Theoretical frameworks guide research by reference to formal theory, and practical frameworks are informed by practitioners' experiences. "A conceptual framework is an argument that the concepts chosen for investigation, and any anticipated relationships among them, will be appropriate and useful given the research problem under investigation" (Lester, 2005, p. 460). Adapting a model for thinking about scientific research by Stokes, Lester argues that educational research can be focused on the pursuit of fundamental understanding, considerations of use, or a blend of the two motives, *use-inspired basic research* (Lester, 2005). Frameworks can be developed to guide research driven by either one or both of these purposes.

It may be noted that, when using the definitions of theory by Niss (2007) and research framework by Lester (2005), both notions include an organisation of concepts and ideas, but that a framework does not need to include claims about phenomena. Thus, a theory may sometimes be thought of as including a framework and claims.

THEORY OF AUTHENTIC TASK SITUATIONS

In the following I will describe a local theory of authentic task situations. First, a conceptual research framework inherent in the theory will be outlined. It is intended for *use-inspired basic research*, and is also presented in Palm (2006) and described in more detail in Palm (2002). As noted above, the concordance between word problems and real-world task situations has been given considerable attention in the literature, but there is a lack of descriptions that capture this relation by specifying, on a fine-grained level, the task characteristics of word problems that emulate out-of-school task situations well. In the following I will use the term authentic for this relation and suggest such characteristics through the framework. After the conceptual framework has been outlined the claims made by the theory are stated. Then the use of the theory for different purposes and the validity of the framework and the theory are discussed. However, first I will provide four examples of word problems that will be used to illustrate the aspects and help exemplify how the framework can be used to analyse tasks.

Example 1.

In a bakery you see a 20 cm long cylinder-shaped Swiss roll. A dissection straight through the cake produces a circular shape with a diameter of 7 cm. The points of time in a day when the Swiss rolls are all sold are normally distributed with mean 5.30 p.m. and standard deviation 15 minutes.
a) What is the volume of the Swiss roll?
b) What is the probability that the Swiss rolls are all sold before 6.00 p.m., when the bakery closes?

Example 2 (from National Pilot Mathematics Test Summer 1992, Band 1-4, paper 1, see Cooper, 1992).

This is the sign in a lift at an office block:

> This lift can carry up to 14 people

In the morning rush, 269 people want to go up in this lift. How many times must it go up?

Example 3 (Carpenter, Lindquist, Matthews, & Silver, 1983).

360 students will go by bus on a school trip. Each bus can hold 48 students.
How many buses are required?

Example 4.

All students in the school will, on the 15th of May, go on a school trip together. You have decided that everyone will go by bus, and that you shall order the buses. You have seen in the student name lists that there are 360 students in the school. Your teacher said that you can order the buses from Swebus, and that each bus can hold 48 students.

Fill in the note below, which you are going to send to Swebus to order the buses.

Swebus – Bus order
Your name:..
School:..
Date of the trip:..
Number of buses to order:..
Other requirements:...
....

Framework for Authentic Tasks

The framework is concerned with the meaning of a concordance between word problems and real-world tasks situations. The point of departure is that the enterprise of developing tasks with such concordance may be viewed as a matter of *simulation*. *Comprehensiveness*, *fidelity,* and *representativeness* are fundamental concepts that will be used in relation to the concept of simulation. The framework is based on the assumption that "if a performance measure is to be interpreted as relevant to 'real life' performance, it must be taken under conditions representative of the stimuli and responses that occur in real life" (Fitzpatrick & Morrison, 1971, p. 239). *Comprehensiveness* refers to "the range of different aspects of the situation that are simulated" (Fitzpatrick & Morrison, 1971, p. 240). Criterion situations are "those in which the learning is to be applied" (p. 237). *Fidelity* refers to the "degree to which each aspect approximates a fair representation of that aspect in the criterion situation" (p. 240). *Representativeness* refers to the combination of comprehensiveness and fidelity (Highland, 1955, cited in Fitzpatrick & Morrison, 1971, p. 240) and will be used as the technical term for the resemblance between a school task and a real-world task situation.

The framework comprises a set of aspects of real-life situations that are reasoned to be important to consider in the simulation of real-world situations. A restriction of comprehensiveness is always necessary. It is not possible to simulate all aspects involved in a situation in the real world and consequently it is not possible to simulate out-of-school situations in such a way that the conditions for the solving of the task will be exactly the same in the school situation. However, the characteristics of the school tasks and the conditions under which they are to be solved can affect the magnitude of this gap, and this gap can affect the similarities in the mathematics used. The proposed aspects were chosen on the basis that a strong argument can be made that the fidelity of the simulations of these aspects clearly has an impact on the extent to which students, when dealing with school tasks, may engage in the mathematical activities attributed to the real situations that are simulated. The match in mathematical activities here refers not only to methods and concepts used in manipulating mathematical objects within the mathematical world in order to obtain mathematical results, but also to the competencies required in the process of creating a mathematical model based on a situation in the "real world", as well as the competencies required for interpreting the obtained mathematical results in relation to the original situation.

The Framework: Aspects of Importance

The aspects of real-life situations considered to be important in their simulation (see Table 1) are:

Table 1. The aspects of real-world situations considered to be important in their simulation.

A. Event	F. Circumstances
B. Question	F1. Availability of external tools
C. Information/data	F2. Guidance
C1. Existence	F3. Consultation and collaboration
C2. Realism	F4. Discussion opportunities
C3. Specificity	F5. Time
D. Presentation	F6. Consequences
D1. Mode	
D2. Language	
E. Solution strategies	G. Solution requirements
E1. Availability	H. Purpose in the figurative context
E2. Experienced plausibility	

A. Event. This aspect refers to the event described in the task. In a simulation of a real-world situation it is a prerequisite that the event described in the school task has taken place or has a fair chance of taking place. For example, picking marbles from an urn and noting their colours (a common event in probability word problems) is not something people do in out-of-school life and therefore does not have a corresponding real event. The events in the examples can all be considered to have a fair chance of happening (a person sees a Swiss roll in a bakery, a number of people want to go up in a lift in the morning, a number of people involved in a team will travel by bus to a game).

B. Question. This aspect refers to the concordance between the assignment given in the school task and in a corresponding out-of-school situation. The question in the school task being one that actually might be posed in the real-world event described is a prerequisite for a corresponding real-world situation to exist. The question in Example 1a is a question that probably would not be asked in the described event, while the questions in the other word problems might be. The owner of the bakery may want to know that an adequate number of Swiss rolls are baked each day. The people in the lift queue may want to know when it may be their turn. The people in Examples 3 and 4 may need to know how many buses to order.

C. Information/data. This aspect refers to the information and data in the task and includes values, models, and given conditions. It concerns the following three subaspects:

C1. Existence. This subaspect refers to the match in existence between the information available in the school task and the information available in the simulated situation. In Example 1 the mean and standard deviation are given, which is information that would not be available in the corresponding real-world situation. This results in a large discrepancy between the mathematics applicable in the school situation (students trying to solve the b-question in Example 1) and the mathematics applicable in the corresponding out-of-school situation (in this situation these statistical measures would not have been used).

C2. Realism. Since students' solution strategies are partly based on judgements of the reasonableness of their answers, and an important reference is reality (Stillman, 1998), the realism of the values given in the school tasks (in the sense of identical or very close to values in the situation that is simulated) is an aspect of importance in simulations of real-life situations.

C3. Specificity. This subaspect refers to the match in specificity of the information available in the school situation and the simulated situation. This match is sometimes important for the possibilities of the students' reasoning to be similar in the in- and out-of-school situations since a lack of specificity can produce a slightly different context and since strategy choice and solution success is dependent on the specific context at hand (see Baranes, Perry, & Stiegler, 1989; Taylor, 1989). For example, the difference between sharing a loaf of bread and sharing a cake can make students reason differently (Taylor, 1989). In addition, if the price of a specific sort of candy is the issue in the out-of-school situation and it is not known in the school situation that the price is about this object then the students will not have the same opportunities to judge the reasonableness of their answers.

D. Presentation. The aspect of task presentation refers to the way the task is conveyed to the students. This aspect is divided into two subaspects:

D1. Mode. The mode of the task conveyance refers to, for example, if the word problem is communicated orally or in written form to the students and if the information is presented in words, diagrams, or tables. Since, for example, all students do not cope equally well with written communication (e.g., Newman, 1977), and mathematical competencies required to handle graphical representations are not the same as those required to handle verbal representations (e.g., Nathan & Kim, 2007) simulation of this aspect can influence the mathematics required or possible to use.

D2. Language use. Linguistic analyses show that in many word problems the semantic, referential and stylistic aspects of these texts are different from texts describing real life situations. Such school tasks require different competencies in interpreting the tasks than the corresponding out-of-school tasks, and thus such language use impedes the possibilities of the same use of mathematics in the in- and out-of-school situations (Nesher, 1980). In addition, an impeding impact of difficult terms (Foxman, 1987; Mousley, 1990), and sentence structure and amount of text (Mousley, 1990), have been reported. Thus, in simulations, it is of importance that the language used in the school task is not so different from a corresponding out-of-school task situation that it negatively affects the possibilities for the students to use the same mathematics as they would have used in the situation that is simulated. The term "dissection" in Example 1a may be a term that impedes understanding in the school word problem.

E. Solution strategies. To be simulated, a task situation includes the role and purpose of someone solving the task. This aspect is divided into two subaspects:

E1. Availability. The availability of solution strategies concerns the match in the relevant solution strategies available to the students solving school tasks and those available to the persons described in the tasks as solving the corresponding tasks in real life beyond school. If these strategies do not match, then the students do not have the same possibilities to use the same mathematics that could have been used in the simulated situation. In Example 4 the students are supposed to take the role of themselves, while in Example 3 it is not known in what role the students are solving the task.

E2. Experienced plausibility. This subaspect refers to the match in the strategies experienced as plausible for solving the task in the school situation and those experienced as plausible in the simulated situation. For example, when a textbook section starts with a description of a particular method for solving tasks, followed by a set of tasks, this may be experienced as a request to use this method and that other methods applicable in the out-of-school situation will not apply to these tasks.

F. Circumstances. The circumstances under which the task is to be solved are factors in the social context (Clarke & Helme, 1998), and are divided into the following subaspects:

F1. Availability of external tools. External tools refer to concrete tools outside the mind such as a calculator, map, or ruler. The significance of this aspect may be visualised by thinking about the difference between the mathematical abilities required to calculate the monthly cost of a house loan using specially designed software (which would be used at a brokers' office) and by doing so only having available a calculator.

F2. Guidance. This subaspect refers to guidance in the form of explicit or implicit hints. Hints in school tasks such as "You can start by calculating the maximum cost", would clearly (if not also given in the simulated situation) cause a vast difference in what the students are expected to accomplish in the two situations.

F3. Consultation and collaboration. Out-of-school task situations are solved solely by oneself, through collaboration within groups, or with the possibility of assistance. In simulations, those circumstances have also to be considered since input from other people can affect which skills and competencies are required to solve a task (Resnick, 1987).

F4. Discussion opportunities. This subaspect refers to the possibilities for the students to ask about and discuss the meaning and understanding of the task. A lack of concordance between in- and out-of-school situations in this subaspect can cause differences in the mathematics used since this communication has been shown to have the power of affecting the experienced meaning of the task and the solution strategies applied (Christiansen, 1997).

F5. Time. Time pressure is known to impede task-solving success. In simulations, it is therefore important that time restrictions are such that they do not cause significant differences in the possibilities of solving the school tasks compared with the situations that are simulated.

F6. Consequences of task solving success (or failure). Different solutions to problems can have different consequences for solvers. Pressures on solvers and their motivations for the task affect the task-solving process and are therefore an aspect to consider in simulations. This aspect may include efforts to promote motivation for word problem solving (people in situations encountered in life beyond school are often motivated to solve those problems). It could also mean putting the products into real use. This could, for example, be done by publishing the results of a statistical survey in the local newspaper or by confronting local politicians with the results. The students could also mark the reduced prices (when working with percentages) when selling self-made products for the purpose of collecting money for people in need (which many schools in, for example, Sweden do). A large project with real consequences is described in Tate (1995). In this project the students used mathematics in their efforts to get liquor stores relocated away from their school neighbourhood.

G. Solution requirements. The notion of solution is to be interpreted broadly, meaning both solution method and the final answer to a task. Judgments on the validity of answers and discussion of solution methods (in textbooks and assessment marking schemes) or phrases in the task text (such as "using derivatives solve the following task") can constitute requirements for the solutions to school tasks. In a simulation, these requirements should be consistent with what is regarded as an appropriate solution in a corresponding simulated situation, and the students should be aware of this.

Example 2 (the lift task) may be solved by dividing 269 by 14 and rounding off the answer upwards to 20. However, in a real-world situation, a realistic assumption would be that people arrive at different points of time, or that some people working on the lower floors would take the stairs, resulting in the lift going up a different number of times than 20 (a similar argument about the links to reality in this task was made by Cooper, 1992). To prevent students from being forced to think differently than they would in corresponding out-of-school situations, calculations and answers based on such assumptions must also receive credit.

H. Purpose in the figurative context. The appropriateness of the answer to a task, and thus the necessary considerations to be made, sometimes depend on the purpose of finding the answer. In other tasks, the whole solution method is dependent on the purpose (see Palm, 2002). Thus, in simulations it is sometimes essential that the purpose of the task in the figurative context is as clear to the students as it is for the solver in the simulated situation (for an example of difference in clarity of the purpose see the short discussion of Examples 3 and 4 under the heading "Validity of the theory" below).

Claims by the Theory

Based on the organised network of concepts in the framework the theory includes a number of claims in the forms of hypotheses. Firstly, in general, the theory hypothesises that there is a positive correlation between the representativeness of simulations, as experienced by the students, and the similarity between the students' behaviours in the in- and out-of-school task situations. As a consequence, the higher the representativeness of a simulation is, the larger will be the proportion of students that makes proper use of their real-world knowledge when working with a word problem, and that will not suspend the requirement that their solutions must make sense in relation to the out-of-school situation that is described in the task. However, in addition to the task text and the task-solving environment, the characteristics of the students themselves affect the way they interact with a task. Thus, individual students may be differently affected by a simulations' representativeness. Furthermore, different aspects of real-world situations affect students' behaviour differently, and the way they affect them may also vary between situations. Some aspects will also be more important for student behaviour than others and the degree of importance will also vary between situations. From this it follows that similarity in student performance between the in- and out-of-school situation will be dependent not only on the number of aspects that are simulated with high fidelity, but also on which aspects that are well simulated. What these most important aspects are will vary from one task situation to another. However, for each word problem, analyses of the task situation may reveal what the most important aspects are and why.

The reason underlying the above claims is the well-known fact that the conditions under which students are set to solve tasks affect their task solving (e.g., Lave, 1988). Thus, conditions similar with respect to important aspects may lead to similar task solving behaviour. For example, Lave (1998) compared arithmetic calculations in the context of shopping in a supermarket, in a simulation of supermarket shopping, and in solving pure arithmetic tasks from a paper-and-pencil test. The students' solution strategies and task solving success differed between the contexts. The tasks encountered under the first two conditions displayed the highest solution rates.

Secondly, a repetitive encounter with word problems that are simulations with a high degree of experienced representativeness and include figurative contexts that are experienced as meaningful affects students so that they increase their engagement in the figurative contexts, and a larger proportion of the students will use their knowledge of the real-world situations described in the tasks in their word problem solving.

The reasons underlying this second claim originate in the important role that beliefs play in mathematical task solving (Schoenfeld, 1985). The students' beliefs must allow them the freedom to act in school as if it was an out-of-school situation. To accomplish this experience for students, the rules of school word-problem solving would have to come closer to the rules of the simulated situations. The students must, for example, believe that their solutions are going to be judged according to the requirements of the real-world situation, and not have to think about what different requirements the teacher might have. But such beliefs are not consistent with the intentions carried by the generic form of the genre of traditional word problems, described by Gerofsky (1999), and since new beliefs are normally integrated in the existing belief system gradually, it is likely to take a frequent encounter with word problems with high representativeness for students to develop beliefs that support serious considerations of the real-world situations described in the tasks. Furthermore, studies on motivation show that significant engagement in a task is enhanced when students experience the task as being meaningful (Ryan & Deci, 2000).

Use of the Theory for Different Purposes

The research framework inherent in this theory of authentic task situations is intended for *use-inspired basic research*. The theory and its framework may be used to guide further research about representativeness by suggesting aspects to be taken into consideration. These aspects can also help organise and synthesise research findings in order to attain a more coherent picture of the acquired knowledge of the influence of the representativeness of a simulation. With such a more coherent picture more well-founded predictions and explanations of students' word problem-solving behaviour could be made. Furthermore, it could facilitate discussions amongst both teachers and researchers about the properties of school tasks that are intended to emulate out-of-school situations, and could be useful in the development and critical analysis of contextualised tasks intended for classroom instruction, textbooks, and assessments, as well as for research purposes.

Validity of the Theory

A theory in education can very seldom be judged by adopting a view of predictions as deterministic in the sense it is used in the physical sciences. However, it is still essential to assess the validity and usefulness of the theory through investigating the theory's claims by conducting empirical studies and analysing how the patterns of the empirical evidence fit with the claims of the theory. This process may lead to refinements of both the claims and the framework inherent in the theory.

Empirical arguments for or against aspects of the theory can be based on studies that have used the framework in their research design. The validity of the theory can also be examined by applying the framework in an analysis of tasks used in studies that did not include the framework in their research design and relate this task analysis to other observed variables in those studies, such as student behaviour. The research framework inherent in this theory of authentic task situations has, so far, been used in the research design of two empirical studies (but see the chapter by Depaepe, De Corte, and Verschaffel in this volume for a third example). The first study investigated the impact of authenticity on students' use of real world knowledge in their solutions to word problems, with the restriction that a higher degree of authenticity has to be accomplished within the frames of the practicalities of normal classroom procedures (Palm, 2008). Word problems from the studies focusing on students' "suspension of sense making" in the '80s and '90s summarised in Verschaffel et al. (2000) were used. The framework was used to guide a revision of these word problems to attain versions of them with higher representativeness. The use of the framework provided a structured set of lenses by which the selection of task properties to change could be made and to attain some control of the differences between the task versions. Two tests, one including the more authentic task versions and one including the less authentic task versions, were randomly administered to 160 fifth-grade students. The students provided written responses, but interview data from all students were also collected. Consistent with the theory the students who were faced with the more authentic task variants both provided written solutions that were consistent with the realities of the "real" situations described in the tasks and activated their knowledge of the "real" situations, whether or not it affected their written solutions, in a significantly higher proportion of the tasks. An example of a pair of tasks included in the study is Examples 3 and 4. Example 4 is considered to simulate the aspects in the framework to a larger extent than Example 3. For example, the consideration in the task development of the aspect Purpose resulted in a clarification of the purpose of the task solving in Example 4 by making the students order the buses by filling in an ordering form. Of the students who were faced with Example 3, 75% provided the answer "8 buses" (and not, for example, a fraction of buses such as 7.5 buses) or gave a realistic comment to why their answer made sense. Of the students who dealt with the more authentic Example 4, 95% provided the answer 8 buses, which was considered to be consistent with the described situation in the task. The difference was statistically significant. DeFranco and Curcio (1997) carried out a similar study on this bus task. In one of the two variants of the task the students were made to believe they were actually ordering the buses through the use of a teletrainer with a person answering at the other end. In this way, the difference between the clarity of the purpose in the in and out-of-school situation was made smaller. Also, in this study, the proportion of students providing "realistic" answers was higher on the more authentic version of the bus task.

The second study is an analysis of Finnish and Swedish national assessments for upper secondary school in which the framework was used as a tool for describing in what way, and to what extent, the word problems in the assessments could be considered authentic or not (Palm & Burman, 2004). The analysis showed, for example, that about 50% of the word problems were considered to both describe an *event* that might occur in life beyond school and include a *question* that really might be posed in that event. About 25% of the tasks also possessed the quality that the *information/data* given in the task was similar to that in some corresponding real-world task situation to such a degree that it required the same mathematics for its solution as would have been required to solve the task in the simulated situation. When also the similarity in the *availability of external tools* between the assessment situation and the real-world task situations was considered, 20% of the tasks were judged to simulate these four aspects with such fidelity that the same mathematics would be required by the assessment tasks and the simulated real-world situations. The results of this study show that the framework can be useful in describing the characteristics of word problems in relation to their authenticity.

SUMMARY AND DISCUSSION

Mathematical word problems may serve several purposes. The study of issues related to some of the purposes, such as providing support for thinking about abstract mathematical concepts, is not the focus of this chapter and may require other theoretical underpinnings than are suggested here. The focus here is on purposes such as facilitating an experience of mathematics as useful in out-of-school situations and practicing solving problems that require respecting circumstances that need to be considered in out-of-school task situations. The importance of attaining these goals has been emphasised by many authors and curriculum documents. To attain these goals, many scholars have promoted the use of tasks that emulate out-of-school task situations, but many have also criticised the word problems most often used today for not living up to such characteristics.

It is of great significance that claims about the impact (or non-impact) of authenticity can be corroborated by empirical evidence. The available body of research on the impact of authenticity is far from sufficient, which influences practitioners working in mathematics education. Developing tasks that simulate important aspects of meaningful task situations with fidelity takes a great deal of time, effort, and money. Today many teachers, textbook writers and professional assessment developers spend a lot of work trying to develop such tasks, motivated by the belief that their effort will be worthwhile. Others do not share this belief and therefore not this direction in their work. Due to the lack of evidence, decisions are many times forced to be based on assumptions. A more extensive body of research about the consequences of the authenticity of mathematical word problems is needed so that practitioners will have better possibilities to base their decisions about task development on empirical evidence grounded in scientific research. This effort would allow a more efficient use of available resources and better opportunities for developing efficient learning environments.

The quality of scientific inquiries in mathematics education, and in all other disciplines, is greatly enhanced by the use of theories and frameworks of different kinds and at different levels to support the research being pursued. To contribute to the theoretical base for the study of authentic word problems and the influence of authenticity on students' performance on word problems, a local theory of authentic task situations has been offered. This theory does not, as of now, make predictions about the learning of new concepts or about transfer of school-learned mathematics to new real-world situations, but is concerned with the prediction and understanding of students' performance on school word problems. Inherent in this theory is a framework conceptualising the idea of concordance between school word problems and out-of-school task situations. This framework can also be used outside the theory, for example in studies of the influence of authenticity on students' affective experiences, transfer, and learning. It can be used to assist in the development of authentic word problems for both instructional and research purposes. For example, if real-world situations involving rich and desired mathematical activities are identified the framework may be used to simulate these situations. It can also be helpful in structuring research studies and the information gathered from them to achieve a more comprehensive picture of the impact of authenticity of mathematical word problems.

REFERENCES

Baranes, R., Perry, M., & Stiegler, J. W. (1989). Activation of real-world knowledge in the solution of word problems. *Cognition and Instruction, 6*, 287–318.

Blum, W., & Niss, M. (1991). Applied mathematical problem solving, modelling, applications, and links to other subjects – State, trends and issues in mathematics instruction. *Educational Studies in Mathematics, 22*, 37–68.

Boaler, J. (1993). The role of contexts in the mathematics classroom: Do they make mathematics more "real"? *For the Learning of Mathematics, 13*(2), 12–17.

Bonotto, C. (2004). How to replace the word problems with activities of realistic mathematical modelling. In H.-W. Henn & W. Blum (Eds.), *ICMI Study 14: Applications and modelling in mathematics education* (Pre-conference Vol., pp. 41–46). Dortmund, Germany: Department of Mathematics, University of Dortmund.

Burton, L. (1993). Implications of constructivism for achievement in mathematics. In J. A. Malone & P. C. S. Taylor (Eds.), *Constructivist interpretations of teaching and learning mathematics* (pp. 7–14). Perth, Western Australia: National Key Centre for School Science and Mathematics.

Carpenter, T. P., Lindquist, M. M., Matthews, W., & Silver, E. A. (1983). Results of the third NAEP mathematics assessment: Secondary school. *Mathematics Teacher, 76*, 652–659.

Christiansen, I. M. (1997). When negotiation of meaning is also negotiation of task. *Educational Studies in Mathematics, 34*(1), 1–25.

Clarke, D. J., & Helme, S. (1998). Context as construction. In O. Björkqvist (Ed.), *Mathematics teaching from a constructivist point of view* (pp. 129–147). Vasa, Finland: Abo Akademi University, Faculty of Education.

Cooper, B. (1992). Testing national curriculum mathematics: Some critical comments on the treatment of "real" contexts for mathematics. *Curriculum Journal, 3*, 231–244.

DeFranco, T. C., & Curcio, F. R. (1997). A division problem with remainder embedded across two contexts: Children's solutions in restrictive vs. real-world settings. *Focus on Learning Problems in Mathematics, 19*(2), 58–72.

Eisenhart, M. A. (1991). Conceptual frameworks for research circa 1991: Ideas from a cultural anthropologist; implications for mathematics education researchers. *Proceedings of the 13th annual meeting of the North American Chapter of the International Group for the Psychology of Mathematics Education* (Vol. 1, pp. 202–219). Blacksburg, VA.

Finnish National Board of Education. (2004). *National core curriculum for upper secondary schools 2003*. Vammala, Finland: Finnish National Board of Education.

Fitzpatrick, R., & Morrison, E. J. (1971). Performance and product evaluation. In R. L. Thorndike (Ed.), *Educational measurement* (2nd ed., pp. 237–270). Washington, DC: American Council on Education.

Foxman, D. (1987). *Assessing practical mathematics in secondary schools*. Windsor, UK: The NFER-NELSON Publishing Company.

Gerofsky, S. (1999). Genre analysis as a way of understanding pedagogy in mathematics education. *For the Learning of Mathematics, 19*(3), 36–46.

Lave, J. (1988). *Cognition in practice*. Boston: Cambridge.

Lester, F. (2005). On the theoretical, conceptual, and philosophical foundations for research in mathematics education. *Zentralblatt für Didaktik der Mathematik, 37*, 457–467.

Mousley, J. A. (1990). Assessment in primary mathematics: The effects of item readability. *Proceedings of the 14th international conference for the Psychology of Mathematics Education* (Vol. 3, pp. 273–280). Mexico.

Nathan, M. J., & Kim, S. (2007). Pattern generalization with graphs and words: A cross-sectional and longitudinal analysis of middle school students' representational fluency. *Mathematical Thinking and Learning, 9* (3), 193–219.

National Council of Teachers of Mathematics. (2000). *Principles and standards for school mathematics*. Reston, VA: National Council of Teachers of Mathematics.

Nesher, P. (1980). The stereotyped nature of school word problems. *For the Learning of Mathematics, 1*, 41–48.

Newman, M. A. (1977). An analysis of sixth-grade pupils errors on written mathematical tasks. *Research in Mathematics Education in Australia, 1*, 239–258.

Niss, M. (1992). Applications and modeling in school mathematics – Directions for future development. In I. Wirzup & R. Streit (Eds.), *Developments in school mathematics education around the world* (Vol. 3). Chicago: National Council of Teachers of Mathematics.

Niss, M. (2007). Reflections on the state of and trends in research on mathematics teaching and learning: From here to Utopia. In F. Lester (Ed.), *Second handbook of research on mathematics teaching and learning* (pp. 1293–1312). Charlotte, NC: Information Age Publishing.

Organisation for Economic Co-operation and Development. (1999). *Measuring student knowledge and skills. A new framework for assessment*. Paris: OECD.

Palm, T. (2002). *The realism of mathematical school tasks – Features and consequences*. Umeå, Sweden: Umeå University.

Palm, T. (2005). Preface. In T. Palm (Ed.), *Proceedings of the 3rd international SweMaS conference*. Umeå, Sweden: Umeå University, Department of Educational Measurement.

Palm, T. (2006). Word problems as simulations of real-world situations: A proposed framework. *For the Learning of Mathematics, 26*(1), 42–47.

Palm, T. (2008). Impact of authenticity on sense making in word problem solving. *Educational Studies in Mathematics, 67*(1), 37–58.

Palm, T., & Burman, L. (2004). Reality in mathematics assessment: An analysis of task-reality concordance in Finnish and Swedish national assessments. *Nordic Studies in Mathematics Education, 9*(3), 1–33.

Resnick, L. B. (1987). Learning in school and out. *Educational Researcher, 16*, 13–20.

Ryan, R. M., & Deci, E. L. (2000). Intrinsic and extrinsic motivations: Classic definitions and new directions. *Contemporary Educational Psychology, 25*, 54–67.

Schoenfeld, A. H. (1985). *Mathematical problem solving*. Orlando, FL: Academic Press.

Silver, E. A., & Herbst, P. G. (2007). Theory in mathematics education scholarship. In F. Lester (Ed.), *Second handbook of research on mathematics teaching and learning* (pp. 39–67). Charlotte, NC: Information Age Publishing.

Stillman, G. (1998). Engagement with task context of applications tasks: Student performance and teacher beliefs. *Nordic Studies in Mathematics Education, 6*(3–4), 51–70.

Tate, W. F. (1995). Returning to the root: A culturally relevant approach to mathematics pedagogy. *Theory into Practice, 34*(3), 166–173.

Taylor, N. (1989). "Let them eat cake" – Desire, cognition, and culture in mathematics learning. In C. Keitel, P. Damerow, A. Bishop & P. Gerdes (Eds.), *Mathematics, education, and society* (pp. 161–163). Paris: Division of Science Technical and Environmental Education, UNESCO.

Verschaffel, L., & De Corte, E. (1997). Teaching realistic mathematical modeling in the elementary school. A teaching experiment with fifth graders. *Journal of Research in Mathematics Education, 28*, 577–601.

Verschaffel, L., Greer, B., & De Corte, E. (2000). *Making sense of word problems*. Lisse, The Netherlands: Swets & Zeitlinger.

Torulf Palm
Umeå Mathematics Education Research Centre (UMERC)
Department of Mathematics Technology and Science Education
Umeå University
Sweden

SUSAN GEROFSKY

2. GENRE, SIMULACRA, IMPOSSIBLE EXCHANGE, AND THE REAL

How Postmodern Theory Problematises Word Problems

INTRODUCTION

It is interesting to treat mathematical word problems historically as a microcosm of the philosophical debate around the nature and relationship of mathematics, language, and reality. Word problems have always been an instantiation of the use of language and story to pose mathematical conundrums – but the purposes of these conundrums, and their purported relationship to "real life" have not remained stable over time.

Elsewhere (Gerofsky, 2004) I have argued that mathematical word problems constitute a written and pedagogical genre which carries within its form echoes of related genres (for example, riddles, parables, puzzles, and competitions of wit), none of which bears any simple, necessary relationship to a presumed practical "reality".

I have also hypothesised a historical change in the pretext for the use of mathematical word problems in Europe at the time of the Renaissance (beginning in the mid-15th century), when knowledge of algebra became widespread (Gerofsky, 2004, pp. 127-132). My conjecture is that, in pre-algebraic societies, mathematical word problems are the only way available to establish mathematical generality, through the "heaping up" of numerous examples in story form. Evidence from the earliest of these stories (from ancient Babylon, about 4500 years ago) to those published in the most recent of school textbooks gives plenty of examples of the fantastical, non-"real" nature of many of these stories (and by extension, the genre itself). With the introduction of algebra to Europe at the time of the Renaissance, mathematical word problems lost their function of expressing generality through exemplification (although it could be argued that for most school students, whose mathematical knowledge is pre-algebraic, word problems might continue to fulfil this function even today). I conjecture that a re-purposing of word problems took place as part of the Renaissance-to-Modernist project, including claims that mathematical word problems were of practical use in a mercantilised, scientised society and would prepare young people for participation in the worlds of trade, science, and engineering. Part of this Renaissance/Modernist claim involved a treatment of language as a transparent medium that matched the realities of that society in an unproblematic way.

It can be argued (for example, in Toulmin, 1992) that the Renaissance-to-Modernist project operated continuously as the paradigm for Western and other societies from the mid-15th century to the mid-to-late 20th century. Assumptions of this project include the presumed separation of, and preference for, rationality over emotion, mind over body, the individual over the collective, empiricism over intuition, consciousness over the unconscious, and a declarative over metaphoric uses of language. This rationalist project is associated with and supported by intellectual and technological advances in science, medicine, mechanical, and industrial processes. Clarity, a rejection of ambiguity, and a presumption of one-to-one mappings between concepts (including mathematical formulae) and practices (including technical and economic praxis) underlay many of these advances. Most of us who are now writing research and theory in mathematics education grew up in societies that favoured these Modernist assumptions.

I contend that our cultural/societal/technological world has changed drastically in the past twenty-five years, and continues to change in ways as extreme as those which distinguished Renaissance from medieval times. With McLuhan (2003), I link changes in our technological service environment, particularly the advent of personal computers, computer networks, and social networking, with changes in culture, perception, and the most fundamental ways of thinking, being, and relating in the world. These changes have been observed and theorised by postmodern and poststructuralist philosophers. If we are interested in making sense of the ongoing changes we are living daily, in education as in other areas of our lives, we would do well to engage with the ideas of these contemporary philosophers.

However, most researchers in mathematics education, including those of us working with mathematical word problems, have continued to work within Modernist paradigms that assume an unproblematic transparency of language, and one-to-one matching or mapping models of the relationship between mathematical representations and "reality" (meaning generally a scientific, engineering, or mercantile reality). In this paradigm, curriculum writers really ought to pay attention to eliminating ambiguity and increasing fidelity to "real life situations" in the word problems they write, and students ought to learn correct ways of interpreting the transparently obvious matchings that connect the language of word problems to their matching real-world situations. Unfortunately for proponents of this project, language is, by its very nature, never unambiguous (see, for example, Lakoff & Johnson, 2003); mathematical models are necessarily neither transparent nor obvious matchings with phenomena, and must by their nature stress and ignore particular features of live situations (Mason & Pimm, 1984); and human consciousness comprises only a small part of human minds, not to mention "reality" (Dehaene, 2001). These considerations were brushed aside as minimal "noise" in the Modernist project, but loom large in postmodern theorising, including scientific theorising in new fields like cognitive science.

Few mathematics education writers have addressed the very useful notions of reality, simulation, and knowledge in our contemporary technocultural environment elaborated by theorists like Bakhtin, Lacan, Zizek, Lyotard, Derrida, McLuhan, Baudrillard, and others (though see Brown, 2008 for a noteworthy exception). These theorists of postmodernity trouble the sense of a transparent, self-evident reality and its representations in a number of ways. For example, Bakhtin, in his work on genre, counters a view of language as a transparent mode of representation, positing that all utterances operate within emergent, mutually referencing, generic environments. Lyotard claims that universalised narratives and absolute knowledge are no longer possible, even as a dream, in the postmodern condition, and all knowledge is contingent, local, and provisional. Lacan's cultural interpretations of Freudian psychoanalytic theory set the inchoate, unknowable, unbearable Real outside the necessary defences created by human culture and psychology, and yet always present. Zizek extends Lacan's concept of the Real to the realms of the arts, politics, and society. McLuhan encourages us to become aware of both the figure and the ground in dealing with culture and technology, pointing out that a narrow focus on content and meaning, or on moralising against changes that have already taken place, makes us wholly unaware of the enormous unintended effects of a changed service environment and its entailments for consciousness, representation, and our notion of reality. Finally Baudrillard's work on simulation and simulacra is especially useful in problematising word problems, as it deals with modes of representation that range so far from the iconic as to supplant reality, creating a world of simulacra that bear no relation to any reality whatever, and interact with other simulacra to create a virtual Real.

In this chapter, I will draw upon some of the ideas of Bakhtin, Lacan, Zizek, McLuhan, and Baudrillard to explore postmodern conceptions of the relationship among language, culture, and reality, and use these concepts to interrogate mathematics educators' claims that we should be able to succeed in matching word problems with real life.

BAKHTIN: GENRES AND "REALITY"

The work of Russian literary and linguistic theorist Mikhail Bakhtin (1895-1975) introduced many new ways of conceptualising speech and writing when it was "discovered" by the West in the 1970s and 1980s. Although Bakhtin came from a background in structural linguistics and literary theory, his ideas about dialogism, addressivity, heteroglossia, the carnivalesque, chronotopes, and speech genres have been taken up by poststructuralist and postmodern theorists, and his work has been considered comparable with Derrida's and Foucault's. Bakhtin's work on genre is most useful in considering questions of reality in relation to mathematical word problems.

Bakhtin defines "speech genres" (which also include written genres like mathematical word problems) as "relatively stable types of utterances" within a particular sphere in which language is used (Bakhtin, 1986, p. 60). While particular literary and rhetorical genres had been studied since antiquity, Bakhtin reframed the concept of a genre to include not only literary forms like the epic or lyric poem, or rhetorical forms like political oration, but *all* forms of language. This was a radical move; in effect, it placed all linguistic activity in the category of generic speech or writing. While Bakhtin emphasised the extreme heterogeneity of speech genres (since the diversity of human activity is productive and ever-changing, and new activity types entail new spoken and written genres), he also asserted the importance of observing and analysing the nature of utterance types or genres as part of any research that involves particular forms of human language and consciousness.

Bakhtin's insistence on the primacy of generic forms in language is closely related to his conception of "chronotopes" (literally, space-time configurations) which are created by writers and speakers working in developing genres, and which form the "givens" for any writer or speaker working in an established genre. A chronotope can be thought of as the distinctive time-space "world" created by a literary or speech genre – for example, the shadowy world of the castle of the Gothic novel, the fictional world of Dickensian London, or the lonely, isolated space station created in many science fiction stories and movies. A chronotope is a cluster of features that involves spatial settings, time schemes, typical plot developments, and character types, and types of language and imagery used in a genre. For example, here is Bakhtin's characterisation of the chronotope of what he calls "adventure time" in a genre of ancient novel he calls "the adventure of ordeal" – the love story genre clearly recognisable in comic or tragic form in innumerable stories from Romeo and Juliet, to folk ballads and tales, and melodramatic, picaresque movies:

> There is a boy and a girl of *marriageable age*. Their lineage is *unknown, mysterious...* They are remarkable for their *exceptional beauty*. They are also *exceptionally chaste*. They meet each other *unexpectedly*, usually during some festive *holiday*. A *sudden* and *instantaneous* passion flares up between them that is as irresistible as fate, like an incurable disease. However, the marriage cannot take place straightaway. They are confronted with obstacles that *retard* and delay their union. The lovers are parted, they seek one another, find one another; again they lose one another, again they find each other. There are the usual obstacles and adventures of lovers: the abduction of the bride on the eve of the wedding, the absence of *parental consent* (if parents exist), a different bridegroom and bride intended for either of the lovers (*false couples*), the flight of the lovers, their journey, a storm at sea, a *shipwreck*, a miraculous rescue, and attack by *pirates, captivity* and *prison,* an attempt on the innocence of the hero and heroine, the offering-up of the heroine as a purifying sacrifice, wars, battles, *being sold into slavery, presumed deaths, disguising one's identity,* recognition and failures of recognition, presumed betrayals, attempts on chastity and fidelity, false accusations of crimes, court trials, court inquiries into the chastity and fidelity of the lovers. The heroes find their parents (if unknown). Meetings with unexpected friends or enemies play an important role, as do fortune-telling, prophecy, prophetic dreams, premonitions and sleeping-potions. The novel ends happily with the lovers united in marriage (Bakhtin, 1981, pp. 87-88).

Herbert J. Gans has outlined similar chronotopes that function in American journalism and determine the selection and narrative formation of "stories" for the news (Gans, 1979) – for example, the chronotopes around the concepts of "small town pastoralism" and "the preservation of social order". (For an interesting recent discussion on the power of these and similar genres in framing news stories on bioethical issues, see Braun, 2007a, and responses by Price, 2007, Chambers, 2007, and Braun, 2007b). Even in the news, which is our source for much of our sense of the larger realities of our world, it's "narrative all the way down" (Chambers, 2007).

The term *schema* (plural *schemata*) has been used by other genre theorists like Swales (1990) for a concept very close to chronotopes. Schemata are culturally-mediated clusters of activities, features, and narrative lines that characterise particular types of events. For example, the North American schema for a birthday party might include games, balloons, singing "Happy Birthday", blowing out candles, eating cake and ice cream, and opening presents, while the Chinese birthday celebration schema might include eating long noodles and eggs, decorating the house with red paper, and receiving gifts of money in red envelopes. The chronotope includes the temporal and narrative aspects of schemata as well as typical spatial, cultural, and social settings. Cultural background knowledge of schemata/chronotopes allows us to make predictions, draw implications, "read between the lines", and read social cues from verbal and written utterances within familiar cultural contexts.

Bakhtin has gone so far as to claim that it is the chronotope that defines genres and generic distinctions (Bakhtin, 1981) – that is to say, a distinctive time-space world of settings, objects, events, character types, and narrative sequences is characteristic of each genre, and in fact becomes its defining feature. These chronotopes can be fresh and surprising in a newly-developing genre, or "fossilised" to reflect an earlier culture in a genre that is well-established and traditional. Later genre theorists like Jamieson (1975) show that the chronotopes of historical antecedents to a genre are carried within the form and referentiality of the genre, often without the writer or speaker being consciously aware of these generic resonances. Another contemporary genre theorist, Miller (1984), finds that a genre carries its typical chronotope not only in terms of temporal-spatial settings, but also in terms of the possible intentions that can be expressed and explored within that genre. She writes that "what we learn when we learn a genre is not just a pattern of forms or even a method of achieving our own ends. We learn, more importantly, what ends we may have." (p. 165)

So if mathematical word problems form a written pedagogic genre within education, and if this genre is defined by its chronotope (presumably a fossilised one, given the four-and-a-half millennia elapsed since our earliest examples of the genre), what relationship can word problems have with reality?

Bakhtin's conceptions of dialogism, chronotopes, and genres presumes a real world, but one that is only known through the mediation of language (and thus genre and culture). In Bakhtin's theory, language can never be a transparent means of reflecting an unproblematic external reality, but a creative and productive means of knowing through dialogic interpretation. Solipsistic interpretations of aspects of reality are avoided through social dialogue (whether amongst people in conversation in the same time and space or between, for example, authors and readers, who may be separated by centuries and great distances), and through a living, evolving relationship and interpenetration between the "real" of experienced lives and generic chronotopes. Bakhtin characterises his concept of the chronotope with an interesting analogy that compares the relationship between chronotope and reality with the relationship of a living organism with its separate but mutually affecting environment:

> However forcefully the real and the represented world resist fusion, however immutable the presence of that categorical boundary line between them, they are nevertheless indissolubly tied up with each other and find themselves in continual mutual interaction; uninterrupted exchange goes on between them, similar to the uninterrupted exchange of matter between living organisms and the environment that surrounds them. As long as the organism lives, it resists a fusion with the environment, but if it is torn out of its environment, it dies. The work and the world represented in it enter the real world and enrich it, and the real world enters the work and its world as part of the process of its creation, as well as part of its subsequent life, in a continual reviewing of the work through the creative perception of listeners and readers... If I relate (or write about) an event that has just happened to me, than I as the *teller* (or writer) of this event am already outside the time and space in which the event occurred. It is just as impossible to forge an identity between myself, my own 'I' and that 'I' that is the subject of my stories, as it is to lift myself up by my own hair. The represented world, however realistic and truthful, can never be chronotopically identical with the real world it represents. (Bakhtin, 1981, pp. 254-256)

So in Bakhtin's theory, *all* representations (including all talking and writing) are generic, and mediated by the language and the chronotopes that characterise the genre; but, at the same time, genres both nourish, and are nourished by, aspects of experienced reality which form their environment, and genres evolve and emerge through dialogic negotiation amongst people, and through contact with aspects of a reality that can never be identical to any representative genre.

Bakhtin's conceptualisation stops short of the most radical postmodern theories of representation through its positing of the existence and influence of an external reality on culturally and linguistically mediated genres. (Note that it is interesting to compare Bakhtin's account above with Baudrillard's concept of "impossible exchange", discussed later in this chapter.) But Bakhtin's genre theory does already pose a very serious and fundamental challenge to those who claim to be able to represent reality through a simple matching process. If all representation (including, for example, news reports, biography, photographs and videotapes, drawings and graphs) is generic and operates within the evolving norms of its chronotope, then there is no "neutral" representation possible. Every human expression operates within generic universes of time, space, storyline, possible intentions and meanings, and these are inescapably linguistically and culturally mediated through dialogue and interpretation. We have no way of representing a "base-level" reality, although our storied, represented knowing is both nurtured by reality and *affects* that reality as well.

LACAN, ZIZEK, AND THE LACANIAN REAL

A similar, perhaps more comprehensive, theory of the relationship between language, culture, and "the Real" comes from the French psychoanalytic theorist, Jacques Lacan (1901-1981). Like Bakhtin's theories, Lacan's work is viewed as bridging structuralist and postmodern approaches. Although the bulk of Lacan's work is a revisiting of Freud's psychoanalytic theory, Lacan has been taken up as much by artists and cultural theorists as by psychoanalysts.

I will refer here as well to the work of Slavoj Zizek (born 1949), the Slovenian philosopher and film and cultural critic whose interpretations of Lacanian theory in terms of cultural phenomena (and vice versa) have won him international fame. Zizek's illustrations of Lacanian concepts in terms of film and popular culture have resonance both in terms of understanding Lacan and making sense of contemporary arts and culture.

Other researchers in mathematics education have taken up ideas from Lacan and Zizek. Notably, Brown and collaborators (Brown & England 2005, Brown & McNamara 2005, England & Brown 2001) have used Lacanian psychoanalytic theory to investigate teacher and learner identity construction; Brown (2001, 2008) and Hardy (2007) have used Lacan's work to critique mathematics education's individualist, "neutral", Modernist traditions; Walkerdine (1988) has explored desire and pleasure in mathematics from a Lacanian point of view. But to my knowledge, no one in mathematics education so far has taken up Lacanian notions of the Real to critique assumptions about representations and applications of mathematics, and it is in this way that I will use a facet of Lacan's oeuvre here.

In Lacan's psychoanalytic theory, there is a sharp distinction between what he terms "reality" and "the Real". "Reality" refers to our socially, linguistically mediated world in the realm of the Symbolic, very similar to Bakhtin's concept of reality as constructed and formulated by the chronotopes of genre. There is nothing basic or necessary about this "reality"; it is constructed out of language, cultural history, and narrative, and always owes a great deal to others who came before us and created these cultural traditions, schemata, and linguistic structures. "Reality" is the social order, regulated through law and socially taken-as-given traditions.

The Real is that which is outside language, symbolism, social structure, and narrative, primary to the Symbolic and not reducible to any kinds of symbols. The Lacanian Real induces anxiety and trauma because it is unmediated and non-categorisable – impossible, inchoate, excessive, unnameable. Lacan describes the Real as "the essential object which is not an object any longer, but this something faced with which all words cease and all categories fail, the object of anxiety par excellence" (Lacan, 1991, p. 164).

To go back a step: Lacan's theory posits a three-part structure to the human psyche, reminiscent of, but not identical to, Freud's id-ego-superego divisions. Lacan's three divisions, the Real, the Imaginary, and the Symbolic, are theorised to develop sequentially in humans, although more than one of these may be present simultaneously.

The Real is the primary state of newborn infants (and, according to Lacan, of non-domesticated animals) where there is no separation of self from environment or from the mother. There are no desires or fantasies, but only needs. Nothing is named or separated; all is one. There is nothing missing or lacking – the Real is what it is, complete, random, excessive.

The Imaginary develops with the child's awareness of another – generally the mother. What was one becomes two, and with this separation, there is a sense of loss. Lacan's Imaginary corresponds to Freud's "mirror stage", which is illustrated by the myth of Narcissus: the self externalises or projects its own image onto the other (the mother), and sees this image as either a figure of perfection or a monster. Lacan identifies the Imaginary with fantasy of all kinds, and claims that it is the Imaginary that is invoked when we fall in love; we strive to make two into one again, to achieve wholeness through union with an imagined other. With the Imaginary, the beginning of a sense of self separate from an other is born, and, with it, fantasy and feelings of lack, as the self demands to be like (and reunited with) its perfected fantasy mirror-image.

With the beginnings of language, the child enters the Symbolic realm, and with language, accepts the laws that regulate society and culture. Lacan calls this symbolic order "the big Other" or, alternately, "the Name of the Father". With language comes the realisation that "two becomes three (or more)" – that there is more to the world than the child and its mother, and that there must be an acceptance of the symbolic order and law for community and culture to function. From this stage on, the person is bound up in language, and desires are formulated in terms of the web of language. Unfulfillable desires are a necessary entailment of the Symbolic order. Lacan goes so far as to include the unconscious as part of the Symbolic, writing that "the unconscious is structured like a language" (Lacan, 1977, p. 203).

Once we are caught up in the Symbolic order, it is impossible to experience the unmediated/ unmediatable Real – and yet the Real continues to have influence in our psychic lives as the immutably material, the not-describable, the undeniable, the horrific. It is the Real that constrains our fantasies and desires and trips us up; the Real constitutes the gaps in our socially-constructed "realities", where language and categories fail.

Zizek uses examples from novels and horror films to illustrate the idea of the irruption or intrusion of the Real into the Symbolic Order. For instance, he gives an example of the traumatic nature of a sidelong glimpse of the Real from Robert Heinlein's science fiction novella, *The Unpleasant Profession of Jonathan Hoag* (Heinlein, 1983). In this story, an American couple learns that our universe is only one of many, designed by mysterious "universe-designing" beings, who had unfortunately overlooked some minor flaws in their design. The couple are advised that by the time they drive home in their car, these flaws will have been repaired, but they must by no means open the window of their car till they arrive home. Through the car window, they see an ordinary sunlit summer scene; and of course an irresistible reason arises that compels them to take the forbidden action of rolling down the car window to talk to a police officer:

> She complied, then gave a sharp intake of breath and swallowed a scream. He did not scream, but he wanted to.

Outside the open window was no sunlight, no cops, no kids – nothing. Nothing but a grey and formless mist, pulsing slowly as if with inchoate life. They could see nothing of the city through it, not because it was too dense but because it was – empty. No sound came out of it; no movement showed in it.

It merged with the frame of the window and began to drift inside. Randall shouted, "Roll up the window!" She tried to obey, but her hands were nerveless; he reached across her and cranked it up himself, jamming it hard into its seat.

The sunny scene was restored; through the glass they saw the patrolman, the boisterous game, the sidewalk, and the city beyond. Cynthia put a hand on his arm. "Drive on, Teddy!"

"Wait a minute," he said tensely, and turned to the window beside him. Very cautiously he rolled it down – just a crack, less than an inch.

It was enough. The formless grey flux was out there too; through the glass, city traffic and sunny street were plain, through the opening – nothing. (Heinlein, 1983, quoted in Zizek, 1991, p. 14)

This "formless grey flux" is, for Zizek, an example *par excellence* of the Lacanian Real, irrupting at the borderline of inside and outside, and at the borderline of familiar "reality" and those gaps or chasms where the realities of our culturally-constructed world fail.

Zizek's citations of literary and cinematic versions of the Real include the 1999 film *The Matrix* and the 1997 film, *Alien Resurrection*. At the climax of *The Matrix*, the protagonist, played by Keanu Reeves, finds out that the world we consider reality is electronically generated and virtual. When he "awakens into the 'real reality' he sees a desolate landscape littered with burned ruins – what remained of Chicago after a global war. The resistance leader Morpheus utters the ironic greeting: 'Welcome to the desert of the real.'" (Zizek, 2002, p. 15). In *Alien Resurrection*, Sigourney Weaver's character, the biological clone of the protagonist in the original *Alien* film, insists on entering a forbidden room on the space station (as the characters in Heinlein's novella insisted on taking the forbidden action of rolling down the car window). There she encounters the unnameable and unbearable horror of the Real: numerous bottled and pickled versions of herself, in foetal or monstrous form, the results of attempts at cloning gone horribly wrong, and finally a barely-surviving monstrous version of herself that looks her in the eye, speaks to her, and which she must kill (Zizek & Fiennes, 2006).

Let me return briefly to mathematical word problems, before addressing the theories of McLuhan and Baudrillard. When mathematics educators call for word problems that match real life situations, clearly what is intended by the term "real life" is not the horrific and inchoate Lacanian Real, nor could it be Bakhtin's closely related concept of a "reality" which can never be equated to any chronotope. The real life referents in word problems are of the nature of Lacan's culturally and symbolically constructed "realities", or Bakhtin's generic chronotopes. These "realities" or choronotopes are inventions of human language and society, created out of a tangential or glancing contact with the Real (which is always present alongside the Imaginary and the Symbolic Order, or alternately, alongside culturally- and linguistically-mediated genres), but more importantly, invented in dialogic response to other examples of the same genre, other traditions and instantiations of a culture.

Film theorist Sobchack elaborates on the fact that instances of a genre (in this case, so-called "genre films") are imitations and responses to one another and to other related chronotopes more than they are imitations of life:

> [Genre films] are made in imitation not of life but of other films. True, there must be the first instance in a series or cycle, yet most cases of the first examples of various film genres can be traced to literary sources, primarily pulp literature [...] And once the initial film is made, it has entered the pool of common knowledge known by filmmaker and film audience alike. Imitations and descendants – the long line of "sons of", "brides of", and "the return of" – begins. (Sobchack, 1975/1986, p. 104)

I have argued elsewhere (Gerofsky, 1999, 2004) that word problems constitute a literary and pedagogical genre within mathematics education. Reading the concept of genre with regard to Bakhtin's chronotopes, or Lacan's "realities", and Sobchack's characterisation of the dialogic, "echoing" nature of genres, it seems very clear that word problems will always be responding primarily to other word problems, and to the related cultural traditions of parables, puzzles, and riddles. There is an insulating quality in this exchange; like an image caught in a series of reflections and distortions in a hall of mirrors, or a sound that enters an endlessly echoing chamber, the chronotopes of genre, or the symbolised "realities" constructed through language allow us to make minimal contact with the dangerous and disturbing Real. Instead, much of our creativity works within the culturally-mediated bounds of mutually-referencing human constructs, playing with and responding to genre, creating new genres in dialogue with earlier ones, creating stories that are in some ways the same, and in other ways different from, those that went before. But we should be clear that new kinds of word problems are far more like other word problems than they are different, and are made in imitation of other word problems far more than they are imitations of the Real.

MCLUHAN: LAWS OF MEDIA, CULTURE, AND TECHNOLOGY

Marshall McLuhan (1911-1980), the Canadian theorist of media, technology, and culture, offers ways to understand *why* we are now in the "postmodern condition" (Lyotard, 1984) and why the Renaissance-to-Modernist project has come to an end. McLuhan's ideas were extended and elaborated by French postmodern theorist Baudrillard (1929-2007) to show that concepts of "reality" have changed radically under postmodern technological and cultural conditions, so that we have all now experienced hyperreality, virtual reality, simulations, and simulacra to some degree. It is with reference to these concepts of a changed experience of reality that I will discuss McLuhan's laws of media.

McLuhan's work comprised a study of the effects of technology (interpreted in its broadest sense) on human perceptions and cultures. One of McLuhan's basic premises was that any technology extends and externalises ("outers" or "utters") part of the human body. For example, a hammer extends the forearm and fist; a bowl extends cupped hands; clothing extends skin; a wheel extends moving feet; number extends fingers (digits) (McLuhan & McLuhan, 1988). Those body parts are stressed or numbed to some degree in the new technological environment – think, for example, of the numbing, immobilising effects of technology on the bodies of people who spend a great deal of time riding in the extended "body" of a car.

Some technologies extend perceptual organs or the nervous system, and McLuhan asserts that these technologies have the effect of altering the balance of the sensorium – that is to say, they alter the relative importance of sight, hearing, touch, etc. in human life and culture, with seismic consequences for both individuals and societies. There are two classes of technology that have particularly significant ramifications in McLuhan's work: the phonetic alphabet, and electric/electronic media.

McLuhan differentiates the phonetic alphabet from other writing systems like ideograms (for example, Chinese characters) or syllabaries (for example, Korean, Hebrew, or Arabic writing systems). Where each ideogram carries a gestalt of sounds, meanings, and associations, and a syllabary character carries a cluster of consonant and vowel sounds and morphemic associations, the phonetic alphabet is the only kind of writing system in which each character carries no meaning at all, but only a single, minimal sound. McLuhan argues that the introduction of the phonetic alphabet and phonetic literacy in a culture entails a violent and dramatic shift in the sensory balance and in modes of consciousness to accommodate this translation of spoken language into these sequential strings of meaningless bits. McLuhan says that when alphabetic literacy comes into a society that has an acoustic sensory bias, there is a rapid and dramatic shift to an overwhelmingly visual bias, and along with it, a shift from a collective, tribal, holistic consciousness to an individual, private, and atomistic one.

This may seem like a great deal to attribute to the single technology of the phonetic alphabet, but McLuhan builds an argument that is convincing in its details and in its explanatory and predictive force. McLuhan considers two significant historical moments when the phonetic alphabet was introduced to societies: Ancient Greece in the time of Plato, and Renaissance Europe, with the introduction of the Gutenberg printing press in the mid-15th century and widespread alphabetic literacy that followed. In both cases he observes that oral, tribal cultures (Homeric Greece and medieval Europe) are overtaken by visual, individualistic cultures. Plato denigrates the Homeric poets, with their orally transmitted "encyclopedia" of culture in the form of orally memorised, improvised, and recited epic poetry, and suggests the epics be abandoned in favour of written, connected, logical, sequential arguments. (Interestingly, Plato was a transitional figure, bridging the oral world of Socrates' dialogues and the newly-alphabetised culture of books).

The Renaissance overthrew the collective, oral, and acoustic consciousness of the Middle Ages in favour of individual consciousness, silent reading, linear rationality, and the revival of the culture and learning the of (alphabetised) Ancient Greeks. McLuhan argues that it is the nature of alphabetic reading, with its extension of the eye as the preferred sensory modality, that brought about a cultural shift to valuing a single point of view (and the innovation of perspective painting), a sense of removed objectivity (only available through an emphasis on vision), and the concepts of privacy, goals, linearity, specialism, rationalism, and a valuing of the continuous, connected, and static (see tetrads on visual space in McLuhan & McLuhan, 1988, pp. 204–205). Modern science and humanism are grounded in these side effects of a societal ocular bias.

McLuhan argues that what was done by the alphabetisation in the Renaissance-to-Modern period is now in the process of being undone in our contemporary world of electric and electronic networked media. McLuhan characterises these media as the extension and "outering" of our nervous systems, so that we are now living *inside* the nervous system of the planet. We are now all connected to everyone else at the level of the nervous system, so that there is no possibility of privacy, the lone individual, or the free-standing genius (as conceived in the Modernist project). In some ways, we are currently "living the Renaissance backward", with a return to an acoustic-tactile collective consciousness and in-depth participation in place of individual consciousness and arms-length objectivity.

The Global Village was McLuhan's term, coined in the 1960s, and what seemed far-fetched in a world connected by television seems obvious now in our world of the Internet and widely available digital technologies. McLuhan could see this process of the extension of the global nervous system beginning in the late 19th and early 20th century with the development of the telegraph, telephone, radio, and electric lighting, accelerated with television and communication satellites, and enormously accelerated with computers, computer networks, and other digital technologies (McLuhan, 2003, 2005). Marshall McLuhan died in 1980, at the very advent of the digital revolution we are still experiencing, but his work predicted many of the phenomena explored in the 1980s and 1990s by postmodern philosophers: the end of privacy, the obsolescence of alphabetic literacy, violence as a quest for identity by tribalised national groups, a rejection of universal grand narratives, and a return to inner landscapes, the performative on a global scale, and holistic, audio-tactile experience. *Wired* magazine recognised the importance of McLuhan's work in 1993, recognising him as the magazine's "patron saint" on its masthead and running special articles about him. McLuhan's work has been a strong influence in the work of French postmodern philosopher, Jean Baudrillard, and it is in Baudrillard's work that we find an articulated account of postmodern "realities" affected by the shift from visual to acoustic culture.

Jean Baudrillard (1929-2007) acknowledged the influence of McLuhan on his work, and along with most French contemporary philosophers, he was also strongly influenced by the work of Lacan and anthropologist Claude Levi-Strauss. Baudrillard's work follows McLuhan in its connections among technology, media, and culture and the ruptures in human consciousness and relation to the world that come as a result of what McLuhan calls the "total service environment" that accrues about a new technology. Baudrillard takes his ideas to a higher philosophical, sometimes apocalyptic pitch than McLuhan, engaging as Zizek does in analyses of very current events in the news and popular culture and using these to build new philosophical arguments.

Baudrillard's ideas about representing "reality" are discussed primarily in relation to his concept of simulations and simulacra in postmodern society, and in his concept of the impossibility of exchange in our contemporary world (and thence, the impossibility of equivalence or representation). Much of Baudrillard's work is focused on the idea of *absence*, particularly the absence of a referent for signs and the absence of a transcendent reality to ground claims of truth and validity. Both these absences are important in our consideration of reality and mathematical word problems, since these problems consist of words and stories often taken to refer to "real-life situations", and since their use in math education is often legitimised by claims to validity in the realm of a greater reality.

In his essay, *Simulacra and Simulations*, Baudrillard (1988) presents the idea of the "precession of the simulacra" in our contemporary globalised, networked, digitised society – the idea that simulations now *precede*, and in fact *supplant* reality, existing entirely without any corresponding or matching referent, and interacting primarily with other simulations:

> It is no longer a question of imitation, nor of reduplication... it is rather a question of substituting signs of the real for the real itself... A hyperreal sheltered ... from any distinction between the real and the imaginary, leaving room only for the orbital recurrence of models and the simulated generation of difference. (p. 170)

Baudrillard's "hyperreal" is best exemplified by the most exuberant excesses of American and now global culture (Las Vegas, various Disneylands) which establish environments based on simulated "nostalgic" or "historical" references to a history that has been altered and fictionalised (viz. Main Street USA, or the Luxor Hotel and Casino).

One step beyond simulation, simulacra arrive prior to any referent, create a virtual experience that is taken as real, and interact with other simulacra and simulations. We are all becoming casually familiar with simulacra through our interactions on the networked social software of Web 2.0. We throw sheep at one another on Facebook, participate in the viral proliferation of video genres on YouTube, and watch our universities use "real" cash to purchase virtual islands for online campuses on Second Life.

Our postmodern world of networked computers and digital media creates strange and hitherto-unknown simulacra that have effects beyond the virtual. An article in *Walrus Magazine* (Thompson, 2004) documents some aspects of the economy of virtual worlds in online fantasy games like EverQuest and Ultima Online. The *Walrus* article documents a young economist's discovery of the economic and governmental systems of an online game, EverQuest (Castronova, 2001). He discovered a strange system where simulacra (virtual money and virtual goods) were traded for US dollars:

> The Gross National Product of EverQuest, measured by how much wealth all the players together created in a single year inside the game...turned out to be $2,266 US per capita. By World Bank rankings, that made EverQuest richer than India, Bulgaria, or China, and nearly as wealthy as Russia. It was the

seventy-seventh richest country in the world. And it didn't even exist. (Thompson, 2004, p. 41)

Not only are there multi-million dollar businesses that trade in game points, game levels, avatars, offshore banking, and currency trading amongst games, but gaming sweatshops in China and Mexico have recently been documented. In these sweatshops, hundreds of low-wage employees are hired to spend long hours and days playing games so that their on-line characters gain powers, levels, and virtual possession, which are then sold through brokers to wealthy buyers.

Simulacra of crime have sprung up as quickly as banks in these virtual worlds. (The Vancouver, British Columbia Police Department recently set up an avatar-led recruiting office in Second Life).

> The [Sims Online] game had a chain of cyber-brothels, run by a character named "Evangeline". Evangeline had organised a handful of Sim women to perform hot-sex chat inside the game for customers, who paid in Simoleans... [It was] later discovered that some of Evangeline's "girls" were underage girls in real life, and that Evangeline herself was a seventeen-year-old boy living in Florida... Soon The Sims Online was on the front page of the New York Times. (Thompson, 2004, p. 46)

Real-life wars are fought using video games and virtual environments, to the point where simulacra may take precedence in creating experiences of war, at least for the privileged:

> The US military has already licensed a private chunk of [online world] **There** and created a simulation of the planet on it. The army is currently using the virtual Baghdad in **There** as a training space for American soldiers. (Thompson, 2004, p. 47)

For reasons like this, Baudrillard made the famous, highly controversial statement that the Gulf War of 1991 had not taken place. Certainly the nature of warfare has changed drastically when both training and missile launches take place in virtual, video game environments and when battles are telecast live by satellite on CNN.

Following McLuhan, it could be argued that the world of technology-mediated simulacra where we now live creates a total service environment that mitigates against a definable real that can be separated from the virtual; the real and virtual are inextricably entangled and mutually affecting.

Baudrillard goes beyond technological arguments to an even more fundamental argument for the impossibility of any representation of the real in any secular society. Using the anthropological concepts of exchange of Levi-Strauss and Marcel Mauss as a fundamental to the circulation of commodities in a society, Baudrillard argues that exchange has become impossible, and thus "reality" exists only as simulacra:

> There is no equivalent of the world. That might even be said to be its definition – or lack of it. No equivalent, no double, no representation, no mirror... There is not enough room both for the world and for its double. So there can

be no verifying of the world. That is, indeed, why 'reality' is an imposture. Being without possible verification, the world is a fundamental illusion. (Baudrillard, 2001, p. 3)

Baudrillard's argument deals with the world or universe as a whole, but also with systems within the world like law, politics, economics, aesthetics, even the field of biology. In any of these systems, it is possible to pretend to be able to represent reality at the micro level, but at the macro level, the entire system is without grounding, unless we posit a "higher reality" through religion or metaphysics (and this is not acceptable in a secular society). Taking politics as an example, Baudrillard writes:

> Politics is laden with signs and meanings, but seen from the outside it has none. It has nothing to justify it at a universal level (all attempts to ground politics at a metaphysical or philosophical level have failed). It absorbs everything which comes into its ambit and converts it into its own substance, but it is not able to convert itself into – or be reflected in – a higher reality which would give it meaning. (Baudrillard, 2001, p. 4)

For "politics", we could substitute "mathematics", since Gödel's Theorem has proved it impossible to devise a mathematical system that is both consistent and complete; or "physics", since quantum mechanics and Heisenberg's uncertainty principle have placed a radical uncertainty and inconsistency at the heart of this field and of our ideas of matter itself.

Baudrillard's concept of impossible exchange leads to a conclusion very much like Lyotard's assertion that, in our postmodern condition, no grand narratives are possible. Writing about economics, Baudrillard says:

> That principle [of a grounding of the field in reality and rationality] is valid only within an artificially bounded sphere. Outside that sphere lies radical uncertainty. And it is this exiled, foreclosed uncertainty which haunts systems and generates the illusion of the economic, the political, and so on. It is the failure to understand this which leads systems into incoherence, hypertrophy and, in some sense, leads them to destroy themselves. For it is from the inside, by overreaching themselves, that systems make bonfires of their own postulates, and fall into ruins. (Baudrillard, 2005, p. 6)

Taking this big, universe-sized idea to our little world of mathematical word problems, there is a kind of unacceptable hubris in claims that there can be a precise equivalence, a transparent matching, an exchange between "reality" and these brief, generic pedagogic stories. To claim that mathematical word problems (or the theorems of physics, or the narratives of history, or novels in the style of "Realism") have a relationship of identity with reality is to "make a bonfire of our own postulates". Baudrillard's concept of reality, like Lacan's "Real", cannot be captured in language or signs of any kind; it cannot be matched up with its equivalent, since it is constitutionally impossible to have an equivalent for reality. Positivistic science, a universe completely marked out with the grid lines of Newtonian physics, Laplace's deterministic project to know all present, past and future eventualities by extrapolation from a complete knowledge of this instant – all of these aspects of the Modernist projects have been foreclosed by the impossibility of providing a grounding or an exchange for reality, and we are left with an unresolvable uncertainty, perhaps mystery, at the heart of things.

CODA: (HOW) CAN WE WORK WITH WORD PROBLEMS?

Mathematics educators who are interested in working with word problems have a great many options available for exploration and development (many of which are described in greater detail in Gerofsky, 2004, pp. 133-154). For example:
- Word problems are closely related to ancestral or antecedent genres including parables, riddles and recreational mathematical puzzles, and educators can profitably explore the resonances among these genres, and experiment with treating mathematical word problems playfully, lingeringly, philosophically, "as if" they were riddles, recreations, or parables.
- Mathematical word problems have the potential to offer memorable imagery that can act as a touchstone for teachers and learners in building and discussing abstract concepts. The imagery that works best may often be anything but "realistic" in its usual interpretation (as matching transparently and unproblematically with the situations of adult work life); for example, learners may find more memorable images in fairy-tale stories of dragons than in stories about mortgage interest rates. The term "realisable" (i.e., imaginable) captures this sense of striking, imaginative imagery, and has been developed in this way by researchers at the Freudenthal Institute (see, for example, Van den Heuvel-Panhuizen, Middleton, & Streefland, 1995).
- Mathematics educators can learn from educators in other fields who work with revitalising generic forms through reframing and re-purposing these forms – see, for example, the inspiring work of language educators Davis and Rinvolucri (1988) in revitalising forms like "the dictation" and "the language lab".
- Mathematical word problems are inherently ambiguous. If mathematics educators are willing to embrace this inevitable ambiguity (rather than holding up mathematics as a realm of absolute clarity and certainty), teachers and students can learn a great deal from the richness of interpretation available in even these brief story problems.
- Mathematics educators can draw learners' attention to the generic nature of word problems and explore the mathematical implications when some features of the genre are held invariant and others are varied or pushed to the limit. Learners become aware of the generic nature of mathematical word problems very early in their experience of schooling, usually by third grade (see, for example, Puchalska & Semadeni, 1987), but this awareness is seldom acknowledged or developed in school.

The approaches to word problems sketched above problematise form as well as content, and involve an awareness of the media of communication, genre, and forms of narrative along with the mathematical concepts these are meant to embody. Researchers and educators who choose to ignore contemporary theoretical developments, and insist on treating mathematical word problems as simple and transparent one-to-one matchings with some purported universally-acknowledged "reality", will simply doom their work to irrelevance. Students know that mathematical word problems are neither transparent nor "real", and (rightly) do not accept word problems as object lessons in the usefulness of mathematics in "real life". It is doubtful if a Modernist "reality-matching" approach was ever more than a pretext for the continued use of word problems in mathematics education. A consideration of contemporary theoretical constructs of the real should help educators grasp the need for more sophisticated consideration of the nature of mathematical word problems, and consequently their uses.

REFERENCES

Bakhtin, M. M. (1981). *The dialogic imagination: Four essays* (C. Emerson & M. Holquist, Trans.). Austin, TX: University of Texas Press.
Bakhtin, M. M. (1986). *Speech genres and other late essays* (V. W. McGee, Trans.). Austin, TX: University of Texas Press.
Baudrillard, J. (1988). Simulacra and simulations. In M. Poster (Ed.), *Jean Baudrillard, selected writings* (pp. 166–184). Stanford, CA: Stanford University Press.
Baudrillard, J. (2001). *Impossible exchange* (C. Turner, Trans.). London: Verso.
Baudrillard, J. (2005). *The intelligence of evil or the lucidity pact* (C. Turner, Trans.). Oxford, UK: Berg.
Braun, J. A. (2007a). The imperatives of narrative: Health interest groups and morality in network news. *The American Journal of Bioethics, 7*(8), 6–14.
Braun, J. A. (2007b). A response to commentators on "The imperatives of narrative: Health interest groups and morality in network news". *The American Journal of Bioethics, 7*(8), W1–W2.
Brown, T. (2001). *Mathematics education and language: Interpreting hermeneutics and post-structuralism (2nd edition)*. Dordrecht, The Netherlands: Kluwer.
Brown, T. (Ed.). (2008). *The psychology of mathematics education: A psychoanalytic displacement*. Rotterdam: Sense Publishers.
Brown, T., & England, J. (2005). Identity, narrative and practitioner research. *Discourse: Studies in the Politics of Education, 26*, 443–458.
Brown, T., & McNamara, O. (2005). *New teacher identity and regulative government: The discursive formation of primary teacher education*. New York: Springer.
Castronova, E. (2001). Virtual worlds: A first-hand account of market and society on the cyberian frontier. Retrieved January, 2008, from http://ideas.repec.org/p/bep/grleeb/2-1-1008.html
Chambers, T. (2007). It's narrative all the way down. *The American Journal of Bioethics, 7*(8), 15–16.
Davis, P., & Rinvolucri, M. (1988). *Dictation: New methods, new possibilities*. Cambridge, UK: Cambridge University Press.
Dehaene, S. (2001). *The cognitive neuroscience of consciousness*. Cambridge, MA: MIT Press.
England, J., & Brown, T. (2001). Inclusion, exclusion and marginalisation. *Educational Action Research, 9*, 335–371.
Gans, H. J. (1979). *Deciding what's news: A study of CBS Evening News, NBC Nightly News, Newsweek, and Time*. New York: Pantheon.
Gerofsky, S. (1999). Genre analysis as a way of understanding pedagogy in mathematics education. *For the Learning of Mathematics, 19*(3), 36–46.
Gerofsky, S. (2004). *A man left Albuquerque heading east: Word problems as genre in mathematics education*. New York: Peter Lang.
Hardy, T. (2007). Participation and performance: Keys to confident learning in mathematics? *Research in Mathematics Education, 9*(1), 21–32.
Heinlein, R. (1983). *The unpleasant profession of Jonathan Hoag*. New York: Berkley.

Jamieson, K. M. (1975). Antecedent genre as historical constraint. *Quarterly Journal of Speech, 61*, 406–415.
Lacan, J. (1977). *The four fundamental concepts of psycho-analysis* (A. Sheridan, Trans.). New York: Norton.
Lacan, J. (1991). *The Seminars of Jacques Lacan: Book II: The ego in Freud's theory and in the technique of psychoanalysis 1954–1955*. New York: Norton.
Lakoff, G., & Johnson, M. (2003). *Metaphors we live by*. Chicago: University of Chicago Press.
Lyotard, J. F. (1984). *The post-modern condition: A report on knowledge* (G. Bennington & B. Massumi, Trans.). Minneapolis, MN: University of Minnesota Press.
Mason, J., & Pimm, D. (1984). Generic examples: Seeing the general in the particular. *Educational Studies in Mathematics, 15*, 277–289.
McLuhan, M. (2003). *Understanding me: Lectures and interviews*. (S. McLuhan & D. Staines, Eds.). Toronto: McLelland & Stewart.
McLuhan, M. (2005). *McLuhan unbound*. (E. McLuhan & W. T. Gordon, Eds.). Corte Madera, CA: Gingko Press.
McLuhan, M., & McLuhan, E. (1988). *Laws of media*. Toronto, ON: University of Toronto Press.
Miller. C. R. (1984). Genre as social action. *Quarterly Journal of Speech, 70*, 151–167.
Price, C. C. (2007). Cinematic thinking: Narratives and bioethics unbound. *The American Journal of Bioethics, 7*(8), 21–23.
Puchalska, E., & Semadeni, Z. (1987). Children's reactions to verbal arithmetical problems with missing, surplus or contradictory data. *For the Learning of Mathematics, 7*(3), 9–16.
Sobchack, T. (1975/1986). Genre films: A classical experience. In B. K. Grant (Ed.), *Film genre reader* (pp. 102–113). Austin, TX: University of Texas Press.
Swales, J. (1990). *Genre analysis*. Cambridge, UK: Cambridge University Press.
Thompson, C. (2004). Game theories: The virtual economist. *The Walrus, 1*(5), 38–47.
Toulmin, S. E. (1992). *Cosmopolis: The hidden agenda of modernity*. Chicago: University of Chicago Press.
Van den Heuvel-Panhuizen, M., Middleton, J. A., & Streefland, L. (1995). Student-generated problems: Easy and difficult problems on percentage. *For the Learning of Mathematics, 15*(3), 21–27.
Walkerdine, V. (1988). *The mastery of reason: Cognitive development and the production of rationality*. London: Routledge.
Zizek, S. (1991). *Looking awry: An introduction to Jacques Lacan through popular culture*. Cambridge, MA.: MIT Press.
Zizek, S. (2002). *Welcome to the desert of the Real*. London: Verso.
Zizek, S., & Fiennes, S. (2006). *Film: The pervert's guide to cinema* [Motion picture]. UK/Austria/ The Netherlands. Lone Star, Mischief Films, Amoeba Film.

Susan Gerofsky
Curriculum Studies, Faculty of Education
University of British Columbia
U.S.A.

UWE GELLERT AND EVA JABLONKA

3. "I AM NOT TALKING ABOUT REALITY"

Word Problems and the Intricacies of Producing Legitimate Text

AN INTRODUCTORY VIGNETTE

In an 8th-grade mathematical textbook, under the running head "Simultaneous Linear Equations in Two Unknowns", the following problem is given:

A man rows a boat downstream for a distance of 66 km in three hours. Then he rows 33 km upstream in three hours.
(a) How fast (in km/h) is the current?
(b) What is the speed of the boat in still water?

There exist myriads of similar word problems. They may differ in the situation they set up, they may state the name of the protagonist or not, they may provide more or less realistic data. Nevertheless, in all of these problems, an activity that is considered to be a recurrent and familiar part of a practice outside school is recontextualised as a school mathematical activity. The task for the students, here, is to consider rowing and flow speed under the gaze of school mathematics, specifically, simultaneous linear equations in two unknowns. Let us get a glimpse of a teacher-student interaction in an 8th-grade mathematics class in Hong Kong, where the teacher and his students try to solve this problem on the whiteboard.

33:22	Teacher:	Look at the question part b. It says what is the speed of the boat in still water. What do we mean by still water is…water that doesn't flow at all. *[in English]*
33:34	Student:	That's what? *[in Chinese]*
33:35	Student:	That's stagnant water. *[in Chinese]*
33:37	Teacher:	Water doesn't flow. It has no movement, water has no movement. *[in English]*
33:40	Student:	Is it possible? *[in Chinese]*
33:42	Teacher:	That er…in English still water means water has no movement. *[in English]*
33:46	Student:	It's not possible. *[in Chinese]*
33:49	Teacher:	That's a…I'm not talking about reality. *[in English]*[1]

Apparently, the teacher and the students do not talk the same language. The students use their first language (Chinese) in order to clarify whether water, supposedly in a natural environment, can, or cannot, exist without any movement. Contrary to that, the teacher uses the official school language (English) in order to engage in a school mathematical argument. At the very moment (33:49), when the teacher realises that the mutual lack of understanding resides not in the differences between first and second language competencies of the students, he explicitly calls on the *recontextualising principle* (see below). He is not talking about reality – but about school mathematics.

In this chapter we discuss the relationships between "words and worlds", which are represented in mathematical word problems, in terms of relationships between domains of practice. These relationships consist in the recontextualisation of out-of-school practices for didactical purposes, including an inescapable relocation and appropriation of the corresponding discourses by pedagogic discourse. The students in the mathematics classroom face these issues as the demands of recognising different forms of discourse and of producing legitimate text.

We take as "word problems" descriptions of school mathematical tasks that contain signifiers that are not from the repertoire of school mathematical technical language. Gerofsky (this volume, p. 22) traces these descriptions back to "Modernist paradigms that assume an unproblematic transparency of language, and one-to-one matching or mapping models of the relationship between mathematical representations and 'reality' (meaning generally a scientific, engineering or mercantile reality)." The assumed unambiguity of language, by which this tradition is informed, is in fact a misleading claim.

After commemorating some interpretations of the dilemma that students face when confronted with these types of tasks, we discuss categories of expression and content of word problems from the perspective of recontextualisation. In the course of the discussion, our focus shifts gradually to interactions of students and their teachers when solving mathematical word problems in the classroom. With our discussion we intend to contribute to developing a language of description that helps organise the empirical text made of these interactions, indicating the structural complexities inherent in mathematical word problems that relate to students' often reported difficulties in this field. We see the students' problems linked to the ways in which the recontextualisation of out-of-school practices operates in mathematics classrooms.

THE DILEMMA OF CALLING ON EVERYDAY EXPERIENCE

Numerous studies report on students' suspension of sense making when solving mathematical word problems (for an overview see Verschaffel, Greer, & De Corte, 2000; see also Palm, this volume). These studies date back to the early 1980s, when a large number of French first and second graders provided numerical solutions for the problem "Sur un bateau il y a 26 moutons et 10 chèvres. Quel est l'âge du capitaine?" (Baruk, 1985; IREM, 1980). The findings from this study have been interpreted differently. Contrary to the mainstream interpretation, for instance, Freudenthal (1982) emphasises the "magic context" that word problems may provide for young children:

> Je ne crois pas que la tension qui existe dans les contextes entre la réalité et la manuel suffice à expliquer des phénomènes comme celui signalé par l'IREM de Grenoble. Il y a encore un autre contexte qui est en jeu dans la formation

de cette attitude mathématique ou plutôt anti-mathématique (...) – le contexte magique. (Freudenthal, 1982, pp. 401-402)

The magic context allows the reading of significance into arbitrary numerical relationships. Such a context is the device by which the apparently absurd mathematical word problem is translated into an authentic problem within the child's imagination. Such argument notwithstanding, "The age of the captain" is generally regarded as the iconic example for many students' suspension of sense making. However, Freudenthal's interpretation suggests that "sense making" is a vague category for exploring students' difficulties.

The suspension of "sense making" when solving word-problems has been explained by the students' conviction of what solving a mathematical task is all about, based on their school mathematical experience of solving typical textbook problems. These tasks describe the substratum of a situation that is supposedly familiar to the students – both the problem and the answer are well defined, no redundant information is given, and no data are missing. The missing quantity is to be calculated straightforwardly, without consideration of situational constraints or issues of validity and implementation of the solution. Critics of the artificial nature of typical textbook problems have pointed out that their unrealistic nature might be the reason for the students' suspension of realistic considerations, even when confronted with allegedly more authentic problems. Carpenter, Lindquist, Matthews and Silver (1983; see also Schoenfeld, 1987) give the following example from the National Assessment of Educational Progress in the U.S.A: "An army bus holds 36 soldiers. If 1128 soldiers are being bussed to their training site, how many buses are needed?" 19% of the students provided the solution "31 remainder 12", about one fifth answered "31". In this line of argument, the students' lack of sense making is interpreted as a *lack of reference to their everyday knowledge* when solving word problems.

On the other hand, Cooper and Dunne (1998, 2000) observe that some students make *too extensive reference to their everyday knowledge* when solving word problems. They studied an extensive database from the Key Stage 2 (ten to eleven year olds) national tests in England. They found that the "misreading" of the tasks, as being situated in a practice outside school mathematics, is linked to the social backgrounds of the students. Working class children were more likely to attempt to solve the tasks by using their everyday knowledge while service class children demonstrated an understanding of word problems as, in fact, being artificial although apparently "real". Cooper and Harris (this volume) elaborate on the problem of using authentic data and provide an example of the benefits of using a de-authenticised version of the same task.

Gates and Vistro-Yu (2003) call the dilemma of interpretation that students face the "Goldilocks Principle" of the reality behind mathematical problems. The successful practice is to use the given numerical or geometrical information and to draw on everyday knowledge only to the extent to which it can make up for the missing information that is needed to solve the task as a school mathematics task (cf. Gellert & Jablonka, 2002a, 2002b).

We regard the tension between the everyday and the academic, which culminates when students have to solve word problems, as an issue of recontextualisation of discourses. It cannot easily be resolved, for example, by making word problems more authentic and interpreting them as problems of mathematical modelling. The example given in the introduction indicates fundamental disparities between teachers' and students' framings of the tasks. However, these differences in the framing are not restricted to "word problems". The following anecdote bears testimony to a more fundamental disruption between the mathematical practices found outside school and their recontextualisation in the classroom. In a 6th-grade mathematics classroom in an Austrian high school in the early 1970s, a girl (who was the best friend of one of the authors) is called to the blackboard and asked to divide a line into three sections of equal length. She draws a line, takes one step backwards, looks for a while at the line, and then draws by eye a very accurate trisection of it. The teacher says: "Thank you, sit down. You have got a good visual judgement. You can become a tailor." Arguably, a tailor does not need to know about constructions with compass and straightedge. The girl left the school after two more years of predominantly unsuccessful participation. Her best friend remained, still puzzled.

STUDIES OF RECONTEXTUALISATION

Word Problems as Mediators Between the Public and the Esoteric Domain

From the viewpoint of Bernstein's theory of pedagogic codes and their modalities (e.g., 1996), pedagogic discourse is defined by the fact that it recontextualises a practice by moving it from its original site in order to use it for a different purpose:

> From one point of view pedagogic discourse appears to be a discourse without a discourse. It seems to have no discourse of its own. Pedagogic discourse is not physics, chemistry or psychology. Whatever it is, it cannot be identified with the discourses it transmits. (Bernstein, 1996, p. 46)

> Pedagogic discourse is constructed by a recontextualizing principle which selectively appropriates, relocates, refocuses and relates other discourses to constitute its own order. (Bernstein, 1996, p. 47)

Bernstein's theory of pedagogic discourse is concerned with the production, distribution, and reproduction of official knowledge and how this knowledge is related to structurally determined power relations. The recontextualisation of knowledge into curriculum involves decisions about what areas of knowledge are to be selected, how these areas are related within the subject, and how they are related to other areas inside or outside school. Indeed, curricula can be usefully described and compared in terms of the strength of the boundaries established between everyday knowledge and the insider's academic knowledge, as well as between the areas that constitute the school subjects. Mathematics curricula for primary and for lower level secondary schools, for example, usually intend to connect school mathematical knowledge to the local and particular of everyday knowledge. This aim is reflected in the high proportion of word problems contained in the curriculum materials for the early grades.

In a critical elaboration of Bernstein's thesis of the ideological transformation of academic discourse by recontextualising it as a pedagogic discourse, Dowling (1996, 1998) identifies two distinct messages in school mathematics texts. One message suggests that mathematics deals with domestic activities. Narratives from the viewpoint of a person acting in a practical situation are used as an introduction into the esoteric domain of mathematics. This strategy supports the view that everyday practical knowledge is constitutive of mathematical knowledge. Many of the word problems found in the introductory chapters of new mathematical topics in textbooks are of this type. However, using domestic activities as a route into mathematics and at the same time restricting its application to those domestic activities forms a myth of participation – mathematical knowledge is constructed as a condition for successful participation in domestic activities.

The second message is, according to Dowling, the myth of reference. It is distributed through problem settings that are constructed mathematically and only retain a trace of non-mathematical significations. It does not remain possible for the learner to evaluate the solution of the problems from a practical point of view. Mathematics appears as having universal descriptive power. Again, the "recipients of this message" are expected to believe that behaving mathematically in such situations would be in their own interests. This type of problem typically appears after a mathematical concept or method has been introduced, sometimes under the heading "applications".

According to Dowling, both of these messages are myths: The application of mathematics in practical domestic activities conceals that mathematics deals with general solution methods, which do not take into account contextual peculiarities. Mathematics is not dealing with the domestic activities. In the episode about the girl solving the task of trisecting a line, the teacher's sarcastic comment points to the fact that different ways of solving a problem are linked to different practices in terms of division of labour.

The expression of domestic activities in mathematical terms conceals the fact that the mathematical structures projected into them are not determined by the structure of the activities; rather, the reference is socially constructed. The word problem from the Hong Kong classroom presented as an introductory vignette, about the man rowing his boat downstream and upstream, may serve as an example. The textbook indicates that the students have to reconstruct the situation under the gaze of school algebra by using simultaneous linear equations. In addition, the movement of the boat and of the current have to be interpreted in terms of school physics. At the end, in the moment when the teacher states that he is not talking about reality, the reference to the activity of rowing a boat is uncovered as a myth.

In order to delve into the recontextualisation of domestic practices in school mathematics texts, Dowling introduces (1996, 1998) and modifies (2007) a relational space of domains of action. He distinguishes between content and expression of a text, both being weakly or strongly institutionalised.

Table 1. Domains of Action (Dowling, 2007, p. 5; layout adjusted)

Expression (signifiers)	Content (signifieds)	
	Strong institutionalisation	Weak institutionalisation
Strong institutionalisation	*Esoteric domain*	*Descriptive domain*
Weak institutionalisation	*Expressive domain*	*Public domain*

According to Dowling, school mathematics text that contains formal mathematics expressed through mathematical symbols is quite different from verbal descriptions of everyday situations and domestic activities – the esoteric and the public domain appear as mutually exclusive. In descriptive domain text, the expression is conventional mathematical language though its object of reference is not institutionalised mathematics. In expressive domain text, a mathematical concept, operation etc. is expressed via non-mathematical signifiers.

Dowling (2009) insistently emphasises that the notion of the public domain is not to be confounded with domestic practices. By casting a school mathematical gaze, domestic practices are recontextualised as the public domain of action, subordinating them to the principles of school mathematics – rowing under the gaze of school mathematics, not rowing as such. For Dowling (1998, p. 136), the public domain is a crucial component of school mathematical practices even if those practices strive for the esoteric domain; the students get access to the esoteric through the public domain. We elaborate on this issue when discussing different trajectories through Dowling's (rather static) domains of action.

Descriptive and Public Domain Text and the Activity of Mathematical Modelling

Descriptive domain text uses strongly classified signifiers, that is, conventional mathematical language, though its object of reference is not institutionalised mathematics but a weakly institutionalised content. In Dowling (1998, p. 134) the descriptive domain is exemplified by an extract from a mathematical textbook (SMP 11-16 Book Y1, CUP, Cambridge, p. 32):

A café orders p white loaves and q brown loaves every day for r days.
What does each of these expressions tell you?
(a) $p + q$ (b) pr (c) qr (d) $(p + q)r$

This school mathematics problem introduces the learner to the translation of a verbal description, which is already including variables, into conventional mathematical symbols, that is strongly institutionalised signifiers. Since the solving of the task requires a translation back to the content of ordering loaves, it remains weakly institutionalised with respect to content. However, on another occasion, Dowling explains the descriptive domain differently:

Descriptive domain text is constituted as *mathematical modelling*, where the expression is strongly institutionalised mathematical language, for example, using conventional algebraic symbols, but the content – that to which the symbols refer – is arbitrary in the context of mathematics per se. (Dowling, 2007, pp. 5-6, emphasis added)

We might wonder whether the SMP textbook problem on white and brown loaves is an example of mathematical modelling or a task developed for practising a sub-skill. The verbal description of the café's ordering is already mathematised by inclusion of the variables p, q, and r. This text is not a weakly institutionalised expression of a typical ordering situation in everyday life. It is not describing any situation, which, in the course of the students' solving process, needs to be mathematised.

If mathematical modelling is understood as the translation of verbal and/or pictorial descriptions of situations to mathematical descriptions (by which identified "problems" can be solved), including a retranslation, than the mathematical modelling text is located in the public domain – similar to standard word problems, such as in the example of the oarsman. The fact that students might use conventional algebraic symbols in order to engage mathematically in verbal descriptions of situations, that is, to cast a school mathematical gaze on those situations – does not locate the problem statement in the descriptive domain. Students who, for example, solve the problem of the man rowing downstream and upstream, may use, as indicated in the page's running head, simultaneous linear equations in two unknowns. This is strongly institutionalised content and expression; nevertheless, the word problem clearly can be located as a public domain activity.

In the terminology introduced by Dowling, standard word problems consisting of short narratives expressed through weakly institutionalised signifiers and problems for mathematical modelling cannot easily be distinguished. As texts, word problems and verbally described situations for mathematical modelling appear both as public domain activities. However, the two types of problems differ with respect to the application of the recontextualisation principle. Whereas, as in the problem of the oarsmen introduced in the vignette, the textbook is explicitly suggesting the school mathematical gaze by the page's running head, in mathematical modelling the students need to choose a particular mathematical gaze from the repertoire of their mathematical techniques or develop suitable ad hoc strategies. This difference is often presented as an argument for the introduction of mathematical modelling in the classroom. But, as we have pointed out, in subordinating one practice to the principles of another (school mathematics) it is always ambiguous to what extent the subordinated practice remains relevant (see the scrutiny on the notion of "still water" in the vignette's word problem), and this issue is even more complicated if the principles of the other practice (school mathematics) are not completely known to the recontextualisers, that is, the students. This is the case when they engage in mathematical modelling tasks.

Transitions from Horizontal to Vertical Discourse

The disparate character of the discourse of everyday situations, and of school mathematics, exacerbates the transition from the public to the esoteric domain. We can draw, again, on Bernstein (1996, 1999) in order to elaborate on this issue. Bernstein distinguishes between horizontal and vertical discourse:

> A horizontal discourse entails a set of strategies which are local, segmentally organised, context specific and dependent, for maximising encounters with persons and habitats.
>
> [A] vertical discourse takes the form of a coherent, explicit, and systematically principled structure. (Bernstein, 1999, p. 159)

In everyday situations, horizontal discourse is predominant. These situations, as the sites of realisation of the discourse, are organised as specialised segments of everyday life. The modes of acquisition and production of horizontal discourse are embedded in that segmentation. Acquisition and production are likely to be local activities and the strategies are often tacitly acquired. Oarsmen acquire a feeling for currents through rowing, not through calculation.

Vertical discourse, by contrast, is not based on a segmental organisation of knowledge, but on a specialised symbolic structure. In the case of school mathematics, this symbolic structure is entered through public domain activity, that is, through recontextualisations of domestic activities. Though the domestic activities are taken from different specialised segments of everyday life, they are all subject to the same recontextualising principle. In mathematics classrooms, for example, in which the introduction of new mathematical procedures, concepts etc. draws on verbal descriptions of everyday situations, the students' participation in classroom interaction is relegated and restricted to horizontal discourse; the agency of the recontextualisation process is on the side of the teacher as the authority of the vertical discourse. Teachers' strategies in organising this process of recontextualisation are described, in the form of interaction patterns, for example, by Voigt (1984, 1985).

By casting a school mathematical gaze onto domestic activities, mathematics teaching aims at erasure of the specificity of the contexts in which the domestic activities are embedded and to which the students' ad hoc strategies are related. The underlying recontextualisation principle mediates the transfer between the horizontal discourse and the vertical discourse, although the differences between the two forms of discourse are mostly obscured. The recontextualisation principle brings about that abstraction (by means of generalisation and conventionalisation) from extra-mathematical contexts to mathematical concepts and structures appears as possible and straightforward, but, actually, this process is a step from the contradictory world to a coherently organised esoteric sphere that has cut off its everyday roots long since (Jablonka & Gellert, 2007).

In the word problem on rowing downstream and upstream a semantic distance between the students and the rowing setting is established by reference to a slightly exceptional distance of 99 km in total and – this is the mathematical result of the word problem – to a highly unrealistic, not to say impossible power of the oarsman. Anyone who could row at a speed of 16.5 km/h (in still water, sic!) over a time period of 6 hours would be the envy of any Cambridge or Oxford boat race crew. Thus, in the word problem the relevance of the domestic setting is minimised through reference to a segment of horizontal knowledge which most of the students (and the teacher?) are not familiar with. It is easier to translate an everyday situation into school mathematics, when this situation is not part of students' everyday experience.

For the students who, in the vignette, argue about the possibility of still water, it is indeed difficult to decide what the teacher is talking about. Presumably, the expression "still water" is weakly institutionalised, because the teacher's attempt of clarification only refers to the problem of English as students' second language. But the teacher is explicitly not engaging in horizontal discourse. The consideration of "still water" in the word problem is based on the mathematical concept of continuity, not on experience with "real" rivers. Is this the expressive domain lurking in word problems?

In mathematics classrooms, verbal descriptions of situations are not only used as introductions to new school mathematical topics, but, as shown in the vignette, also serve as what often has been called "applications". In that case, the students need to use their esoteric domain knowledge in order to solve a public domain problem. This activity is differently coded in, for example, textbooks. Rarely is a word problem given in the form of "Set up two simultaneous linear equations in two unknowns and calculate the solution." More often, the esoteric domain knowledge to be applied is presented as the page's running head or as a chapter title. In fact, it is not necessary to use simultaneous linear equations to solve the word problem about the man rowing downstream and upstream. Addition and division would do as well. Students who are actually setting up two linear equations in the two unknowns "speed of current" and "speed of the boat" for solving this problem are not only used to public domain activities in the mathematics classroom. They are also aware of the coding of the particular piece of esoteric domain knowledge used as the principle to which the rowing practice is to be subordinated. This is a process of a twofold recognition: recognising verbal descriptions of everyday situations as public domain text plus recognising the particular esoteric domain knowledge that affects the recontextualisation of the domestic activity.

In "applications", specialised knowledge of school mathematics, which consists of a coherent body of assembled symbolic structures, is projected onto segments of localised activities. By the very virtue of the recontextualisation principle, which refocuses and selectively appropriates context specific discourse, any meaning within the horizontal discourse is disrupted. Given this disruption, it is highly problematic to have students evaluate their numerical solutions of word problems in terms of the local situational context described in the problem. Even if an average speed of 16.5 km/h sounds very fast, in classroom activity it does not matter that no "real" oarsman would be as fast as the one presented in the word problem: we are not talking about reality. There is no escape from the arbitrariness of this kind of evaluation.

In the course of students' acquisition of school mathematical knowledge, the descriptive domain text configures a (first) passage from local everyday situations, recontextualised as a school mathematical activity, towards the strongly institutionalised esoteric knowledge of formal mathematics. In this case recontextualisation is a principle that organises activities into a hierarchy. The purpose of the second passage, "application", is then of doubtful value, particularly because of the countless and arbitrary segments from horizontal discourse, to which these "applications" refer. If the arbitrariness and innumerability of "contexts of applications" is regarded as a pedagogic device by which the generalising character of school mathematics can be pointed to, then exemplars and principles are confused.

STUDENTS SOLVING WORD PROBLEMS: INTRICACIES OF PRODUCING LEGITIMATE TEXT

As has been argued, mathematical classroom practices with their associated activities (such as solving word problems) are generated through recontextualisation of discourses. Particularly, but not exclusively, in primary and lower secondary education, a gaze is cast from the esoteric domain onto domestic activities, resulting in a subordination of domestic practices to the principles of school mathematics – in order to provide an entrance to the latter. This is the public domain. As Dowling (1998) has demonstrated for the case of the SMP scheme in England, in school systems where students have been grouped according to their mathematical achievement, there are some students who are more or less deprived of any esoteric domain activities. For these students, school mathematics is restricted to public domain activities, as the pedagogy is aiming implicitly at students' identification with manual occupations as prolongations of those domestic activities. This is the myth of participation.

For other students, mathematics curricula sketch routes from the public domain to the esoteric domain: Weakly institutionalised expressions need to be transformed into strongly institutionalised expressions, as the reference of these expressions shifts towards strongly institutionalised school mathematical meanings. The transformations of expression and content do not necessarily coincide since there is no straightforward step from public to esoteric domain text. Whereas the first is based on horizontal knowledge (although under the gaze of school mathematics), the second is based on vertical knowledge. For the students, the shift from weakly institutionalised to strongly institutionalised expressions and contents translates into intricacies of adequate participation in the mathematics classroom, that is, of producing legitimate text.

A glance into another 8th-grade classroom may illustrate these intricacies. The lesson takes place in Berlin (Germany), where a teacher is making use of the presence of a researcher, who is asked to present a verbal description of a problem farmers face when exchanging parts of their properties:

31:01 Teacher: Well, now we want to address ourselves to the following problem. *[draws a square on the board]*
31:17 For that purpose we look at this square, please. This is supposed to represent a square plot of land owned by a

		farmer. Now you have to tell the rest, would you please tell the story?
31:39	Researcher:	The neighbour approaches the farmer and says "It would be very advantageous for my planning if you could give me a strip of one meter of your land from the cross side *[teacher points to the upper horizontal edge of the square]*, I then would give you in return a strip of one meter from my property on the other edge" *[teacher points to the right vertical edge of the square]*. Would you agree?
32:20	Teacher:	Okay.
32:26	Anton:	No…it isn't the same…um…um.
32:28	Student:	Unfair.
32:41	Student:	No…well…because he then has less…You can…you can already see that from the drawing that you would then get less from that plot.
32:47	Student:	Well…somehow…well I would refuse because this is
32:48	Teacher:	Wait…I didn't get that…this is such a mumbling
32:48	Student:	I would refuse because somehow…um…you have a piece …you haven't such a corner…plot there around.
32:58	Teacher:	No you have…um…what's the shape of the new plot…it's not a square anymore…but it's still at least a rectangle. So you would refuse because you'd prefer a square over a rectangle. *[laughter]*
33:15	Student:	I mean…um…want to take away on one side and put on the other side…where…oh where is then the neighbour's garden…on the left side or there below?
33:22	Martin:	Thus it is around.
33:23	Teacher:	It is around.
33:24	Student:	But that's a bit illogical…isn't it?
33:27	Student:	Why?
33:29	Teacher:	That's…that is…um
33:30	Martin:	Man
33:30	Teacher:	uninteresting. Our question is…um…whether the one concerned…well…whether he should exchange…whether this is favourable…or whether…um…it doesn't matter or…it is just what it is about…whether for this very farmer who now is up to mischief in there…it is…um…yes a problem.
33:56	Kerstin:	Well I would say…I would assume…um…if I…in this piece he wants to…I don't know…steal from me…if I hadn't anything there…I mean a shed and stuff…then I could as well take the meter down there because the area is the same.
34:15	Martin:	Ey?
34:16	Teacher:	Ah…that was…is the area the same?
34:16	Felix:	Yeah

34:17 Teacher: That is the good question.
34:20 Student: No...isn't the same...because...um...before...well now... he is missing exactly one piece...he has the full side and now he has from his shorter plot also...um...only the shorter half from the bottom...and so he misses exactly one square meter.
34:33 Teacher: Yes.[2]

Is the researcher's story presenting an activity from the public domain? The story is clearly situated as an out-of-school activity, farmers exchanging parts of their property. Before the story is told, the teacher has already cast a mathematical gaze on that domestic activity – a square on the blackboard is supposed to represent the farmer's plot – thus the teacher has made a part of the recontextualisation principle explicit. However, the student who first justifies an answer by what she can "already see from the drawing" is apparently undecided about the status of the square drawn on the blackboard. By referring to her cursory consideration of the drawing, this student reminds us of the Austrian girl dividing a line into three sections by visual judgement. Of course, a square could reasonably be considered a strongly institutionalised mathematical artefact, thus locating the combination of story and drawing on the blackboard as a descriptive domain activity. But in that case, any of the student's argument should have been produced as referring to the institutionalised aspect of a square – and not to visual judgement. The square drawn by the teacher is reinforcing the mathematical gaze, which is already present, but not always visible to all students in the mathematics classroom.

In the course of the conversation, the teacher takes up the ambiguous status of the square in the form of an irony, namely to prefer a square over a rectangle – on the surface the students seem to capture the working of the irony. In fact, if the teacher's utterance had not been framed (by himself) as an irony, it would have provided a route to a mathematical argument, since if the perimeter of the two polygons were the same, than the square is the maximum rectangle with respect to area. But the irony disguises this argument. The teacher is aiming at another mathematical argument, that is, towards an application of the binomial formulas (that have been the topic of the previous lesson). However, by his reaction, the students are oriented towards more mundane arguments, such as the location of the other farmer's garden, and to imaginable quality characteristics of the plot. The student Kerstin takes apparently for granted that to talk about "shed and stuff" is a relevant contribution to the collective solution. Anyway, her contribution is not acceptable within any domain of action in the mathematics classroom, since she has largely ignored the mathematical perspective on the farmer's problem. Finally, the teacher is relocating the students' perspectives by explicating the "good question" for the researcher's story.

The tensions between mathematical tasks presented as a public domain problem, and the didactical impetus to ascend to the esoteric domain of mathematical content and expression, culminate in the domains of transition: the expressive as well as the descriptive domain. If a domestic activity is already recontextualised as a public domain text, that is, subordination of the domestic activity under the principles of school mathematics, what then is the effect of reformulating the public domain problem by means of mathematical expressions? Do the students still need to be aware of the particularities of the corresponding domestic activity? If not, then mathematics is used rather algorithmically, as a universal technology with a technological fascination in itself.

For the expressive domain, its didactical character is even more evident. How can strongly institutionalised content be coherently communicated by weakly institutionalised expressions, for example, fractions as parts of pizzas or vectors as arrows? The expressive domain can be interpreted as an attempt of translating esoteric domain text into an exoteric one. As such, it cannot open up a route into the esoteric, because the principles of its retranslation are unknown for the one who is not already familiar with the content that is expressed.

We interpret the students' difficulties when solving word problems, which serve as a pedagogic device aiming at providing a route from the public to the esoteric domain, as a consequence of the implicitness of the recontextualisation principle in classroom discourse. Discovering the principle is left to the students' aptness of guessing the criteria for what counts as a legitimate school mathematical text, a skill that is linked to their ability of recognising the status of the school mathematical activity of solving word problems as located in the descriptive domain. If the problem statements consist of public domain text, the acquisition of the recontextualisation principle is in fact impossible.

Making the principles of recontextualisation explicit, that is, explaining the status of constructions with compass and straightedge as opposed to visual judgement and measurement, explicitly referring to the concept of continuity, drawing the students' attention to looking for invariants, could have helped in the examples from classrooms to which we referred in the chapter.

Teachers differ in their practices when dealing with "words and worlds" in respect to their attempts in guarding against obscuring the difference between outside school and school mathematical discourses. Strategies include the acceptance of non-mathematical solutions, allowing a discussion of the context before moving to a mathematical solution, contrasting the mathematical solutions with the students' everyday experiences, critically discussing the artificiality of the problems, pointing out the difference and independency of the mathematical structure, getting students to make their assumptions about the problem context explicit and comparing alternative meanings, or, in opposition to maximising authenticity, deliberately making the problems inauthentic (e.g., Chapman, 2006; Jablonka, 2004; Sethole, 2005). All these practices reduce the implicitness of the recontextualisation principle, in contrast to a strategy which attempts to disguise the disruption between different discourses by introducing a series of "translation steps".

NOTES

[1] Transcript from *The Learner's Perspective Study* (http://extranet.edfac.unimelb.edu.au/DSME/lps/)
[2] Transcript from *The Learner's Perspective Study* (http://extranet.edfac.unimelb.edu.au/DSME/lps/)

REFERENCES

Baruk, S. (1985). *L'âge du capitaine: De l'erreur en mathématiques.* Paris: Seuil.
Bernstein, B. (1996). *Pedagogy, symbolic control and identity: Theory, research, critique: Vol. 5. Class, codes and control.* London: Taylor & Francis.
Bernstein, B. (1999). Vertical and horizontal discourse: An essay. *British Journal of Sociology of Education, 20,* 157–173.
Carpenter, T. P., Lindquist, M. M., Matthews, W., & Silver, E. A. (1983). Results of the third NAEP mathematics assessment: Secondary school. *Mathematics Teacher, 76,* 652–659.
Chapman, O. (2006). Classroom practices for context of mathematics word problems. *Educational Studies in Mathematics, 62,* 211–230.
Cooper, B., & Dunne, M. (1998). Anyone for tennis? Social class differences in children's responses to national curriculum mathematics testing. *The Sociological Review, 46,* 115–148.
Cooper, B., & Dunne, M. (2000). *Assessing children's mathematical knowledge: Social class, sex and problem-solving.* Buckingham, UK: Open University Press.
Dowling, P. (1996). A sociological analysis of school mathematics texts. *Educational Studies in Mathematics, 31,* 389–415.
Dowling, P. (1998). *The sociology of mathematics education: Mathematical myths/pedagogical texts.* London: Falmer Press.
Dowling, P. (2007). Organising the social. *Philosophy of Mathematics Education Journal, 21,* online without pagination.
Dowling, P. (2009). *Sociology as method: Departures from the forensics of culture, text and knowledge.* Rotterdam, The Netherlands: Sense Publishers.
Freudenthal, H. (1982). Fiabilité, validité et pertinence: Critères de la recherche sur l'enseignement de la mathématique. *Educational Studies in Mathematics, 13,* 395–408.
Gates, P., & Vistro-Yu, C. (2003). Is mathematics for all? In A. Bishop, M. A. Clements, C. Keitel, J. Kilpatrick & F. Leung (Eds.), *Second international handbook of mathematics education* (pp. 31–74). Dordrecht, The Netherlands: Kluwer.
Gellert, U., & Jablonka, E. (2002a). Tasks and questions used in international assessment of mathematical literacy. In L. Bazzini & C. Inchley (Eds.), *Mathematical literacy in the digital era: Proceedings of the 53rd conference of the Commission Internationale pour l'Étude et l'Amélioration de l'Enseignement des Mathématiques (CIEAEM), Verbania, Italy, July 21–27, 2001* (pp. 114–118). Milano: Ghisetti e Corvi Editori.
Gellert, U., & Jablonka, E. (2002b). Testing the validity of test items. In L. Bazzini & C. Inchley (Eds.), *Mathematical literacy in the digital era: Proceedings of the 53rd conference of the Commission Internationale pour l'Étude et l'Amélioration de l'Enseignement des Mathématiques (CIEAEM), Verbania, Italy, July 21–27, 2001* (pp. 327–331). Milano: Ghisetti e Corvi Editori.
IREM (Équipe "Élementaire" de l' I.R.E.M. de Grenoble) (1980). Quel est l'âge du capitaine? *Bulletin de l'Association des Professeurs de Mathématique de l'Enseignement Public, 323,* 235–243.
Jablonka, E. (2004). *Structure in diversity: Initiation into mathematical practice in classrooms from Germany, Hong Kong and the United States.* Habilitation Thesis. Berlin: Freie Universität Berlin.
Jablonka, E., & Gellert, U. (2007). Mathematisation – Demathematisation. In U. Gellert & E. Jablonka (Eds.), *Mathematisation and demathematisation: Social, philosophical and educational ramifications* (pp. 1–18). Rotterdam, The Netherlands: Sense Publishers.
Schoenfeld, A. H. (1987). What's all the fuss about metacognition? In A. H. Schoenfeld (Ed.), *Cognitive science and mathematics education* (pp. 189–215). Hillsdale, NJ: Erlbaum.
Sethole, G. (2005). From the everyday, through the inauthentic, to mathematics: Reflection on the process of teaching from contexts. In H. L. Chick & J. L. Vincent (Eds.), *Proceedings of the 29th conference of the International Group for the Psychology of Mathematics Education* (Vol. 4, pp. 169–175). Melbourne: PME.

Verschaffel, L., Greer, B., & De Corte, E. (2000). *Making sense of word problems*. Lisse, The Netherlands: Swets & Zeitlinger.

Voigt, J. (1984). *Interaktionsmuster und Routinen im Mathematikunterricht: Theoretische Grundlagen und mikroethnographische Falluntersuchungen*. Weinheim, Germany: Beltz Verlag.

Voigt, J. (1985). Patterns and routines in classroom interaction. *Recherches en Didactique des Mathématiques, 6*, 69–118.

Uwe Gellert
Department of Educational Science and Psychology
Freie Universität Berlin
Germany

Eva Jablonka
Institute of Mathematics
Luleå University of Technology
Sweden

WOLFF-MICHAEL ROTH

ON THE PROBLEMATIC OF WORD PROBLEMS – LANGUAGE AND THE WORLD WE INHABIT

Discussion of Part I: Theoretical Perspectives

Bertrand Russell has said that in mathematics we never know what we are talking about. This means that nowadays *mathematics is not concerned with truth, but with validity*. Not with whether it necessarily applies to the world as it is, but whether it makes logical sense within its own boundaries and according to its own rules. (Barr, 1964, p. 162)

Educators often exclaim, "Mathematics is everywhere," sometimes suggesting that it is the language of nature. If it were like this, we should see it and students should not have as many difficulties as they have with story problems in textual form that mathematics educators refer to as contextual and contextualising {word problems}. Perhaps we should accept the statement of the introductory quote, whereby *mathematics* is not about truth but about validity; and validity questions are different in the everyday world than they are in mathematicians' mathematical praxis. Here I emphasise the term mathematics, because people use numbers in their lives without doing (mathematicians') mathematics. Thus, in a recent study, I show how the different concerns of fish culturists lead, in the hatchery, to very different forms of knowing and different practices than those that characterise mathematicians and students of mathematics (Roth, 2005). We do know that students do have difficulties with the story genre in mathematics education, although it is used to the present day, to paraphrase Susan Gerofsky, to "heap up" massive amounts of examples to establish the generality of mathematics. After years of conducting research involving {word problems}, I am not so sure about the nature of the concept or practice, and therefore bracket the term indicating thereby that I use it only provisionally. There is research, and Torulf Palm refers to it, suggesting that adults reason very differently in their everyday life contexts and on {word problems} (e.g., Lave, 1988). Such research questions the relationship between experiences in and of the everyday life-world and the world projected in the stories of {word problems}.

This commentary is written by someone who has an extended relation with the research concerning {words}, {problems}, and {word problems} in school classrooms and educational research (involving scientists and technicians) and who has had ample occasion to think about the relationship between words and the world, both the one in which {word problems} appear and the one that the {word problems} *are said to* denote or be a model of. Although part of my training has been as an applied mathematician, my everyday life is remarkably un-mathematical and protected from the "mathematical gaze" (Uwe Gellert and Eva Jablonka) that I might take on other issues. I doubt that there is a need for transferring "school mathematics to new real world situation," as Palm appears to hold. The suggestion that mathematics is everywhere may just be a myth. My task here is to comment on the chapters or themes that they have articulated and the issues that they have raised. Because conversations shift more easily when they are not anchored somehow in a concrete entity that in a way grounds what is happening, I take below a brief excerpt from a research project concerned with practicing scientists' readings of graphing tasks.

When we read a text, we do not do so innocently, as blank slates to be imprinted by a copy of the text. In reading/interpreting a text, our practical understanding precedes, accompanies, and concludes our explaining; but explaining develops our practical understanding (Ricœur, 1991). We always read from a specific cultural, historical, and biographical position – a particular chronotope, as Gerofsky calls it following Mikhail Bakhtin – each of which comes with its own *sup*positions, *presup*positions, *dis*positions, *op*positions, or *com*positions. My own intellectual biography has led me to appreciate the positions on language and culture taken by Bakhtin (and his collaborators Pavel Medvedev and Valentin Vološinov) and by the French philosophers Jacques Derrida and Paul Ricœur.[1] My thinking about the problematic of {word problems} therefore lies closest to Gerofsky – perhaps not surprisingly, both Marx and Freud intersect in and are topics of the writings of Derrida and the Bakhtin circle. Other than in Gerofsky, however, what stands out for me in the works of these authors, and what has shaped my thinking, is their articulation of language as a non-self-identical aspect of our lives. Being non-self-identical, we cannot ever say what a language (genre, word) *is*, for in use, there is only flow and development, continuous translation at the very instance of language use. More so than any one of the chapter authors, I think of language as an ideology, a form of consciousness that stands in a constitutive (but indeterminate and not determining) relationship with the worlds we inhabit.

In addition to the position on language, my recent thinking has been influenced by, and in turn influenced the development of, cultural-historical activity theory, a theory based on Marxist (dialectical-materialist) ideas of the relationship between knowing and doing. The theory, developed in the former USSR by psychologists and philosophers including Lev S. Vygotsky, Alexei N. Leont'ev, Evald Il'enkov, and Felix Mikhailov (among others) insists on societally relevant activity systems and the associated form of irreducible individual|collective consciousness and ideal|material processes as the *minimal unit* for the analysis of productive processes and cognition.[2] The irreducibility of societal activity – farming, manufacturing, and, relevant here, schooling – immediately implies that none of its structural moments can be understood independently of other structural moments and independently of activity. In making thematic the dialectical, mutually presupposing and mutually constituting structural *moments* we overcome the dualisms – mind and body, individual and collective – that have plagued traditional philosophy, cognitive science, and (cognitive) psychology. The theory particularly emphasises the *constitutive* role of affect in individual|collective cognition and consciousness, because without affect, "the thought process appear[s] as an autonomous flow of 'thoughts thinking themselves,' segregated from the fullness of life, from the personal needs and interests, the inclinations and impulses, of the thinker" (Vygotsky, 1986, p. 10).

CONTEXT IN CONTEXT

To anchor my reading of the three preceding chapters and my discussion, I use a concrete situation from my research that asked practicing scientists to interpret graphs that were embedded in some scientific narrative. My research team and I invited practicing scientists to read graphs and associated problem stems that we had culled from introductory university-level science courses in the domain of the scientists. In this way we wanted to create a reference for gauging the performances of high school and college students on graph and data interpretation tasks presented in story form. For comparison purposes, we constructed parallel sets of tasks that also were from introductory courses but in another science domain. One of these tasks involved a population model used in theoretical biology to theorise the stability or instability of a population given birth and death rate curves (Figure 1). The present fragments from a think aloud/interview protocol come from a session involving a 30+-year veteran physics professor (Annemarie) who not only had published regularly but also had received university teaching awards. The research assistant is an undergraduate student (David) in the process of completing a co-op term as part of his double major in physics and anthropology.

When is a {Word Problem}?

My first comment concerns the nature of the {word problem}. Gerofsky writes that it constitutes something like a historically evolved genre typical for texts that appear in school mathematics. Palm appears to accept the traditional formulation that the content of a {word problem} pertains to some real-life situation – after all, there are populations approximately behaving as modelled and the graph depicts an important model in theoretical biology. His question might concern the level to which the real-world situation is modelled, which, as some of our biologist participants have shown, fits well with a variety of populations. Gellert and Jablonka, too, leave the nature of the {word problem} unquestioned and simply ask about the relationship between the words on the paper and the worlds that these words are about. But do these different formulations – here rendered in my translation and therefore already and inherently no longer the thing itself, the original chapters – do justice to the contents of Figure 1? Perhaps yes. Perhaps no. Perhaps both yes and no. Perhaps, this is my predilection, all of these possibilities simultaneously.

I personally prefer taking a Wittgensteinian and cultural-historical activity theoretic position, according to which we cannot ask about the nature of a thing independent of its concrete use by people *in* situation *for* a particular purpose, *in-order-to* achieve something *on-the-basis-of* grounds (reasons) that are inherently intelligible to others. I do have this preference without asking others to abandon their own, which might differ from mine. And, like theirs, I cannot provide the (entire) grounds for this preference, which is given to me. I suspect that Bakhtin, too, might have characterised the text, in the same way as he characterised poems and novels, that is, as utterances that are moments of irreducible acts that require, as the counterpart of/to the utterance, its effect.[3] As Bakhtin (1978) suggests, every poetic work asks for a response, a social evaluation, and we cannot know the response (social evaluation) to (of) a text unless we follow its readers. Studying utterances, including {word problems}, does not lead us anywhere because the minimum unit of analysis requires us to think of its social evaluation, which speakers/authors already take into account and look for in the response they receive. That is, texts are not simply produced: they are produced *for* others and *in-order-to* elicit specific responses, which are monitored by the speaker/author and which become constitutive to his/her subsequent turns.

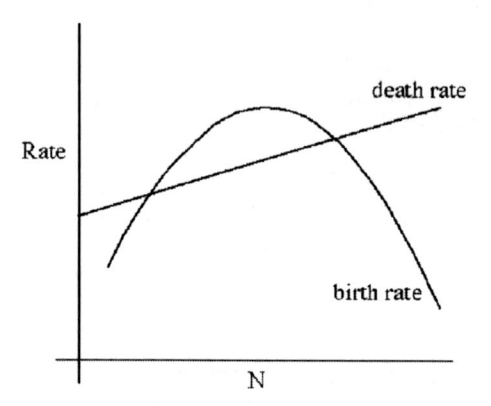

In our derivation of the logistic model, we assume that, as N increased, birth rates declined linearly and death rates increased linearly. Now, let's assume that the birth and death rates follow a quadratic function (e.g., $b = B_0 + (k_b)N - (k_c)N^2$), such that the birth and death rates look like the figure. Such a function is biologically realistic if, for example, individuals have trouble finding mates when they are at very low density. Discuss the implication of the birth and death rates in the figure, as regards conservation of such a species. Focus on the birth and death rates at the two intersection points of the lines, and on what happens to population sizes in the zones of population size below, between, and above the intersection points.

Figure 1. Graph interpretation task presented to professional biologist (university, public sector) and physicists (university)

DISCUSSION PART I

The social evaluation is available to the speaker/author in the response. Thus, it is in and through the concrete act of reading that "an organic, historical, and actually connection is established between the meaning and act (utterance), between the act and the concrete sociohistorical situation" (p. 120). More so, "[a]ll of these evaluations interpenetrate and are dialectically connected. . . . Social evaluation unites the minute of the epoch and the news of the day with the aim of history" (p. 121). The question of what the content or function of Figure 1 is therefore has to be studied *empirically* so that one can show how the entity is taken up and mobilised performatively in some concrete, societally relevant activity. If this is the case then we cannot just analyse individual utterances, but always have to take utterance pairs as the minimal unit. This is the approach taken in conversation analysis (ten Have, 1999), on which I draw here as the analytical method of choice.

Doing a Problem and Making Societal Activity

The fact that students do not just engage in tasks such as the one displayed here in Figure 1 (or the ones mobilised by the chapter authors) is generally overlooked in the mathematics educational literature and by the authors of all three chapters in particular. If we were to ask a child or adolescent in the morning what they are doing during the day, they would probably say something like "I'm going to school." That is, what they do in the course of the day is shaped by the consciousness of their participation in schooling, but it is only in and through their action that this schooling comes about. Students have to collude to bring about schooling as we know it; and when they do not co-operate in the desired ways, institutional structures and processes are mobilised – suspension, expulsion, in some instances even imprisonment – to bring a school back to the status quo. This orientation to the ongoing societal form of activity also is noticeable in instances such as the think aloud/interview protocols that I gathered from scientists, as the following example shows.

The session concerning the population graph begins with Annemarie's turning the page staring at the task sheet (Figure 1), and then uttering whether she is to read aloud. The question mark at the end of the sentence indicates that her pitch rises toward the end of the sentence so that together with the grammatical structure, this utterance proffers the first part of a question|response pair. Whether the utterance functions as a question *in this conversation* depends on, and cannot be independently established from, the second constitutive part of the unit. Each pair, according to Bakhtin, is a unit that includes both utterance and its social evaluation.[4]

Fragment 1
```
001 A:  do you want me to read it out loud?
002 D:  sure, if youd like to
003     (1.41)
004 A:  .hhhhhhhh (1.33) okay:::=ra:te (1.68) n in our
        derivation of the logistic model we assumed that as
```

59

In the present instance, the second part of the pair (turn 002) begins with an affirmative adverb, "sure," and continues, "if you'd like to." There follows a conversationally long pause (turn 003), long in-breaths, pauses, and an aborted beginning ("okay, rate") before Annemarie actually starts reading aloud the text below the graph. That is, if we take turns 002 and 004 as a unit, then we can read it as an invitation|acceptance pair: David invites her to read aloud if she would like to, and Annemarie begins to read aloud, thereby accepting the invitation. In both turn pairs, we see what conversation analysts have come to denote as the preferred action, which is affirmation and acceptance (of invitations). But preferred actions do not *have to be* taken. Any situation, therefore, also could have been otherwise. If we had known only that Annemarie and David are professor and student in her department, respectively, we might have been surprised overhearing the first turn pair. Why would a professor ask her student whether she should read aloud the text that contains a task statement? Has research not shown that usually teachers initiate with a question, students respond, and the teacher provides an evaluation, which leads to the well known interaction pattern denoted by the acronym I-R-E? Why would the student invite the professor to read the text, which asks the reader to respond to a question?

Of course, the information I have provided thus far solves the puzzle: the undergraduate student is a member of a research team conducting a study of graphing among scientists. Annemarie and David here are oriented to the purpose of the present situation of realising a think-aloud/interview protocol. They are both oriented to the societal activity of doing social science research and they collaborate in setting up the conditions required for realising the activity in a concrete way. But knowing that they participate in a research task does not *explain* or *determine* their behavior. Rather, we need to understand the think-aloud/interview protocol also as a product of their conversational actions. This latter aspect is important, because any action has the potential to destabilise the current activity and turn it into something else: any form of participation has to be thought as marginal|central so that it allows the activity to transform itself into something completely different (Goulart & Roth, 2006). This, in fact, eventually happens in the course of this particular session, when Annemarie, frustrated by not getting a grip on the asked-for interpretation, invites David to assist her in producing it. The think-aloud/interview protocol turns into, and is completed as, a tutoring session.

Here, then, we clearly see a radical changeover in what is being accomplished by the collective actions of participants and a change in the function of the graph and its co-text. Initially it was configured as an object of activity, associated with the motive of producing data for a research project in the form of a recorded and subsequently transcribed text. However, the object subsequently becomes an object of and site for a tutoring session. The recorded talk (and gestures) therefore not only accomplished some task, not only was *about* a graph, but also simultaneously constituted the activity for what it was and became; and it was in and through the talk that the activity changed into a very different one. The talk that the graph and its co-text occasioned was very different from what one might have anticipated. To me, this means that we cannot, as the chapter authors seem to be doing, talk about the ontology of {word problems} as such. Rather, one has to find in each concrete situation of interest the problematic that {word problems} occasion and bring forth. Both as objects of and function in a specific activity, {word problems} differ from situation to situation, they are not the same: they do not have a stable ontology (Roth, Bowen, & Masciotra, 2002).

We must not assume that students take up the problematic that educators believe to be embodied in {word problems} and that students take up the problematic in their horizontal or vertical discourse (Gellert and Jablonka). We should not be satisfied to work with a theory, as Palm does, focusing only on the relationship between texts and the world we inhabit. I am not saying that the authors are wrong but I read their work as highlighting one-sided expressions of a more complex whole activity, here: schooling. If we do not include the activity as level of analysis, then we cannot get at phenomena such as the production and reproduction of failure in certain societal classes, the working-class poor, African Americans, First Nations, or Mexican (il/legal) immigrants. Gellert and Jablonka point out that working-class students, for example, drew on their everyday knowledge – it just turns out that mobilising such knowledge often leads to failure, as science educators have found out when identifying "misconceptions." It is precisely the inaccessibility of the textual form of the {word problem} that leads to the production of failure and the low scores on standardised examination because school language – in {word problems} and sequentially ordered classroom talk – is more like that found in middle- than in working-class culture (Eckert, 1989). It is precisely this level of analysis that allows us to make relevant the Foucauldian and (neo-) Marxian analyses of school mathematics culture – e.g., in the work of Valerie Walkerdine – and the way its genres and sequentially ordered talk in classroom interactions lead to the production and reproduction of statistically detectable achievement differences along the lines of gender, race, or class. That is, with our choices of units of analysis, we may make invisible the function of {word problems} to reproduce particular social classes, gender differences, race, and so on.

Problematising {Word} and {Problem}

I do not think that as a research community, we have yet a good handle on the concept of {word problem}; we do not even have a good handle on the terms of this composite term, {word [language]} or {problem}. Generally accepted in the mathematics education literature is the term {word problem}. In the foregoing chapters, we do not see the question about the signified of this signifier. Thus, Gellert and Jablonka's Chinese students do face a first problem (breakdown), but it has little to do with what mathematics educators consider to be the problem stated in the riddle of the rower and his speed. In the episode, the Chinese students draw on their everyday knowledge when in fact it would be advantageous to "suspend the requirement that their solutions must make sense in relation to the out-of-school situation" (Palm). The latter problem consists of a translation from the text into two mathematical equations[5], which then can be solved according to a standard algorithm (solving two equations with two unknowns). The problem that the Chinese students discuss is the possibility of "still water." We do not have the Chinese text available nor the semantic of the terms they use in Chinese, perhaps using everyday vernacular, which hides what the mathematics educator wants to be the problematic. The importance of the semantic field, which I have articulated in several studies, also arises here in the concept of "still water," which denotes not only stagnant bodies of water but also non-sparkling, tap water. Accordingly, the boat could not be rowed in (a glass of) still water; but this is only one of the concrete possibilities within the semantic field of the word.

When we parse the term {word problem}, we get "word," a term that is often used to refer to any textual or verbal form. The term "problem" is semantically rich, but in the context of mathematics and mathematics education it is used to denote propositions that require specific actions to be done. Etymologically, the term derives from the ancient Greek πρόβλημα (problema), a question proposed for a solution or set task. In the previous section, we already see how a first problem arises that has nothing to do with the graph but with bringing about a particular kind of organisation. As for Gellert and Jablonka's students, semantic issues also arose for the scientists in my studies, as exemplified in Fragment 2.

Fragment 2
```
013  A:  <<p>focus on the birth and death rates (0.70) at the
         two intersection points of the lines.> (0.93) and on
         'what happens to ^population sizes in the ↑zones of
         population size 'below (0.64) be↑tween and ab↑ove the
         inter[sec]tion
014  D:         [uum]
015  A:  points.
016      (1.20)
017      .HHhssssss. <<f>i can hardly absorb what that means.>
018      (2.02)
019      <<pp>discuss the implication of the birth and death
```

The transcript shows the pauses and intonations that Annemarie produces as she reads the final words of the text below the graph. There is pause (turn 016) followed by a loud in-breath and hissing sound before the loud ("<<f> . . . >") articulation of "I can hardly absorb what that means" (turn 017). Another pause succeeds before Annemarie re-reads, with a very low voice intensity, parts of the figure caption. Listening to the actual tape, her intonations can be heard as frustration, displeasure, and disgust. The computer-aided analysis of her prosody exhibits features consistent with the published psychological research – increased speech intensity, pitch, first formant, and a decrease in the second formant in the sounds that go with "between" and "above" and the statement about difficulties in absorbing the meaning of the text.[6] But toward the end of the fragment, Annemarie has returned to the text, the prosody having returned to normal, expressing what can be heard as a resolution to the attempt of finding out. This is a new and different problem, a problem in its own right: what the problem is that she has been asked to address.

Here, then, Annemarie's problem is not one of interpretation. She tells the listener that she does not understand the meaning of the text and thereby states the real problem that she is currently facing. It is not one of translation but one of comprehending what is there. This problem therefore is related to understanding the text, not one of providing the sought-for problem, which is one of translation of the graph/text into a textual rendering.

The situation also points us to the nature of language, which is to be understood, as researchers of bilingualism tell us (e.g., Katibi, 1985), as non-self-identical with itself. Here, Annemarie is facing a text that contains only words with which she is already familiar, there is a quadratic equation of the type that she uses in her own teaching, and the syntax of the sentences is not in any way different from the syntax of other sentences she might encounter in her everyday work. More so, as a teacher, we might think that she should be familiar with the kind of genre displayed here, which, following Gerofsky, I take to be particular to school (and psychological laboratory) settings. In what happens subsequently, David provides such translations, which consist of other forms of English text accepted by both as having the same topic. Eventually, Annemarie understands what she is asked to do. That is, a translation from English to another such English allowed her to understand what she is asked to do and how to do it. English, as any language, is non-self-identical, which provides opportunities to translate it into itself but differently so that the same ideas are articulated differently, some of which are intelligible to particular individuals whereas other forms are not.

This immediately allows us to return to the Gellert and Jablonka's Chinese students. They require an additional translation, one that provides a Chinese equivalent to the language of instruction, itself a translation from mathematical language into the vernacular forms that students are familiar with. If such a translation were not to occur, students would not ever be able to understand what teachers are talking about (in [mathematical] English), who would be, in an interesting twist of vernacular English, "speaking nothing but Chinese" or "speaking in tongues."

The texts that students are confronted with in their mathematics classes, those that teachers and textbooks denote by the signifier {word problem}, therefore do not constitute genres of the type totally foreign to students in the way Gerofsky articulates this issue. The fact is that the very use of these genres presupposes their own intelligibility on the part of students who are not yet familiar with this genre. There is therefore a contradiction at the very heart of teaching mathematics using {word problems}. These texts, to be properly understood by students unfamiliar with mathematical topics – for the Chinese students it is the algebra of solving two equations with two unknowns – and unfamiliar with the genre, themselves have to provide a pedagogy that assists students in understanding first the text and then the task. In part, the texts do so by using words that also show up in everyday conversations, whether these pertain to a man rowing a boat on a river or birth rate, death rate, and population. However, as Gerofsky justly points out, we need to be careful in mistaking what is described in the texts for us, mathematics educators, as a model of the world outside schools. We do not know whether students have experience in using such phrases "A man rows a boat downstream for a distance of 66 km in three hours" even if they are rowers themselves. In fact, as I know from my own rowing experience (including runner-up in world championships), such phrases never occur in the conversations of rowers. Gellert and Jablonka therefore rightly point out that from a practical experience, the situation sketched in the sentence does not even make sense from a single rower's perspective, pointing again to the genre-specific nature of the sentences we find in {word problems}.

Finally, in this episode we see emotions at work, and it is the concurrent frustration with not getting it and the resolve to find out from which emerges the shift of the nature of the concretised activity: from a think-aloud/interview to a tutoring session. None of the three chapters topicalises affect, which nevertheless is important in understanding *what* is problematic, whether the {word problem} is the problem, or whether the problematic once identified in the way mathematics educators intended it is actually taken up. It makes a difference, for it is part of the (un/conscious) choice to engage in expansive or defensive learning, the former related to the life activity as a whole, the second related to making it through school in an unscathed way. This problem often does not pose itself in middle-class schools, but become a major point of contestation in many inner-city schools of the US – if we admit their low performance on standardised (state) examinations as a measure of students' competencies in understanding and doing {word problems}. I do not dwell on this issue, as the chapter authors do not address it, but I do believe with Vygotsky (1986) that we cannot understand cognition (here related to {word problems}) if we do not see in emotions the constitutive moment of thinking, speaking, and being conscious.

The Text and the World

Gerofsky points to the genre nature of mathematical {word problem}; that is, {word problems} constitute a form of text that has its own history and historical development, which can be understood only by seeing in them expressions of culture generally and mathematical culture more specifically. Gellert and Jablonka feature the nice quote of a teacher who suggests that he is not talking about reality in and with his story problem involving a rower. All three chapters point us to the problematic issues concerning the relationship between the content of the text and the world of which this text is said to be a representation or model. I do not think that we can take {word problems} as simple models ("myths" for Gellert and Jablonka) of the world in the way I read Palm as suggesting. But I do not think, as I read Gellert and Jablonka apparently doing, that students exhibit "lack of sense making" when they, for example, suggest that it takes 31 remainder 12 when asked for the number of 36-seat buses are required to transport 1128 soldiers. These answers *precisely* are an expression of the sense they made, and it is the researchers' problem not to have sought understanding what the (students') world is like within which "31 remainder 12" *is* a reasonable and intelligible answer. If there are so many students reading the text in such a way that "31 remainder 12" is a reasonable answer (why would students give answers that they themselves

DISCUSSION PART I

consider to be unreasonable?), then the possibility of reading the text in this way is already enabled in language itself, in the unavoidable gap between language as intended (illocution) and the effect it brings about (perlocution). In their answers, students merely and despite themselves concretise one such possibility.

With Bakhtin (1978) and Ricœur (1991), I take the world of the text to be a different world than the world of the utterance. The relationship between the two worlds and between the languages that appear in each generally is taken as unproblematic in mathematics education, where {word problems} are thought to allow students to connect with their "real-world" experiences. However, literary theorists have for some time pointed out that written texts have their own laws that are very different from those that describe the texts we produce as part of living in the world. Thus, "if the world is to be represented in literature, ideological *refraction*, cognitive, esthetic, political, or religious refraction, *is an obligatory and irrevocable preliminary condition* for the world's entrance into the structure and content of literature" (Bakhtin, 1978, p. 17-18, my emphasis). The world as it appears in the text of the {word problem} cannot be taken as a mirror image, but is the result of an obligatory *refracting* transformation following the laws of the text rather than that of the world. But, of course, in real concrete reading and engagement with a text, the two worlds come together because the textual world occasions events (e.g., interpretations, struggles, contests) in the lived-in world. The text, Bakhtin says, is artistically shaped and follows artistic laws just as the texts appearing in mathematics books are shaped for didactic purposes that are different from the purposes in which the objects denoted in the text appear in the outside world. This is the case even when the text is an auto/biography, where the relation of the main protagonist and the living person is not to be taken as identical. The {word problem} texts, as Gerofsky rightly points out, embody a Bakhtinian chronotope; but its relation to the chronotope of the world inhabited by embodied people has to be taken as problematic, even if, as Gellert and Jablonka point out, mathematicians and mathematics educators cast a school mathematical gaze onto domestic activities.

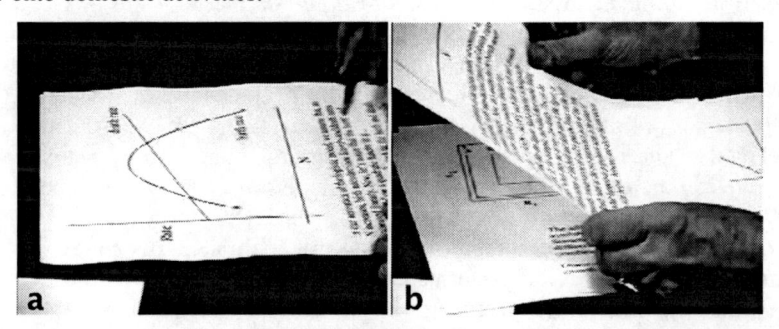

Figure 2. Annemarie formulates that she needs the paper "further away" to overcome her "trouble getting out." a. This overlay shows how she moves the hand/pen downward while uttering "getting out." b. She moves the task sheet away and lifts it off the table

Less than a minute after Fragment 2, Annemarie makes another statement about her process, having a problem "getting out," a statement followed by her moving the sheet further away from herself (Figure 2).

Fragment 3
```
025    so the first sentence <<p>is not (0.20) relevant to
       this right? (0.20) i=am> i=m having trouble (0.15)
       n::=getting out ((movement along text with pencil))
       (0.37). <<pp>as long as> i need it further away.
       (0.47) ((Literally moving paper further away.)) .hhh
       whats here?
```

In this instance, Annemarie articulates in different forms being caught in the text, unable to get out of it. To get out and to gaze at rather than be in the situation, she moves the sheet aware from her (Figure 2). In her practice, and as she articulates herself, the world of the text and graph is a different one, it is a part of the world distinct from the world she currently inhabits. To understand, she requires taking an objective gaze on this other world rather than being completely immersed in and confounded with it. Consciousness has to make this world strange by making it other than itself, turn it into an object and thereby to objectify it, before she can subjectify the objective in a concurrent movement of consciousness folding back over itself.

All three chapters deal with the relation of the world in the text and the world students can experience outside the text. There may be a relation, but it is not a simple one. The world can be understood as "the ensemble of references opened up by the texts" (Ricœur, 1991, p. 149). In classical texts, this might be the "world" of the Greek. The referent of all literature then no longer is "the *Umwelt* of the ostensive references of dialogue, but the *Welt* projected by the nonostensive references of every text that we have read, understood, and loved" (p. 149). This statement is consistent with the idea that "in the novel, the entire world and all of life are given in the cross section of the *integrity of the epoch*. Then events depicted in the novel should somehow *substitute for* the total life of the epoch" (Bakhtin, 1978, p. 43). From this perspective, then, understanding a text also means "to light up our own situation or, if you will, to interpolate among the predicates of our situation all the significations that make a *Welt* of our *Umwelt*" (Ricœur, 1991, p. 149, original emphasis). This *Umwelt* is that of school mathematics culture and its relation to the natural world rather than a mirror image of the natural world itself. We can therefore expect students to be successful in doing {word problems} once they are familiar with this culture rather than with the world they inhabit outside school. The widely reported disjunction exhibited by college physics students of highly successful performances on {word problems}, on the one hand, and on their flagrant "misconceptions" of physics phenomena, on the other hand (e.g., Clement, 1982), testifies to the radical differences between the two worlds. One can be successful in the world of {word problems} without being successful in the world they are intended to model.

Understanding the relationship between the world projected by the text of {word problems}, on the one hand, and the world that students inhabit as part of being, on the other hand, is their primary problem. It is not a relationship that ought to be taken for granted, as it is only through a refracting process that the world that is familiar to us, our *Umwelt* (life-world), comes to be presented in the text. In my own research I could show that when this transformation of *Umwelt* into text and text into Umwelt is familiar, students do really well in both objectifying and representing the material world in a variety of inscriptions (mathematical, statistical, graphical, textual) and to envision material world contexts of which written text may be taken to be the refracted versions (Roth, 1996). In fact, it turns out that eight-grade students outperformed science teacher candidates who had already completed bachelor and masters degrees in science on {word problems} that required them to interpret scientific data embedded in a story form.

CODA

The three foregoing chapters provide us with interesting perspectives on the nature of a particular practice of school mathematics culture, the use of stories for teaching mathematical procedures and thinking. The three chapters, each in its own ways, raise concerns with the idea that there is a simple relation between the mundane, everyday-experienced world, on the one hand, and the world projected in the stories, on the other hand. The mathematics educator may now ask, what am I to do now that I have learned about the problematic nature of {word problems}?

First, rather than thinking that the lived-in world outside school could be a resource in the understanding the world projected in school textbooks, mathematics educators are probably better off in thinking about the special laws and narrative functions that underlie the stories in mathematics textbooks, laws and functions that are very different from those that students encounter in their everyday life-worlds.

Second, it might be profitable if we, mathematics educators, not only were focusing on what students do with {word problems}, how they succeed or fail, but also were looking at the institutional context that produces a populace in which there have to be 7% structural unemployment and welfare recipients not even looking for work to allow capitalist markets to reap profits. My conclusion is that {word problems} have marginally to do with the world as students experience it outside school; and they have everything to do with the world they do and will experience in school. Each term in this incompossible statement is but a one-sided expression of societal reality that we contribute to make and in turn experience. If anything is authentic in school task situations (Palm) where {word problems} are employed then it is the employment of these stories in and for the purpose of producing grades, which students use as a currency to access jobs and institutions of higher learning. The relationship of the stories to aspects of the world we, students and teachers, inhabit is much more tenuous and part of the ideology of the {word problem} itself.

Third, mathematics educators and teachers may have to rethink the relationships between the two worlds and how to mobilise how they can inform each other. The two worlds have everything to do with one another because the language of the {word problem} and the one they talk use the same words, though with very different semantic fields, syntax, and intonations. It is the same English (German, French, Chinese) that has to be translated into another such English (German, French, Chinese) so that students can and do make sense in all worlds, inside and outside the classroom and in the {word problem} itself. And all of these worlds are but moments of the world. The multiple relations within and between these worlds have not received proper attention by mathematics educators. I have the hunch that Bakhtin (1977) already provide us with a framework for studying these relations in their focus on the problem of reported speech generally and direct, indirect, and quasi-direct discourse more specifically.

NOTES

[1] Some of the readings I am thinking of here are Bakhtin (1986) on speech genres, Bakhtin (1977) on ideology, Bakhtin (1981) on the dynamic underlying the change in the genres. I am thinking about Derrida (1998) on monolingualism and the non-self-identical nature of language, which always is coming from the other and returning to the other. And I am thinking of Ricœur's (2004) marvellous treatment concerning the question of translation, which highlights, as does Derrida, the continual translations that occur in every language use.

[2] In our research, we developed the convention of joining contradictory moments by means of the Sheffer stroke "|", a logical operation meaning that two entities A and B are incompatible when they are joined as A|B. In our work, this expression therefore is consistent with the dialectical materialist insistence that whole units, like A|B, always expresses themselves one-sidedly, as A or as B.

[3] In this, Bakhtin is not unlike John L. Austin (1962), who created his speech act theory much later, but who theorised the speech act as including performative (locutionary), intentional (illocutionary) and effectual (perlocutionary) moments.

[4] Consistent with historically developed conversation analytic practices, I use the following convention: (1.41) – time in 1/100th of a second; .hh – aspiration, where the number of "h" letters indicates length in 1/10th of a second; okay:: – colons indicate lengthening of sound by about 1/10th of a second per colon; okay=rate – equal sign indicates "latching," that is, lack of separation between two words; <<p>focus> – bracketed talk is in "piano" voice; <<pp>discuss> – bracketed words are spoken pianissimo (low volume); <<f>i can> –bracketed talk is in fortissimo (louder than usual); [sec] [uum] – overlapping brackets in subsequent lines indicate overlap; .HH – capital letters suggest louder than usual sound; ↑– significant upward jump in pitch; 'what – rising pitch in word; – ^population – rising-falling pitch; ((movement)) –transcriber's comments are enclosed in double parentheses.

[5] I am using the term *translation* in the sense that Claude Janvier (1987) articulated it.

[6] I do these analyses using the freely available software for linguists named PRAAT (www.praat.org). Interested readers may contact me for more information.

REFERENCES

Austin, J. (1962). *How to do things with words*. Cambridge, MA: Harvard University Press.
Bakhtin, M. (1981). *The dialogic imagination*. Austin, TX: University of Texas Press.
Bakhtin, M. M. (1986). *Speech genres and other late essays*. Austin, TX: University of Texas Press.

Bakhtin, M. M. [Medvedev, P. N.] (1978). *The formal method in literary scholarship: A critical introduction to sociological poetics.* Baltimore: Johns Hopkins University Press.

Bakhtine, M. M. [Volochinov, V. N.] (1977). *Le marxisme et la philosophie du langage. Essai d'application de la méthode sociologique en linguistique.* Paris: Les Éditions de Minuit.

Barr, S. (1964). *Experiments in topology.* New York: Thomas Y. Crowell.

Clement, J. (1982). Students' preconceptions in introductory mechanics. *American Journal of Physics, 50,* 66–71.

Derrida, J. (1998). *Monolingualism of the Other; or, The prosthesis of origin.* Stanford, CA: Stanford University Press.

Eckert, P. (1989). *Jocks and burnouts: Social categories and identity in the high school.* New York: Teachers College Press.

Goulart, M. I. M., & Roth, W.-M. (2006). Margin|center: Toward a dialectic view of participation. *Journal of Curriculum Studies, 38,* 679–700.

Have, P. ten (1999). *Doing conversation analysis: A practical guide.* London: Sage.

Janvier, C. (1987). Translation processes in mathematics education. In C. Janvier (Ed.), *Problems of representation in the teaching and learning of mathematics* (pp. 27–32). Hillsdale, NJ: Erlbaum.

Katibi, A. (1985). Presentation. In Bennani-Boukous-Bounfour-Cheng-Formentelli-Hassoun-Katibi-Kilito-Meddeb-Todorov, *Du bilinguisme* (pp. 9–10). Paris: Denoël.

Lave, J. (1988). *Cognition in practice: Mind, mathematics and culture in everyday life.* Cambridge: Cambridge University Press.

Ricœur, P. (1991). *From text to action: Essays in hermeneutics, II.* Evanston, IL: Northwestern University Press.

Ricœur, P. (2004). *Sur la traduction.* Paris: Bayard.

Roth, W.-M. (1996). Where is the context in contextual word problems? Mathematical practices and products in Grade 8 students' answers to story problems. *Cognition and Instruction, 14,* 487–527.

Roth, W.-M. (2005). Mathematical inscriptions and the reflexive elaboration of understanding: An ethnography of graphing and numeracy in a fish hatchery. *Mathematical Thinking and Learning, 7,* 75–109.

Roth, W.-M., Bowen, G. M., & Masciotra, D. (2002). From thing to sign and "natural object": Toward a genetic phenomenology of graph interpretation. *Science, Technology, & Human Values, 27,* 327–356.

Vygotsky, L. S. (1986). *Thought and language.* Cambridge, MA: MIT Press.

Wolff-Michael Roth
Lansdowne Professor, Applied Cognitive Science
University of Victoria, BC
Canada

PART II: SOCIOCULTURAL FACTORS

FRANK J. SWETZ

4. WORD PROBLEMS: FOOTPRINTS FROM THE HISTORY OF MATHEMATICS

A PERSPECTIVE

Historically it is interesting, and a bit telling, that some of the earliest written communication consisted of "word problems." These exercises in mathematics learning are thousands of years old and first appeared in the Tigris-Euphrates basin, Ancient Mesopotamia. Archaeological excavations in this region have unearthed thousands of clay tablets whose contents reveal the evolution of written communication (Schmandt-Besserat, 1992). The earliest tablets recovered contain imprints of clay tokens, concrete mathematical counters, whose impressions designated numerical values. Gradually this system of symbols became incorporated into a more flexible form of writing, the cuneiform script. It appears that the initial products of this process were numerical tablets, records containing data on societal activities such as harvest amounts or taxes collected, and "problem texts," that is clay tablets whose contents present a collection of problems for which a mathematical solution is sought or a particular problem with an answer and solution process outlined. A dig at a temple precinct from the Sumerian city of Shuruppak unearthed the oldest know mathematics word problem from the fourth millennium BCE:

> [Given] A granary of barley. [If one man received] 7 *sila* [of grain]. What are its men? [i.e. how many men can be given a ration?] (Robson, 2007, p. 75).

A scribe answering this question had to know a granary capacity, 2400 *gur*, where 1 *gur* = 480 *sila*, and a correct answer in sexagesimal notation is provided. While the contents of such problems appear rather mundane now, their very existence attests to the importance of "word problems."

Word or story problems are a natural extension of an oral teaching situation where instead of a transitory verbal confrontation with a problem a prolonged involvement results. Eventually, the written form allows for a standardisation of problems and establishes a record of important mathematical knowledge and the situations upon which that knowledge is to be applied. In a sense, it is an instrument of socio-mathematical indoctrination. It specifies what mathematics is important and what situations warrant its use. As such, word problems provide an historic testimony to the societal uses and the changing passage of mathematics over time; specifically how mathematics was used and what were its societal applications. They are the "footprints" in the history of mathematics and its teaching. Mathematically speaking, they show where we have been and the direction in

L. Verschaffel et al. (eds.), Words and Worlds: Modelling Verbal Descriptions of Situations, 73–91.
© *2009 Sense Publishers. All rights reserved.*

which we are proceeding. Their path delineates a journey of involvement and understanding and illustrates the power of mathematics. A good tracker can tell much from footprints. A deer hunter following his quarry can determine if the deer is moving fast, whether it has jumped, foraged for acorns on the forest floor, or been joined by companions; and may even determine where it might be overtaken. Similarly, word problems leave a trail. They can tell their pursuer how mathematics was used, for what tasks, and reveal societal concerns and priorities.

Word problems as an extension of an oral tradition of learning supplemented that tradition and eventually replaced it by becoming a means for self-study. Before the appearance of "books," they served as the "bare bones" collection of knowledge that had to be preserved and promoted. The appearance of word problem texts followed the rise of urbanisation in southern Mesopotamia and the formation of a highly centralised state. Most of the problem texts excavated were school texts intended for the training of scribes for state service. Mesopotamia's ascendancy initially rested upon agriculture which in turn depended on irrigation and water conservancy (Powell, 1988). In the theory of social anthropologist Karl Wittfogel such "hydraulic societies" share common characteristics, principle among which is the existence of a dominant bureaucracy whose task is to initiate and maintain public works projects such as the construction of dikes, canals, grain storage facilities, land usage, and tax collection (Wittfogel, 1957). All of these topics are evident in the extant problem tablets. Within these collections of problems emerge a pattern of societal concerns and a chain of situations demanding mathematical consideration (see Figure 1).

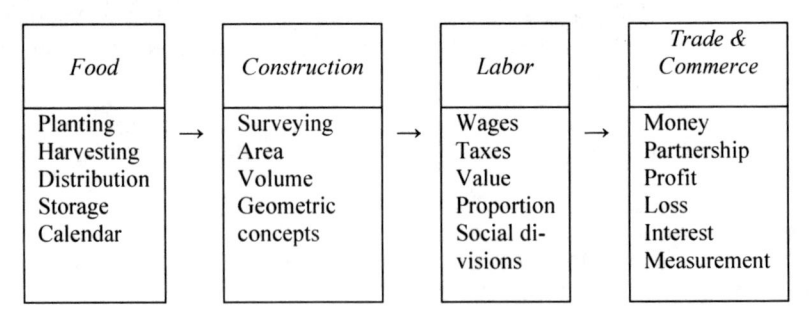

Food	Construction	Labor	Trade & Commerce
Planting Harvesting Distribution Storage Calendar	Surveying Area Volume Geometric concepts	Wages Taxes Value Proportion Social divisions	Money Partnership Profit Loss Interest Measurement

Figure 1. Schema of problem development as based on human needs

Scribal problem solving efforts follow a strict procedure and are designed to obtain a number. Numeric computation is stressed. Problem situations are frequently couched in the measurement of everyday objects and activities. Scribes are asked to find the area of fields, the lengths of canals, the amount of dirt removed from an excavation, or the number of bricks required for a structure (Nemet-Nejat, 1988):

> I have two fields of grain. From the first I harvest $^2/_3$ a bushel of grain/unit area; from the second, ½ bushel/unit area. The yield of the first field exceeds the second by 50 bushels. The total area of the two fields together is 300 square units. What is the area of each field? (Van der Waerden, 1983, p. 158)

FOOTPRINTS FROM THE HISTORY OF MATHEMATICS

> A man carried 540 bricks for a distance of 30 rods. [For this] They gave him 1 *ban* of grain. Now he carried 300 bricks and finished the job. How much grain did they give him? [1 *ban* = 10 *sila* (liters)] (Robson, 2007, p. 115).

Despite this seemingly close association with daily events, the resulting mathematical scenarios are often unrealistic. The situation setting is merely a backdrop for the mathematics. Mathematics dominating the application is best illustrated in geometrically conceived problems.

> A triangular piece of land [in form of right triangle] is divided among six brothers by equidistant lines constructed perpendicular to the base of the triangle. The length of the base is 390 units and the area of the triangle is 40,950 square units. What is the difference in area between adjacent plots of land? (Neugebauer & Sachs, 1945, p. 52)

And there are problems undesignated in their mathematical intent, for example "the measuring of stones."

> I found a stone but did not weigh it; after I subtracted $1/7$ and then again subtracted $1/13$ [of the remainder] I weigh it at one manna. What was the original weight of the stone? (Katz, 2003, p. 27)

Problem collections with similar subjects and formats are found in other hydraulic societies of the ancient world, Egypt and China. One of the few extant collections of Egyptian word problems is found in the Rhind papyrus. This collection of 85 problems compiled in approximately 1650 BCE was prepared for scribal training. Each problem is associated with an aspect of Egyptian daily life:

> Divide 100 loaves among 10 men including a boatman, a foreman, and a doorkeeper, who received double portions. What is the share of each? (Chace, 1979, p. 84)

> How many cattle are in a herd when $2/3$ of $1/3$ of them makes 70, the number due as tribute to the Owner? (Chace, 1979, p. 102)

The theory that the great pyramids of Egypt were built by slave labour gangs has been put to rest. It is now realised that they were constructed by skilled labourers who were paid for their work in rations of grain, bread, and beer. Egyptian problem collections affirm this fact.

Perhaps the most organised, comprehensive, and influential collection of word problems from the ancient world is found in the Chinese *Jiuzhang suan shu* (ca 100 CE). The two hundred and forty-seven problems of this collection together with their solution procedures and attached commentaries served the bureaucratic needs of the Chinese Empire. Each of its nine chapters is devoted to specific applications of mathematics:
- Field measurement
- Processing millet and rice
- Short width: measurement and surveying
- Construction consultations: engineering works

- Impartial taxation: taxes and labour assignment
- "Excess and deficiency": linear equations
- Way of calculating by tabulation: systems of equations
- Right triangles: surveying.

This collection became a mathematical classic, served as a Chinese reference for over a thousand years and was adopted in the surrounding countries, becoming a mathematical manual for Japan and Korea.

Westward on the shores of the Mediterranean, Greek civilisation had been developing as a series of independent city-states supported by maritime trade. The Greek empire was not a hydraulic society and its intellectual characteristics and priorities differed from those of its oriental neighbours to the east. While mathematics was needed for social and economic concerns, a dichotomy was established between applied mathematics, *Logistica*, calculation, and theoretical mathematics, *Arithmetica*, aspects of numbers and shape worthy of philosophical consideration. *Logistica*, the "less worthy" mathematics, was undertaken by slaves, craftsmen, and merchants. No records of their mathematical problems remain. In the hydraulic societies, mathematical problems had become an end in themselves and resulted in a specific numerical answer whereas for the Greeks problems were a beginning from which theories evolved (Høyrup, 1985). The earliest surviving collection of Greek word problems is found in the Palatine collection of the grammarian Metrodorus (ca 500 CE). The forty-six arithmetical problems are stated as riddles and appear to be compiled for intellectual recreation (Page, Rouse, & Capps, 1916).

Word problem collections would play a prominent role in the teaching of commercial mathematics and the introduction of the Hindu-Arabic numerals and their computational algorithms into Medieval and Early Renaissance Europe. As textual forms became more elaborate, the number of problems introduced into a discourse decreased; however, problem scenarios would be repeated and a standardisation of word problems emerged. Word problems now became a supplement and reinforcement for more textual instructional forms. They now appeared in arithmetic books but still their emphasis could vary as to the existing social conditions and the intent of the author. English writers of the sixteenth century such as Robert Recorde (1546) and Humphrey Baker (1568) presented problems that appealed to craftsmen and tradesmen. Recorde also posed problems related to warfare and military affairs, as did several other authors of arithmetic texts such as Rudolff (1526), Tartaglia, and Digges (1579).

Eighteenth and nineteenth century popularisation of mathematics saw the rise of periodicals – newspapers, almanacs, and journals that published collections of word problems for the mathematical edification and education of their readers. One very influential such journal was the *Ladies' Diary* published in England from 1704-1841 (Perl, 1979). Challenge problems would be offered to readers and their correct solutions published in later additions. When the first mathematical periodical, the *Mathematical Correspondent*, was published in the United States in 1804 it emulated the *Diary* in its exposition and use of problems (Hogan, 1977).

PROBLEM FORM AND PRESENTATION

Earliest written problems were simple statements and resulted in a question, the words of the mathematics master or instructor captured for permanence and reuse. They tested basic comprehension and operational methods: find a sum; divide the amount, etc. But gradually they became more demanding, requiring analysis of data and synthesis of solution methods. Their social relevance and psychological appeal were increased by reference to daily activities. Such referencing could result in problems with realistic data resulting in realistic solutions or in pseudo-realistic settings where impractical answers resulted. This later class of problems was usually conceived to demonstrate mathematical concepts rather than be utilitarian. Subclasses of realistic problems to emerge in Europe by the sixteenth century were scientifically based problems whose answers entailed both knowledge of mathematics and the new emerging sciences. A third class of word problems were developed as recreational, intellectual challenges. In most early problem collections such "riddles" or "puzzles" were interspersed among the practical mathematics problems and they stood as an assertion that mathematics was also a pure intellectual activity transcending the realm of daily activities. Perhaps the simplest and most enduring of these recreational problems are ones of the form "guess my number" as found in the Rhind Papyrus:

> What quantity whose whole and seventh added together gives nineteen? (Chace, 1979, p. 66)

And in the early United States:

> There are two numbers whose sum is equal to the difference of their squares; and if the sum of the squares of the two numbers be subtracted from the square of their sum, the remainder will be 60. What are the two numbers? (Watson's *Connecticut Almanack*, 1777)

A fascination with geometric progressions appears in many early recreational problems and spans various cultures. The Rhind Papyrus introduces the "seven cats":

> [There are] seven houses; in each 7 cats; each cat kills 7 rats; each rat would have eaten 7 ears of spelt; each ear of spelt will produce 7 *hekat*. What is the total of them all? How much *hekat* of grain is thereby saved? (Chace, 1979, p. 112)

Two thousand years later, an independent Chinese version in *Master Sun's Manual* (ca 400 CE), replaced the Egyptian culturally preferred number seven by the Chinese special number nine:

> Now there is sighted 9 embankments; each embankment has 9 trees; each tree has 9 branches; each branch holds 9 nests; each nest has 9 birds; each bird has 9 young; each young has 9 feathers and each feather has 9 colours. Find the quantity of each (Lam & Ang, 1992, p. 181).

When the British monk, Alcuin of York, became educational advisor to Charlemagne in 781 he compiled a collection of mathematical word problems for the training of court pages. His *Propositiones ad acuendos jevenes* was a collection of 56 riddle type problems (Hadley & Singmaster, 1992). This is the first Latin collection of such problems. It, too, considered questions of progressions:

> A ladder has 100 steps. On the first step sits 1 pigeon; on the second 2; on the third 3, and so on up to the hundredth. How many pigeons are there in all? (Hadley & Singmaster, 1992, p. 121)

When Leonardo of Pisa published his influential *Liber Abaci* in 1202 he included several of Alcuin's problems among his collection of problems (Sigler, 2002). Once established, problem types and scenarios provided templates upon which future problems would be composed for other environments.

MATHEMATICAL CONTENT

Several years ago while conducting a workshop for thirty experienced secondary school teachers, I was shocked to learn they knew so little about the origins of mathematics. Quite simply, they did not know when or why the mathematics they had been teaching for years originated. Since a prolonged prevalence of a mathematical concept attests to its importance, the teachers had a limited appreciation for the mathematics itself.

The mathematical content evident in word problems compiled a millennium before the Christian Era reveals that the calculators of the time could perform all the basic operations known today with a high degree of accuracy. They could extract square and cube roots to several decimal places, and knew correct formulae for area and volumes. They worked with linear and quadratic equations and understood the concepts of arithmetic and geometric progressions, approximated the value of π to workable accuracy, and knew the mathematical relationship popularly known as the "Pythagorean Theorem." Pythagoras flourished in the fifth century BCE; however, problems whose required solution demonstrates a knowledge of the relationship that bears his name are found in many problem collections that predate him by centuries. For example, these Old Babylonian (2000–1600 BCE) problems:

> A beam of length ½ [stands against a wall]. The upper end has slipped down a distance $1/10$.
>
> How far did the lower end move? (Van der Waerden, 1983, p. 59)
>
> [Given] a gate. The height is ½ rod, 2 cubits, the breadth 2 cubits. What is the diagonal? (Robson, 2007, p. 140)

The variety and scope of the twenty-four right triangle problems given in the ninth chapter of the *Jiuzhang* indicate that Chinese surveyors and mathematical clerks were well aware of the "Pythagorean Theorem" at an early date. In particular, two of the problems in this collection, "the broken bamboo" and the "reed in the pond" have since appeared in different forms in several cultures.

> A bamboo shoot 10 ch'ih tall has a break near the top. The configuration of the main shoot and its broken portion forms a triangle. The top touches the

ground 3 ch'ih from the stem. What is the length of the stem left standing? (Swetz & Kao, 1977, p. 44)

This problem again appears in the ninth-century Sanskrit mathematical classic *Ganita-Sara* by Mahavira and still later in Philippi Calandri's *Arithmetic* published in Florence in 1491 (See Figure 2).

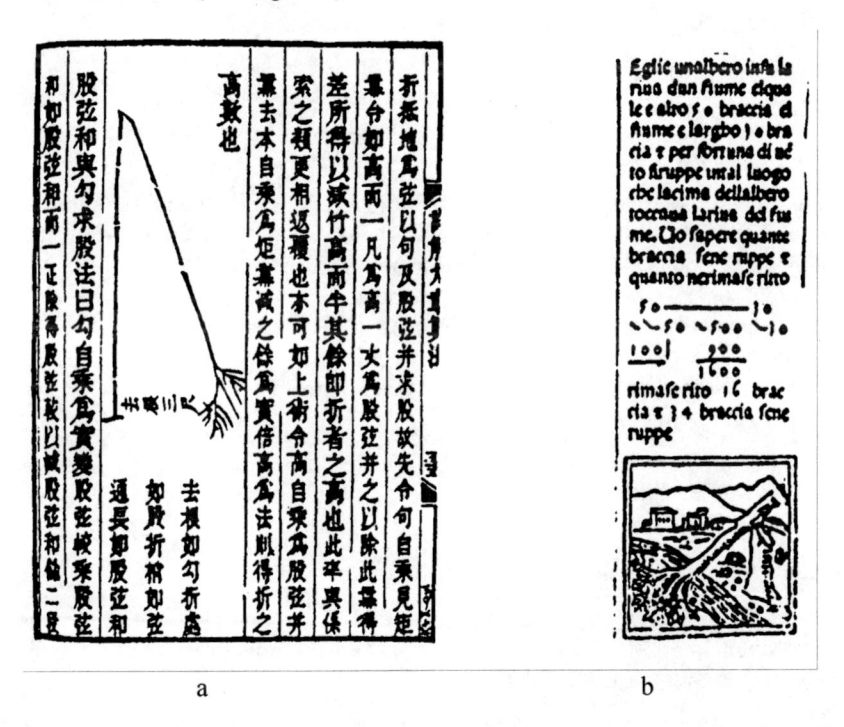

Figure 2. (a) Jiuzhang bamboo problem (China ca 100); (b) Calandri's broken tree problem

In the center of a square pond whose side is 10 *ch'ih* grows a reed whose tip reaches 1 *ch'ih* above the water level. If we pull the reed towards the bank, its top becomes even with the surface of the water. What is the depth of the pond and the length of the plant? (Swetz & Kao, 1977, p. 30)

In a more picturesque Hindu version of this problem published by Bhaskara (1114–ca 1182), the reed becomes a lotus and red geese occupy the pond. (Colebrooke, 1817, p. 66)

There are some instances where the first appearance of a mathematical technique is given in a problem. For example, the first known example of the Chinese "Remainder Theorem" appears in a problem from *Master Sun's Manual* (400 CE):

Now there are an unknown number of things. If counted by threes there is a remainder of two; if counted by fives there is a remainder of three and if counted by sevens there is a remainder of two. Find the number of things. (Lam & Ang, 1992, p. 104)

From the thirteenth century onwards, Chinese word problems demonstrated techniques for numerical root extraction for higher degree equations. This facility was not common in Europe until the appearance of the Ruffini-Horner method in 1819. A typical problem of this type is:

There is a tree 135 *bu* from the southern gate [of a walled city]. The tree can be seen if one walks 15 *bu* from the northern gate and then 208 *bu* in the eastward direction. Find the diameter of the walled city. (Li Zhi's *Ceyuan haijing*, 1248)

Using modern notation and allowing the radius of the city to be represented by X, the conditions result in the equation: $4X^4 + 600X^3 + 22500X^2 - 11681280X - 788486400 = 0$ and X is correctly found to be 120 (Libbrecht, 1973, p. 134).

Word problems posed as simple statements intended to foster mathematical thinking have often served as a seed for mathematical research. Consider the "pursuit problem" where one creature, person, animal, is pursuing another. The first known appearance of this problem once again comes from the Chinese *Jiuzhang*, chapter 6, problem 14, where we find:

A hare runs 100 *bu* ahead of a dog. The dog pursuing at 250 bu is 30 *bu* short. Tell me in how many *bu* will the dog catch up with the hare? (Shen, Crossley, & Lun, 1999, p. 330)

Alcuin's European version is:

A dog chasing a rabbit, which has a start of 150 feet, jumps 9 feet every time the rabbit jumps 7. In how many leaps does the dog overtake the rabbit? (Hadley & Singmaster, 1992, p. 115)

By the early Middle Ages, the European alteration by Abraham ben Ezra (ca 1140) had replaced the animals by travellers, which were probably more relevant to the contemporary scene:

Reuben sets out from his city on the morning of the first day of the new moon to go to meet his brother Simon in Simon's town. On the same day, Simon also leaves his town to go see Reuben in his city. The distance between the two places is 100 miles. We ask when will they meet? (Sanford, 1927, p. 72)

The situation has been personalised by the insertion of particular names. Still later, the situation was generalised further by the insertion of couriers. "Courier problems" with various routes taken remained popular among German and Italian writers of the sixteenth century (Smith, 1917). In 1732, the French mathematician Pierre Bouguer proposed a pursuit problem before the French Academy in which he envisioned a merchant ship and a pirate ship. The merchant flees the pirate on a course perpendicular to that of the pirate who pursues. Bouguer sought the *courbe de poursuite* or curve of pursuit. This situation initiated a topic of mathematical research that exists until the present day, namely interception and pursuit analysis (Nahin, 2007).

Another simple problem that has spawned some interesting variations is the "river crossing" problem. Alcuin of York first gave it in his *Propositiones* as:

> Three friends each with a sister needed to cross a river. Each of them coveted the sister of another. At the river they found a small boat in which only two of them could cross at once. How could they cross the river without any of the women being defiled by the men? (Hadley & Singmaster, 1992, p. 111)

The following three problems in Alcuin's collection involve the same situation with different subjects, namely wolf, goat, and cabbage, and overweight people and hedgehogs. Perhaps the licentious implications prompted continual interest in this problem. Luca Pacioli asserts that four or five couples will require a three-person boat. Tartaglia in 1556 claimed that four couples could cross in a two-person boat, challenging Pacioli. Finally Gaspar Bachet de Meziriac, who published his own collection of recreational problems, *Problèmes plaisants et délectables* (1612), refuted Tartaglia. Interest in this problem was resurrected in the nineteenth century by the French mathematician Anatole Lucas. In 1879, one of Lucas' students, De Fontenay, introduced an island into the situation that allowed four couples to complete the transit in twenty-four crossings (Pressman & Singmaster, 1989). Since that time Rouse Ball has concluded that $6n - 7$ crossings are required for n couples (Ball, 1987). The cultural variants of this particular problem are also interesting and will be examined later.

WHERE THE FOOTPRINTS LEAD: SOCIETAL AND CULTURAL RELEVANCE

Mathematical historian D. E. Smith in his early twentieth century examination of problem collections was impressed by the amount of societal and cultural information conveyed by word problems (Smith, 1918). Word problems, by their content and emphasis, are vehicles for societal indoctrination either explicitly or implicitly. The mathematical tracker can discern the subject's activities during a journey. Much factual and historical information can be revealed from word problems.

In ancient Mesopotamia, the transition from the fourth millennium to the Old Babylonian Period is marked by a lessening of despotic bureaucratic rule: city states express their independence; collective agriculture is replaced by smaller holdings; royal workshops are replaced by private handicraft; royal traders become independent merchants and individuals are allowed to use identification seals, a practice formerly reserved for royalty. There is a shift of importance from the state and its apparatus to individuals. A new self-confidence is evident in scribal writing (Høyrup, 1985). Written mathematical problems become more creative, algebraic in their conception, and more personally directed as mental challenges rather than mere exercises.

A contrast exists in reviewing Chinese problem collections where a striking similarity and rigid form of problem posing and solving is maintained over centuries. In the Confucian tradition, classics written by masters were to be revered, copied, and perhaps respectfully commented upon. In mathematics instruction, the standard was also followed whereby all texts imitated a canon of problem forms, recipes. In the nineteenth century, collections of problems were still appearing that mirrored the situation depicted in the first century *Jiuzhang*. This dogmatic adherence to set problem forms and standards stifled creativity and limited mathematical advances in the Chinese Empire. The mathematical question "What if?" did not appear, defeating the rise of theoretical mathematics (Swetz, 1996).

While, initially, the Japanese emulated their Chinese neighbours and adopted China's mathematical classics and problem collections for the instruction of their scholars and bureaucrats, by the Endo Period (1603–1867) they began evolving their own problem forms. The Endo Period was a time when Japan retreated into isolationism, removing itself from feared western encroachment. It was a time for cultural introspection and renewed reverence for traditional customs. In 1627 the mathematician Yoshida Kōyu published *Jingoki* (Treatise on Eternal Mathematical Truth) in which he set a new mathematical standard by concluding his work with a list of twelve unsolved problems. These were taken up by readers who, in turn, published their solutions and offered further challenge problems. A popular wave of problem solving evolved based mainly on the solution of complex and fancifully conceived geometric problems involving circular properties and dealing with finding the lengths of chords, arcs, etc. Common people, such as farmers, now openly became involved in problem solving and, as a gesture of thanksgiving, and perhaps an expression of bravado for solving a problem, they inscribed their problems and solutions on wooden plackets and hung them in the local temple or Shinto shrine (Fukagawa & Pedoe, 1989). Often these tablet problems, *sangaku*, bore the challenge, "See if you can prove this!" Historically, such a movement in problem posing and solving appears unique to the Japanese. One of the Kōyu problems is as follows:

> There is a log of precious wood 18 feet long whose bases are 5 feet and 2 ½ feet in circumference. Into what lengths should this log be cut to trisect its volume? (Cooke, 1997, p. 248)

And a *sangaku* in modern notation:

> The centers of a loop of n circles of radius r [i.e. touching circles] form the vertices of an n-gon. Let S_1 be the sum of the [parts of the] areas of the circles inside [the n-gon], and S_2 the sum of the [parts of the] areas of the circles outside [the n-gon]. Show that $S_2 - S_1 = 2\pi r^2$ (Fukagawa & Rigby, 2002, p. 27).

The rise of European mercantile capitalism in the late Middle Ages saw an accompanying renewed interest in numerical computation and problem solving. From the twelfth through the fifteenth centuries a wave of manuscripts and eventually books appeared that promoted a use of Hindu-Arabic numerals and their associated algorithms, and commercial problem solving. Problems now accompanied more theoretical explanations but they still supplied the majority of practical instruction. When the first printed arithmetic book, *Treviso Arithmetic,* appeared in Italy in

1478, its 123 pages of text included sixty-two problems. A variety of business issues were covered by such problems as the computation of interest, determination of profit and loss, and the mathematics of partnership (Swetz, 1987). The situational descriptions provided in these problems reveal much about the daily life of the times: oxen were used for ploughing; important centres of European trade included Venice, Lyons, London, Antwerp; the commodities most often traded included cloth, wool, brass, rice. In Siena, the rental price of a house was 30 lire a year, while in 1640 Florence the price was 300 lire. Beef selling for 1 grosso for 3 pounds in 14th century Italy was intended for the wealthy, as were spices such as pepper, ginger, and sugar. Sixteenth century Italian bread prices stand at 20 ounces for ½ penny. The existence of social class structure based on purchasing power is obvious. Relative quality of some products can be judged from the information given: Spanish linen sold for 94 to 120 ducats per hundredweight while Italian linen fetched 355 ducats for the same amount. A predominance of monetary exchange problems indicates the confused state of monetary standards. This fact is further confirmed by considerations of barter indicating unreliability of money supply. Travel times and multiple custom duties testify to the difficulty of moving commodities. Even hotel life is revealed in a German problem from 1561 that describes a *Gausthaus* with 8 rooms, each room with twelve beds and each bed sleeping 3 guests. The reader is asked to compute the payment due. Frequent reference to the wool industry, a primary source of European income at this time, is found in many books:

> A man bought a number of bales of wool in London, each bale weighing 200 pounds, English measure, and each bale cost him 24 florin. He sent the wool to Florence and paid carriage, duties and other expenses amounting to 10 florin. He wishes to sell the wool in Florence at such a price as to make 20% on his investment. How much should he charge a hundred weight of 100 London pounds, which are equivalent to 133 Florentine pounds? (Ghaligai, 1521, fol. 31v)

Changing social, political, and economic needs saw the situational content of word problems change accordingly. The rise of animal husbandry in Europe was accompanied by the appearance of "pasturage problems":

> Two men rent a pasture for 100 livres, on the understanding that two cows are to be counted as equivalent to three sheep. The first puts in 60 cows and 85 sheep; the second 80 cows and 100 sheep. How much should each pay? (Trenchant, 1566, p. 178)

The early Christian church forbade the charging of interest in financial transactions and the policy was affirmed by the church's Council of Vienna in 1311. However, commerce demanded the lending of money. With the church's approval, Jewish moneylenders and bankers filled this void, giving loans and charging interest. Compound interest, an unpleasant prospect to labour under, was often associated with Jewish moneylenders:

> A Jew lends a man twenty florins for four years and every half year he reckons the interest on his capital. I ask how much the twenty florins will amount to in four years if a florin earns 2 d. a week? Find the interest on the interest (Riese, 1522, fol. 6V).

After the Lateran Council of 1515, allowing Christians to charge interest, attention to interest computation in problem situations increased.

By the sixteenth century, the needs of European warfare began to find their way into mathematical word problems (Digges, 1579). For example, in order to blunt cavalry charges against infantry, in the fifteenth century, the Swiss devised the use of square phalanx formations of pike men and halberdiers. Formed into a tight square formation and with their weapons pointed outward, this defensive formation was called a "hedgehog." The mathematics of square troop arrangements became a subject of problems:

> There is a capitian, whiche hath a greate armie & would gladly marshall them into a square battaile, as large as might be. Wherefore in his first proofe of a square forme, he had remaining 284 too many. And prouving again by putting 1 moare in the fronte, he founde wante of 25 men. How many soldiers had he as you guesse? (Recorde, 1542, fol. G)

Although the introduction of artillery in warfare made such formations obsolete, this problem continued in arithmetic books until the nineteenth century.

An interesting trail to follow is that of an appealing word problem through variant forms over time. A problem that has endured in almost all cultures is the "cistern problem." Probably originating in the Mediterranean world of ancient Greece or Rome, the problem initially concerned water flowing in a fountain. A version given in the Palatine collection of 500CE goes as follows:

> I am a brazen lion; my spouts are my two eyes, my mouth and the flat of my right foot. My right eye fills a jar in two days, my left eye in three, and my foot in four. My mouth is capable of filling it in six hours. Tell me how long all four together will take to fill it? (Page, Rouse, & Capps, 1916, p. 31)

In 16th century agricultural Europe, milling became the subject:

> A man wishes to have 500 *rubii* of grain ground. He goes to a mill that has five stones. The first of these grinds 7 *rubii* of grain in an hour, the second grinds 5, the third 4, the fourth 3, and the fifth 1. In how long a time will the grain be ground and how much done by each stone? (Clavius, 1583, p. 191)

Subsequently, the same mathematical situation has been depicted regarding trade, sails on a ship (Borghi, 1484), companions drinking wine (Buteo, 1559), animals devouring a sheep (Calandri, 1491), and, in perhaps its most recurrent form concerning labour:

> If two men or three boys can plow an acre in $\frac{1}{6}$ of a day; how long will it require three men and two boys to plow it? (Brooks, 1863, p. 191)

One Victorian version given in J. H. Smith's *Arithmetic* (1880) reflects on a miner's working conditions:

> If 5 pumps each having a length of stroke of 3 feet working 15 hours a day for 5 days, empty water out of a mine; how many pumps with a length of stroke 2½ feet, working 10 hours a day for 12 days, will be required to empty the same mine; the strokes of the former set of pumps being performed 4 times as fast as the other? (p. 120)

Another problem that has left a long and winding trail is Alcuin's "River Crossing" situation. From the Catholic Church's moral concern with the innocence of young women, the problem takes on social class distinctions. A 1624 version has three masters and their valets crossing the river but each master hates the others' valets and will do them harm if given the opportunity. In 1881, Cassell's *Book of Indoor Amusements* depicts the situation with violent servants who will rob any outnumbered master. Ten years later, at the height of British imperialism and the carrying out of the white man's burden theory, the problem becomes one of missionaries and cannibals where the missionaries must keep from being eaten by their travelling companions (Pressman & Singmaster, 1989).

Most problems considered in early American arithmetics reflected on the nation's emergence as a trading power. Such problems provide a wealth of information on the mercantile conditions of the time:

> Shipped for the West Indies 223 quintals of fish, at 155.6 d. per quintal; 37000 feet of boards at $8^{1}/$_{3}$ per 1000; 12000 shingles at ½ guin per 1000; 19000 hoops at $1½ per 1000, and 53 half *joes* [Portuguese coins]; and in return, I have 3000 gallons of rum at 1s. 3d. per gallon; 2700 gallons of molasses, at $5½ d. per gallon; 1500 pounds of coffee at 8½ d. per pound and 19 cwt of sugar at 12 s. 3 d. per cwt and my charges on the voyage were £37 12s, pray, did I gain or lose, and how much, by the voyage? (Pike, 1788, p. 133).

A later problem appearing in the 1814 issue of *The Analyst* reflects on the human cost of the plantation economy of the West Indies:

> If out of a cargo of 600 slaves, 200 die during a passage of 6 weeks from Africa to the West Indies; how long must the passage be that one half the cargo may perish? Supposing the degree of mortality to be the same throughout the passage, that is, the number of deaths at any time to be proportional to the living at the same time (Douglas, 1814, p. 21).

When, in 1776, England's thirteen American colonies broke away and became the United States of America, each colony was an independent civic and political entity within itself. This independence was reflected in the monetary systems they employed. All were different. As a commercial nation, the problems of monetary exchange, both foreign and domestic, became a major concern for the fledgling United States. This issue was evident in the mathematical word problems of this time (Swetz, 1993).

A different kind of track is problems with a political or social agenda. Problems can reveal societal divisions; favourite groups can be designated and viewed in a good light while undesirables can also be recognised. One of the most curious of such designations is the "Josephus Problem" named after the first century Jewish historical figure, Flavius Josephus, who found himself trapped together with forty colleagues in a cave by the Roman army. Facing imminent death, the group chose suicide. Josephus arranged himself and his companions in a circle wherein from a certain point every third man would be killed until all were eliminated. Josephus chose his position so that he became the last man standing and so survived. A popular form of this problem comes from the tenth century and involved Turks and Christians:

> A sinking ship must cast off passengers to survive. There are 15 Christians and 15 Turks aboard. The captain, himself a Christian, arranges the passengers in a circle where every ninth person will be thrown overboard. How should he make the arrangement so that the Christians survive? (Smith, 1958, p. 541)

An eighteenth century Japanese version has a stepmother arranging her children, both stepchildren and her own offspring, in a circle upon which a selection scheme will be applied to disinherit some children. She wishes to have her children benefit from the process, but miscounts, and all are disinherited. A problem with a moral!

Another problem that has lent itself to discriminating situations is that of the "Hundred Fowls." Originating in China in about the fifth century, the problem initially involved chickens, ducks, and sparrows, thus the "Fowls" designation. Its solution results in a linear indeterminate equation for which a practical value is required. A twelfth century Islamic version places Christians and Jews at a disadvantage:

> A Turkish bath has 30 visitors in a day. The fee for Jews is 3 dirhams, for Christians 2 dirhams and for Muslims ½ dirham. Thirty dirhams were earned by the bath. How many Christians, Jews and Muslims attended? (Rebstock, 2007)

More stringent propaganda can be found in more modern word problem collections. In the early twentieth century the United States was attempting to instil democratic principles in the Philippines and remove Spanish colonial traditions (Swetz, 1999). Special textual materials were produced to help introduce these new ideals into the subject population. Arithmetic problems focused on the evils of the existing tenant land holding situation:

> Pedro is a tenant on Mr. Santos' farm. He has rented 4 hectares of rice land. After the cutting is paid for, Mr. Santos is to have for the use of the land one half of what rice is left and Pedro will take the other half for himself. If 45 *cavans* grow on each hectare, and one sixth is given for cutting, how many *cavans* will the cutters get? How much will be left? What will be Mr. Santos' share? What will be Pedro's share?

The problem series goes on to point out that Pedro is in debt to Mr. Santos for seed rice and also for products purchased at Mr. Santos' store. After a series of calculations, the student/reader finds that Pedro comes out of this situation even deeper in debt (Bonsall, 1905, p. 113).

Landlord exploitation was also a frequent topic in Chinese Communist textbooks:

> In the old society, there was a starving family who had to borrow 5 *dou* [200 pounds] of corn from the landlord. The family repaid the landlord three years later. The greedy landlord demanded 50% interest compounded annually. How much corn did the landlord demand at the end of the third year? (*New York Times*, March 9, 1969, p. 18)

The cost of "undesirables" is considered in Nazi textbooks used in Germany in 1941:

> Every day, the state spends RM 6 on one cripple; RM $4\frac{1}{2}$ on one mentally ill person; RM $5\frac{1}{2}$ on one deaf and dumb person; RM $5^3/_5$ on one feeble-minded person; RM $3\frac{1}{2}$ on one alcoholic; RM $4^4/_5$ on one pupil in care; RM $2\frac{1}{10}$ on one pupil at a special school; and RM $9/_{20}$ for one pupil at a normal school.

Then followed a series of questions emphasising the cost to the state for "inferiors," such as:

> Calculate the expenditure of the state for one pupil in a special school and one pupil in an ordinary school over eight years and state the amount of higher cost engendered by the special school pupil. (Pine, 1997, p. 27)

PEDAGOGICAL IMPLICATIONS

Word problems are composed to teach mathematics. For thousands of years they were the primary means for such instruction. Their compilation required an investment of time and thought. The process of devising problems entailed selecting the mathematic principles to be communicated and embedding them in a situation that provided motivation, either societally bound, intellectual, or both. It should be noted that many early problem collections were prologued by motivational comments; for example, the author of the Rhind Papyrus promises its reader that the text provides "insights into all that exists" and "knowledge of powerful secrets" (Chace, 1979, p. 27). Sun Zi, in the introduction to his arithmetic classic (ca 400), assures his reader that "mathematics governs the length and the breadth of the heavens and earth; affects all creatures" (Lam & Ang, 1992, p. 151). Such admonitions as to the power and usefulness of mathematics were carried on by Robert Recorde in his sixteenth century efforts to popularise mathematics in England, and became a standard feature in early American mathematics books.

Further motivation is then built into the problem sequence. Problems develop from simple statements issuing a challenge: "Find me a number...." to directed dialogues stressing social and economic relevance, to extended story situations that employ "human interest" to draw the reader into the drama:

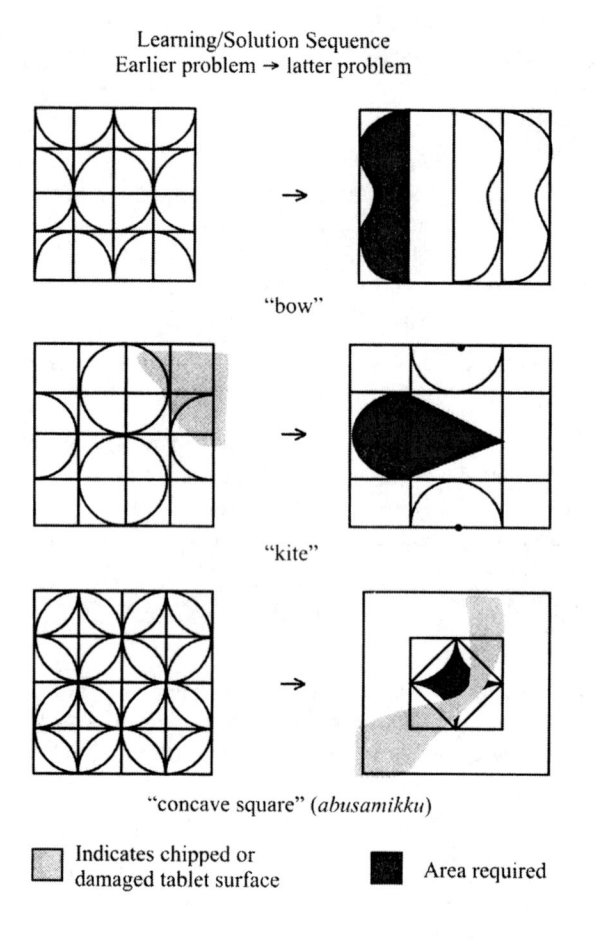

Learning/Solution Sequence
Earlier problem → latter problem

"bow"

"kite"

"concave square" (*abusamikku*)

Figure 3. Sequence of "find the area" problems for Old Babylonian period

The Burgomaster and council of the city of Oppenheym employed a learned writing master for the city, telling him if he would serve them faithfully for a year they would give him 100 guilders, a horse, and a suit of clothes. The school master taught no longer than three months when he was obliged to take leave of the council and, for his services of three months, they gave him the horse and the clothes and said, "Now take the horse and the outfit of clothes and go on your way." The writing master received them gladly and went happily on his way. The question is what was the value of the horse and the clothes since they served as three month's reckoning? (Köbel, 1514, fol. 78 r)

Pedagogical ordering is evident in many collections of problems, progressing from simple problems to more complex; from single procedure solutions to those requiring multiple computing techniques; from concrete based problems to the abstract (Swetz, 1995). A learner's confidence is established before he/she ventures into higher levels of involvement. An early visual example of this principle is evident in the BM 15285 cuneiform tablet from the Old Babylonian period that presents a series of geometric configurations. As the scribal students progress through the series they encounter more intricate geometrical situations to unravel (see Figure 3).

In the historical period up through the nineteenth century word problems were carefully chosen for their impact and used to supplement instruction. They were a major part of the instruction. As the design of textbooks changed, stressing more theoretical aspects of mathematics, a reliance on the instructional power of word problems has decreased. Word problems no longer make a statement as to the importance and power of mathematics. Unfortunately, they have often been reduced to a status of "busy work" or employed as a means of punishment.

CONCLUSION

The mathematical footprints we have been following from the Late Bronze Age to the present have led us on a long trail. At the start, the trail was quite narrow but it soon broadened, became well travelled, and began to branch in different directions, each wandering away from the main path. Word problems revealing economic conditions, illustrating trade and commerce, reflecting on contemporary events, scientific advancement, social movements, warfare, and so on, deserve exploration. Perhaps some accompanying essays will undertake this task. Word problems remain a valuable resource to teach mathematics but also, in their historical examination, to supply an understanding of the development of mathematical ideas, their priorities and their interrelationship with the real world.

REFERENCES

Bachet de Meziriac, C. G. (1612). *Problèmes plaisants et délectables qui se font par les nombres.* Lyons: Pierre Rigaud.
Baker, H. (1568). *The well spring of sciences.* London.
Ball, R. (1987). *Mathematical recreations and essays.* New York: Dover.
Bonsall, M. (1905). *Primary Arithmetic.* Manila: World Book Co.
Borghi, P. (1484). *Qui comenza la nobel opera de arithmetica.* Venice.
Brooks, E. (1863). *The normal written arithmetic.* Philadelphia: Sower, Potts & Co.
Buteo (1559). *Logistica.* Lyons: Gulielmum Rouillium.
Calandri, P. (1491). *Arithmetica.* Florence: Morgiani & Petri.
Chace, A. B. (1979). *The Rhind mathematical papyrus.* Washington, DC: The National Council of Teachers of Mathematics.
Clavius, C. (1583). *Arithmetica prattica.* Rome.
Colebrook, H. T. (1817). *Algebra, with arithmetic and mensuration from the sanscrit of Brahmegupta and Bhascara.* London: John Murray.
Cooke, R. (1997). *The history of mathematics: A brief course.* New York: John Wiley & Sons.
Digges, T. (1579). *An arithmeticall militare treatise named Stratioticos.* London.
Douglas, W. (1814, March 1). Question 2. *The Analyst,* p. 21.

Fukagawa, H., & Pedoe, D. (1989). *Japanese temple geometry problems*. Winnipeg, Canada: Charles Babbage Research Centre.

Fukagawa, H., & Rigby, D. (2002). *Traditional Japanese mathematics problems of the 18th and 19th centuries*. Singapore: Science Culture Technology Press.

Ghaligai (1521). *Summa de Arithmetica*. Florence: Bernardo Zucchetta.

Hadley, J., & Singmaster, D. (1992). Problems to sharpen the young. *The Mathematical Gazette*, 76(475), 102–126.

Hogan, E. R. (1977). George Baron and the "Mathematical Correspondent". *Historia Mathematica, 4*, 157–172.

Høyrup, J. (1985). Varieties of mathematical discourse in pre-modern socio-cultural contexts: Mesopotamia, Greece and the Latin Middle Ages. *Science and Society, 69*(1), 4–41.

Katz, V. (2003). *A history of mathematics*. New York: Addison-Wesley.

Köbel, J. (1514). *Rechenbuch auff linien und ziffern*. Augsburg, Germany.

Lam, L. Y., & Ang, T. S. (1992). *Tracing the conception of arithmetic and algebra in ancient China: Fleeting footsteps*. Singapore: World Scientific.

Libbrecht, U. (1973). *Chinese mathematics in the thirteenth century: The Shu-shu chiu-chang of Ch'in Chiu-shao*. Cambridge, MA: MIT Press.

Nahin, P. J. (2007). *Chases and escapes: The mathematics of pursuit and evasion*. Princeton, NJ: Princeton University Press.

Nemet-Nejat, K. R. (1988). Cuneiform mathematical texts as training for scribal professions. In E. Leichty (Ed.), *A scientific humanist: studies in memory of Abraham Sach* (pp. 285–300). Philadelphia: University of Pennsylvania Press.

Neugebauer, O., & Sachs, A. (1945). *Mathematical cuneiform texts*. New Haven, CT: American Oriental Society.

New York Times. (1969, March 9). China's new math and old problems. p. 18.

Page, T. E., Rouse, W. H. D., & Capps, E. (Eds.). (1916). *The Greek Anthology in the Loeb Classical Library* (Vol. 5, pp. 27–107). Cambridge, MA: Harvard University Press.

Perl, T. (1979). The Ladies' Diary or the Woman's Almanack, 1704–1841. *Historia Mathematica, 6*, 36–53.

Pike, N. (1788). *A new and complete system of arithmetic composed for the use of citizens of the United States*. Newburyport, ME.

Pine, L. (1997). Nazism in the classroom. *History Today, 47*, 22–27.

Powell, M. A. (1988). Evidence for agriculture and waterworks in Babylonian mathematical texts. *Bulletin on Sumerian Agriculture, 4*, 161–172.

Pressman, I., & Singmaster, D. (1989). "The Jealous Husbands" and "The Missionaries and Cannibals." *The Mathematical Gazette, 73*(4640), 3–81.

Rebstock, U. (2007, July). *Mathematics in the service of the Islamic community*. Paper presented at the Fifth European Summer University on History and Epistemology in Mathematics Education, Prague, Czech Republic.

Recorde, R. (1546). *The ground of arts*. London: Reynold Wolff.

Riese, A, (1522). *Rechnung auff der linien und federn*. Erfurt, Germany.

Robson, E. (2007). Mesopotamian mathematics. In V. Katz (Ed.), *The Mathematics of Egypt, Mesopotamia, China, India and Islam* (pp. 58–181). Princeton, NJ: Princeton University Press.

Rudolff, C. (1526). *Künstliche rechnung mit der ziffer und mit den zal pfenningen*. Vienna.

Sanford, V. (1927). *The history and significance of certain standard problems in algebra*. New York: Teachers College Press.

Schmandt-Besserat, D. (1992). *Before writing: From counting to cuneiform*. Austin, TX: University of Texas Press.

Shen, K. S., Crossley, J. N., & Lun, A. (1999). *The nine chapters on the mathematical art*. Beijing: Science Press.

Sigler, L. E. (2002). *Fibonacci's Liber Abaci*. New York: Springer.

Smith, D. E. (1917). On the origin of certain typical problems. *American Mathematical Monthly*, *24*(64), 64–71.
Smith, D. E. (1918). Mathematical problems in relation to the history of economics and commerce. *American Mathematical Monthly*, *25*, 221–223.
Smith, D. E. (1958). *History of mathematics* (Vol. 2). New York: Dover.
Smith, J. H. (1880). *A treatise on arithmetic*. London: Rivingtons.
Swetz, F. J. (1987). *Capitalism & arithmetic: The new math of the 15th century*. Chicago: Open Court.
Swetz, F. J. (1993). Back to the present: Ruminations on an old arithmetic text. *Mathematics Teacher*, *86*, 491–496.
Swetz, F. J. (1995). To know and to teach: Mathematical pedagogy from an historical context. *Educational Studies in Mathematics*, *29*, 73–88.
Swetz, F. J. (1996). Enigmas of Chinese mathematics. In R. Calinger (Ed.), *Vita Mathematica* (pp. 87–97). Washington, DC: Mathematical Association of America.
Swetz, F. J. (1999). Mathematics for social change: United States experience in the Philippines, 1898–1925. *Bulletin of the American Historical Collection Foundation*, *27*, 61–80.
Swetz, F. J., & Kao, T. I. (1977). *Was Pythagoras Chinese?* University Park, PA: The Pennsylvania State University Press.
Trenchant, J. (1566). *L'Arithmetique*. Lyons: Degabiano & Girard.
Van der Waerden, B. L. (1983). *Geometry and algebra in ancient civilizations*. New York: Springer.
Watson, E. (1777). *Watson's Connecticut almanacke 1777*. Hartford, CT.
Wittfogel, K. A. (1957). *Oriental despotism: A comparative study of total power*. New Haven, CT: Yale University Press.

Frank J. Swetz
The Pennsylvania State University (Emeritus)
Harrisburg, Pennsylvania
U.S.A.

BARRY COOPER AND TONY HARRIES

5. REALISTIC CONTEXTS, MATHEMATICS ASSESSMENT, AND SOCIAL CLASS

Lessons for Assessment Policy from an English Research Programme

INTRODUCTION

In recent years increasing attention has been paid to comparative performance in mathematics, both across and within societies. The findings of both the Programme for International Student Assessment (PISA) by the Organisation for Economic Cooperation and Development (OECD) and the Trends in International Mathematics and Science Study (TIMSS) have generated enormous debate within many countries concerning comparative performance. In parallel, in those countries such as England that have a national curriculum and an associated annual and exhaustive programme for testing mathematical achievement, there is a continuous debate about changing "standards" and the contribution of various types of schools to the "need" for mathematically skilled workers. Much of this debate in the media and the political classes takes place without reference to the nature of the assessment that has been used to produce the results employed in these often heated discussions. In the between-countries context, some occasional critical reference is made to the tests themselves, noting the difficulty of producing a test that is fair across systems, given differing national curricula (e.g. Brown, 1996). Harlow and Jones (2004) have also shown, by interviewing children, that some science items used in TIMSS do not provide valid access to what children know and understand.

However, it is less common to raise the issue we will address in this chapter of whether test items in mathematics are fair or, more strictly, equally valid across social groups *within* a particular society. Given that the results of tests within our research setting, England, are used to compare schools with differing social compositions as well as to make placement decisions as children, for example, move from primary to secondary schools, any differential validity by social class or gender becomes not just a technical matter but also one that might impact on social justice. In this chapter, we will employ one particular item to illustrate some relations between social class, gender and validity. We will draw on interviews with children as they undertake two forms of this item in order to demonstrate how easy it is to modify items so that validity interacts differently with such factors as social class and gender. The work reported forms just one part of a programme of work carried out in England by the authors and other colleagues over the past 15 years and, to begin, we will describe this programme, its purpose and some of its key conclusions (Cooper, 1992, 1994, 1998a, 1998b, 2004; Cooper & Dunne, 1998,

2000a, 2000b; Cooper & Harries, 2002, 2003, 2005). Not only is this larger programme the context for the detailed analysis to follow, but it also has demonstrated that the problem we will address is not one peculiar to some particular items, but has a general character.

England introduced a national curriculum in 1988 and an associated programme of national testing of all children at several ages followed. At the ages of 10-11 and 13-14, the ages addressed in our programme of research, the national assessment has included timed paper and pencil tests, taken towards the end of the last year in primary school and the third year in secondary school. These tests cover the whole content of the national curriculum and, importantly, they contain many items that embed the mathematical task in some supposedly realistic context. In mathematics education circles in general, it is thought that such contextualisation of mathematics is both motivating and useful for future domestic and occupational life, especially for those children who find mathematics more difficult (for a critical discussion of such assumptions, see Dowling, 1988). In line with such beliefs, many of the items in these tests set their tasks in such contexts as a shopping trip, a sports event, or some sort of consumer or traffic survey. Cooper (1992, 1994) wondered, given what was known sociologically about the relationship between socio-cultural backgrounds and the mode of response to a variety of test contexts, whether there might not be unintended negative consequences for working-class children of such contextualisation. Bernstein (1996) and Bourdieu (1986) and their co-workers (e.g., Holland, 1981) had shown that working-class individuals were more likely to respond to test-like situations by drawing on 'local' and/or 'functional' rather than 'esoteric' and/or 'formal' (more 'distancing') perspectives. There was also earlier relevant work by Luria and others (discussed at length in Cooper, 2004). Any such social class based predisposition to respond differently to problems posed raises potential problems for test items which realistically contextualise mathematics. A few examples might make this point clearer. We will discuss three. The first belongs to the general class of division with remainder problems, the second to problems concerned with combinations, and the third concerns probability.

In the early versions of the English secondary testing programme an item appeared which asked children to say how many times a lift would need to go up, in the "morning rush", if it could carry up to 14 people and 269 wished to go up in the lift (Schools Examination and Assessment Council (SEAC), 1992). Just one correct answer was allowed in the marking scheme, namely 20 times. To achieve this answer the child must not only carry out a calculation successfully, but must also make reference to a limited range of realistic considerations: lifts go up in whole numbers, the lift never has fewer, where possible, than 14 passengers or ever more than this, and no-one use the stairs. A child must not employ too many realistic considerations, wondering for example whether impatient people might turn to the stairs or crush more than 14 into the lift. Such a strategy, given the marking scheme, would lead to failure. We might wonder whether all children would have a similar "feel for the game" here (Bourdieu, 1998). For evidence that they don't, see Cooper and Harries (2005).

The second example is taken from the primary tests in 1993 (SEAC, 1993). Children were asked to reflect on a mixed doubles tennis competition. They were given a picture of 3 girls' names in one bag and 3 boys' names in another, and asked to find all the possible ways boys and girls could be paired and write the pairs down. The answer scheme required nine pairs. A little thought might make us wonder whether children, especially those more predisposed to introduce realistic considerations when faced with such tasks, might only provide 3 pairs, simply because these pairs could then begin to play tennis in various combinations (Cooper, 1994). In fact, this is exactly what some children do, rather than produce the esoteric nine pairs. More importantly, it can be shown, through interview-based work, that many children, even though they initially give three pairs, are quite capable of providing nine (Cooper & Dunne, 2000a). Around ten percent of Cooper and Dunne's primary school sample fell into the set that provided three pairs initially but moved to nine when they were asked, as they turned the page of the test booklet, whether they had all the pairs. Working class children were especially likely to fall into this set. The tennis item has a form which causes it to generate *false negatives* in assessment terms. Some children who are capable of undertaking the combinatorial act do not initially demonstrate this in the written test context.

Our third example is one that generates *false positives* and, as will be seen later, is also an item that is treated differently by children from different social class backgrounds. Since this item and our revision of it will be discussed at length later, we will only briefly mention its problematic character at this point. The item gives some numerical data from a traffic survey, and then asks the children to estimate some likelihoods on the basis of these data (see Figure 1). As will be shown later, children could gain the marks on this item without making any reference at all to the given data but by instead drawing on their knowledge of typical frequencies of cars, lorries, etc. in their everyday worlds. The item therefore can generate false positives. As we will show, working class children were more likely than others to call up their everyday knowledge.

Such false positives and negatives are, from the assessment perspective, a technical problem in the sphere of validity. Given that Cooper and Dunne (2000a) provided evidence that there are social class and gender differences in the manner in which children respond to such items, we can see that there is a problem of *differential* validity. Cooper and Dunne also carried out a quantitative analysis of children's relative performance on realistically contextualised and purely mathematical items, drawing on data from three written tests taken by children aged 10-11. A key finding was that differences between the social classes were larger for the contextualised class of items than for the non-contextualised. Furthermore, these differences in performance by class on the two types of item were large enough to make a substantial difference to life chances were the tests to be used in selection processes (Cooper & Dunne, 2000a, chapter 5). Summarising, we can see that, all else being equal, the proportions of non-contextualised and contextualised items, and also the balance of contextualised items tending to produce false negatives and positives, are both likely to have consequences for the fairness between social classes of a written test. Taken as a whole, and in conjunction with other work

> The children in Year 6 of a school conduct a traffic survey outside of the school for 1 hour.
>
> | Type | Number that passed In one hour |
> |---|---|
> | car | 75 |
> | bus | 8 |
> | lorry | 13 |
> | van | 26 |
>
> When waiting outside the school they try to decide on the likelihood that a **lorry** will go by in the next minute.
>
> Put a ring round how likely it is that a **lorry** will go by in the next minute.
>
> certain　　very likely　　likely　　unlikely　　impossible
>
> They also try to decide on the likelihood that a **car** will go by in the next minute.
>
> Put a ring round how likely it is that a **car** will go by in the next minute.
>
> certain　　very likely　　likely　　unlikely　　impossible

Figure 1. The original traffic item used by Cooper and Dunne (2000a)

showing similar differences between social groups in their mode of responding to mathematics problems (Boaler, 1994; Lubienski, 2000), this body of work does suggest that more attention needs to be paid to the ways in which contextualising test items might disadvantage some children.

In our more recent work, we have been exploring ways in which test items can be rewritten to make it clearer whether none at all, a little, or some fuller reference to realistic considerations is required. We have, for example, asked children to reflect on four different answers "other children" have given to a version of the lift item in order to assess their willingness to introduce a range of realistic considerations (Cooper & Harries, 2002, 2003, 2005). As part of these studies we have also asked children to respond to a revised version of the traffic item with the survey data shown in Figure 2. Here, quite deliberately, the given data do not parallel typical everyday experience. We expected that this simple revision would move

REALISTIC CONTEXTS, MATHS ASSESSMENT, AND CLASS

this item out of the class of items generating false positives, but into the class that might disadvantage working class children. In this work children were asked some questions probing their solution processes immediately after they had completed each pencil and paper task. Clearly, by asking children to comment on the traffic task after they had completed it, we moved the test item out of its original paper and pencil context. Without this move, we would have had no evidence concerning how children made use or otherwise of the frequency data provided in the item. We have no reason to believe that the nature of the children's solution processes was affected by our adding this subsequent questioning.

Type	Number that passed In one hour
car	13
bus	8
lorry	50
van	10

Figure 2. Data from the revised traffic item

In the remainder of the chapter we will report our findings concerning children's response to this revised item, after having initially summarised some findings from the earlier work concerning the original traffic item. During our discussion of the revised item, we will employ Boolean analytic methods especially suited to our medium sized non-random sample, which we shall explain before their use in a later section. These methods produce configurational explanatory accounts rather than the net effects accounts produced by regression methods (Ragin, 2006a, 2006b). We turn now to the findings from Cooper and Dunne (2000a) for the original traffic item.

THE TRAFFIC ITEM OLD AND NEW

The original traffic item employed reported numbers from the survey in line with what might be found in everyday life (Figure 1). The official mark scheme for this original item awarded a mark for giving "unlikely" as the answer for the lorry and a mark for either of "likely" or "very likely" for the car (SEAC, 1993). As reported elsewhere (Cooper & Dunne, 2000a), there are class differences in the mode of response to this item. As part of the earlier study, Cooper and Dunne interviewed more than a hundred children aged 10-11 attending three primary schools as they worked at this item. Once the children had circled two answers, they were asked how they had decided upon these responses. Children decided upon their answers either by reference to the given data, as the item designers presumably intended, or, alternatively, they drew on their everyday knowledge of traffic on roads or on a blend of the given data and their everyday knowledge. As can be seen from Table 1, these responses were related to social class background (Cooper & Dunne, 2000a); for our class scheme, see Table 2. Whilst there was clearly not a one-to-one relation between social class background and mode of response, it was amongst the working class children that responses drawing only on everyday experience, or on a mix of this and the given data, were more likely to occur.

Table 1. Distribution of response strategies by social class (original traffic item)

	Uses given data alone	Uses everyday knowledge and given data	Uses everyday knowledge alone	Totals
Service class	38 (64.4%)	10 (16.9%)	11 (18.6%)	59
Intermediate class	16 (53.3%)	10 (33.3%)	4 (13.3%)	30
Working class	16 (50.0%)	6 (18.8%)	10 (31.3%)	32
Totals	70 (57.9%)	26 (21.5%)	25 (20.7%)	121

Turning to gender, while it was the case that girls were about equally likely as boys to use just their everyday knowledge (19.2% against 22.5%), it was also the case that they were twice as likely as boys to employ a mixed response (30.8% against 15.5%). A configurational view of the relation between class, gender and mode of response is shown in Table 3. Here, it is clearly working class girls who are most likely to employ everyday knowledge, either solely or in conjunction with reference to the given data, as the basis of their solution process.

We have space for one illustrative example of a response making no apparent reference to the given data (Cooper & Dunne, 2000a):

A working class boy – response 'realistic'

[He circles unlikely for lorry – one mark, very likely for car – one mark.]

BC: Now, how did you decide on those two?

Child: Cos, because the lorry, there's not as many lorries around as there is cars.

BC: What were you thinking of, whereabouts?

Child: Outside of school, more parents would come to like collect a child in a car than they would in a lorry.

BC: That's true, right, OK, did you look at these numbers at all here? Did you read that part?

Child: No.

BC: OK so you did the question without looking at that part?

Child: Yep.

Table 2. Social class categories employed (see Goldthorpe, Llewellyn, & Payne, 1987)

7-fold categories	Occupational groups	3-fold categories
Upper service	Higher-grade professionals, administrators, and officials; managers in large industrial establishments; large proprietors.	Service class
Lower service	Lower-grade professionals, administrators, and officials; higher-grade technicians; managers in small industrial establishments; supervisors of non-manual employees.	
Routine non-manual	Routine non-manual workers: routine non-manual employees in administration and commerce; sales personnel; other rank-and-file service workers	Intermediate class
Petty bourgeoisie	Petty bourgeoisie: small proprietors and artisans, etc., with and without employees Farmers: farmers and smallholders and other self-employed workers in primary production	
Supervisors etc.	Lower-grade technicians; supervisors of manual workers	
Skilled manual	Skilled manual workers	Working class
Semi- and un-skilled manual	Non-skilled workers: semi- and unskilled manual workers (not in agriculture, etc.) Agricultural labourers: agricultural and other workers in primary production	

Table 3. Responses involving some reference to the everyday by class and gender (original traffic item)

Class	Sex	Number	Uses everyday or mixed response (proportion)
Working	Girl	12	0.67
Intermediate	Boy	17	0.47
Intermediate	Girl	13	0.46
Working	Boy	20	0.40
Service	Girl	25	0.40
Service	Boy	34	0.32

Because the given data in the original item are broadly in line with what children would normally experience in their extra-school lives, it was possible, as this transcript shows, to gain the full marks for this item without paying any attention to the given data. Because of this feature, the item, from the point of view of assessing children's purely mathematical competence, generates false positives. Some children are awarded marks who have not reasoned about probabilities using the given data and who might not, in fact, have been able to do so.

In our recent work, we have interviewed children while they worked through a number of revised items (Cooper & Harries, 2005). One of these comprised the revised traffic item with the new data shown in Figure 2. Our rationale for the revision was straightforward. Given the results from Cooper and Dunne's earlier work, we wished to explore children's responses to an item where there was a deliberate conflict introduced between typical everyday experience (more cars, fewer lorries) and the given data (more lorries, fewer cars). In doing so, we had, of course, written a revised item which should not generate false positives. We will now discuss children's responses to this revised item. The discussion draws on research with 55 children from four primary schools in the North East of England (Cooper & Harries, 2005). As a result of the procedure used to select children for the study (teachers were asked to supply children with a range of attainment in mathematics rather than pay attention to social background) our sample became skewed away from service class backgrounds (see Table 4). One interview failed to record and we shall therefore use data for 54 cases in this paper.

Table 4. The sample by social class background and gender (Cooper & Harries, 2005)

	Service class		Intermediate class		Working class		All social classes	
	Boys	Girls	Boys	Girls	Boys	Girls	Boys	Girls
School B	0	0	3	2	3	5	6	7
School E	0	0	0	1	6	5	6	6
School N	2	5	4	3	1	1	7	9
School S	0	0	3	3	4	4	7	7
Totals	2	5	10	9	14	15	26	29

We will analyse, using Boolean configurational methods, children's responses to this revised traffic item, which appeared as the second item in the booklet they were asked to work through during a one-to-one interview. We must briefly explain some basic elements of these methods first. We will draw on the account in Cooper and Glaesser (2007).

QUALITATIVE COMPARATIVE ANALYSIS (QCA): A BRIEF INTRODUCTION

The variety of Boolean method we will employ is Ragin's *Qualitative Comparative Analysis* (QCA). QCA has been developed over a period of some twenty years (Ragin, 1987, 2000, 2006a, 2006b) and provides an alternative to the linear additive analytic approaches characterising regression-based methods. Until recently, QCA has been used mainly in the field of political science, and especially in the context of macro-comparative work employing small to medium sized samples. More recently, some researchers have begun to explore its use with large *n* samples (Cooper, 2005, 2006; Cooper & Glaesser, 2007; Ragin, 2003, 2006b).

In QCA, sets of cases for analysis are constructed by bringing together individuals who share similar positions on a range of factors. Then, in place of the attempt to determine the net effects of variables that characterises regression, QCA sets out to determine which configurations of conditions characterising cases are either necessary and/or sufficient for particular outcomes to be achieved (see also Boudon, 1974). The focus is on cases and their features, rather than on relations between variables and their net effects abstracted from the cases. Although QCA does allow statistical tests to be incorporated in some of its analyses, its main concern is not with statistical inference from sample to population but is rather to provide an alternative method of describing "causal" patterns in datasets, one grounded in set theory.

Boolean equations have a different functional form to the regression equations with which sociologists are familiar. Here, taken from a recent paper contrasting the two approaches (Mahoney & Goertz, 2006), is a crisp set[1] example, where the upper and lower case letters indicate respectively the presence or the absence of 'qualitative' factors:

$$Y = (A*B*c) + (A*C*D*E)$$

In these Boolean equations the symbol * indicates Logical AND (set intersection), the symbol + indicates Logical OR (set union), and upper case letters indicate the presence of a factor, lower case letters indicate its absence. In this example of causal heterogeneity, $Y = (A*B*c) + (A*C*D*E)$, the equation indicates that there are two causal paths to the outcome Y. The first, captured by the *causal configuration* A*B*c involves the presence in the case of features A and B, combined with the absence of C. The second, captured by A*C*D*E, requires the joint presence of A, C, D and E. Either of these causal configurations are sufficient for the outcome to occur, but neither is necessary, given the existence of an alternative causal route. The factor C behaves differently in the two configurations. For the moment, we are assuming in these remarks that there are no empirical exceptions to the relations embodied by the equation.

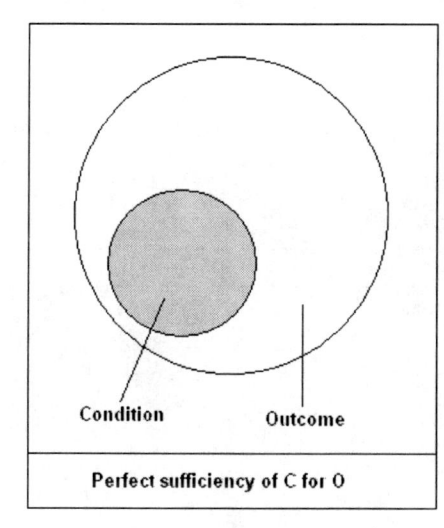

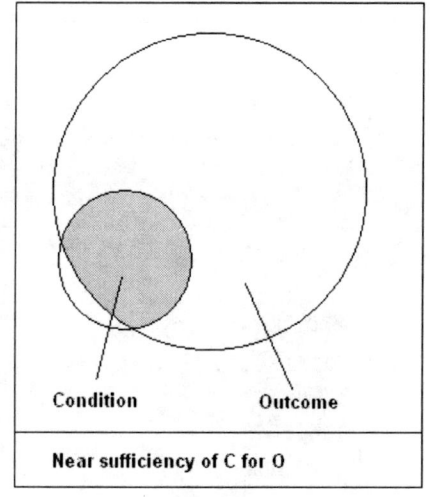

Figure 3. Venn diagrams for perfect and near sufficiency

Sufficiency, understood causally or logically, involves a subset relation. If, for example, a single condition is always sufficient for an outcome to occur, the set of cases with the condition will be a subset of the set of cases with the outcome (see the left hand panel of Figure 3). Given the condition, we obtain the outcome. In real applications, perfect sufficiency is unlikely to be found, and the right hand panel of Figure 3 will apply, where most but not all of the set of cases with the condition also are members of the outcome set. In the crisp set case, the proportion of the condition set who are also members of the outcome set can be used as a measure of the degree of *consistency* of the empirical relation with a relation of perfect sufficiency.

The right hand panel of Figure 3 illustrates a quasi-sufficient relation that might be described as only 'nearly always sufficient'. Here, the condition set is almost completely contained within the outcome set. Figure 3 can also illustrate, in its simplest form, the concept of explanatory *coverage*, analogous to variance explained in the regression approach. The proportion of the outcome set that is overlapped by the condition set can be used as a measure of the degree to which the outcome is covered ("explained") by the condition. In Figure 3, coverage – at around a fifth – can be seen to be low in both Venn diagrams. This condition is clearly not a necessary one for the outcome to occur. We return now to the revised traffic item.

THE REVISED TRAFFIC ITEM: RESULTS

The likelihoods initially chosen by the 54 children are shown in Table 5. Because the given data show many more lorries than cars being observed in an hour, we would expect, were the children to be drawing on these given data, to rank the chance of seeing a lorry in the next minute as higher than a car. We can see from a glance at Table 5 that the results suggest something other than the given data seems to have been taken into account by the respondents, since the distributions of chosen likelihoods are much more similar to each other than an observed ratio of 50 lorries to 13 cars ought, mathematically, to justify. Table 6 shows the distribution of the children's pairs of responses across the three categories of lorry more likely, lorry and car equally likely, or car more likely. Only 34 of the 54 children in fact rank the lorry as being more likely, with 11 actually ranking the car as more likely[2].

Table 5. Revised traffic item: answers for lorry and car

	Lorry		Car	
	Frequency	Percent	Frequency	Percent
Certain	4	7.4	2	3.7
Very likely	18	33.3	5	9.3
Likely	27	50.0	27	50.0
Unlikely	4	7.4	19	35.2
Impossible	1	1.9	1	1.90
Total	54	100.0	54	100.0

REALISTIC CONTEXTS, MATHS ASSESSMENT, AND CLASS

Table 6. Revised traffic item: response patterns across 54 cases

	Frequency	Percent
Lorry more likely	34	63.0
Same	9	16.7
Car more likely	11	20.4
Total	54	100.0

Table 7. Truth table from fs/QCA for the outcome CAR_MORE_LIKELY_OR_SAME

SERVICE_CLASS	WORKING_CLASS	BOY	NUMBER	OUTCOME	CONSIST
0	1	0	15		0.733
0	1	1	14		0.357
0	0	0	8		0.250
1	0	0	5		0.200
0	0	1	10		0.100
1	0	1	2		0.000

Who are the children, by class and gender, producing each of these three outcome categories? We will explore this by collapsing the three response categories in Table 6 to just two, contrasting those children who argue that the lorry is more likely to go by in the next minute with those who argue, contrary to the given data, that it is not. We have undertaken a QCA analysis, using dummy factors for class, of the model CAR_MORE_LIKELY_OR_SAME = Function(SERVICE_CLASS, WORKING_CLASS, BOY). Table 7 is the associated truth table produced within the QCA software. The first row, 010, for example, represents the Boolean configuration service_class *WORKING_CLASS* boys, i.e. it is the working class girls in our sample. The final column gives the proportion for each configuration that argues that cars are more likely than lorries or equally likely. This number, e.g. 0.733 for the working class girls, is also, in this simple case, the measure of consistency with a relation of sufficiency. To proceed to the next stage of producing a QCA solution the analyst must determine a threshold for quasi-sufficiency and enter noughts or ones into the penultimate column to mark this. This decision determines which configurations will be allowed into the final minimised solution produced by the software. We have done this, using a threshold of 0.7, and have also re-labelled the configurations, removing the dummy factors, in Table 8.

The configuration WORKING_CLASS*GIRL has by far the highest consistency level at 0.73 with a relation of sufficiency and also a fairly high explanatory coverage index of 0.55, accounting for 11 of the 20 cases with this outcome. If a lower threshold is set (of 0.35^3) it is possible to generate the solution WORKING_CLASS with a rather low overall consistency with sufficiency of 0.55 but a high coverage of 0.80. In words, children from working class backgrounds are more likely than not to provide a pair of answers inconsistent with the given data and they comprise, in this sample, a large majority of those who do. In fact,

103

since the coverage index in this simple case is equivalent to a measure of consistency with a relation of necessity (Ragin, 2006a) we can see that, in this sample, being working class is close to being a necessary condition for providing this response pair. If we explore the solution for the complementary outcome of the lorry being more likely than the car (Table 9), setting a threshold for quasi-sufficiency of 0.7, we obtain the solution "working_class" (i.e. NOT WORKING CLASS), with an overall consistency of 0.84 and coverage of 0.62. Basically, not being a member of the working class seems to lead, in the vast majority of cases, to an answer pair consistent with the given data.

Table 8. Relabelled truth table for the outcome CAR_MORE_LIKELY_OR_SAME

Class	Sex	Number	Car more likely or as likely as lorry	Consistency with sufficiency
Working	Girl	15	1	0.73
Working	Boy	14	0	0.36
Intermediate	Girl	8	0	0.25
Service	Girl	5	0	0.20
Intermediate	Boy	10	0	0.10
Service	Boy	2	0	0.00

Table 9. Truth table for the outcome LORRY_MORE_LIKELY

Class	Sex	Number	Lorry more likely	Consistency with sufficiency
Service	Boy	2	1	1.00
Intermediate	Boy	10	1	0.90
Service	Girl	5	1	0.80
Intermediate	Girl	8	1	0.75
Working	Boy	14	0	0.64
Working	Girl	15	0	0.27

We can now ask whether this pattern of class and gender based responses has arisen from the tendency observed in Cooper and Dunne's earlier work, i.e. for there to be a relation between class, gender, and the chosen mode of response. To explore this, we have, as did Cooper and Dunne, coded children's answers to our request during the interview, made immediately after they had written their two answers, to explain their answers. Children have been coded as either using a mix of given data and everyday knowledge, only given data, or only everyday knowledge. Illustrative examples of each coding are shown below.

Example 1. Uses both the given data and everyday knowledge (working class boy):

TH: Okay, can you tell me how you decided on the answers? For example if you look at the lorry, the first one, why did you choose that answer?

REALISTIC CONTEXTS, MATHS ASSESSMENT, AND CLASS

Child: Because if in 1 hour, 50 go past, then the next lorry that would come in the next minute, there might be one and there might not, so I put likely.

TH: Okay, why did you not put "very likely"?

Child: Because that's over an hour and this is in 1 minute.

TH: Okay. What about the car? Why did you choose the answer for the car?

Child: 'Cause usually people go round in cars and also that's higher than any of the others and that was in 1 hour as well.

TH: So can you tell me why they are both likely?

Child: 'Cause lorries are usually for business work and there are lots of shops down XXXXXX Lane [*a local street*] and there would rather be lorries to deliver things to the people and there would be cars to go down the streets to go to the shops.

TH: Right. So when you were answering those questions did you just use this table or did you use your own knowledge of what happens on the street?

Child: I used both.

Example 2. Uses given data alone (intermediate class boy):

BC: Right, how did you decide on "likely" for the lorry?

Child: Because the lorry goes past 50 times in a minute and there's 60 minutes in an hour so it's like 5 out of a 6th chance that it will go.

BC: What about the car? How did you decide on "unlikely" for the car?

Child: Because the car goes and there's only 13 go past in an hour and that's only a sixth so it's unlikely and it's not impossible because some cars have gone past.

BC: Okay. ... Did you think about anything apart from this table when you were working it out?

Child: No.

BC: You didn't think about cars outside or anything?

Child: No.

Example 3. Uses everyday knowledge alone (intermediate class girl):

BC: How did you decide on "likely" for a lorry?

Child: Because if you're in a lorry, it's not often that a lorry comes round our streets.

BC: Right, and how about car, how did you decide on "very likely" for car?

Child: Many people usually have cars.

BC: Right, were you thinking of streets that you know? Okay. What about those numbers here? Did you use those at all? Did you read those numbers?

105

Child: Yes.

BC: Why didn't you use those then?

Child: Don't know.

BC: Was it because you knew about cars and lorries already. Was that it do you think?

Child: Yes

The first question is whether there is a relation between class and response mode. Table 10 shows clearly that there is such a relation. No child amongst the small number of service class children uses everyday knowledge alone and the working class children are most likely to employ this mode of response. Turning to gender, while there is no overall gender difference in the proportions using only the given data, girls are twice as likely as boys to use only their everyday knowledge in responding to the revised item.

Table 10. The revised traffic item: social class, gender and mode of response

Sex	Class	Uses everyday experience alone	Uses both in mix	Uses given data alone	Total
Girls	Service	0 (00.0%)	1 (20.0%)	4 (80.0%)	5 (100.0%)
	Intermediate	1 (12.5%)	0 (00.0%)	7 (87.5%)	8 (100.0%)
	Working	5 (33.3%)	3 (20.0%)	7 (46.7%)	15 (100.0%)
	Total	6 (21.4%)	4 (14.3%)	18 (64.3%)	28 (100.0%)
Boys	Service	0 (00.0%)	0 (00.0%)	2 (100.0%)	2 (100.0%)
	Intermediate	0 (00.0%)	4 (40.0%)	6 (60.0%)	10 (100.0%)
	Working	3 (21.4%)	2 (14.3%)	9 (64.3%)	14 (100.0%)
	Total	3 (11.5%)	6 (23.1%)	17 (65.4%)	26 (100.0%)

The second question is whether the response mode can explain the relationship between the answers given for lorry and car. Table 11 shows the relation between our coding of children's mode of response and the three response categories set out in Table 6. There is a clear relation here between response mode and the nature of the pair of answers. Those children who employ their everyday knowledge, either wholly or partly, are much less likely to argue that the lorry is more likely than the car.

We will now use QCA to explore the potential relations *Class, gender → response mode → the relationship between the two answers*, since it appears from these various two-way tables to offer a plausible two-step model of the relation between class and gender and the answers given. First, what are sufficient conditions for not introducing any everyday knowledge into the solution process? Which children decide just to use the given data? Table 12 is the relevant truth table. Using QCA with a threshold for a configuration to enter the solution of equal to or greater than 0.8 generates the Boolean solution, SERVICE_CLASS + working_class*boy,

REALISTIC CONTEXTS, MATHS ASSESSMENT, AND CLASS

Table 11. Revised traffic item: likelihood of lorry and car by mode of response

	Lorry more likely	Same	Car more likely	Total
Uses everyday experience alone	0 (00.0%)	2 (22.2%)	7 (77.8%)	9 (100.0%)
Uses both in mix	4 (40.0%)	4 (40.0%)	2 (20.0%)	10 (100.0%)
Uses given data alone	30 (85.7%)	3 (08.6%)	2 (05.7%)	35 (100.0%)
Total	34 (63.0%)	9 (16.7%)	11 (20.4%)	54 (100.0%)

Table 12. Truth table for using the given data by class and gender

Class	Sex	Number	Uses given data only	Consistency
Service	Boy	2	1	1.00
Intermediate	Girl	8	1	0.88
Service	Girl	5	1	0.80
Working	Boy	14	0	0.64
Intermediate	Boy	10	0	0.60
Working	Girl	15	0	0.47

with an overall consistency of 0.87. At this high level of quasi-sufficiency, it is children from the service class OR girls who are not from the working class who nearly always employ just the given data. It is the working class children and boys from the intermediate class who are less likely to do so.

Now, what is the empirical relation between using the given data and an answer pair giving the lorry as more likely? If we use a very simple QCA model, LORRY IS MORE LIKELY THAN CAR = Function(USES GIVEN DATA ALONE), we obtain the solution that this factor is 0.86 consistent with sufficiency with a solution coverage of 0.88, i.e. it is not only close to being sufficient for the outcome but also close to being necessary for it.

Taking these two steps together, we can see that being from a service class background or being an intermediate class girl, is a nearly sufficient condition for using just the given data, and that, in turn, using the given data is a nearly sufficient condition for stating that the lorry is more likely than the car to go by in the next minute.

CONCLUSION

It is important first to note some limitations of the work reported here. We obviously do not have a perfectly representative sample for the work with the revised item. We had low numbers of children from the service class, especially so in the case of boys. We have also collected data for the revised item from a different region of England (the North East) from that for the data for the original item (the South East). We cannot rule out some impact of regional cultural differences on our findings. The reader should bear these facts in mind. However, in spite of these limitations, given the strong relations described between social class, gender and the mode of response, we believe our findings should be taken seriously, especially given the context of the earlier body of work on class and response mode described in our introduction.

We have turned an item that produced false positives into one that, while avoiding this problem, is associated with considerable class differentiation. The revised item may also be producing false negatives, as did the tennis item discussed in our introduction. Since we did not explore this possibility systematically in our interviews, we can only speculate on this. It does seem likely though, that many of the children who failed to use the given data could in fact have reasoned sensibly from them, had they not been predisposed to use their everyday knowledge in lieu of these data.

Most work on differential validity and differential item functioning is statistical (and often focuses on multiple choice items). This is obviously valuable and important. However, rather than identifying poorly-behaving items via statistical methods, what we have been trying to do is to explore, via case-based methods, the effects of one particular class-based mechanism that can lead to invalidity and/or differential validity when contextualised items are employed in tests, while also incorporating gender into our analyses. We have shown that even a very simple revision of the relation between given data and typical everyday experience might impact dramatically on the distribution of success and failure on an item by social class and gender.

Our simple exercise and its results, alongside those of the larger programme of work in which we have been involved, have several lessons, we believe, for test designers. We would argue that test developers would do well to pay greater attention to relevant sociological accounts of cultural differences when making decisions about the nature of contextualised assessment items, since there clearly are predictable social class differences in predispositions to respond in one mode rather than another to such items. More attention to this area during test design could also be expected to reduce the proportions of false positives and false negatives generated during testing. Furthermore, our work has convinced us that putting more energy into interview-based trials of items and a little less into statistical analyses of differential item functioning would be a productive move where validity is concerned.

NOTES

[1] Crisp sets are those in which a case can simply be in or out of a set (e.g. the set of Protestants). On the fuzzy set variant, see Ragin (2000, 2006a).

[2] The data from the earlier project are not in a form that allows a comparable analysis to be undertaken.

[3] This is better understood as a threshold for possibility than sufficiency, of course. A consistency figure of 0.35 indicates that is possible that working class boys will produce this outcome.

REFERENCES

Bernstein, B. (1996). *Pedagogy, symbolic control and identity: Theory, research, critique.* London: Taylor & Francis.
Boaler, J. (1994). When do girls prefer football to fashion? An analysis of female underachievement in relation to 'realistic' mathematic contexts. *British Educational Research Journal, 20*(5), 551–564.
Boudon, R. (1974). *The logic of sociological explanation.* Harmondsworth, UK: Penguin.
Bourdieu, P. (1986). *Distinction: A social critique of the judgement of taste.* London: RKP.
Bourdieu, P. (1998). *Practical reason.* Cambridge, UK: Polity Press.
Brown, M. (1996). FIMS and SIMS: The first two IEA International Mathematics Surveys. *Assessment in Education, 3*(2), 193–212.
Cooper, B. (1992). Testing National Curriculum Mathematics: Some critical comments on the treatment of "real" contexts for mathematics. *The Curriculum Journal, 3*(3), 231–243.
Cooper, B. (1994). Authentic testing in mathematics? The boundary between everyday and mathematical knowledge in national curriculum testing in English schools. *Assessment in Education, 1*(2), 143–166.
Cooper, B. (1998a). Assessing national curriculum mathematics in England: Exploring children's interpretation of key stage 2 tests in clinical interviews. *Educational Studies in Mathematics, 35*(1), 19–49.
Cooper, B. (1998b). Using Bernstein and Bourdieu to understand children's difficulties with "realistic" mathematics testing: An exploratory study. *International Journal of Qualitative Studies in Education, 11*(4), 511–532.
Cooper, B. (2004). Dilemmas in designing problems in "realistic" school mathematics: A sociological overview and some research findings. In M. Olssen (Ed.), *Culture and learning: Access and opportunity in the classroom.* Greenwich, CT: Information Age Publishing.
Cooper, B. (2005). Applying Ragin's crisp and fuzzy set QCA to large datasets: Social class and educational achievement in the National Child Development Study. *Sociological Research Online, 10*(2). Retrieved from http://www.socresonline.org.uk/10/2/cooper.html
Cooper, B. (2006, April). *Using Ragin's Qualitative Comparative Analysis with longitudinal datasets to explore the degree of meritocracy characterising educational achievement in Britain.* Paper presented at annual meeting of the American Educational Research Association, San Francisco.
Cooper, B., & Dunne, M. (1998). Anyone for tennis? Social class differences in children's responses to national curriculum mathematics testing. *The Sociological Review, 46*(1), 115–148.
Cooper, B., & Dunne, M. (2000a). *Assessing children's mathematical knowledge: Social class, sex and problem-solving.* Buckingham, UK: Open University Press.
Cooper, B., & Dunne, M. (2000b). Constructing the "legitimate" goal of a "realistic" maths item: A comparison of 10-11 and 13-14 year-olds. In A. Filer (Ed.), *Assessment – Social practice and social product: Socio-cultural perspectives on educational assessment and testing.* London: Falmer/Taylor & Francis.
Cooper, B., & Glaesser, J. (2007, September). *Exploring compositional effects with crisp and fuzzy set methods: Individual and school level social class as conditions for educational achievement in the British National Child Development Study.* Presented to the annual conference of the British Educational Research Association, University of London, Institute of Education.
Cooper, B., & Harries, A. V. (2002). Children's responses to contrasting "realistic" mathematics problems: Just how realistic are children ready to be? *Educational Studies in Mathematics, 49*(1), 1–23.
Cooper, B., & Harries, A. V. (2003). Children's use of realistic considerations in problem solving: Some English evidence. *The Journal of Mathematical Behavior, 22*(4), 449–463.
Cooper, B., & Harries, A. V (2005). Making sense of realistic word problems: Portraying working class "failure" in a division with remainder problem. *International Journal of Research and Methods in Education, 28*(2), 147–169.
Dowling, P. (1988). The contextualising of mathematics: Towards a theoretical map. In M. Harris (Ed.), *Schools, mathematics and work.* London: Falmer.

Goldthorpe, J. H., Llewellyn, C., & Payne, C. (1987). *Social mobility and class structure in modern Britain*. Oxford, UK: Clarendon Press.

Harlow, A., & Jones, A. (2004). Why students answer TIMSS science test items the way they do. *Research in Science Education, 34*(2), 221–238.

Holland, J. (1981). Social class and changes in orientation to meaning. *Sociology, 15*(1), 1–18.

Lubienski, S. T. (2000). Problem solving as a means toward mathematics for all: An exploratory look through a class lens. *Journal for Research in Mathematics Education, 31*(4), 454–482.

Mahoney, J., & Goertz, G. (2006). A tale of two cultures: Contrasting quantitative and qualitative research. *Political Analysis, 14*(3), 227–249.

Ragin, C. C. (1987). *The comparative method*. Berkeley, CA & Los Angeles: California University Press.

Ragin, C. C. (2000). *Fuzzy set social science*. Chicago: Chicago University Press.

Ragin, C. C. (2003). *Recent advances in fuzzy-set methods and their application to policy questions*. Retrieved from http://www.compasss.org/Ragin2003.PDF

Ragin, C. C. (2006a). Set relations in social research: Evaluating their consistency and coverage. *Political Analysis, 14*(3), 291–310.

Ragin, C. C. (2006b). The limitations of net-effects thinking. In B. Rihoux & H. Grimm (Eds.), *Innovative comparative methods for policy analysis: Beyond the quantitative-qualitative divide*. New York: Springer.

Schools Examinations and Assessment Council. (1992). *Mathematics tests 1992: Key Stage 3*. SEAC/University of London.

Schools Examinations and Assessment Council. (1993). *Pilot standard tests: Key Stage 2 Mathematics*. SEAC/University of Leeds.

Barry Cooper
School of Education
University of Durham
U.K.

Tony Harries
School of Education
University of Durham
U.K.

MARILYN FRANKENSTEIN

6. DEVELOPING A CRITICALMATHEMATICAL[1] NUMERACY THROUGH *REAL* REAL-LIFE WORD PROBLEMS

INTRODUCTION: ALL MATHEMATICAL WORD PROBLEMS
ARE NON-NEUTRAL

A great honour was conferred on me a few years ago when right-wing conservative Lynne V. Cheney (1998), former USA Vice-President Dick Cheney's wife, trashed my work because I stated that in mathematical texts, "A trivial application like totalling a grocery bill carries the non-neutral message that paying for food is natural." (Frankenstein, 1983, p. 328). Contrary to Cheney's claim that I would not want students to solve problems totalling grocery bills, I certainly would want students to solve such problems – comparing grocery bills in poor neighbourhoods with those in rich neighbourhoods, for example, or problems comparing the costs of the packaging with the costs of the food, for another example, or countless mathematical investigations that could relate to issues of hunger and capitalism where tens of millions of tons of surplus food rot for the profit of a few (Mittal, 2002) while approximately 40 million people die from hunger and hunger-related illness every year and "available evidence indicates that up to 20,000,000 citizens [living in the USA] may be hungry at least some period of time each month."[2] (National Council of Churches, 2007).

I argue that all real-life mathematical word problems contain non-numerical "hidden" messages, and that, if those problems are presented as neutral, they can stifle creative thought and questioning, by increasing the aspects of our society that people take for granted.

Gill (1988) gives another example: mathematical texts that "neutrally" define "profit" as the difference between the selling price and the cost price. In contrast, she argues that a Marxist definition of profit as ultimately unpaid labour "suggests that if the total of goods or capital in a social system is unequally divided between people at different levels in the social-industrial hierarchy, exploitation is necessarily taking place" (p. 122). In an analysis of real-life mathematical word problems in Greek elementary school texts, Chassapis (1997) found that more than 70% of the examples, applications, and problems for the fifth and sixth grades were "financial, and especially commercial, situations devoid of any pertinent social relationships....to all appearances existing on their own beyond any human agency and away from any space, time, or social structure...." (p. 26).

Moreover, the "hidden" messages do not just come from the subtexts of the problem statements. MacKernan (2000, p. 45) contends that in England, increasingly, teachers need "to start discussing what we are not allowed to teach." He presents many government statistics and suggests mathematical investigations that could *not* take place in the classroom – questions, for example, about why the UK is responsible for almost a fifth of the world's arms exports.

There has, in recent years, been a push to include real-life mathematical word problems in the curriculum. Verschaffel, Greer, and De Corte (2000) presented a comprehensive analysis of pedagogical concerns about practices involving word problems that lead students to suspend their sense-making critical capabilities. Contributions to this present volume extend that analysis in various directions. In this chapter, I discuss how teachers can try to develop students' critical political capabilities through using mathematics word problems that challenge the mainstream narrative of how our society works.

First, I'll discuss some political concerns about other aspects of the non-neutral "hidden" curriculum that results from particular selections of real-life data used to create contrived and/or context-narrow word problems. In the body of the chapter, I'll suggest various categories of *real* real-life mathematical word problems, illustrating how to go about creating such problems so they are presented in a broad enough context for students to appreciate how understanding numbers and doing calculations can illuminate meaning in real life. In conclusion, I will discuss some pedagogical and political questions about the real-life use of *real* real-life mathematical applications, returning to the issue of the non-neutrality of knowledge, and addressing the question of teaching difficult, pessimistic perspectives.

The main goal of a criticalmathematical literacy is not to understand mathematical concepts better, although that is needed to achieve the goal. Rather it is to understand how to use mathematical ideas in struggles to make the world better. In other words, the question to be investigated about my criticalmathematical literacy curriculum is not "Do the *real* real-life mathematical word problems make the mathematics more clear?" The key research questions are "Do the *real* real-life mathematical word problems make the social justice issues more clear?" and, "Does that clarity lead to actions for social justice?"

PROBLEMS WITH REAL-LIFE MATHEMATICAL WORD PROBLEMS

Real-Life Mathematical Word Problems Without Real Meaning

Mathematical word problems are all too easy to satirise (Figure 1). In a French study (IREM de Grenoble, 1980), a 7-year-old was asked the following question: "You have 10 red pencils in your left pocket and 10 blue pencils in your right pocket. How old are you?" When he answered: "20 years old," it was not because he didn't know that he was 7 in real life, or because he did not understand the relevant mathematical concepts. Rather it was, as Pulchalska and Semadeni (1987, p. 15) conclude, because the unwritten social contract between mathematics students and teachers stipulates that "when you solve a mathematical problem... you use the numbers given in the story... Perhaps the most important single reason

Figure 1. A satirical view of word problems

why students give illogical answers to problems with irrelevant questions or irrelevant data is that those students believe mathematics does not make any sense".

Pedagogically, that kind of "social contract" is a political problem – the political implications of "educating" people to accept nonsensical statements uncritically in order to "fit in" hardly need to be stated. Moreover, it is also politically problematic even when mathematical word problems do not ask nonsensical questions, but use real-life numerical data without *real* meaning, but only as "window dressing" to practice a particular mathematical skill. First, when assumptions about what are the "natural" conditions of real life (e.g., heterosexual families) are used as the "window dressing" context for mathematical problems, students who do not fit those "natural" categories are disrespected and/or made invisible. Further, the "hidden curriculum" about what is "natural" gets reinforced, making it less likely that students will question these taken-for-granted assumptions. Second, the *real* significance of the "window-dressed" real-life data is also hidden. When no better understanding of the data is gleaned through solving the mathematics problem created from the data, using real-life data masks how other mathematical operations, as well as other non-mathematical investigations, could be performed that would illuminate those same data. It gives a "hidden curriculum" message that using mathematics is not useful in understanding the world – mathematics is just pushing around numbers, writing them in different ways depending on what the teacher wants.

Real-Life Mathematical Word Problems Without Real Real Context

There are, of course, curricula that contain real-life mathematical word problems that involve using numbers to gain more information to help make real-life decisions. However, often these problems assume everyone's real-life context is the same. By contrast, Greer, Verschaffel, and Mukhopadhyay (2007, p. 96) stated that "if a decision is made to mathematise situations and issues that connect with students' lived experience, then it brings a further commitment to respect the diversity of that experience across genders, classes, and ethnicity". Take the following example:

> It costs $1.50 each way to ride the bus between home and work. A weekly pass is $16.00. Which is the better deal, paying the daily fare or buying the weekly pass?

It was found that inner-city African-American students "transformed the 'neutral' assumptions of the problem – all people work 5 days a week and have one job – into their own realities and perspectives" (Tate, 1995, p. 440). In their experience, a job (such as cleaning) might mean making several bus trips every day and working more than 5 days a week. If items of this type are used for assessment, with assumptions about the "right" answer, the implications are clear, given that, as Tate (1995, p. 440) puts it: "the underpinnings of school mathematics curriculum, assessment, and pedagogy are often more closely aligned with the idealised experience of the White middle class".

Apple (1992, pp. 424-425) concludes that the NCTM Standards (1989) do not address "the question of *whose problem* ... by focusing on the reform of mathematics education for 'everyone', the specific problems and situations of students from groups who are in the most oppressed conditions can tend to be marginalised or largely ignored (see Secada, 1989, p.25)." The Standards do not contain, for example, suggestions for mathematical investigations that would illustrate how the current US government's real-life de-funding of public education, through funding formulas based on property taxes, creates conditions in which the real-life implementation of the NCTM student-centered pedagogy is virtually impossible except in wealthy communities (Kozol, 1991).

Real-Life Mathematical Problems Without Enough Real Context

Those "neutral" real-life mathematical word problems that do include a real-life context like totalling grocery bills still omit the larger contexts of individual economic differences within a system where a 1997 report from the US Department of Agriculture declared that 11 million citizens, including 4 million children, "live in households categorised as moderately or severely hungry." (Sarasohn, 1997, p. 14).

Other "neutral" real-life mathematical word problems involve numerical descriptions that omit the larger contexts that created the reality of those descriptions. For example, *Multiplying People, Dividing Resources* (Zero Population Growth, 1994) contains a worksheet of real-life mathematical word problems designed to help students conceptualise large numbers. In the section on "Explanations/ Applications," there is their "neutral" comment that:

> When Columbus arrived in the Americas in 1492, there were probably 5 million Native Americans living in the area of the United States, and 57 million in the two American continents. World population at that time was about 425 million, and did not reach one billion until approximately 1810. . . . In 1994, the United States has approximately 260 million people within its borders . . .

Hidden in this real-life context is the larger context of what happened to those Native Americans. Although there is some academic debate about the number of people living North of Mexico in 1492 (ranging from about 7 million to 18 million),

> There is no doubt, however, that by the close of the nineteenth century the indigenous population of the United States and Canada totalled around

250,000. In sum, during the years separating the first arrival of Europeans in the sixteenth century and the infamous massacre at Wounded Knee in the winter of 1890, between 97 and 99 percent of North America's native people were killed (Stannard, 1992, p. 432).

For a real-life project-based example, Brown and Dowling (no date) comment on a mathematics study card in England that asks students to do various measurements in order to "study the problems of the disabled" (p. 23). They note that if the activity were really about real-life study, students would be involved in asking disabled people about their problems, instead of using their physical situation as "window dressing" for measurement exercises. Further, they remark that the larger institutional context is hidden: "The card is not about the ways in which able-bodied society handicaps disabled people...No mention is made of financial difficulties or difficulties relating to state 'aid,' 'compensation,' insurance, ... nor does the card make any reference to physical or emotional pain, social isolation..." (pp. 22-23).

REAL REAL-LIFE MATHEMATICAL WORD PROBLEMS[3]

Real real-life mathematical problems occur in broad contexts, integrated with other knowledge of the world. I (Frankenstein, 1983) contend, along with Freire (1970; Freire & Macedo, 1987) that the underlying context for critical adult education, in this case criticalmathematical literacy, is "to read the world." In that case, mathematical skills and concepts are learned in order to understand the institutional structures of our society.

Below are various categories of problems that, of course, overlap in different ways. The overarching activity is gaining a better analysis of the issue through understanding the meaning of the numbers, and gaining more knowledge about the issues through performing relevant calculations. The purpose of discussing the examples in this manner is to show many types of situations in which numbers can be used to make sense of the world, and then to make justice in the world.

Understanding the Meaning of Numbers

The *real* real-life mathematical word problems whose solutions involve understanding the meaning of numbers focus on using different kinds and arrangements of numbers (e.g., fractions, percents, graphs) to:
- describe the world
- reveal more accurate descriptions of the world
- understand the meaning of the sizes of numbers that describe the world
- understand the meanings that numbers can hide in descriptions of the world
- understand the meanings that numbers cannot convey in descriptions of the world.

Understanding the meaning of the numbers is needed to understand the meaning of these situations, situations that illuminate the way our world is structured.

Using numbers to describe the world. Example:

> Although Helen Keller was blind and deaf, she fought with her spirit and her pen. When she became an active socialist, a newspaper wrote that "her mistakes spring out of the... limits of her development." This newspaper had treated her as a hero before she was openly socialist.
>
> In 1911, Helen Keller wrote to a suffragist in England: "You ask for votes for women. What good can votes do when ten-elevenths of the land of Great Britain belongs to 200,000 people and only one-eleventh of the land belongs to the other 40,000,000 people? Have your men with their millions of votes freed themselves from this injustice?" (Zinn, 1980, p. 337).

Students are asked to discuss how numbers support Helen Keller's main point and to reflect on why she sometimes uses fractions and other times uses whole numbers. Information about the politics of knowledge is presented as a context in which to set her views, including class discussions about Keller's militant answer to the editor of the *Brooklyn Eagle* (Zinn, 1980, p. 338) and about why so many children's books ignore her socialist activism (Hubbard, 2002).

Using numbers to reveal more accurate descriptions of the world. Example: Students are asked to read articles that present numbers that counter taken-for-granted assumptions that many view as "natural" facts about the world. I use an editorial on "The wrong face on crime," (Jackson, 1994) which gives myriad "counter-intuitive" data such as "white Americans are ... three times more likely to be violently assaulted by another white person than by an African-American;" and a newspaper article which shows that in spite of widespread belief that "illegal"[4] immigrants are robbing tax payers through their use of hospital emergency rooms and public education, not only do "illegal" immigrants pay sales and other such taxes, but they also pay over $6 billion in Social Security and about $1.5 billion in Medicare taxes, without collecting any of the benefits from those taxes (Porter, 2005).

Understanding the meaning of the sizes of numbers that describe the world. Example: Students are asked to discuss what numerical understandings they need in order to understand the political and personal implications of the chart shown in Table 1. These figures were compiled in time-and-motion studies conducted by General Electric, and published in a 1960 handbook to provide office managers with standards by which clerical labour should be organised.

To understand more deeply how numbers underpin worker control, we discuss historical examples, like that of William Henry Leffingwell who, in the early 1900's:

> ... calculated that the placement of water fountains so that each clerk walked, on the average, a mere hundred feet for a drink would cause the clerical workers in one office to walk an aggregate of fifty thousand miles each year

just to drink an adequate amount of water, with a corresponding loss of time for the employer. (This represents the walking time of a thousand clerks, each of whom walked only a few hundred yards a day.) (Braverman, 1974, pp. 310-11).

Table 1. Estimated time for various operations (Braverman, 1974, p. 321)

Open and close	Minutes
Open side drawer of standard desk	0.014
Open centre drawer	0.026
Close side drawer	0.015
Close centre drawer	0.027

Chair activity	Minutes
Get up from chair	0.039
Sit down in chair	0.033
Turn in swivel chair	0.009

We also look at contemporary examples, including situations where "managers kept computer spreadsheets monitoring employee use of the bathroom" and female workers were told "to urinate into their clothes or face three days' suspension for unauthorised expeditions to the toilet" (Robin, 2002, D5).

According to the Bureau of Labor Statistics, in 1979, 25 percent of employees in medium- to large-sized companies did not have paid rest breaks during which they could go to the bathroom. By 1993, the last year for which there are statistics, that number had jumped to 32 percent. . . Not until 1998 did the federal government, under pressure from the labor movement, even maintain that employers had to grant employees an ill-defined "timely access" to the bathroom. (Robin, 2002, p. D5)

Scharf (2003) gives another current example where employees' talk to customers is "scripted" by management:

Fast-food drive-through window workers must greet customers almost instantly – often within three seconds from the time the car reaches the menu board. Digital timers . . . measure how long it takes the worker to issue the greeting, take the order, and process the payment. ... Former McDonald's CEO Jack Greenberg claimed that unit sales increase 1% for every six seconds saved at the drive-through.

To look at such outrages even more deeply, we think about the theory behind the "scientific management" of workers. Braverman (1974) states that the idea is to conceive of the worker as a general-purpose machine operated by management, displacing labourers as the subjective element of the labour process and transforming them into objects.

This mechanical exercise of human faculties according to motion types, which are studied independently of the particular kind of work being done, brings to life the Marxist conception of "abstract labor."... The capitalist sees labor not as a total human endeavor, but [abstracts it] from all its concrete qualities in order to comprehend it as universal and endlessly repeated motions, the sum of which, when merged with the other things that capital buys – machines, materials, etc. – results in the production of a larger sum of capital than that which was "invested" at the outset of the process. Labor in the form of standardized motion patterns is labor used as an interchangeable part ... (pp. 180-2)

Understanding the meanings that numbers can hide in descriptions of the world.
Example: Students are given data of employment status for various categories of workers such as "employed part-time, want full-time work," and "not employed, want a job now, have not looked for work in the last year." They are asked to decide which categories should count as unemployed, which are in the labour force, and to calculate their unemployment rate, and compare it with the rate calculated using the categories counted by the government.

Discussion brings out that there is political struggle involved in deciding who counts as unemployed. In 1994, the USA official definition gave an unemployment rate of 5.1%, whereas considering additional categories of discouraged workers as unemployed changes the rate to 9.3%. Further, there are other groups we could count, such as the 2.5 million people who worked full-time, year round, in 1994 and earned below the official poverty line (Sklar, 1995). And there are many other political decisions to make about how to count unemployment (Figure 2):

Figure 2. The counting of jobs

Even more sophisticated ways of making the unemployment data seem "low" are also considered. For example, students need to use algebra to show why removing an unemployed worker from the labour force makes the unemployment rate go down.

Several years ago BLS changed the criteria for determining labor force status so that the higher the job turnover, the lower the official unemployment rate. To illustrate: workers who expected to begin a new job but who were not yet working were formerly counted as unemployed. Now most are defined as out of the work force and are no longer included in the unemployment statistics. Moreover, the worker who left with the intention of seeking another job is defined as out of the work force until that person applies for another job. To be counted as unemployed requires an "active" effort to find work. . . . Neither the worker who expects to begin a job nor the individual who just left the same job are collecting a paycheck. Yet the official unemployment rate among them is zero. The greater the job turnover, the more this situation is replicated, and the larger the gap between the official and real unemployment rates. (Brill, 1999, p. 40).

This is a case in which the larger context of the politics behind the collection of data is important to include. In 1994 the Bureau of Labor Statistics stopped issuing its U-7 rate, a measure that included various categories of discouraged workers not counted for the official government unemployment rate, so now researchers will not be able to determine "alternative" unemployment rates (Saunders, 1994). Then, in 2003, the "mass layoff" statistics (layoffs putting 50 or more workers out of a job) were dropped by the Bureau of Labor Statistics. Boothby (2003) reports that in November 2002 there were 2,150 mass layoffs affecting 240,000 workers.

Finally, more extended discussion brings up a number of related criticalmathematical issues such as the effects of racism and sexism resulting in differential unemployment rates and incomes. In 1986, even with a college degree, blacks had higher unemployment rates than whites (13.2% to 5.3%); blacks with a college degree even had higher unemployment than whites with only a high school diploma (13.2% to 10.1%). Folbre (1987, charts 4.7, 4.12) explains that:

> One way to measure the combined effect is to multiply the median earnings of the different groups by the percentage of the labor force of that group that is employed. This provides an estimate of the typical earnings of a member of the labor force. . . . individual black men working full-time in 1983 earned 75% of what white men earned, but a typical black man in the labor force earned only 52% of what a typical white man earned – because the black man was far more likely to be unemployed.

Of course, the broadest theoretical context examines why 100% employment cannot exist in a capitalist economic system, because that would create a situation in which the workers would have too much power to change the conditions of their exploitation.

Understanding the meanings that numbers cannot convey in descriptions of the world. Example: Following this is an example of art encoding quantitative information. The numbers are the data of our world – our wars; the art allows us to understand the quantities in ways we could not understand from the numbers alone.

As Toni Morrison states: "Data is not wisdom, is not knowledge" (quoted in Caiani, 1996, p. 3).

The famous memorial in Washington, D.C. by artist Maya Lin lists the names of 57,939 Americans killed during the Vietnam War. In "The other Vietnam Memorial" (Museum of Contemporary Art in Chicago, IL), Chris Burden etched 3,000,000 names onto a Rolodex-type structure, standing on its end, that fills the entire room in which it is displayed. The names represent the approximate number of Vietnamese people killed during the US war on Vietnam. Since many of their names are unknown, Burden created variations of 4000 names taken from Vietnamese telephone books. Also, the museum notes comment that by using the form of a common desktop object that functions to organise professional and social contacts, Burden underlines the unrecognised loss of Vietnamese lives in US memory.

Understanding the Calculations

The *real* real-life mathematical word problems whose calculations are an integral part of understanding a situation focus on:
– verifying/following the logic of an argument
– understanding how numerical descriptions originate
– using calculations to restate information
– using calculations to explain information
– using calculations to reveal the unstated information.

The purpose underlying all the calculations is to understand better the information and the arguments, and to be able to question the decisions that were involved in choosing which numbers to use and which calculations to perform.

Verifying/following the logic of an argument. Example: Students are asked to read an excerpt from "The One-Percent Solution", the letter to the editor criticising one of the examples in the excerpt, discuss the arguments made, and fill in all the details of the mathematical operations the writer performed to back up his argument. (One of the nice pedagogical aspects of this exercise is that the letter writer, correcting one mathematical mistake made by Dollars & Sense, makes another mathematical error himself.)

The excerpt from "The One-Percent Solution" (*Dollars & Sense*, December 1989, p. 32) is as follows:

> Both the sheer volume of numbers and, in an era of multi-trillion-dollar national debts, their overwhelming magnitude obscure their true meaning. ... Divorced from both the decisions of the powerful and the effects on the powerless, the numbers just numb. A percentage point here, a percentage point there; what's the difference?

As the following examples demonstrate, the difference can be dramatic indeed.

- A one percentage point reduction in the poverty rate, from 13.1% to 12.1%, would lift 2.4 million people above the poverty line, including over 600,000 children.
- A one percentage point decrease in the official unemployment rate, from 5.3% to 4.3%, would mean 1.2 million people working and an additional $75 billion in annual output.

The letter to the editor, titled "One percent is bigger than it looks" (Dollars & Sense, April 1990, p. 22) reads as follows:

> I have a comment on your "Economy in Numbers" (December 1989). You state that a 1% decrease in the average number of hours worked each week would create the equivalent of 17,000 new full-time jobs. I think this estimate is much too low.
>
> Average weekly hours for production or non-supervisory workers in the private sector in 1988 was 34.7. A 1% reduction would be 0.347 hours. Total employment in 1988 was 116.7 million. Assuming this average weekly hours estimate applies to all workers, a 1% reduction in hours would mean that the existing work force would work a total of 40.49 million fewer hours per week. If both labor productivity and total labor demand remained unchanged, 1.167 million additional workers working 34.7 hours per week would be required, nearly 70 times the *Dollars & Sense* estimate!
>
> Of course, productivity tends to increase when the length of the work is reduced (workers might have a specific number of tasks they must perform in a shorter time period) so there would be some reduction in labor demand. Surely, however, it would not be as much as implied by your estimate.
>
> In closing, I find *Dollars & Sense* an excellent publication. Keep up the good work!
>
> Andrew Sharpe, Head of Research, Canadian Labour Market and Productivity Centre, Ottawa, Canada.

Understanding how numerical descriptions originate (Seeing how raw data are collected, transformed, and summarised into numerical descriptions of the world). Example: Students are asked to read the excerpt below so that they are thinking about issues of how to teach and how people learn mathematics at the same time that they are learning the mathematics. Then, they are asked to: describe the study's methodology (i.e., what procedures were followed in the study, what the "raw" data consisted of, and how the raw data were transformed and summarised); rewrite the findings described by creating a chart; discuss which presentation of the data is clearest, and why; list conclusions they can and cannot draw from the data; and indicate what other information they would want in order to clarify the data or strengthen and/or change their conclusions. The excerpt to be analysed is as follows (Sklar, 1993, p. 53):

Sixty-six student teachers were told to teach a math concept to four pupils – two White and two Black. All the pupils were of equal, average intelligence. The student teachers were told that in each set of four, one White and one Black student was intellectually gifted, the others were labelled as average. The student teachers were monitored through a one-way mirror to see how they reinforced their students' efforts. The "superior" White pupils received two positive reinforcements for every negative one. The "average" White students received one positive reinforcement for every negative reinforcement. The "average" Black student received 1.5 negative reinforcements for each positive reinforcement, while the "superior" Black students received one positive response for every 3.5 negative ones.

Using calculations to restate information (Changing the quantitative form). Example: Students study a letter I wrote (Frankenstein, 2002) responding to an article by Howard Zinn (2002) in which he argues that the numerical descriptions of the deaths from the US war on Afghanistan can obscure those horrors. To dramatise my argument that numbers can illuminate the meaning of data and deepen connections to our humanity, I conclude that the 12 million children who die every year from hunger "are dying faster than we can speak their names." (Frankenstein, 2002, p. 23).

Using calculations to explain information. Example: Students are asked what calculations to perform to understand how declining block rate structures, like the one illustrated in the chart below, transfer money from the poor to the rich, and to propose other kinds of payment structures. The Rate Watcher's Guide (Morgan, 1980) details that a 1972 study conducted in Michigan, for example, found that residents of a poor urban area in Detroit paid 66% more per unit of electricity than did wealthy residents of nearby Bloomfield Hills. Researchers concluded that "approximately $10,000,000 every year leave the city of Detroit to support the quantity discounts of suburban residents."

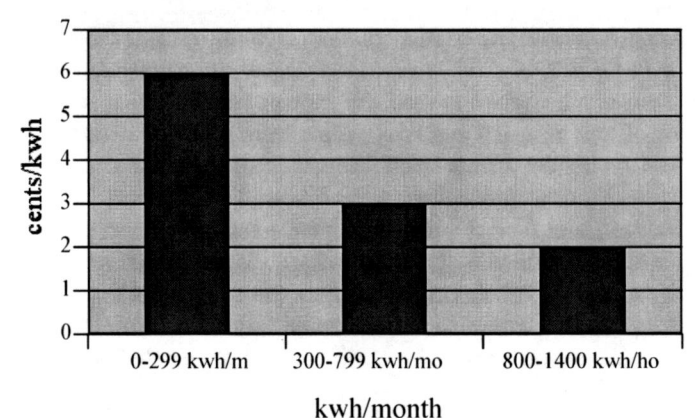

Figure 3. Declining block rate structure

Using calculations to state the unstated information. Example: Students learn about percents while analysing the following political poster in the context of the politics of language where people who constitute a majority of the world's population are referred to as "minorities." Students also see that numbers are "behind" many economic, political, and/or social issues even if there are no numbers "visible" in the picture (Figure 4).

Figure 4. Los Angeles Hispanics and other recent immigrants are demanding their piece of the pie (Guardian, 1978, Mario Torero, with Zapilote, Rocky, El Lton, and Zade)

CONCLUSION: PEDAGOGICAL AND POLITICAL DIMENSIONS OF TEACHING THROUGH *REAL* REAL-LIFE MATHEMATICAL WORD PROBLEMS

Pedagogical Dimensions

Following ABC's 1983 airing of a film about *The Day After* a nuclear war, the network presented a panel discussion, chaired by Ted Koppel, of mostly conservative government officials and Carl Sagan, a liberal scientist. At one point, Sagan refuted the then Secretary of State Schultz's contention that the Administration was already disarming, pointing out that "its current build-up calls for an increase in the number of strategic warheads, from 9,000 to 14,000." Koppel turned to Sagan and said "... I must confess statistics leave my mind reeling and, I suspect, everybody else's too." (Manoff, 1983, p. 589)

Certainly, students need enough mathematics so that their heads do not reel from comparing the size of two numbers! As a prerequisite to accomplishing the goal of a Freirean "reading of the world" using a criticalmathematical literacy, students need confidence that they can learn enough mathematics to use as part of understanding public and community service issues. Some of this confidence is gained from analysis of mystifications about learning mathematics, such as "there is only one correct method for solving a particular mathematical problem" and "only some people have mathematical minds" (Frankenstein, 1984). Of course, there is an emotional part of analysing these aspects of mathematics learning. When students realise that their teacher has confidence in them and expects, with studying, that they will learn the mathematics, they can begin to let go of the negative expectations many have internalised from past mathematics learning experiences.

Some confidence is gained from analysis of the societal uses of mathematics "anxiety." For example, I think it is important to address issues of "the politics of language" in order for students to understand how the label "mathematically anxious" can have contradictory effects. Naming that situation can initially reassure students that their feelings about mathematics are so common that educators have a name for them. However, the label can also focus the problem inward, "blaming the victims" and encouraging solutions directed solely *at* them. The label can direct attention away from the broader social context of how their learning got mystified, and what interests might be served by widespread mathematics "anxiety" and avoidance.

Some confidence is gained from understanding the politics of knowledge that have discounted some people's knowledge and privileged others' knowledge. For example, I ask students to reflect on Freire's (Freire & Macedo, 1987) insistence that "the intellectual activity of those without power is always characterised as non-intellectual." (p. 122) and on Marcuse's (1964) argument that:

> In this society, the rational rather than the irrational becomes the most effective mystification...For example, the scientific approach to the vexing problem of mutual annihilation – the mathematics and calculations of kill and over-kill, the measurement of spreading or not-quite-so-spreading fallout... is mystifying to the extent to which it promotes (and even demands) behavior which accepts the insanity. It thus counteracts a truly rational behavior – namely, the refusal to go along, and the effort to do away with the conditions which produce the insanity (pp. 189-190).

Once students are confident in their ability to learn mathematics, and motivated to reason quantitatively about public and community issues, then the question is: How much of the structure of mathematics must be demystified in order for students to be able to use numerical data for demystifying the structure of society?

It is important for students to understand enough concepts behind the basic algorithms to be able to use those rules comfortably in many different situations. However, as Lange and Lange (1984) found, although mathematics education can be empowering in a more general way, it is not necessarily the best approach in working with people on specific empowerment issues. The piece-rate workers they were organising in the textile industry in the southern United States were struggling with a pay system made intentionally obscure. The Langes' experience was that teaching the concepts of ratios and fractions behind that rate system was not the most effective way to empower the workers in their struggle for decent pay. It was more empowering to create a slide-rule distributed by the union that did the pay calculations for the workers, making the mathematical problem disappear, so that the workers could "focus on the social and economic relations underlying the way they are treated and paid" (p. 14).

Brown and Dowling (no date) argue for a research-based mathematics education – "an approach which centralises the consideration of social inequalities as a goal in itself, and which subordinates the mathematics as one of a number of possible means." In my context, my curriculum is loosely organised by a linear thread of underlying mathematical concepts (i.e., the meaning of whole numbers, then fractions, later percents, and so on). But, the lessons also involve non-linear explorations of *real* real-life public and community issues and much interdisciplinary content.

However, in thinking about what numeracy citizens need to solve *real* real-life problems, I am not advocating getting rid of college preparatory mathematics. As Powell and Brantlinger (2008) argue, teaching "traditional" mathematics with understanding to students who have been marginalised from college or certain professions is another form of criticalmathematics education appropriate to that context. I would argue that all citizens need the criticalmathematics I am describing, but it does not need to replace more "traditional" mathematics.

Political Dimensions

I suspected trouble when, at a 1981 National Council of Teachers of Mathematics (NCTM) Conference, the president of the organisation opened the meeting by stating that Ronald Reagan's election was great for mathematics teachers. But, I did not suspect how outraged the teachers would be by the biases in my real-life word problems. They did not accept my argument that no mathematical word problems are neutral.

A few years after my NCTM audience was furious at my biased word problems, the NCTM journal, *The Mathematics Teacher*, (March 1984, December 1984) was running multi-page spreads advertising a US Navy slide show "Math and Science: START NOW!" Toll-free phone numbers to arrange for a class presentation by a Navy representative were included. They published one critical letter that focused on the inappropriateness of the Navy starting recruiting drives in junior high school and questioned why there were no ads from government groups "whose mandate is more closely tied to social and environmental problems" (Milne, 1984). The editor answered that the Navy paid for the ad and any government agency could do likewise. He did not publish my strong critique that accepting an ad from the Navy implied:

> ... a certain level of support – especially since the NCTM's Executive Director is quoted in the ad as saying "Without hesitation, we endorse the project"!! In addition, your ad policy will be skewed towards those governmental agencies with the largest advertising budgets – therefore, those agencies, such as the military, which are favored by the current administration, will also be favored by NCTM ad policy. Finally, we did pay for the ad – not through our NCTM dues as you stated – but certainly, through our tax dollars.

As discussed in Frankenstein and Powell (1994), the epistemology of Paulo Freire is in direct opposition to the NCTM's and other dominant educational institutions' paradigm of positivism which views knowledge, though a product of human consciousness, as neutral, value-free, objective, and completely separate from how people use it. Learning, in this view, is the discovery of static facts and their subsequent description and classification (Bredo & Feinberg, 1982). On the other hand, Freire insists that knowledge is not static; that there is no dichotomy between objectivity and subjectivity, or between reflection and action; and that knowledge is not neutral.

For Freire, knowledge is continually created and re-created as people act and reflect on the world. Knowledge, therefore, is not fixed permanently in the abstract properties of objects, but is a process in which gaining existing knowledge and producing new knowledge are "two moments in the same cycle" (Freire, 1982). Embedded in this notion is the recognition that knowledge requires subjects; objects to be known are necessary, but they are not sufficient.

> Knowledge...necessitates the curious presence of subjects confronted with the world. It requires their transforming action on reality. It demands a constant searching (Freire, 1973, p. 101).

Knowledge, therefore, is a negotiated product emerging from the interaction of human consciousness and reality; it is produced as we, individually and collectively, search and try to make sense of our world.

Because of the unity between subjectivity and objectivity, people cannot *completely* know particular aspects of the world – no knowledge is finished or infallible. As humans change, so does the knowledge they produce. In connection with this, Lerman (1989) theorises that objective statements are publicly-shared social constructions. At particular moments in history, communities of people discuss, debate, revise, adopt, and challenge concepts and theories. Thus knowledge, "objective" beyond the visions of individual subjects, does not have the "transcendental existence" that positivists ascribe to it (Lerman, 1989, p. 219). Through constant search and dialogue, we continually refine our understandings and theories of reality and, in so doing, act more effectively.

Further, action and reflection are not separate moments of knowing. On the one hand, reflection that is not ultimately accompanied by action to transform the world is meaningless, alienating rhetoric. On the other hand, action that is not critically analysed cannot sustain progressive change. Without reflection, people cannot learn from each other's successes and mistakes; particular activities need to be evaluated in relation to larger collective goals. Only through praxis – reflection and action dialectically interacting to re-create our perception and description of reality – can people become subjects in control of organising their society.

This praxis is not neutral. Knowledge does not exist apart from how and why it is used, and in whose interest. Even, for example, in the supposedly neutral technical knowledge of how to cultivate potatoes, Freire asserts that:

REAL REAL-LIFE WORD PROBLEMS

> ... there is something which goes beyond the agricultural aspects of cultivating potatoes.... We have not only...the methods of planting, but also the question which has to do with the role of those who plant potatoes in the process of producing, for what we plant potatoes, in favor of whom. And something more. It is very important for the peasant...to think about the very process of work – what does working mean? (Brown, 1978, p. 63).

In Freire's view, people produce knowledge to humanise themselves. Overcoming dehumanisation involves resolving the fundamental contradiction of our epoch: domination against liberation.

One final point: the *real* real-life context illuminated by the *real* real-life mathematical word problems in my adult criticalmathematical literacy curriculum are outrageously horrible. How can these topics be taught without discouraging people and thereby stopping resistance? The context of my students' lives is such that many have been involved in our struggle to change this situation. And different groups of us have experienced some victories. However, given the resources of those in power to regroup, we wind up fighting the same battles over and over and often initial victories are overturned or co-opted. Nevertheless, those of us who are committed to the struggle for a just liberatory world keep fighting.

Audre Lorde (1988) reminds us in *A Burst of Light* that:

> ... hope [is] a living state that propels us, open-eyed and fearful, into all the battles of our lives. And some of those battles we do not win. But some of them we do. (p. 80)

If you can walk, you can dance ... (Figure 5).

Figure 5. Yes we can!

NOTES

[1] When Arthur Powell and John Volmink and I formed the Criticalmathematics Educators Group (CmEG) in 1991, following a conference we organised in October 1990, we decided to use one word to describe critical mathematics because of our hope that one day all mathematics education will be critical. See Powell and Brantlinger (2008) for a perspective on various ways of interpreting criticalmathematics education. In the future we intend to create a web site for the group, which will include the archive of the five CmEG Newsletters we distributed between 1991 and 1997.

[2] Related to the politics of language, The Progressive (2007, p. 11) cites a Washington Post article indicating that the United States Department of Agriculture will no longer use the word "hunger" to describe people who cannot get enough food to eat; instead these people will be described in official government documents as having "very low food security."

[3] Due to space limitations the examples are presented in an abbreviated form. I am developing these and others into a collection of columns for various websites and newsletters. Since June 2008, they have been appearing in *Numeracy Briefing*, edited by Europe Singh. For more information contact them at numeracy@basicskillsbulletin.co.uk. If any reader is interested in syndicating these columns, free of charge, contact me at marilyn.frankenstein@umb.edu

[4] I use quotes around illegal to draw attention to who gets to make the laws that determine who is "legal" and who is "illegal".

REFERENCES

Apple, M. (1992). Do the standards go far enough? Power, policy, and practice in mathematics education. *Journal for Research in Mathematics Education, 21*, 412–431.

Boothby, B. (2003, March/April). Layoff stats given pink slip. *Dollars & Sense.* pp. 4–5.

Braverman, H. (1974). *Labor and monopoly capital.* New York: Monthly Review Press.

Bredo, E., & Feinberg, W. (Eds.). (1982). *Knowledge and value in social and educational research.* Philadelphia: Temple University Press.

Brill, H. (1999, September). Partners in deceit: The bureau of labor statistics (BLS) and the census bureau. *Z Magazine,* pp. 39–44.

Brown, C. (1978). *Literacy in 30 hours: Paulo Freire's process in Northeast Brazil.* Chicago: Alternative Schools Network.

Brown, A., & Dowling, P. (n.d.). *Towards a critical alternative to internationalism and monoculturalism in mathematics education.* Working Paper No. 10, London: University of London, Institute of Education.

Caiani, J. (1996). Art, politics, and the imagination. *Resist Newsletter, 5*(6), 1–3; 11.

Chassapis, D. (1997). The social ideologies of school mathematics applications: A case study of elementary school textbooks. *For the Learning of Mathematics, 17*(3), 24–27.

Cheney, L. V. (1998). Politics in the schoolroom. In U. Colombo, R. Cullen & B. Lisle (Eds.), *Rereading America: Cultural contexts for critical thinking and writing* (4th ed., pp. 263–276). Boston: Bedford, St. Martins.

Dollars & Sense. (1989, December). The economy in numbers: The one-percent solution.

Folbre, N. (1987). *A field guide to the United States economy.* New York: Pantheon.

Frankenstein, M. (1983). Critical mathematics education: An application of Paulo Freire's epistemology. *Journal of Education, 165*(4), 315–340.

Frankenstein, M. (1984). Overcoming math anxiety by learning about learning. *Mathematics and Computer Education, 18*(3), 169–180.

Frankenstein, M. (2002, April 8). Letter to the editor. *The Nation,* p. 23.

Frankenstein, M., & Powell, A. B. (1994). Toward liberatory mathematics: Paulo Freire's epistemology and ethnomathematics, In P. McLaren & C. Lankshear (Eds.), *Politics of liberation: Paths from Freire* (pp. 74–99). New York: Routledge.

Freire, P. (1970). *Pedagogy of the oppressed.* New York: Seabury.

Freire, P. (1973). *Education for critical consciousness.* New York: Seabury.

Freire, P. (1982, July 5–15). Education for critical consciousness. Unpublished Boston College course notes taken by Frankenstein, M.

Freire, P., & Macedo, D. (1987). *Literacy: Reading the word and the world.* South Hadley, MA: Bergen & Garvey.

Gill, D. (1988). Politics of percent. In D. Pimm (Ed.), *Mathematics teaching and children* (pp. 122–125). Milton Keynes, England: Open University.

Greer, B., Verschaffel, L., & Mukhopadhyay, S. (2007). Modelling for life: Mathematics and children's experience. In W. Blum, P. L. Galbraith, H.-W. Henn & M. Niss (Eds.), *Applications and modelling in mathematics education: The 14th ICMI Study* (pp. 89–98). Berlin: Springer.

Hubbard, R. S. (2002, Fall). The truth about Helen Keller: Children's books about Helen Keller distort her life. *Rethinking Schools*, pp. 10–11.

Institut de Reserche sur l' Enseignement des Mathématiques (IREM) de Grenoble (1980). *Bulletin de l' Association des professeurs de Mathématique de l' Enseignement Public, 323*, 235–243.

Jackson, D. Z. (1994, August 19). The wrong face on crime (Op-ed). *The Boston Globe.*

Kozol, J. (1991). *Savage inequalities.* New York: Crown.

Lange, B., & Lange, J. (1984, May/June). Organizing piece-rate workers in the textile industry. *Science for the People,* pp. 12–16.

Lerman, S. (1989). Constructivism, mathematics and mathematics education. *Educational Studies in Mathematics, 20,* 211–223.

Lorde, A. (1988). *A burst of light.* Ithaca, NY: Firebrand.

MacKernan, J. (2000). Not for the classroom. *Mathematics Teaching, 172*(September), 40–45.

Manoff, R. K. (1983, December 10). The week after. *The Nation,* pp. 588–589.

Marcuse, H. (1964). *One-dimensional man.* Boston: Beacon.

Milne, R. (1984, September). Navy ad (Letter to the editor). *The Mathematics Teacher.*

Mittal, A. (2002, February). On the true cause of world hunger: An interview by Derrick Jensen. *The Sun.* Retrieved December 8, 2008, from http://www.foodfirst.org/achive/media/interviews/2002/amittalsu.html

Morgan, R. E. (1980). *The rate watcher's guide.* Washington, DC: Environmental Action Foundation.

National Council of Churches. (2007). Hunger: Myth & realities. Retrieved December 8, 2008, from http://rehydrate.org/facts/hunger.html

National Council of Teachers of Mathematics. (1989). *Curriculum and evaluation standards for school mathematics.* Reston, VA: Author.

Porter, E. (2005, April 5). Illegal immigrants are bolstering social security with billions. *New York Times.* Retrieved December 8, 2008, from http://www.nytimes.com/2005/04/05/business/05immigration.html

Powell, A. B., & Brantlinger, A. (2008). A pluralistic view of critical mathematics. In J. F. Matos, P. Valero & K. Yasukawa (Eds.), *Proceedings of the Fifth International Mathematics Education and Society conference* (pp. 424–433). Lisbon, Portugal: Centro de Investigacao em Educacao, Universisdade de Lisboa, and Department of Education, Learning and Philosophy, Aalborg University, Denmark.

The Progressive. (2007, January). No comment: Word deprivation. p. 11.

Pulchaska, E., & Semadini, Z. (1987). Children's reaction to verbal arithmetic problems with missing, surplus or contradictory data. *For the Learning of Mathematics, 7*(3), 9–16.

Robin, C. (2002, September 29). Lavatory and liberty: The secret history of the bathroom break. *The Boston Globe,* p. D1, D5.

Sarasohn, D. (1997, December 8). Hunger on main Street: Food banks are straining, but the worst is yet to come. *The Nation,* p. 13, 14, 16, 18.

Saunders, B. (1994, September 26). Numbers game. *The Nation, 259*(9), 295–296.

Scharf, A. (2003, October). Scripted talk: From "Welcome to McDonald's" to "Paper or plastic?" employers control the speech of service workers. *Dollars & Sense.* Retrieved December 8, 2008, from: http:/www.dollarsandsense.org/archives/2003/0903scharf.html

Secada, W. (1989). Agenda setting, enlightened self-interest, and equity in mathematics education. *Peabody Journal of Education, 66*, 22–56.
Sharpe, A. (1990, April). One percent is bigger than it looks. *Dollars & Sense*.
Sklar, H. (1993, July/August). Young and guilty by stereotype. *Z Magazine*, pp. 52–61.
Sklar, H. (1995, June). Back to the raw deal. *Z Magazine*. pp. 10–12.
Stannard, D. E. (1992, October 19). Genocide in the Americas: Columbus' legacy. *The Nation*. pp. 430–434.
Tate, W. F. (1995). School mathematics and African American students: Thinking seriously about opportunity-to-learn standards. *Educational Administration Quarterly, 31*, 424–448.
Verschaffel, L., Greer, B., & De Corte, E. (2000). *Making sense of word problems*. Lisse, The Netherlands: Swets & Zeitlinger.
Zero Population Growth. (1994). *Multiplying people, dividing resources*. Washington, DC: ZPG Education Program.
Zinn, H. (1980). *A People's History of the United States*. New York: Harper & Row.
Zinn, H. (2002, February 11). The others. *The Nation*. Retrieved December 8, 2008, from http://www.thenation.com/doc/20020201l/zinn

Marilyn Frankenstein
University of Massachusetts
Boston
U.S.A.

JO BOALER

CAN MATHEMATICS PROBLEMS HELP WITH THE INEQUITIES IN THE WORLD?

Discussion of Part II: Sociocultural Factors

INTRODUCTION

Is it possible that the writing of mathematics problems, in particular the decisions that are made with regard to context and story-line, can help with the inequalities that pervade our world? I find this an interesting and alluring idea and one that is offered as a distinct possibility by the three chapters in this section. Yet the three authors offer this possibility in completely different ways, that are all worthy of serious attention. The first author, Frank Swetz, does not pose this question or idea in his writing, but his chapter's juxtaposition with the other two make this question an irresistible one to ask of his work. Marilyn Frankenstein, and Barry Cooper and Tony Harries differ in that their chapters add to their history of work considering the relationship between mathematics contexts and inequality. In the following, I will review the three different ways that mathematics problems may help tackle inequality offered by the three chapters, and then I will offer a fourth possibility, that has emerged from recent research on an interesting mathematics approach that was highly successful at promoting equity.

THE ROLE OF HISTORY IN FIGHTING INEQUALITY

Frank Swetz provides a fascinating historical survey. In reviewing the mathematics word problems that were written thousands of years ago, we are taken upon a delightful journey, giving insights into the ways mathematics was used to communicate the workings of society. Swetz has collected a rich and detailed set of problems spanning thousands of years, and he points out, quite rightly, that the mathematics word problems written for different times "leave a trail", revealing "societal concerns and priorities" (p. 74). Travelling along this trail with Swetz was extremely interesting for me, as I learned about the issues and assumptions of different times as well as the ways in which mathematics was deemed to be helpful.

All historical records give us insights into events that took place in the past, but it may be that the mathematics word problems that have been uncovered from different time periods play an unusual and particularly useful role. It is well recognised that any historical account is layered with analysis and interpretation. As Henry Stimson famously wrote, "history is often not what actually happened but what is recorded as such" (http://hnn.us/articles/1328.html). Historians, like any other people, have particular persuasions and personal understandings that inevitably pervade their accounts of the past. But can the same be said for mathematics word problems? Perhaps the ways in which mathematics problems were formed in Ancient Mesopotamia or Egypt, for example, with everyday proceedings described in order to present a perplexing problem, give a particular, less subjective account of historical events and relationships? Swetz mentions, for example, the way in which ancient Egyptian mathematics problem collections have helped show that the pyramids of Egypt were built by skilled labourers and not slave labour gangs, as once believed. The role played by the mathematics problems formed in different times in our piecing together of events in the past is an interesting one.

The examples Swetz sets out, providing something akin to mathematical windows into the past, communicate a great deal about society, making them fascinating to read. But what of their potential in combating inequality? History has an important role to play in promoting an awareness of past oppressions and helping us avoid the mistakes of the past, so well captured in the famous quote that "those who forget history are doomed to repeat it" and Swetz gives us some interesting examples of societal inequities portrayed through mathematics. The following is not a problem that Swetz offers as an example of gender inequality but I certainly see it in this way. It comes from a collection compiled by the British monk, Alcuin of York, in 781:

> Three friends each with a sister needed to cross a river. Each of them coveted the sister of another. At the river they found a small boat in which only two of them could cross at once. How could they cross the river without any of the women being defiled by the men? (Hadley & Singmaster, 1992, p. 111)

Swetz adds that in related problems the "subjects" were replaced by "wolf, goat and cabbage, overweight people and hedgehogs." A sentence that somehow added to my sense of insult for the role of women in the problems! Swetz is more explicit in his presentation of the ways the following problem reflects social inequities, in particular of landlord exploitation, communicated in Chinese Communist textbooks:

> In the old society, there was a starving family who had to borrow 5 dou [200 pounds] of corn from the landlord. The family repaid the landlord three years later. The greedy landlord demanded 50% interest compounded annually. How much corn did the landlord demand at the end of the third year? (*New York Times*, 1969, March 9, p. 18)

Swetz also describes the cultural inequalities communicated in problems, as in the following example from a Nazi textbook from Germany in 1941:

> Every day, the state spends RM6 on one cripple; RM $4\frac{1}{2}$ on one mentally ill person; RM $5\frac{1}{2}$ on one deaf and dumb person; RM $5\frac{3}{5}$ on one feebleminded person; RM $3\frac{1}{2}$ on one alcoholic; RM $4\frac{4}{5}$ on one pupil in care; RM $2\frac{1}{10}$ on one pupil at a special school; and RM $\frac{9}{20}$ for one pupil at a normal school.

These data are followed by a series of questions emphasising the cost of "inferiors" to the state. Such problems, in the hands of a knowledgeable and skilful teacher, provide the potential for rich conversations that are both mathematically interesting and important in the promotion of awareness of inequalities. Other problems Swetz tells us about offer the potential for more positive awareness raising. As the world continues to face the issue of female under-representation at the highest mathematical levels (Herzig, 2004a, 2004b; Boaler, 2009), how interesting it was to read that the *Ladies Diary*, published in England from 1704-1842 (Perl, 1979) which included mathematics problems as challenges for its readers, became the prototype for the first mathematics periodical The *Mathematical Correspondent*, published in the United States in 1804. This little known fact, communicating the knowledge that women of Georgian and Victorian Britain were so interested in mathematics, and played such an influential role, provides important opposition to the persistent media idea that women are mathematically inferior to men (Boaler, 2002).

In taking us upon a journey of "mathematical footprints" Swetz makes his mission clear – he communicates the idea that teachers need to understand history in order to know about the "origins of mathematics". This seems correct, although I disagree with his harsh logical deduction that as "prolonged prevalence of a mathematical concept attests to its importance", teachers who do not know about the origin of mathematics have "a limited appreciation for the mathematics itself" (p. 78). There are many ways in which we may appreciate mathematics that are not hampered in any way by a lack of knowledge of the ways mathematics was used in the past; such an awareness may enhance mathematical appreciation but it does not define it. But I have concentrated, in this response, upon the potential of the mathematics problems Swetz introduces us to, in raising awareness of the social, cultural, and gender inequalities of the past and the ways that they are communicated through, and connected to, mathematics. My doing so has been prompted both by the chapter's juxtaposition with two chapters that deal more explicitly with issues of equity and the enormous potential of the problems to which we have been introduced. Whether or not the mathematics problems of the past are used to prompt discussion and awareness of the inequities in society, they provide a great opportunity to promote another, critical, awareness. Mathematics is a human activity, a social enterprise, that cannot be separated from life and, whilst school children continue to be disadvantaged by the prevailing view that mathematics is an abstract and irrelevant subject, separate from the issues of the world, any uncovering and publicising of the ways in which mathematics is entwined in our lives, and in the most important issues for society, is a very important task indeed.

THE ROLE OF MATHEMATICS PROBLEMS IN EXPOSING INJUSTICE AND INEQUALITY

In Marilyn Frankenstein's chapter she describes an important agenda to which she has dedicated her career and probably a lot more, in using mathematics problems to expose social injustice. This agenda also includes teaching students the mathematics they need to make sense of the world and to recognise inequality when they experience it. I use the word "agenda" deliberately as I see Frankenstein's mission, as she does herself, as overtly political. As she describes in her chapter Frankenstein gives students mathematics problems and mathematical data, such as the following:

> Fast-food drive-through window workers must greet customers almost instantly – often within three seconds from the time the car reaches the menu board. Digital timers . . . measure how long it takes the worker to issue the greeting, take the order, and process the payment. ... Former McDonald's CEO Jack Greenberg claimed that unit sales increase 1% for every six seconds saved at the drive-through.

Frankenstein uses this example to highlight the ways that management "displace" labourers and transform them "into objects". It is clear from this chapter and other writing of Frankenstein and her contemporaries (see for example, Gutstein, Lipman, Hernandez, & de los Reyes, 1997) that mathematics problems can be used to fight injustice, precisely by exposing the nature of societal injustice and inequality to students. Frankenstein also makes a strong case for the non-neutrality of mathematics, of knowledge, and of mathematics problems. Indeed, she argues that every "real world" problem contains hidden messages, which is an interesting claim worthy of some thought. The questions I am left with, in reading this interesting and provocative chapter, concern the political work in which Frankenstein is engaged. For before we rush out and rejoice in the role of mathematics problems and contexts in highlighting and fighting inequality through the kinds of examples Frankenstein provides, we have to recognise that such examples make many students and teachers extremely uncomfortable, if not angry. Frankenstein gives us some indication of this response in describing the "outrage" of teachers at a National Council for Teachers of Mathematics (NCTM) conference when presented with the problems. Some years ago, when I was a professor at Stanford University in the United States, I shared the mathematics curriculum of Rico Gutstein (2006), which has also been compiled in order to highlight inequalities. The curriculum was the focus of a reading group held with the students learning to be mathematics teachers; together we read the problems and discussed their use. This was an interesting experience for me because the students were, in the main, committed to issues of equity and saw their role as mathematics teachers as that of teaching mathematics as well as promoting equity. One of the students was an ex-marine with a conservative viewpoint, but he was far from typical of the group. When we discussed the problems, and their potential use in the classroom, many of the students became what I can only describe as uncomfortable. They wanted to be able to use the problems to promote equity and their discomfort was not because of a lack of commitment but because they felt they didn't have the knowledge of the issues raised in the problems to discuss them. They worried that students might ask them questions about the situations described, such as the exploitation of Mexican workers, that they felt unable to answer. They were worried, too, that if they exposed students to a world of inequality it might upset them or lead to their underachievement, particularly in culturally diverse classrooms. The teachers' discomfort probably spoke to an issue that Frankenstein raises of mathematics teachers commonly believing that their job is entirely neutral, objective, and apolitical. But for those teachers who recognise their power, perhaps even their responsibility, in helping students recognise and deal with injustice then these curriculum ideas sit a lot more comfortably.

In reading this chapter, we learn a lot about the types of problems and data Frankenstein uses and she makes a very good case that mathematics problems can be used to "read the world" and expose the sources of social inequity. The questions I am left with concern the particular social interactions that constitute students' learning about inequality. For I see the success of Frankenstein's work as being a great deal to do with the teacher (Frankenstein), as well as the students with whom she works. I would like to learn more about the ways the problems are used, the issues that are raised, the nature of the conversations that unfold, the tensions and concerns communicated, the prior experiences of the teachers, the most empowering moments that ensue, and so on. As with any analysis of learning, I find it most helpful to position the research lens, particularly in a set of chapters united by a "sociocultural theme", on the community of learners and the practices that are jointly constituted. Greeno and the Middle-school Mathematics through Applications Project (MMAP) propose that learning situations be analysed in terms of the constraints and affordances they offer (Greeno & MMAP, 1998) and, as I read, I wanted to learn about the constraints and affordances of Frankenstein's activity system. This is not a criticism of the chapter, as it may not have been the book's purpose, but the proposal to use mathematics problems to empower and educate students is fundamentally a question of learning, which always occurs at the intersection of teachers, students, and content, in a community of learners (Boaler, 2000; Greeno & MMAP, 1998; Hawkins, 1974; Lave & Wenger, 1991). That I was left wondering about the communities and the interactions and practices that emerged as students worked in these ways is perhaps a reason to read further, and to continue learning about the potential of such problems in the promotion of social justice.

Frankenstein describes herself as a fighter; in fact she is a lot more than this as her work has opened a space and a possibility. She and her colleagues have created an idea that is important. Not all teachers will be comfortable using the problems and data she uses, but they may take the idea further, finding opportunities to empower and educate students in the fight against societal inequalities, and that is very important indeed.

THE ROLE OF MATHEMATICS PROBLEMS IN CAUSING INEQUALITY

In the chapter by Cooper and Harries we have yet another very different but interesting example of the relationship between the context of mathematics problems and equality. But this time the subject is not the value of problems, but the danger of certain types of problem in creating inequalities. The country in which their work is located is England – a country that has, in my view, enough well documented ways of oppressing working-class children (such as extreme and widespread use of ability grouping) without providing further barriers to their achievement through mathematics assessments. But the work of Cooper and Harries, with their colleague Mairead Dunne, has shown us that this is exactly what happens when contexts are used in mathematics assessments. This is particularly true when the contexts prompt students to consider the "real world" when forming their answers, but then penalise them for doing so. In the chapter by Cooper and Harries, which adds to the considerable body of scholarship produced by Cooper and colleagues, we learn about the impact of contexts which may tempt students to use their own knowledge from the real world, instead of, or in addition to, the data or facts given in a question, thus causing them to get the wrong answers. The authors have demonstrated repeatedly that this phenomenon not only exists but is related to social class, with students from working class homes being more likely to use their own knowledge when this is not the intention of the test designers. This finding, showing a clear route between test design and social class inequality, is extremely important.

In addition to the social class inequalities that result when certain contexts are used, I have shown that certain contexts prompt girls, more than boys, to engage with real world variables, thus compromising their performance (Boaler, 1994), and Zevenbergen has shown that students of a particular linguistic or cultural background are similarly disadvantaged (Zevenbergen, 2000). It is interesting to consider why it might be girls, language learners and working-class students who are the students who are more likely to consider real world variables and less likely to play the school context game (Boaler, 2008a; Wiliam, 1997), and Cooper and Dunne (1998) provide a fascinating analysis of the reason for this phenomenon amongst working-class students. But in some senses it does not matter which students are disadvantaged by such contexts, as long as we know that considerable numbers of students are disadvantaged by the contexts, which serve to hide their knowledge of mathematics. The work of Cooper, Harries, Dunne and others should prompt a major review of context use in mathematics assessments.

A review of contexts to determine and understand which contexts lead to inequality would involve examining the exact nature of contexts that prompt students to consider real world variables and then penalise them for doing so. Cooper and Harries provide a number of examples of these in their chapter, including a question asking students how many times a lift would need to go up in the rush hour, which seems to lead to a use of real world knowledge. Other contexts, for example a question asking what fraction of a pizza is left if someone takes one of four equal slices, do not prompt the use of real world knowledge. How are these contexts different? Could we set out guidelines for those who design assessments, to halt the systematic inequalities which Cooper and Harries show so clearly?

A second issue raised by the work of Cooper and Harries concerns the difference between contexts used in assessments and those used in classrooms. In the classroom, teachers can always be flexible and respond to a students' understanding and use of context, whereas in a formal assessment this does not happen. This means that contexts can be used in classrooms and in particular ways in classrooms that would be highly inappropriate in an assessment situation. But this does not mean that any type of classroom context use is helpful. I, and others, have argued that contexts should only be used if students are given the opportunity to engage with the situations given, or the contexts help to give meaning to a problem, without requiring that students ignore all that they know about the real world (Boaler, 1993, 2008a; Verschaffel, Greer, & De Corte, 2000). Contexts can be extremely powerful in the mathematics classroom but they should only be used when they are realistic, and when the contexts offer something to the students, such as increasing their interest or providing a model of a mathematical concept. A realistic use of context is one where students are given real situations that need mathematical analysis, for which they do need to consider the variables, rather than ignore them. For example, students could be asked to use mathematics to predict population growth. This could involve students interpreting newspaper data on the population, investigating the amount of growth over recent years, determining rates of change, building linear models ($y=mx+b$) and using these to predict population growth into the future. Such questions are excellent ways to interest students, motivate them, and give them opportunities to use mathematics to solve problems. Contexts may also be used to give a visual representation, helping to convey meaning. It does not hurt to suggest that a circle is a pizza that needs dividing into fractions, but it does hurt to offer questions such as this:

> A pizza is divided into fifths for 5 friends at a party. Three of the friends eat their slices but then 4 more friends arrive. What fractions should the remaining 2 slices be divided into?

Everyone knows that when extra people turn up at a party more pizza is ordered or people go without slices. In such questions, students are invited into the world of parties and friends while at the same time being required to ignore everything they know about parties and friends (Boaler, 2008a).

An insensitive use of contexts, particularly when students are invited to engage in the real world, but then penalised for doing so, results in classroom inequalities. In addition, students learn, over time, to ignore the real world portrayed in mathematical contexts, which is, in itself, a serious issue. As students learn to answer nonsensical questions about pizza slices being divided among friends, trains travelling towards each other on the same track, or people painting houses all day at identical rates, they come to believe that mathematics classrooms are strange places in which common sense cannot be used. Over time, schoolchildren realise that when you enter *Mathsland* you leave your common sense at the door (Boaler, 2008a; Verschaffel et al., 2000).

The issue of context use in classrooms and in assessments is complex and important, but the fundamental message I take from the work of Cooper and Harries, as well as other authors (Verschaffel et al., 2000) and several other chapters in this volume), is that contexts that require students to engage partly in the real world, whilst at the same time ignoring everything they know about the real world, should not be used. It seems we have reached a place of significant understanding of the impact of contexts, as displayed in the various chapters in this book, but that the understanding shared by academics in mathematics education has not reached a broader audience, which is something we should all work to change.

CONCLUSION

The three chapters in this section are rich and varied, each one giving us a greater understanding of the ways that contexts may fundamentally shape students' experiences and relationships with mathematics. Swetz teaches us about the ways that contexts may give students access to a greater understanding of the world and the role of mathematics within it; Frankenstein teaches us about the ways that contexts may be used to increase students' awareness of inequality and their ability to deal with inequalities through mathematics; and Cooper and Harries teach us the ways in which some contexts can create inequalities through their use in assessments. In my own research, I recently found that mathematics problems and contexts contributed to the promotion of equity in a different way. As part of a four year study of different mathematics approaches, involving over 700 students, I found that one approach contributed to the promotion of equity through the use of mathematics problems that could be viewed and answered in different ways, combined with a teaching approach that valued the contribution of different and varied student perspectives. Interestingly, this contributed to equity, not through contexts that raised issues of equity directly – indeed many of the problems were abstract with no context – but through teaching students to appreciate diverse perspectives and viewpoints. As students became more open-minded about the different ways in which other students could contribute to the mathematics problems, whatever their social class, ethnicity, gender, or achievement level, students became more open-minded about the value of different students in general. This resulted in very impressive working relations between students and high levels of respect that crossed traditional barriers of gender, social class, ethnicity, and mathematical achievement. In addition, all of the achievement differences between students of different cultural groups that were in place when students started at the school, diminished or disappeared, and students told us that there were no ethnic cliques at the school because of the mathematics approach used. In other places, I have argued that mathematics, as a discipline, has a particular role to play in this regard. Whereas in an English class students may agree to differ on their perspectives on an essay or poem, in the equitable mathematics classes I studied, students were taught that they needed each other's perspectives and they should work together in finding the "right answer" to the problems (see Boaler, 2008a, 2008b; Boaler & Staples, 2008). In the classrooms I studied, the mathematics problems did not increase awareness of historical issues, nor did they raise issues of poverty, employment discrimination or other inequalities in society, but the nature of the open problems fundamentally contributed to the promotion of equity.

I started this section review asking whether mathematics problems can help with the inequities in the world. Although this claim sounds bold, our three authors show clearly the ways in which they can. Mathematics, as a subject, has the power to crush children's confidence and to result in traumatic learning experiences (Boaler, 2008a). This power, coupled with the intensity of the relationship many students (and adults) have with mathematics, makes the work of these three authors all the more important. The contexts students meet, in mathematics classrooms and assessments, contribute to their understanding of mathematics and the world and the relationship between the two. These authors have shown us that they can also help with the inequities that persist in our schools and in our classrooms, in varied and important ways.

REFERENCES

Boaler, J. (1993). The role of contexts in the mathematics classroom: Do they make mathematics more "real"? *For the Learning of Mathematics, 13*(2), 12–17.
Boaler, J. (1994). When do girls prefer football to fashion? An analysis of female underachievement in relation to "realistic" mathematics contexts. *British Educational Research Journal, 20*, 551–564.
Boaler, J. (2000). Exploring situated insights into research and learning. *Journal for Research in Mathematics Education, 31*, 113–119.
Boaler, J. (2002). Paying the price for "sugar and spice": Shifting the analytical lens in equity research. *Mathematical Thinking and Learning, 4*, 127–144.
Boaler, J. (2008a). *What's math got to do with it? Helping children love their least favorite subject – and why it's important for America.* New York: Viking.
Boaler, J. (2008b). Promoting "relational equity" and high mathematics achievement through an innovative mixed ability approach. *British Educational Research Journal, 34*, 167–194.
Boaler, J. (2009). *The elephant in the classroom: Helping children learn and love maths.* Souvenir Press: London.
Boaler, J., & Staples, M. (2008). Creating mathematical futures through an equitable teaching approach: The case of Railside School. *Teachers' College Record, 110*, 608–645.
China's new math and old problems. (1969, March 9). *New York Times*, p. 18.
Cooper, B., & Dunne, M. (1998). Anyone for tennis? Social class differences in children's responses to national curriculum mathematics testing. *The Sociological Review, 46*, 115–148.
Greeno, J. G., & MMAP. (1998). The situativity of knowing, learning and research. *American Psychologist, 53*, 5–26.
Gutstein, E. (2006). *Reading and writing the world with mathematics: Toward a pedagogy for social justice.* New York: Routledge.
Gutstein, E., Lipman, P., Hernandez, P., & de los Reyes, R. (1997). Culturally relevant mathematics teaching in a Mexican American context. *Journal for Research in Mathematics Education, 28*, 709–737.
Hadley, J., & Singmaster, D. (1992). Problems to sharpen the young. *The Mathematical Gazette, 76*(475), 102–126.
Hawkins, D. (1974). *I, Thou, and It. The informed vision.* New York: Agathon Press.
Herzig, A. (2004a). Becoming mathematicians: Women and students of color choosing and leaving doctoral mathematics. *Review of Educational Research, 74*, 171–214.
Herzig, A. (2004b). Slaughtering this beautiful math: Graduate women choosing and leaving mathematics. *Gender and Education, 16*, 379–395.
Lave, J., & Wenger, E. (1991). *Situated learning: Legitimate peripheral participation.* Cambridge, UK: Cambridge University Press.
Perl, T. (1979). The Ladies Diary or the Woman's Almanack, 1704–1841. *Historia Mathematica, 6*, 36–53.
Verschaffel, L., Greer, B., & De Corte, E. (2000). *Making sense of word problems.* Lisse, The Netherlands: Swets & Zeitlinger.
Wiliam, D. (1997). Relevance as MacGuffin in mathematics education. *Chreods, 12*, 8–19.
Zevenbergen, R. (2000). "Cracking the code" of mathematics classrooms: School success as a function of linguistic, social and cultural background. In J. Boaler (Ed.), *Multiple perspectives on mathematics teaching and learning* (pp. 201–224). Westport, CT: Ablex Publishing.

Jo Boaler
University of Sussex
U.K.

PART III: PROBING STUDENTS' CONCEPTIONS

LIEVEN VERSCHAFFEL, WIM VAN DOOREN, LIMIN CHEN,
AND KATRIEN STESSENS

7. THE RELATIONSHIP BETWEEN POSING AND SOLVING DIVISION-WITH-REMAINDER PROBLEMS AMONG FLEMISH UPPER ELEMENTARY SCHOOL CHILDREN

INTRODUCTION

Recent recommendations for the reform of school mathematics suggest an important role for problem posing. For example, *The Principles and Standards for School Mathematics* in the U.S. (National Council of Teachers of Mathematics, 2000) call for students to "formulate interesting problems based on a wide variety of situations, both within and outside mathematics" (p. 258) and recommend that students should make and investigate mathematical conjectures and learn how to generalise and extend problems by posing follow-up questions. Similarly, other national curricular documents plea for (more) instructional attention to the acquisition of problem-posing skills (e.g., Ministry of Education of Peoples' Republic of China, 2001; *Ontwikkelingsdoelen en eindtermen voor het gewoon basisonderwijs van het Ministerie van de Vlaamse Gemeenschap*, 1997).

Since the late eighties, there is also growing interest among researchers in problem posing (see e.g., Brown & Walter, 1993; English, 1998a; Kilpatrick, 1987; Silver, 1994). The most frequently cited motivation for curricular and instructional interest in problem posing is its perceived potential value in assisting students to become better problem solvers. To explore this potential value, several studies have been set up to investigate the relationship between word problem solving and word problem posing (e.g., Cai & Hwang, 2002; Ellerton, 1986; Silver & Cai, 1996). In these studies students were typically asked to generate one or more problems (sometimes of different levels of difficulty) starting from a given situational description, a picture, or a number sentence, and, afterwards, the quality of the mathematical problems generated by the students was compared with their problem-solving capacities.

Silver and Cai (1996), for instance, asked large groups of sixth- and seventh-grade students to pose three questions (that could be answered using the given information) based on the following brief written story-problem description: "Jerome, Elliot, and Arturo took turns driving home from a trip. Arturo drove 80 miles more than Elliot. Elliot drove twice as many miles as Jerome. Jerome drove 50 miles". The questions posed by the students were examined according to their solvability, linguistic and mathematical complexity, and these measures of problem posing were compared to students' performance on a problem-solving test involving eight mathematical problems from various mathematics content areas. It was found that students generated a large number of solvable mathematical problems, many of which were linguistically and mathematically complex, and that nearly half the students generated sets of closely related problems. It was also found that good problem solvers generated more mathematical problems and more complex problems than poor problem solvers did.

A more recent international comparative study by Cai and Hwang (2002) revealed a close relationship between word problem solving and word problem posing. A sample of Chinese sixth-grade students and a comparable sample of U.S. sixth-grade students were administered three pairs of problem-solving and problem-posing tasks. Each pair of problem-solving and problem-posing tasks involved one mathematical situation (e.g., the first three figures of an increasing square dot pattern consisting, respectively, of 9, 16, 25 dots). The problem-solving task for this situation included three (standard) word problems built around this situation, whereas the problem-posing task required students to generate one easy, one moderately difficult, and one difficult problem starting from the same situation. For Chinese students, the variety of problems posed was clearly associated with their problem-solving success; moreover, the complexity of the self-generated problems was positively associated with the use of abstract problem-solving strategies. For the U.S. sample, the relationship between the variety and type of problems posed and problem-solving success was much weaker. Cai and Hwang (2002) suggested that the stronger link between problem solving and problem posing for Chinese students might be attributable to the fact that the U.S. students used less abstract problem-solving strategies.

Besides ascertaining studies revealing the existence of a relationship between problem posing and solving, some design experiments have been realised wherein new instructional approaches have been designed, implemented, and evaluated, in which problem posing is incorporated into the mathematics curriculum and used as a vehicle to improve students' problem-solving ability (English, 1997a, 1997b; 1998a, 1998b; Rudnitsky, Etheredge, Freeman, & Gilbert, 1995; Verschaffel, De Corte, Lowyck, Dhert, & Vandeput, 2000). In general, these latter studies revealed that having students engage in some activities related to problem posing (e.g., making up word problems according to mathematical stories) may have a positive influence not only on their word problem-posing abilities but also on their problem-solving skills and their attitudes towards mathematical problem solving and mathematics in general.

Another topic that has attracted the attention of many researchers in mathematics education concerns the role of real-world knowledge and realistic considerations in pupils' solutions of arithmetic word problems. Since the nineties, several researchers have addressed this issue by carefully looking at pupils' approaches to, and solutions of, "non-standard" or "problematic" arithmetic word problems wherein – contrary to the traditional standard problems – the appropriate mathematical model or solution is neither obvious nor indisputable, at least if one seriously takes into account the realities of the context evoked by the problem statement (Cai & Silver, 1995; Greer, 1993; Silver, Shapiro, & Deutsch, 1993; Verschaffel, De Corte, & Lasure, 1994). By analysing pupils' reactions to these non-standard problems, these researchers provided strong empirical evidence that most elementary school children perceive school word problems as artificial, routine-based tasks that are unrelated to the real world, and, accordingly, approach these problems in a way that has little to do with genuine mathematical modelling and applied problem solving (see Van Dooren, Verschaffel, Greer, & De Bock, 2006; Verschaffel, Greer, & De Corte, 2000, for overviews of this research). More specifically, instead of going through the different phases of a genuine modelling process (understanding, modelling, analysis, interpretation, evaluation, and communication) they go through a superficial process whereby a particular mathematical model is triggered more or less automatically by certain conspicuous elements in the problem situation (e.g., certain key words in the problem statement), there is no serious attempt to understand and analyse the problem situation, and the result is immediately computed and communicated as the answer, without referring back to the original problem situation to verify that it is a meaningful response to the original question, or to check its reasonableness.

One of the most frequently studied types of non-routine problems in this line of research are the division-with-remainder (DWR) problems, i.e. problems wherein the dividend and the divisor are both integers and wherein the division results in a non-integer outcome that still needs to be interpreted and evaluated in relation to the real-world constraints of the problem setting. This kind of problem was used with a stratified sample of 13-year-olds in the *Third National Assessment of Educational Progress (NAEP)* in the U.S. (Carpenter, Lindquist, Matthews, & Silver, 1983): "An army bus holds 36 soldiers. If 1128 soldiers are being bussed to their training site, how many buses are needed?" Of about 70% of the students who correctly carried out the division 1128 by 36 to get a quotient of 31 and remainder of 12, only 23% (of the total number of students) gave the answer as 32 buses, 19% gave the answer as 31 buses, and 29% gave the answer as "31, remainder 12". A similar division problem appeared on the 1983 version of the *California Assessment Program (CAP) Mathematics Test for Grade 6*, and was answered correctly by about 35% of the sixth-graders in California (Silver et al., 1993). As in the NAEP assessment, most students erred by giving non-whole-number answers or rounding the outcome of the division to its nearest whole-number predecessor. Since then, numerous studies involving this type of problem have been done in different countries, basically leading to similar results and conclusions (for an overview see Verschaffel et al., 2000). In an early reflection upon these results, Hilton (1984, p. 8) asserted that:

> the separation of division from its context is an appalling feature of traditional drill arithmetic... the solution to the division problem 1000 ÷ 12 should depend on the context of the problem and not the grade of the student.

Inspired by these "dramatic" results on the above-mentioned NAEP item, and in line with Hilton's (1984) suggestion, Streefland (1988, p. 81) proposed the following problem-posing task:

> Invent stories belonging to the numerical problem "6394 divided by 12" such that the result is, respectively:

- 532
- 533
- 532 remainder 10
- 532.83 remainder 4
- 532.83333
- About 530.

However, Streefland himself never reported systematic findings or even anecdotal data on children's reactions to this nice problem-posing task presented in the context of an ascertaining study or a design experiment.

From the studies on problem posing, we can conclude that this activity has a potential value in assessing and improving children's problem-solving capacities. However, an important feature of the problem-posing research up to now is that it has investigated the relationship between problem posing and solving especially, and even almost exclusively, for standard word problems that can be unproblematically modelled by one ore more operations with the numbers given in the problem statement. Stated differently, no research investigated this relationship for problematic problem situations, wherein students have to use their commonsense knowledge and real-world experience when trying to model and solve the problem (Verschaffel et al., 2000). At the basis of the present study was the expectation that, especially for this kind of non-standard problems, looking at children's problem-posing processes and skills may have a great diagnostic value, because of the unfamiliar or non-routine nature of word problem posing (as opposed to the ritual scholastic activity of solving school word problems, which elicits (quasi-) automatised behaviour) and because of its potential to reveal modelling difficulties during the phases of the modelling cycle that are most interesting from a modelling perspective, namely the establishment of an appropriate link between the understanding of the problem situation and the development of a mathematical model (= modelling) and the interpretation of the result of the computational work in terms of the original problem situation (= interpretation).

RESEARCH QUESTIONS AND HYPOTHESES

Based on the above literature review and the results of a pilot study (Chen, Van Dooren, Chen, & Verschaffel, 2005), we made the following predictions. First, as in the previous studies on realistic mathematical modelling, we expected to find that upper elementary school children in Flanders would show great difficulties with solving such problems realistically. Second, these findings were expected to show up also in students' problem-posing performance, although we had no clear expectations about children's relative performance on the two tasks. On the one hand, it could be argued that, because of the unfamiliarity of the problem-posing task, performance on this task will be worse than on the parallel problem-solving task. On the other hand, because the problem-posing task confronted children with the fact that the same division can result in different responses (while this idea was left implicit and had to be discovered by the children themselves in the problem-solving task), it could be argued that performance on problem solving would be worse. Third, as in the studies on the relationship between solving and posing of standard word problems, we expected a significant positive relationship between students' ability to pose and solve non-standard problems. Finally, we wanted to assess the impact of a number of subject variables, such as pupils' age, mathematical ability, and gender, as well as of some task variables, namely order of test administration and interval between the two tests. With respect to the latter two task variables, we anticipated that children's performance on the problem-solving test would be better when they had to do this test after the problem-posing test, and that their performance on the problem-posing test would be better when they had to do this test after the problem-solving test, and that the transfer effect would be greater when the interval between the two tests was smaller.

METHOD

Participants

Participants were 245 children from two elementary schools in Flanders: 84 fourth graders (9-year-olds), 92 fifth graders (10-year-olds), and 69 sixth graders (11-year-olds). There was about an equal number of boys and girls in the sample and also in the three different grade levels. All children were administered a mathematics achievement test (Dudal, 2002). This test distinguishes five achievement levels ranging from level A to level E. Pupils with an A or B score were considered as mathematically strong, those with a C score as medium, and those with D or E as weak.

Materials

In the problem-posing task, students were instructed to generate three questions or stories. In the problem-solving task, they were asked to solve three problems that were closely related to the questions or stories to be generated. Besides producing a numerical answer, they were also explicitly asked to write down the solution process or some explanation for each problem-solving task.

Problem-posing (PP) task. Invent three story problems that belong to the numerical problem $100 \div 8 = ?$ such that the answer to the story problem is, respectively
(a) 13   (PP1)
(b) 12   (PP2)
(c) 12.5 (PP3).

Problem-solving (PS) task. Solve the following three problems and write down how you arrived at the answer:
(a) 100 children are being transported by minibuses to a summer camp at the seaside. Each minibus can hold a maximum of 8 children. How many minibuses are needed? (*answer: 13 buses*) (PS1)

(b) Grandfather gives his 6 grandchildren a box containing 80 balloons, which they share equally. How many balloons does each grandchild get? (*answer: 13 balloons*) (PS2)
(c) A tailor sold a large piece of cloth with a length of 50 meters. He wants to cut it into 4 pieces of the same length. How long is each piece? (*answer: 12.5 meters*) (PS3).

To minimise the possible role of specific number effects, we worked with two number clusters: $100 \div 8 = ?$ (see above examples) and $70 \div 4 = ?$ (*answer, respectively 18, 17 or 17.5*) in the PP task. For the same reason, we worked with two number clusters for each PS task: $100 \div 8 = ?$ (*answer: 13*) and $70 \div 4 = ?$ (*answer: 18*) for PS1, $80 \div 6 = ?$ (*answer: 13*) and $50 \div 4 = ?$ (*answer: 12*) for PS2, and $50 \div 4 = ?$ (*answer: 12.5*) and $100 \div 8 = ?$ (*answer: 12.5*) for PS3.

Procedure and Task Administration

The two tests were administered collectively in the context of a regular mathematics classroom activity.

For the PP test, the test administrator (the fourth author) extensively explained and showed the students what was expected from them. Students were first given a mathematical situation ("Pete has 10 apples, Ann has 6 apples") and asked to make up three relevant mathematical questions and, second, a numerical equation (76 + 28 = 104) and asked to generate different word problems that fit this equation. Examples of appropriate and inappropriate questions or problems were discussed with the whole class until all pupils understood the problem-posing instruction and also what would be considered as a correct question or word problem for a given situation or numerical expression.

Because of pupils' familiarity with word problem solving, instructions for the PS test were less extensive. Using a simple example of a typical word problem, the test administrator explained what was expected from the pupils, emphasising that if, for whatever reason, they could not answer a problem, they were invited to (try to) record the reason for their failure.

Afterwards, the teacher asked the students to do the PP or the PS test. Each test took at most 30 minutes. During the test administration, the experimenter herself checked very carefully whether all students also articulated and explained their responses.

In each of the three grade levels, about half of the pupils got the PP test first and the PS test second (PP-PS group), whereas the other half got these two tests in the reverse order (PS-PP group). Moreover, half of the pupils from the PP-PS and the PS-PP group got the two tests with an interval of only two days (short interval group) whereas for the other half the interval was almost one month (long interval group).

Data Coding

Pupils' answers to the three PS items were coded using a schema that was an elaboration of the classification schema developed by Verschaffel et al. (1994). The classification schema comprised 14 categories, which were, in a second stage, reduced to three general categories: realistic reaction, no reaction, other reaction.

Realistic reactions (RR) comprise all cases wherein a pupil either gave the (most) correct numerical response that also took into account the real-world aspects of the problem context, as well as cases wherein there was a clear indication that (s)he tried to take into account these real-world aspects, without, however, giving the mathematically and situationally (most) accurate numerical answer.

No reactions (NR) were all those cases wherein a pupil did not give a numerical response and did not give any further written comment that indicated that (s)he was aware of the realistic modelling difficulty that prevented him/her from answering the problem.

Other reactions (OR) were all other cases without any indication that the pupil was aware of the realistic modelling difficulty, for example mathematically correct but situationally inaccurate responses, computational errors, etc.

Here are examples of answers to PS1, illustrating the coding of answers as RR and OR.

Realistic reactions (RR)
- "100 ÷ 8 = 12.5, so 13 minibuses are needed" (situationally most appropriate numerical answer)
- "100 ÷ 8 = 12 remainder 4, so 12 minibuses are needed and something extra for the remaining children" (other answer that properly takes into account the problem situation)
- "100 ÷ 8 = 16.5, so 17 minibuses are needed" (technical error but situationally appropriate)
- "100 ÷ 8 = 12.5, I do not know how to answer this problem; my result is 12.5 but half buses do not exist" (no answer, but accompanied with a clear indication of an accurate situational interpretation).

Other reactions (OR)
- "100 ÷ 8 = 12.5, so 12.5 minibuses are needed" (mathematically correct but situationally inappropriate numerical answer)
- "100 ÷ 8 = 12.5, so 12 minibuses are needed" (other answer, that does not properly take into account the situation)
- "100 ÷ 8 = 16.5, so 16.5 minibuses are needed" (technical error and situationally inappropriate numerical answer)
- "100 x 8 = 800, so 800 minibuses are needed" (wrong-operation error, without any indication of a situationally appropriate interpretation).

Pupils' self-generated problems in reaction to the three PP items were coded using a schema that was an elaboration of the classification schema developed by De Corte and Verschaffel (1996). This elaborated schema comprised of 20 categories, which were, just as the categories of the PS coding schema, reduced to three main categories: realistic reaction, no reaction, and other reaction.

Realistic reactions (RR) comprise all cases wherein a pupil generated a mathematically and situationally accurate problem, but also those cases wherein the child posed another problem, an incomplete problem or even no problem at all, but expressed in whatever way clear awareness of the realistic modelling problem involved in the task.

No reactions (NR) were all those cases wherein a pupil did not generate any problem and also did not give any further explication that suggested awareness of the realistic modelling difficulty that prevented him/her from succeeding in the problem-posing task.

Other reactions (OR) were all remaining cases, including mathematically correct but situationally inaccurate problems, mathematically and situationally inaccurate problems, incomplete problems without any indication of awareness of the realistic modelling difficulty, etc.

Typical examples of student-generated problems for PP1, together with their code, are given below.

Realistic reactions
- "100 students take boats. One boat takes at most 8 students. How many boats are needed?" (mathematically and situationally accurate problem)
- "100 children need transportation to go to the theatre. They go by car. A car can hold 8 children. So, 13 cars are needed." (problem with an answer in stead of a question at the end, but providing clear evidence of a situationally correct interpretation)
- "Teacher Laura has 100 sweets and wants to divide them among her 8 pupils. How many sweets does each child get? Afterwards they all additionally get half of a sweet." (even though the problem cannot be simply be modelled by $100 \div 8 = ?$, it was scored as RR because of the pupil's clear and meaningful struggling with the realistic modelling complexity).

Other reactions
- "In the class of Teacher Tine there are $100 \div 8$ children. How many children are there in the class of Teacher Tine?" (besides the fact that the problem comprises an unacceptable computational command (namely $100 \div 8$), the situation does not call for rounding up to the next natural number (13)
- "A man buys 100 flowers. He wants to distribute them equally among his 8 grandchildren. How many flowers does each grandchild get?" (problem with an appropriate underlying mathematical model, namely $100 \div 8 = ?$, but leading to another response than the requested one, namely 12 instead of 13
- "100 children are participating in a running competition. 8 children fall during the competition. How many children reach the finish?" (problem leading to an inappropriate mathematical model, namely $100 - 8 = ?$)
- "The teacher asks Jan to make the following sum in the mathematics class: $100 \div 8 = ?$ Do you know the result?" (no real word problem, since the required

operation (100 ÷ 8 = ?) is simply given as a symbolic problem, without a "real context").

RESULTS

Results for the PS Task

Overall, the percentage of realistic reactions (RR) on the three PS items was 57%. As shown in Table 1, the percentages of RRs on the three PS items were, respectively, 44%, 71%, and 56%. So, the percentage of RRs in PS2 was somewhat more than that in PS1 and PS3, whereas the reverse was true for the other answers (ORs).

The finding that PS2 yielded more RRs than PS1 is in line with most previous studies showing higher percentages of realistic answers for the balloons item than for the buses item, although there are also a few studies that report opposite results (see Verschaffel et al., 2000). Moreover, we were somewhat surprised that PS3 did not yield more RRs, taking into account that, for this item, the outcome of the computation is at the same time the (correct) answer to the word problem (and, can, thus, according to our terminology, be considered as a "standard problem").

A more detailed look at the responses revealed that almost all RRs belonged to the subcategory of both mathematically and situationally accurate responses (for PS1, PS2, and PS3, respectively, 97%, 98%, and 95% of all RRs, and 97% overall). Of the "other responses" on PS1, PS2, and PS3, 57%, 41%, and 52% respectively, and 52% overall, were computationally correct but situationally inaccurate. So, about half of the ORs were the direct and clear result of a situationally incorrect interpretation of a correctly computed division with a remainder, whereas for the other half the role of the realistic modelling difficulty in the actual response to the word problem remained unclear.

Table 1. Percentages (and absolute numbers) of realistic reactions (RRs), no reactions (NRs), and other reactions (ORs) for the three problem-solving (PS) items

	PS1	PS2	PS3	Total
RR	44%	71%	56%	57%
	(107)	(173)	(138)	(418)
NR	2%	3%	4%	3%
	(5)	(7)	(9)	(21)
OR	54%	27%	40%	40%
	(133)	(65)	(98)	(296)

The results of Table 2, which show the percentage of pupils who succeeded in solving three, two, and one problem, indicate that the Flemish upper elementary school pupils performed rather weakly on these non-standard problems requiring realistic sense-making. Only a quarter of the students produced three situationally accurate answers or reacted three times in a way that reveals attention to the realistic modelling complexity involved in the problem.

Table 2. Percentages (and absolute numbers) of pupils who produced three, two, one, and zero realistic reactions (RRs) in the problem-solving (PS) task

3 RR	2 RR	1 RR	0 RR	Total
29%	28%	29%	14%	100%
(70)	(69)	(70)	(36)	(245)

Results for the PP Task

Table 3 shows the percentages of appropriate math stories for the three PP items. Overall, there were 27% RRs, which is considerably lower than 57% RRs for the corresponding PS task. As for the PS task, the number of children who gave no reaction at all (NRs) was small, meaning that the majority of the reactions belonged to the category of ORs.

Table 3. Percentages (and absolute numbers) of realistic reactions (RRs), no reactions (NRs), and other reactions (ORs) for the three problem-posing (PP) items

	PP1	PP2	PP3	Total
RR	13%	39%	31%	27%
	(31)	(95)	(76)	(202)
NR	6%	2%	7%	5%
	(15)	(6)	(16)	(37)
OR	81%	59%	62%	67%
	(199)	(144)	(153)	(496)

The PP1, PP2 and PP3 item elicited, respectively, 13%, 39%, and 31% realistic reactions (RR's). So, as for the PP task, the number of RRs for PP2 was considerably higher than for PP1, and was even somewhat higher than for PP3.

A closer look revealed that the percentages of RRs to PP1, PP2, and PP3 that were both mathematically and situationally accurate was, respectively, 22%, 65%, and 84% (overall percentage: 66%). Of the other subcategories of reactions that were coded as RRs, problems that were not (completely) accurate from a mathematical point of view but that showed that the pupil had struggled with the realistic modelling difficulty, were the most frequent category. For the PP1 item, such reactions were responsible for 77% of all RRs.

Of the ORs, problems that were mathematically correct but situationally inaccurate – such as generating the word problem "A man buys 100 flowers. He wants to distribute them equally among his 8 grandchildren. How many flowers does each grandchild get?" for PP1 – was the most frequent subcategory (28% overall; 33% for PP1, 21% for PP2, and 28% for PP3, respectively). Another subcategory that occurred almost as frequently was the construction of word problem that led to another mathematical outcome than the correct one or that involved other numbers as givens than the ones provided in the task, such as "There are 100 words written on the blackboard. The teachers wipes off 8 words. How many words are there still on the blackboard?" for PP2 (26% overall; 23%, 33%, and 25% for PP1, PP2, and PP3, respectively).

The results of Table 4, which show the percentage of pupils who succeeded in producing three, two, one, and none RRs to the problem-posing task, indicate that the Flemish pupils have great difficulties in posing word problems that do not simply require the generation of a problem situation that correctly matches a given number sentence but also demands a situationally accurate interpretation of the outcome. Only 6% of the students produced three realistic answers, which means that they either gave three times the most realistic response or demonstrated at least awareness of the realistic modelling complexity. Apparently, thinking of meaningful contexts that ask for rounding up, rounding down, and keeping as a decimal the outcome of a division with remainder, and distinguishing between these different contexts, is a very difficult task for children.

Table 4. Percentage (and absolute number) of pupils who produced three, two, one, and zero realistic reactions (RRs) in the problem-posing (PP) task

3 RR	2 RR	1 RR	0 RR	Total
6%	19%	26%	49%	100%
(15)	(46)	(65)	(119)	(245)

The Effect of Task and Subject Variables

Effect of type of task. The above-mentioned discussion of the results of the two kinds of tasks already revealed that the pupils performed considerably better on the PS task (57%) than the PP task (27%). A logistic regression analysis showed that the difference was statistically significant, $\chi^2(1) = 93.12$, $p < .01$, which was the case for each of the three tasks too, $\chi^2(1) = 60.17$, $p < .01$ for task 1, $\chi^2(1) = 51.56$, $p < .01$ for task 2, and $\chi^2(1) = 37.69$, $p < .01$ for task 3.

Effect of age. Percentages (and absolute numbers) of RRs of the fourth, fifth and sixth graders on the PS and PP tests are given in Table 5. The logistic regression analysis showed that, as expected, the percentage of RRs for PS increased with

Table 5. Percentages (and absolute numbers) of realistic reactions (RRs) of the fourth, fifth and sixth graders on the problem-solving (PS) and problem-posing (PP) tasks

	4th grade (n = 84)	5th grade (n = 92)	6th grade (n = 69)
PS	29% (74)	62% (172)	83% (172)
PP	17% (44)	27% (75)	40% (83)

age, $\chi^2(2) = 29.02$, $p < .01$. The contrast analysis shows that sixth graders performed better than fifth graders, $\chi^2(1) = 19.88$, $p < .01$, who in turn performed better than the fourth graders, $\chi^2(1) = 51.34$, $p < .01$.

On PP we also found a main effect of age, $\chi^2(2) = 13.02$, $p < .01$. Again, we found significantly better performances for sixth graders than for fifth graders, $\chi^2(1) = 5.45$, $p = .02$, and for fifth graders than for fourth graders, $\chi^2(1) = 4.53$, $p = .03$.

There also was an interaction effect between type of task and age, $\chi^2(1) = 12.39$, $p < .01$. The difference between PS and PP was significant in each grade, $\chi^2(1) = 23.37$, $p < .01$ for sixth grade, $\chi^2(1) = 20.49$, $p < .01$ for fifth grade, and $\chi^2(1) = 4.64$, $p = .03$ for fourth grade, but differences in percentage of RRs between PS and PP increased with grade (a difference in favour of PS of 12%, 35%, and 43% for fourth, fifth, and sixth graders, respectively), mainly due to the fact that, with age, PS performance grew considerably more than PP performance.

Effect of mathematical achievement. The results for mathematical achievement are given in Table 6. The logistic regression analysis revealed a significant effect of mathematical achievement on PS performance, $\chi^2(2) = 9.50$, $p = .01$. As expected, mathematically strong pupils produced more RRs on PS than pupils with a medium achievement level, $\chi^2(1) = 9.25$, $p < .01$, who, in their turn, performed better than their mathematically weaker peers, although not significantly, $\chi^2(1) = 3.10$, $p = .08$.

Table 6. Percentages (and absolute numbers) of realistic reactions (RRs) on the problem-solving (PS) and the problem-posing (PP) tasks for mathematically strong, medium, and weak pupils

	Mathematical achievement level		
	Strong ($n = 140$)	Medium ($n = 49$)	Weak ($n = 56$)
PS	68% (284)	49% (72)	37% (62)
PP	36% (151)	21% (31)	12% (20)

As far as PP is concerned, the logistic regression analysis revealed also a significant effect of mathematical achievement, $\chi^2(2) = 20.30$, $p < .01$, again with mathematically strong pupils producing more RRs than mathematically medium ones, $\chi^2(1) = 10.26$, $p < .01$; the difference between this group and the weaker ones was statistically not significant, $\chi^2(1) = 3.39$, $p = .07$. Finally, there was no significant interaction effect between type of task and mathematical achievement.

The finding that realistic problem-solving and problem-posing performance is related to mathematical achievement in combination with the finding that there was an overrepresentation of mathematically strong pupils in our sample, implies that our results concerning Flemish upper elementary school pupils performance in solving and posing DWR problems realistically are to some extent an overestimation of their actual skills.

Effect of gender. Given that some previous studies have suggested that gender might affect pupils' problem-solving and/or problem-posing competence (Leder, 1992) and/or have an impact on their disposition towards realistic mathematical modelling (Verschaffel, 2002), we also analysed the effect of that factor (see Table 7). Even though the performance of the boys was somewhat better on both tasks, we found no statistically significant effect of gender on PS, $\chi^2(1) = 0.02$, $p = .89$, or on PP, $\chi^2(1) = 0.61$, $p = .43$. Also the interaction of gender and mathematical achievement level was not significant either for PS, $\chi^2(2) = 2.42$, $p = .30$, or for PP, $\chi^2(2) = 1.71$, $p = .43$, indicating that gender effects were absent both for the stronger, and for the medium and weaker pupils.

Table 7. *Percentages (and absolute numbers) of realistic reactions (RRs) on the problem-solving (PS) and problem-posing (PP) tasks according to gender*

	Boys (n = 120)	Girls (n = 125)
PS	61% (219)	53% (199)
PP	29% (106)	26% (96)

Effect of order. As explained in the Methods section, about half of the pupils got the PP test first and the PS test second (PP-PS group), whereas the other half got these two tests in the reverse order (PS-PP group). Percentages (and absolute numbers) of RRs on PS and PP for both groups of pupils (PP-PS and PS-PP) are given in Table 8.

Table 8. *Percentages (and absolute numbers) of realistic reactions (RRs) on the problem-solving (PS) and the problem-posing (PP) tasks for the pupils from the PS-PP and the PP-PS groups*

	PP-PS group (n = 95)	PS-PP group (n = 150)
PS	59% (168)	56% (250)
PP	29% (83)	26% (119)

The expectation was that the pupils from the PP-PS group would perform better on the PS task than those from the PS-PP group. Similarly, we expected the pupils from the PP-PS group would perform weaker on the PP task than those from the PS-PP group. As Table 8 shows, however, the differences were small and they were not statistically significant, $\chi^2(1) = 0.00$, $p = .95$ for PS performance, and $\chi^2(1) = 0.64$, $p = .42$ for PP performance. So, unexpectedly, for neither of the tasks was there a (positive) transfer effect from one task to the other.

Effect of magnitude of time interval between the two tests. We also experimentally manipulated the interval between the two tests (i.e. a short versus a long interval, respectively of two days versus three weeks). Although the percentages of RRs on PS were somewhat higher on the delayed tests for both the PS test (61% versus 57%) and the PP test (30% versus 21%), neither of these differences was statistically significant, $\chi^2(1) = 0.62$, $p = .43$ for PS and $\chi^2(1) = 2.86$, $p = .09$ for PP.

Relation Between Performance on PS and PP

The results of the overall comparison between pupils' performances on the two kinds of tasks are given in Table 9. There was a significant relationship between the two variables, indicating that students with a higher global score on the three PP tasks performed better on the three PS tasks than pupils with a lower score (*Spearman* $\rho = 0.34$, $p < .01$).

Table 9. *Distribution of pupils according to the number of realistic reactions (RRs) on the problem-solving (PS) and the problem-posing (PP) tasks*

		0 RR	1 RR	PP 2 RR	3 RR	Total
PS	0 RR	27	7	2	0	36
	1 RR	40	18	8	4	70
	2 RR	32	22	12	3	69
	3 RR	20	18	24	8	70
	Total	119	65	46	15	245

Finally, we also analysed the relationship between PS and PP at the item level. This analysis revealed that the general significant correlation was also found for each of the three items, although correlations were quite small (0.18, 0.15, and 0.23 for task 1, 2, and 3 respectively).

GENERAL DISCUSSION

Recent research has documented a close relationship between problem posing and problem solving in (elementary) arithmetic. However, most studies have investigated the relationship between problem posing and problem solving only by means of standard problem situations without realistic modelling complexities. The present study aimed at filling that gap by investigating this relationship for non-standard problem situations, and, more particularly, division-with-remainder problem (DWR) situations, which have elicited already quite a lot of problem-solving research in the past, but, until recently, were not subjected to a systematic analysis from a problem-posing perspective.

Groups of fourth, fifth, and sixth grade pupils from elementary schools in Flanders were administered a set of 3 DWR-items both in a problem-solving (PS) and a problem-posing (PP) task setting. The analysis focused on (a) the realistic nature of pupils' reactions to both kinds of tasks, (b) the impact of various subject and task variables on pupils' performance, and (c) the relationship between performances on the two types of tasks.

First, pupils' rather weak overall performance on the PS task, and the finding that this relatively weak performance was to a large extent due to the fact that they provided a lot of mathematically correct but situationally inappropriate responses, largely confirmed the conclusion from previous research with DWR-problems (for an overview see Verschaffel et al., 2000), namely that students have great difficulty with problem situations about division that require the activation of realistic considerations and sense-making to give a proper interpretation of a non-integer quotient. Complementary to that previous research, our results indicate that these problems with realistic modelling not only apply to DWR problems for which the situationally most reasonable answer is the whole number that is next or previous to the computational outcome of the division, as was found in previous studies, but also to DWR problems with the decimal number that directly results from the calculation as their situationally most appropriate response.

Second, our study yielded further evidence for upper elementary school pupils' difficulties with realistic mathematical modelling of school word problems by showing that they perform weakly not only when having to *solve* word problems that demand realistic interpretations, but also when they have to *pose* such problems starting from given divisions requiring certain numerical responses. Actually, pupils' performance on this problem-posing task was even considerably worse than for the problem-solving task – not only in general terms but also for each of the three items separately. The finding that children in general also performed weakly and behaved unrealistically on the unfamiliar and challenging problem-posing task suggests that pupils' tendency to neglect their real-world knowledge when doing mathematical modelling is not simply due to their lack of alertness or mindfulness when doing (seemingly) routine word problems, but is (also) caused by genuine cognitive difficulties with flexibly switching between the mathematical operation of division and real-world situations that can be modelled by it. However, the results for the PP test also revealed that pupils also made a lot of other errors that were not directly due to realistic modelling difficulties but rather to their unfamiliarity with problem posing as such.

Third, the analysis of the effects of the different subject and task variables revealed that the ability to properly take into account real-world considerations when solving or generating DWR-problems increased, as expected, with age and mathematical achievement level. On the other hand, no gender effect was found. Neither did we find a (positive) transfer effect of the solution of either task towards the other task, not even among those pupils who got the second task only a few days after the first one.

As far as the relationship between problem posing and problem solving is concerned, the integrated and comparative analysis of the two kinds of data revealed that pupils' problem-solving performance was significantly correlated with their problem-posing performance. However, the correlation was not high, mostly because there were many pupils who solved realistically one or more items without generating a situationally accurate problem themselves or vice versa.

From a methodological point of view, the present study suggests that problem posing can be a valuable research method to shed light on certain (problematic) aspects of pupils' (realistic) mathematical modelling. By somehow starting at the opposite side of the modelling cycle (Verschaffel et al., 2000) and confronting pupils with a given mathematical model and asking them to generate a real-world situation that matches that model – instead of giving them the more familiar task of formulating a mathematical model that fits with a given problem situation – and by comparing pupils' performances and difficulties for the two kinds of modelling tasks, one can shed new light on these skills and processes. In particular, the fact that problem posing is an unfamiliar, challenging, open-ended task that invites pupils more strongly to get highly involved in the task and to activate all their cognitive efforts than in a traditional word problem-solving task, may help to test the importance of certain hypothetical explanations for pupils' tendency to neglect real-world knowledge and realistic considerations when doing school word problems, such as the explanation that they only behave unrealistically because of a lack of attention and motivation.

Finally, from an educational perspective, even though our study was an ascertaining study and, therefore, does not yield data that demonstrate the instructional value of problem posing, it provides support to Streefland's (1988) claim that the problem-posing task he invented and that was quoted at the beginning of this chapter, may have a great instructional potential to help pupils become aware of the fact that mathematical modelling is not a simple and straightforward process, and, more particularly, that the outcome of computational work cannot immediately and uncritically be considered as *the* (numerical) response to a mathematical application problem, but always needs to be interpreted and evaluated in relation to the original problem situation, taking into the real-world constraints of that situation. In our own design experiments about realistic modelling in general (Verschaffel & De Corte, 1997; Verschaffel et al., 1999), we have had some positive experience with the problem-posing tasks that were used in the present study and also found some empirical evidence that upper elementary school children are better at meaningfully responding to DWR-problems after they have been involved in this problem-posing activity. However, more systematic and focused intervention studies are needed to assess the relative merits of problem posing compared to interventions that are solely based on problem-solving activities.

ACKNOWLEDGEMENT

This research was partially supported by Grant GOA 2006/01 "Developing adaptive expertise in mathematics education" from the Research Fund KULeuven, Belgium.

REFERENCES

Brown, S. I., & Walter, M. I. (Eds.). (1993). *Problem posing: Reflections and applications.* Hillsdale, NJ: Erlbaum.
Cai, J., & Hwang, S. (2002). Generalized and generative thinking in U.S. and Chinese students' mathematical problem solving and problem posing. *Journal of Mathematical Behavior, 21,* 401–421.
Cai, J., & Silver, E. A. (1995). Solution processes and interpretations of solutions in solving division-with-remainder story problems: Do Chinese and U.S. students have similar difficulties? *Journal for Research in Mathematics Education, 26,* 491–497.
Carpenter, T. P., Lindquist, M. M., Matthews, W., & Silver, E. A. (1983). Results of the third NAEP mathematics assessment: Secondary school. *Mathematics Teacher, 76,* 652–659.
Chen, L., Van Dooren, W., Chen, Q., & Verschaffel, L. (2005). The relationship between posing and solving division with remainder problems among Chinese elementary school children. *Mediterranean Journal for Research in Mathematics Education, 4*(2), 85–109.
De Corte, E., & Verschaffel, L. (1996). An empirical test of the impact of operations intuitive models of operations on solving word problems with a multiplicative structure. *Learning and Instruction, 6,* 219–242.
Dudal, P. (2002). *Leerlingvolgsysteem Wiskunde: Toetsen 4 – Basisboek* [Mathematics Achievement Tests: Tests for Grade 4 – Basic Book.]. Antwerpen, Belgium/Apeldoorn, The Netherlands: VCLB & Garant.
Ellerton, N. F. (1986). Children's made-up mathematics problems: A new perspective on talented mathematicians. *Educational Studies in Mathematics, 17,* 261–271.
English, L. D. (1997a). The development of fifth-grade children's problem-posing abilities. *Educational Studies in Mathematics, 34,* 183–217.
English, L. D. (1997b). Promoting a problem posing classroom. *Teaching Children Mathematics, 4,* 172–178.
English, L. D. (1998a). Children's problem posing within formal and informal contexts. *Journal for Research in Mathematics Education, 29,* 83–106.
English, L. D. (1998b). *Problem posing in middle school classrooms.* Paper presented at the annual meeting of the American Educational Research Association, San Diego, CA.
Greer, B. (1993). The modelling perspective on wor(l)d problems. *Journal of Mathematical Behavior, 12,* 239–250.
Hilton, P. (1984). Current trends in mathematics and future trends in mathematics education. *For the Learning of Mathematics, 4*(1), 2–8.
Kilpatrick, J. (1987). Problem formulating: Where do good problems come from? In A. H. Schoenfeld (Ed.), *Cognitive science and mathematics education* (pp.123–147). Hillsdale, NJ: Erlbaum.
Leder, G. (1992). Mathematics and gender: Changing perspectives. In D. A. Grouws (Ed.), *Handbook of research on mathematics teaching and learning* (pp. 597–622). New York: Macmillan.
Ministry of Education of Peoples' Republic of China (NCSM). (2001). *Chinese National Curriculum Standards on Mathematics.* Beijing, China: Beijing Normal University Publishing House.
National Council of Teachers of Mathematics. (2000). *Principles and standards for school mathematics.* Reston, VA: NCTM.
Ontwikkelingsdoelen en eindtermen. Informatiemap voor de onderwijspraktijk. Gewoon basisonderwijs [Standards. Documentation for practitioners. Elementary education]. (1998). Brussel: Ministerie van de Vlaamse Gemeenschap, Departement Onderwijs, Afdeling Informatie en Documentatie.
Rudnitsky, A., Etheredge, S., Freeman, S., & Gilbert, T. (1995). Learning to solve addition and subtraction word problems through a structure-plus-writing approach. *Journal for Research in Mathematics Education, 26,* 467–486.
Silver, E. A. (1994). On mathematical problem posing. *For the Learning of Mathematics, 14*(1), 19–28.
Silver, E. A., & Cai, J. (1996). An analysis of arithmetic problem posing by middle school students. *Journal for Research in Mathematics Education, 27,* 521–539.
Silver, E. A., Shapiro, L. J., & Deutsch, A. (1993). Sense making and the solution of division problems involving remainders: An examination of middle school students' solution processes and their interpretations of solutions. *Journal for Research in Mathematics Education, 24,* 117–135.
Streefland, L. (1988). Reconstructive learning. In A. Borbas (Ed.), *Proceedings of the twelfth international conference for the Psychology of Mathematics Education* (Vol. 1, pp. 75–91). Veszprem, Hungary: OOK Printing House.

Van Dooren, W., Verschaffel, L., Greer, B., & De Bock, D. (2006). Modelling for life: Developing adaptive expertise in mathematical modelling from an early age. In L. Verschaffel, F. Dochy, M. Boekaerts & S. Vosniadou (Eds.), *Instructional psychology: Past, present and future trends* (pp. 91–112). Oxford, U.K.: Elsevier.

Verschaffel, L. (2002). Taking the modeling perspective seriously at the elementary school level: Promises and pitfalls (Plenary lecture). In A. Cockburn & E. Nardi (Eds.), *Proceedings of the 26th annual conference of the International Group for the Psychology of Mathematics Education* (Vol. 1, pp. 64–82). School of Education and Professional Development, University of East Anglia, UK.

Verschaffel, L., & De Corte, E. (1997). Teaching realistic mathematical modeling in the elementary school. A teaching experiment with fifth graders. *Journal for Research in Mathematics Education, 28,* 577–601.

Verschaffel, L., De Corte, E., & Lasure, S. (1994). Realistic considerations in mathematical modeling of school arithmetic word problems. *Learning and Instruction, 4,* 273–294.

Verschaffel, L., De Corte, E., Lasure, S., Van Vaerenbergh, G., Bogaerts, H., & Ratinckx, E. (1999). Design and evaluation of a learning environment for mathematical modeling and problem solving in upper elementary school children. *Mathematical Thinking and Learning, 1,* 195–230.

Verschaffel, L., De Corte, E., Lowyck, J., Dhert, S., & Vandeput, L. (2000). *Supporting mathematical problem solving and posing in upper elementary school children by means of Knowledge Forum.* Deliverable of project No. 2017 CL-Net: Computer Supported Collaborative Learning Networks in Primary and Secondary Education.

Verschaffel, L., Greer, B., & De Corte, E. (2000). *Making sense of word problems.* Lisse, The Netherlands: Swets & Zeitlinger.

Lieven Verschaffel
Centre for Instructional Psychology and Technology
Katholieke Universiteit Leuven
Belgium

Wim Van Dooren
Centre for Instructional Psychology and Technology
Katholieke Universiteit Leuven
Belgium

Limin Chen
College of Teachers' Professional Development
Shenyang Normal University
China

Katrien Stessens
Centre for Instructional Psychology and Technology
Katholieke Universiteit Leuven
Belgium

ZIQIANG XIN

8. REALISTIC PROBLEM SOLVING IN CHINA

Students' Performance, Interventions, and Learning Settings

INTRODUCTION

Many studies have consistently documented (Cai, 2007; Fan, Wong, Cai, & Li, 2004; Stevenson et al., 1990) that Chinese students outperformed their counterparts in Western countries (e.g., United States) in mathematics achievement. This phenomenon has stirred experts' and teachers' desires for further exploration (Cai, 2007; Moy & Peverly, 2005). In the past decades, Verschaffel, Greer, and others (Greer, 1993; Verschaffel, De Corte, & Lasure, 1994, 1999) have done seminal work on students' solutions of word problems that are problematic from a realistic point of view (so-called P-items). In this chapter I will address the question how Chinese students perform on these P-items. I will answer this question by reviewing and discussing the available research, especially ours, on Chinese students' realistic problem solving and how it is influenced by prevailing and alternative instructional settings.

BACKGROUND: FOCUSING ON REALISTIC MATHEMATICS IN CHINA

Similar to the situation in which many Western students have been challenged by the famous "shepherd's age" problem (e.g., *There are 125 sheep and 5 dogs in a flock. How old is the shepherd?*') (Greer, 1997; Nesher, 1980), in China, children are often confronted with word problems such as: *There were 5 birds on a tree. If one bird was shot down by a hunter, how many birds are left?* Most Chinese young children would answer "4", as they normally do in the classroom. Nevertheless, a more realistic answer would be "none, because all of the other birds would be frightened away by the sound of the shot".

By contrast with standard problems (S-problems) mostly used in school mathematical education, the above problems are examples of problematic problems (P-problems) (Verschaffel et al., 1994). Successful solutions to these P-problems not only require a mastery of basic arithmetic operations and computations, but also call for real-world knowledge and real-life experiences, since these problems can not be properly solved by means of straightforward arithmetic calculations with the given numbers.

An increasing number of Western scholars have critically argued that current school instruction given for arithmetic word problems is likely to develop in children a tendency to exclude real-world knowledge and realistic considerations from their solution processes (Cooper & Harries, 2003, 2005; Greer, 1993, 1997; Mayer,

L. Verschaffel et al. (eds.), *Words and Worlds: Modelling Verbal Descriptions of Situations, 161–176.*
© *2009 Sense Publishers. All rights reserved.*

2004; Verschaffel et al., 1994, 1999; Yoshida, Verschaffel, & De Corte, 1997). For many children in elementary school, emphasis has been put on syntax and arithmetic rules rather than treating the problem statement as a description of some real-world situation to be modelled mathematically. As a result, some children perform well on S-problems but fail on the parallel P-items that additionally require considerations of real world knowledge. How about Chinese children's performance on these P-problems? In fact, realistic mathematical teaching has been emphasised by some educational theorists for a long time in China, but up to now there has been only limited rigorous empirical research on realistic problem solving.

The reflection and research on realistic problem solving in China is partly rooted in the movement of Realistic Mathematics Education starting from the 1970s in the Netherlands (Van den Heuvel-Panhuizen, 2000). As a leading figure of that movement, Freudenthal (1968, 1991) suggested that the overall goal of mathematics education is that students must be able to use their mathematical understanding and tools to solve problems. This goal implies that they should learn "mathematics so as to be useful" (Freudenthal, 1968). During the teaching process, mathematics must be connected to reality, stay close to children's experience, and be relevant to society. In brief, just as mathematics arose from the mathematisation of reality, so must learning mathematics also originate from mathematising reality. Freudenthal's view has directly affected Chinese mathematics education to some degree. In 1987, Freudenthal visited some universities in Beijing and Shanghai and presented a series of lectures and seminars (see Freudenthal, 1991). Thenceforward, many Chinese educators (Sun, 1995; Zhang, 2005; Zhao, 2006) have become interested in his view of realistic mathematics education.

The research on realistic problem solving by Greer (1993), Verschaffel et al. (1994, 1999), and others has affected and strengthened a new wave of emphasis on realistic mathematics education worldwide, including China. Lots of Chinese educators (Chen, Verschaffel, & Chen, 2006; Cheng, Gu, & Wang, 2001; Wong, 1997; Xin, 2006; Xin & Zhang, 2005) have participated in the discussion on realistic mathematics, but, so far, little empirical research on students' realistic problem solving has been conducted in China (for exceptions, see Liu & Chen, 2003; Xin, Lin, Zhang, & Yan, 2007; Xin & Zhang, 2009; Xu, 2006, 2007). Based on these investigations, the level of Chinese students' realistic solving of P-problems will be discussed next.

CHINESE CHILDREN'S PERFORMANCE: REALISTIC CONSIDERATIONS AND ANSWERS

The above-mentioned empirical research has revealed that Chinese children also have a strong tendency to exclude real-world knowledge and realistic considerations from their solution processes to P-problems. For example, in an early study (Liu & Chen, 2003) with a sample of 148 students from 4th and 6th grade in Beijing, it was found that only one fourth (26%) of the students' solutions of problems were from a realistic point of view (attending to realistic considerations), whereas half (48%) of the responses showed a strong tendency to exclude real world knowledge (in the rest of the cases, no answer was given). The testing material in this study consisted of 12 P-problems, namely the ten P-items taken from Verschaffel et al. (1994) and two others from Greer (1997). However, Liu and Chen (2003) did not examine the participants' performance on standard word problems simultaneously. Moreover, because the test items used in this research differed partly from those employed in the original studies, it was difficult to compare and explain their findings. In addition, in this study only "realistic considerations" were examined as an index of children's ability of solving P-problem, whereas in fact children's performance can be differentiated into "realistic considerations" and "correct answers", because not all children who can give realistic considerations can also reach correct solutions.

Given the aforementioned limitations, we (Xin et al., 2007; Xin & Zhang, 2005) carefully translated the complete set of ten P-items and their matched S-items developed by Verschaffel et al. (1994), and used them to investigate Chinese elementary school children's ability to solve word problems in a realistic way. So, each problem pair consisted of an S-problem asking for the straightforward application of one or more arithmetic operations with the given numbers and a parallel P-problem in which the mathematical modelling assumptions were problematic, at least if one seriously takes into account the realities of the context called up by the problem statement. The ten P-problems are listed here.

(1) Wang Ming and Yang Wen go to the same school. Wang Ming lives at a distance of 17 km from the school and Yang Wen at 8 km. How far do Wang Ming and Yang Wen live from each other?
(2) Grandfather gives his 4 grandchildren a box containing 18 balloons, which they share equally. How many balloons does each grandchild get?
(3) Xiao Ping was born in 1978. Now it's 2004. How old is he?
(4) Mr. Lee wants to have a rope long enough to stretch between two poles 12 m apart, but he has only pieces of rope 1.5 m long. How many of these pieces would he need to tie together to stretch between the poles?
(5) This flask is being filled from a tap at a constant rate. If the depth of the water is 4 cm after 10 seconds, how deep will it be after 30 seconds?

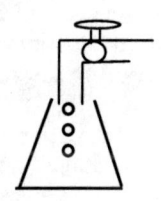

(6) Xiao Qiang has 5 friends and Xiao Jun has 6 friends. Xiao Qiang and Xiao Jun decide to give a party together. They invite all their friends. All friends are present. How many friends are there at the party?
(7) Mr. Lee has bought 4 planks of 2.5 m each. How many planks of 1 m can he get out of these planks?
(8) What will be the temperature of water in a container if you pour 1 cup of water at 80°C and 1 cup of water at 40°C into it?

(9) 450 soldiers must be bussed to their training site. Each army bus can hold 36 soldiers. How many buses are needed?

(10) Xiao Ming's best time to run 100 m is 17 seconds. How long will it take him to run 1 km?

As in the study by Verschaffel et al. (1994), for each problem, children were required to report how they arrived at the answer and then write down both the computations and the final answer in the "answer area". In addition, they were asked to fill in the "comments area", expressing their feelings or explaining their difficulties if they were not able to solve the problem.

Referring to Verschaffel et al. (1994), children's reactions to P-problems can be divided into "realistic considerations" and "correct answers". "Realistic considerations" refer to any trace (either in the answer area or the comments area) of hesitancy to perform simple and straightforward mathematical operations, attributable to the activation and use of real-world knowledge. For example, all cases such as children's criticism of the problem statement, supplementation of the answer with certain qualifying comments, or indication that there is no simple or single answer, would be coded as "realistic considerations".

"Correct answers" were encoded only for data in the answer area. The realistic answer to "birthday party problem", for example, is that Xiao Qiang and Xiao Jun have 11 friends *at most* present at the party, because they may have common friends. The realistic answer to "mixture problem" is that the water temperature is between 40°C and 80°C. Because the mathematical modelling assumptions of most of this kind of problems were problematic, there existed not one but a certain range of possible solutions to a P-problem. If children could give the range of solutions, their answers were regarded to be correct.

Furthermore, the coding of information in the "answer area" and "comments area" partially overlapped. Concretely, "realistic considerations" can be coded according to information in the comments area (even when an incorrect or no answer was given according to the information in the answer area), whereas "correct answers" (in the answer area) must be realistic answers resulting from realistic considerations and effective use of real-world knowledge elicited by the problem statement. That is to say, the student's optimal performance on a P-problem is generating a correct answer, i.e., a realistic answer, that is based on a realistic consideration. A "realistic consideration" reflects the activation of real-world knowledge, but it is anyhow only a step in the direction of a correct solution of a P-problem. By distinguishing "realistic considerations" and "correct answers", it is possible to achieve a fine-grained understanding of the specific levels of "realism" children could reach in their attempts to solve P-problems.

Two hundred and two children from an ordinary primary school in Beijing participated in the study: 48 4th graders (mean age: 10.15 years), 89 5th graders (mean age: 11.09 years), and 65 6th graders (mean age: 11.91 years). As expected, the results showed that the children performed well on the standard problems (84% correct). The results further showed that only 37% of the responses took realistic considerations into account on the P-items and that even fewer of the responses (18%) resulted in realistic answers. Though the results for the P-items were considerably higher than what has been reported in Western studies (Greer, 1993;

Verschaffel et al., 1994; for an overview see Verschaffel, Greer, & De Corte, 2000), these results do not meet the overall objective of mathematics education. So, it can be concluded, based on the above results, that there is also an overt lack of ability in solving P-problems among Chinese primary school children.

Later, we (Xin & Zhang, 2009) used the same testing materials to investigate another similar sample and the results confirmed this conclusion. One hundred and nineteen children from an ordinary primary school in Weifang City, in East China's Shandong Province, participated in the study. This sample consisted of 34 children of grade 4, 43 children of grade 5, and 42 children of grade 6. Mean ages of the children in each grade were 10.59, 11.49 and 12.24 respectively. The results showed that 88% of the answers to the S-problems were correct, while only 27% of the P-items elicited realistic considerations and only 22% yielded correct answers.

Both of the above studies have shown a great difference between the percentages of correct answers and realistic considerations. This difference pattern has also been supported by a study by Xu (2006) on 207 6th graders in a city located in East China's Zhejiang Province. Her results, using similar testing materials (actually, she used only 7 pairs of P- and S-problems from the study by Verschaffel et al., 1994) showed the percentage of realistic considerations was 37%, which was again much higher than the percentage of correct answers (27%).

To sum up, it can be concluded that Chinese children in elementary schools, like their Western peers, demonstrate a strong tendency of neglecting realistic demands when solving P-problems.

Moreover, children's performance on P-problems differed for different age groups. Our research (Xin et al., 2007; Xin & Zhang, 2009) has shown differences in abilities to solve P-problems among the different age groups involved. In the study of Xin et al. (2007), the percentages of children in grade 4, 5 and 6 offering realistic considerations to the P-problems were 22%, 35% and 51% respectively, and the percentages of correct answers were 10%, 17% and 26%. The pattern of grade differences in the study of Xin and Zhang (2009) was quite similar: the percentages for each grade were 17%, 26%, 36% for realistic considerations, and 17%, 20%, 28% for correct answers. This finding could be attributed to the accumulation of children's everyday experiences and knowledge of mathematics and other relevant subjects. Taking the "temperature problem" as an example, successful solutions require some basic knowledge of physics, which Chinese children start to learn in the first year of junior high school, making the problem difficult for children in primary school. Another factor to take into account is that children are inclined to make reference to their everyday experiences when their classroom experiences are scarce or insufficient. This is reflected in their comments such as "I never tried this in classroom", "I never conducted this kind of experiment", or "to solve this problem calls for common sense". It could be assumed that the lack of knowledge and experiences gained in classroom, to a certain degree, made these children seek solutions from a more realistic perspective. With the increase of everyday experiences and common sense, children's abilities of realistic problem solving improved gradually.

Furthermore, it is notable that word problem characteristics have an effect on children's realistic solving. Consistent with the existing literature (Yoshida et al.,

1997), P-problems with different content were found to have quite distinct levels of difficulty evidenced by the different percentages of correct answers and realistic considerations (Xin et al., 2007). If judged by the percentage of realistic considerations made by the children, the most difficult problem in Xin et al.'s (2007) study was the date of birth item, and the least difficult was the balloon problem. The complete list of P-problems in order of descending number of realistic considerations is: balloon (70%), soldiers (69%), home distance (48%), "birthday party" (44%), "mixed temperature" (43%), "water depth" (27%), running time (26%), planks (17%), rope (16%) and date of birth (10%). Therefore, making realistic considerations has much to do with the characteristics of the problems themselves. Moreover, the nature of the realistic considerations that need to be taken into account also varies considerably among the P-problems.

Solving P-problems requires children to go through a series of cognitive steps, such as representing the problem statement, establishing a mathematical model, choosing a solution and evaluating the outcome. For different P-problems, children might be required to take realistic considerations into account at different stages (Verschaffel et al., 2000). Take the birthday party problem as an example. Children are required to take realistic considerations into consideration at the initial stage of representing the problem statement, for they can not arrive at a correct answer unless they have a good understanding of friendship. Other problems, however, require children to use real-world knowledge at the situational model establishing stage (e.g., the problems about rope, plank, and running time), or even only at the outcome evaluating stage (e.g., the problems about the balloons and soldiers). As was found in Western research (see Verschaffel et al., 2000), our study (Xin et al., 2007) has indicated that children performed better when they had to behave realistically at the outcome evaluating stage than at the beginning representation and model establishing stages, at least for these samples of P-problems.

IMPROVING CHILDREN'S PERFORMANCE: POSSIBLE INTERVENTIONS

As mentioned above, contrasted to the solution of S-problems, children demonstrate a strong tendency to exclude real-world knowledge and realistic considerations from their solution processes when solving P-problems. So it is necessary to seek some effective methods to improve students' performance on this latter type of problems. It has been documented by some pilot studies that pre-test written or verbal warnings aimed at improving the disposition towards more realistic arithmetic word problem solving did not produce the expected positive effect (Reusser & Stebler, 1997; Yoshida et al., 1997). It was argued that warning instructions are not effective enough to change the established stereotyped response patterns in the children's cognitive structure (Yoshida et al., 1997). Another type of pre-test instructional intervention termed "process-oriented instruction" was proposed in one of our experimental studies (Xin et al., 2007), which aimed to help children not only notice problem situations that were problematic from a realistic point of view, but also consider the (in)appropriateness of applying straightforward arithmetic operations in their solutions. The study involved a sample of 60 children (male: 32, female: 28; 4th graders: 33, 5th graders: 27) and was conducted to examine whether such a "process-oriented instruction", was more helpful than the "warning instruction" for the activation of realistic considerations in children's realistic word problem solving.

In this study, we also administered the 10 pairs of S- and P-problems (see above), but we added two pre-test interventions, namely a "warning instruction" versus a "process-oriented instruction" printed on the top of the test sheets. In the "warning instruction", as in the studies by Reusser and Stebler (1997) and Yoshida et al. (1997), the children were told firstly that "some of the problems are not as easy as they seem to be", whereas in the "process-oriented instruction", they were asked at the beginning of the test to consider the following two questions that would be helpful to their solutions: (1) What are the real-life situations behind the problem statements? (2) Is it appropriate to solve these problems by using straightforward arithmetic operations? Participants were asked to read the instructions before they began solving the problems. The two tests with different instructions were administered collectively and the test papers were randomly distributed to the participants. In the end, 28 test papers (two pupils dropped out) with warning instruction and 30 test papers with process-oriented instruction were available for analysis.

The results of the study (Xin et al., 2007) showed that the difference in the percentages of realistic considerations reached marginal significance between the two instructions (warning vs. process-oriented) (21% vs. 28%, $z = 1.92$, $p = 0.055$). However, no significant difference was found in the use of correct answers (17% vs. 20%, $z = 0.94$, $p > 0.05$).

In summary, the warning instruction was arguably less effective because it could not change children's existing stereotyped response patterns (Greer, 1997), which are very resistant to change. Examining children's word problem solving behaviours in the classroom, we found that they often started by working out a certain type of computation based on the information embedded in the statements (e.g., cue words, numbers etc.). By doing so, they only activated the model for the S-problems as well as the relevant operations and strategies; however, their realistic world knowledge and experiences were apparently not activated and used in this process. As Gravemeijer (1997) stated, children's problem solving behaviours, *like their everyday automatic behaviours,* are the result of adaptation, in this case to the classroom environment.

By contrast, process-oriented instruction, calling for mindful processing, not only partially activated children's real-world knowledge and experience, but also, at least to some extent, raised their critical awareness of the appropriateness or otherwise of straightforward arithmetic operations. So, compared with the warning instruction, the process-oriented instruction was more likely to motivate and help the participants to use realistic considerations. Nevertheless, it was not very effective in helping them to arrive at the correct answers. In other words, the process-oriented instruction was able to make children more aware of the importance of taking realistic considerations, but did not promote them to take further realistic actions in their actual problem-solving process, leading to correct responses to P-problems.

Why did the process-oriented instruction failed to significantly help children arrive at correct or realistic answers? One possible reason for this was that making realistic answers demanded from children more knowledge than just activating realistic considerations. For example, to solve the home distance problem, participants should give different solutions regarding the two homes located in the same or opposite directions on the way to the school. Furthermore, when the two homes and the school are not located on a straight line, knowledge of trigonometry is needed for an accurate answer. Actually, if children gave the possible range of two homes' distance (all solutions between $17 - 8$ and $17 + 8$), they were also regarded as solving it correctly. However, in the case of the home distance problem, like most P-problems, primary school students may realise its complexity, but they do not have enough knowledge to successfully solve it. Another reason that the process-oriented instruction did not resulted in a significant gain over the warning instruction may be that it was too weak an encouragement for changing their stereotyped beliefs about, and approaches to, word problem solving, even though they were aware of the importance of utilising realistic considerations. For instance, children are typically accustomed to find one specific solution to a word problem, but not to integrate several possible solutions.

THE IMPACT OF LEARNING SETTINGS: COGNITIVE HOLDING POWER

There are many causes leading students to neglect realistic considerations during word problem solving. In the previous section we showed that some direct conditions, such as the pre-test instructions (Xin et al., 2007), had an influence on Chinese children's performance. Another study by Xu (2007) found that the methods of investigation served as another factor. Concretely, while solving the same P-problems, children who were interviewed individually had better achievements than those tested collectively (Xu, 2007). However, more studies have attributed children's tendency to neglect realistic context to unfavourable mathematics classroom practice and culture (Alacaci & Pasztor, 2002; Cobb & Bauersfeld, 1995; McNeal & Simon, 2000). For example, when learners experience conflict between their personal sense-making and the need to produce expected "correct" answers, most of them choose to give the expected answers and give up their personal insights, because the school mathematics culture generally rewards conformity and punishes personal sense-making (Alacaci & Pasztor, 2002; for a thorough discussion also see Verschaffel et al., 2000). So it is necessary to evaluate the impact of the classroom learning setting on students' realistic problem solving. The pressure of the learning setting on students' use of different cognitive procedures has been conceptualised by Stevenson (1990, 1998) as "cognitive holding power". This conceptualisation is outlined next.

Generally, knowledge can be differentiated into declarative knowledge (such as information, facts, assertions, propositions) and procedural knowledge (such as techniques, skills, ability to achieve goals). Procedural knowledge can be further differentiated into two types (Stevenson, 1990). First order procedures are those automated procedures that enable the achievement of specific goals, e.g., knowledge how to hammer a nail, play a familiar piece of music, and apply a particular mathematical algorithm. Second order procedures are those procedures which achieve more general purposes by operating on specific procedures in order to enable the interpretation of new situations, the solving of problems, and the learning of new skills, combining existing knowledge in new ways and enabling far transfer (Perkins & Salomon, 1989; Stevenson, 1990, 1998).

It is argued by Stevenson and Evans (1994) that settings or environments can press students into using first or second order cognitive procedures and can be regarded as having first or second order cognitive holding power. A setting possessing first order cognitive holding power (FOCHP) presses students into the utilisation of specific procedures, which is conceived as one where the environment poses goals for the student which can be achieved through the direct execution of existing specific procedures or the direct acquisition (from the teacher) of the required specific procedures. In such an environment, students merely listen to what a teacher says and copy what a teacher does in learning how to accomplish specific tasks. Most of them are unaware of the thinking strategies used in the lesson and not responsible for controlling them. So they have no chance to develop and use second order procedures. However, a setting possessing second order cognitive holding power (SOCHP) presses a student into the utilisation of second order procedures. Such a setting poses unfamiliar goals for the student, and elicits the execution of second order procedures to deal with new situations and problems. Second order procedures are used to make links between the features of the task and setting, and existing knowledge; generate ideas; try out and test problem-solving strategies; monitor the effectiveness of approaches; and check results. In this conceptualisation, specific procedures are seldom used directly, but are selected, organised, and applied under the controlling of second order procedures (Stevenson & Evans, 1994).

Cognitive holding power produced by mathematics classroom settings was shown to have a strong influence on children's realistic problem solving, for instance in a recent study by Xin (2008) about a kind of complex word problems about a rectangle's area. Currently, in Chinese mathematics classroom practice, many teachers mainly focus on pressing students to use first rather than second order procedural knowledge so that students could perform well in all kinds of exams (Xin, 2008). It can be hypothesised that, as a result, a lot of students may get poor performance on non-standard, problematic problems. To solve P-problems students have to possess second order procedural knowledge. Thus they should learn in classroom settings which are characterised by high levels of second order cognitive holding power (Stevenson, 1986, 1998; Stevenson & Evans, 1994). However, the relation between cognitive holding power produced by instructional settings and children's realistic problem solving has been given no systematic attention up to now except for a recent study by Xin and Zhang (2009).

In that study, a sample of 119 Chinese 4-6th graders was administrated the word problem test which has been used by Xin et al. (2007) as well as the Chinese version (revised by Xin, Chi, & Ning, 2005) of the Cognitive Holding Power Questionnaire (CHPQ) originally developed by Stevenson (1998). The revised CHPQ focuses on cognitive holding power as perceived by students in mathematics classes in primary and junior schools. It consists of 30 questions scored on a 1-5

Likert scale. FOCHP is measured by 13 items, e.g., "The teacher encourages students to copy what he (she) does" and "I feel I have to work exactly as I am shown in mathematical classroom", which reflect students' perception of a learning environment that presses them to use first order procedural knowledge. SOCHP is measured by 17 items, e.g., "The teacher encourages students to find links between the things they learn" and "I try out new ideas in mathematical classroom", which indicate the students' perception of a learning environment that presses them to use second order procedural knowledge.

The results of that study (Xin & Zhang, 2009) showed that (1) second order cognitive holding power (SOCHP) perceived by children in mathematics classrooms predicted their performance on P-problems (for correct answers, $R^2 = 0.08$; for realistic considerations, $R^2 = 0.05$) but not on S-problems; (2) the relationship between first order cognitive holding power (FOCHP) and children's correct answers to P-problems was mediated (the mediating effect accounted for 61% of the total effect) by second order cognitive holding power (SOCHP).

It is an interesting finding that SOCHP could significantly predict children's performance (correct answers and attention to realistic considerations) on P-problems, but not on S-problems. By pressing students into working things out for themselves, finding links, trying out ideas, checking results, the learning settings with SOCHP could promote the use of second order procedures. According to Stevenson's (1986, 1998) argument, engagement in learning activities that demand the use of second order procedures can help students achieve far transfer, in which there is no obvious similarity between the learning tasks and transfer tasks. In current instructional practice, children are mainly taught to deal with S-problems, whereas P-problems are unfamiliar and difficult because they usually require children to flexibly reorganise their first order procedures under the direction of second order procedures, so as to adapt to unconventional problem situations. In this sense, if learning settings possess higher SOCHP which can promote the utilisation of second order procedures, children's realistic problem solving that usually demands this type of procedures would be better. In contrast, children often automatically solve S-problems, which are familiar for them and don't need far transfer. So SOCHP could significantly predict children's performance on P-problems but not on S-problems.

As for FOCHP, it had no significant relation with children's attention to realistic considerations, but the relationship with children's correct answers to P-problems was significant, which indicated that although FOCHP could not facilitate children to consider the realistic context, it did offer basic knowledge required to solve P-problems. Furthermore, the influence of FOCHP on children's correct answers was indirect with SOCHP as a mediator. By pressing students into following instructions or procedures provided by the teacher, the settings possessing FOCHP could foster the learning and acquiring of first order procedural knowledge and skills which second order procedural knowledge has to be operated on. In this sense, FOCHP is a prerequisite to successfully solve P-problems, but not a sufficient condition.

To sum up, settings possessing SOCHP can promote children to consider realistic contexts and enable them to acquire second order knowledge necessary to solve

P-problems, while the role of FOCHP lies in that it enables children to acquire first order procedural knowledge required by second order procedural knowledge. In this sense, SOCHP is a key factor for children to learn how to solve P-problems.

REALISTIC CONSIDERATIONS ON THE REALITY OF CHINESE MATHEMATICAL EDUCATION

Many studies (Cooper & Harries, 2003, 2005; Greer, 1993; Mayer, 2004; Verschaffel et al., 1994, 1999; Yoshida et al., 1997) on English, American, Belgian and Japanese children have consistently indicated that primary school children lack the ability to solve P-problems. Several studies (Liu & Chen, 2003; Xin et al., 2007; Xin & Zhang, 2009; Xu, 2006, 2007) in China have revealed that Chinese children are also not good at realistic problem solving, as compared to their better achievements in other mathematical areas (Cai, 2007; Fan et al., 2004; Stevenson et al., 1990; Zhang & Zhou, 2003).

To focus on the causes of Chinese children lacking ability in solving realistic word problems, we have to first give a glance to the tradition of mathematical education in China. For a very long time (at least since the 1960s), the "two basics", including training students' basic knowledge and basic skills through intensive practice, have been the core goal of elementary and secondary mathematical education in China. Since the 1990s the idea of "ability training" has become popular in China, thus mathematics became a tool for developing students' abilities of basic computation, spatial imagination, logic, and analysis. The view of realistic mathematics education has not been fully recognised, though some educators have recently started to call on and propagandise it (Cheng et al., 2001; Sun, 1995; Wong, 1997), as explained above. Recently a new wave of elementary curriculum reform occurred. The scope, intensity and speed of this reform are unprecedented. The new "Mathematics Curriculum Standards for Full-time Compulsory Education" was announced by Ministry of Education of China in 2001. The "new standards" stress the relationship of mathematics and reality. It is emphasised that by following mathematical education, students are prepared for future life development, learn to apply mathematical thinking to everyday life and the study of other related subjects, learn the value of mathematics and feel the close relationship between mathematics, nature and human society, and develop their creativity, practical abilities, and personalities through mathematics learning. However, although new goals have been established and new textbooks have been published, it will still take a very long time to fully achieve the new standards.

In current Chinese mathematical instructional practice, there are many obstacles to the development of children's ability of realistic problem solving.

First, in China the problems in textbooks and examinations are not so realistic (Zhang, 2005), which partly determines the contents of teaching. For example, whether P-problems are involved in all kinds of examinations, especially the senior high school entrance examination and the college entrance examination, will have great influence on daily teaching and learning of this type of problems. If, in most cases, children go through a totally abstract process while solving arithmetic word problems in classrooms, such as the problem statement being de-contextualised, and children merely facing the abstract language symbols, it is impossible to demand their realistic considerations while solving P-problems. All of these make the classroom word problem solving far different from that in real life situations; therefore, it is quite easy for children to be inclined to neglect realistic considerations when solving P-items (Greer, 1997).

Second, classroom and school culture influence (non-)realistic word problem solving. As many scholars (Brousseau, 1984; Kazemi & Stipek, 2001; Verschaffel et al., 2000) have argued, from their everyday learning practices children have acquired a set of implicit word problem solving standards and expectations, e.g., they believe that all the problems presented and raised by the teachers can be solved, that all the information that is needed for their solutions can be found in the provided conditions, that every problem has only one answer, or that the use of realistic knowledge to solve word problems is "wrong" and will be punished. These implicit beliefs and rules relating specifically to students' mathematical activities (or "sociomathematical norms", as Cobb & Bauersfeld (1995) or Kazemi & Stipek, (2001) would call them), impede children from using realistic knowledge in their solutions.

What's more, the values and attitudes held by teachers (e.g., the ideas about how to teach and what the essence of mathematics is) could be another important factor affecting children's performance in realistic problem solving. Some teachers regard the objective of mathematics as developing students' mathematical thinking, whereas others value training in basic arithmetic operations or computations more. The latter would probably make children focus only on the results of arithmetic computations instead of the real situations imbedded in word problem statements. Many previous studies (Alacaci & Pasztor, 2002; Cobb & Bauersfeld, 1995; Kazemi & Stipek, 2001; McNeal & Simon, 2000) have provided empirical evidence supporting the hypothesis that biased mathematical instruction and classroom culture will have an influence on children's realistic problem solving, and this is also true for Chinese primary school children. As shown above, if students are required to obey teachers' directions and demonstrations and have no opportunity to facing new tasks with their own insights, they can not develop second order cognitive procedures needed for realistic problem solving. So cognitive holding power possessed by learning settings heavily affects children's mathematical abilities (Xin & Zhang, 2009).

It has been universally recognised by constructivists that the construction of mathematical knowledge should be contextual and related to real life (Xin, 2006). However, children's lack of ability to solve P-problems makes us realise that we still have a long way to go towards the reform of mathematical education. We suggest the following tentative guidelines for improving educational practice.

First, students should be confronted with more P-problems in their daily lessons and examinations. The standard word problems offered in traditional classrooms should be replaced, or at least supplemented by various realistic or problematic ones reflecting daily life. Thus students should have the opportunity to reference their real lives, which will make them realise the variety and complexity of problems and solutions. Otherwise, they will only know that if there are two numbers in the problem, the answer will be found by adding, subtracting, multiplying or dividing these two numbers (Greer, 1993). They will never consider the applicability of these arithmetic operations and other approaches (e.g., approximations, qualitative answers) to P-problems.

Second, teachers should apply more effective instructional approaches. Simply exposing students to P-problems may not be enough, so teachers should apply powerful instructional methods that explicitly aim at the development of the proper concepts, skills, and attitudes that are needed for realistic modelling of problem situations, and realistically considering the applicability of operations, and realistically interpreting the outcomes of arithmetic calculations (Verschaffel et al., 1999; Verschaffel & De Corte, 1997).

For example, cooperative learning may be helpful. Cooperative learning usually results in higher level reasoning, more frequent generation of new ideas and solutions, and greater transfer of what is learned from one situation to another than does competitive or individualistic learning (Roger & Johnson, 1994). Thus, students may realise that there are different ways of representing and solving the same P-problem, and they may learn to compare these alternatives and select the best one. This point of view has been supported by studies on English children (Cooper & Harries, 2005) and Swedish students (Wyndhamn & Säljö, 1997). For example, in the study by Cooper and Harries (2005), when the children were required to comment on some competing answers produced by other children, they were more willing and able to introduce realistic thinking during their problem solving.

It was shown that process-oriented instruction is an alternative instructional option in promoting realistic considerations (Xin et al., 2007). Under this type of instruction, students are reminded to consider the real situations behind problem statements and to think over the applicability of using straightforward arithmetic operations while solving P-problems. Taking a long view of the matter, new sociomathematical norms should be established, in which word problems are conceived as exercises in mathematical modelling, with a focus on the assumptions and the appropriateness of the model underlying any proposed solution (Verschaffel & De Corte, 1997). When pupils are immersed in a classroom culture that favors these norms, their abilities to solve P-problems may develop to some degree.

Third, learning settings with high cognitive holding power, especially high second order cognitive holding power, should be created. Our studies (Xin, 2008; Xin & Zhang, 2009) have suggested that the settings forcing students to use second order procedure knowledge could improve their realistic problem solving. Furthermore, based on the finding that the teacher can be an effective agent in creating second order cognitive holding power, regardless of the school or the year level at which they teach (Stevenson, 1998), we must emphasise the role of teachers in promoting students' abilities.

Finally, when paying much attention to children's realistic problem solving, we should not excessively criticise children's tendency to neglect real world context. In a sense, in the given circumstances, it is mostly more beneficial for students to ignore real-world knowledge and focus on formal calculations, which can make them quickly master the formal rules and theories. The key question is how to make students link the mathematical theories or principles to real life closely and make them know when to consider the realistic context. Just as Inoue (2005) stated, "the real challenge for educators would be to find a way to effectively teach students not to fall into a too simplistic understanding of the world while simultaneously acquiring theoretical models for viewing the big picture of the world" (p. 82).

CONCLUSIONS

Based on the above review of the literature on Chinese students' performance on realistic problem solving and its correlates, it can be concluded that, like their Western counterparts, Chinese pupils lack the ability to solve P-problems. Their performance on these problems is related to many factors, such as pre-test instructions (warning vs. process-oriented) and (first or second order) cognitive holding power as perceived by students in mathematics classrooms. In order to promote students' realistic problem solving, according to the tradition and reality of mathematics education in China, a series of measures should be taken, including supplementing P-problems in daily teaching and exams, designing effective instructional approaches, and establishing learning settings with high second order cognitive holding power.

ACKNOWLEDGEMENT

This chapter was written with support (project 30500162) from the National Natural Science Foundation of China.

REFERENCES

Alacaci, C., & Pasztor, A. (2002). Effects of flawed state assessment preparation materials on students' mathematical reasoning: A study. *Journal of Mathematical Behavior, 21*, 225–253.

Brousseau, G. (1984). The crucial role of the didactical contract in the analysis and construction of situation in teaching and learning mathematics. In H. G. Steiner (Ed.), *Theory of mathematics education: ICME 5 topic area and miniconference* (pp. 110–119). Bielefeld, Germany: Institut für Didaktik der Mathematik der Universität Bielefeld.

Cai, J. (2007). *Empirical investigations about Chinese and U.S. students' learning of mathematics: Insights and recommendations.* Beijing, China: Educational Sciences Publishing House.

Cheng, G., Gu, L., & Wang, J. (2001). On mathematics class and real life. *Educational Science, 17*(3), 31–33.

Chen, L., Verschaffel, L., & Chen, Q. (2006). Discussion on the relationship of problem posing to the development of students' ability. *Journal of Mathematics Education, 15*(3), 31–34.

Cobb, P., & Bauersfeld, H. (1995). *The emergence of mathematical meaning: Interaction in classroom cultures.* Hillsdale, NJ: Erlbaum.

Cooper, B., & Harries, A. V. (2003). Children's use of realistic considerations in problem solving: Some English evidence. *Journal of Mathematical Behavior, 22*, 449–463.

Cooper, B., & Harries, A. V. (2005). Making sense of realistic word problems: Portraying working class "failure" in a division with remainder problem. *International Journal of Research & Methods in Education, 28*, 147–169.

Fan, L., Wong, N.-Y., Cai, J., & Li, S. (2004). *How Chinese learn mathematics: Perspectives from insiders.* Singapore: World Scientific.

Freudenthal, H. (1968). Why to teach mathematics so as to be useful. *Educational Studies in Mathematics, 1*, 3–8.

Freudenthal, H. (1991). *Revisiting mathematics education: China lectures*. Dordrecht, The Netherlands: Kluwer.
Gravemeijer, K. (1997). Commentary solving word problems: A case of modeling? *Learning and Instruction, 7*, 388–397.
Greer, B. (1993). The mathematical modeling perspective on world problems. *Journal of Mathematical Behavior, 12*, 239–250.
Greer, B. (1997). Modeling reality in mathematics classrooms: The case of wor(l)d problems. *Learning and Instruction, 7*, 293–307.
Inoue, N. (2005). The realistic reasons behind unrealistic solutions: The role of interpretive activity in word problem solving. *Learning and Instruction, 15*, 69–83.
Kazemi, E., & Stipek, D. (2001). Promoting conceptual thinking in four upper-elementary mathematics classrooms. *The Elementary School Journal, 102*, 59–80.
Liu, R., & Chen, H. (2003). An investigation on mathematical realistic problems. *Psychological Development and Education, 19*, 49–54.
Mayer, R. E. (2004). Teaching of subject matter. *Annual Review of Psychology, 55*, 715–744.
McNeal, B., & Simon, M. A. (2000). Mathematics culture clash: Negotiating new classroom norms with prospective teachers. *Journal of Mathematical Behavior, 18*, 475–509.
Ministry of Education of China. (2001). *Mathematics curriculum standards for full-time compulsory education*. Beijing, China: Beijing Normal University Press.
Moy, R., & Peverly, S. T. (2005). Perceptions of mathematics curricula and teaching in China. *Psychology in the Schools, 42*, 251–258.
Nesher, P. (1980). The stereotyped nature of school word problems. *For the Learning of Mathematics, 1*, 41–48.
Reusser, K., & Stebler, R. (1997). Every word problem has a solution: The social rationality of mathematical modeling in schools. *Learning and Instruction, 7*, 309–327.
Roger, T., & Johnson, D. W. (1994). An overview of cooperative learning. In J. Thousand, A. Villa, & A. Nevin (Eds.), *Creativity and collaborative learning* (pp. 31–44). Baltimore: Brookes Press.
Stevenson, H. W., Lee, S., Chen, C., Lummis, M., Stigler, J., Liu, F., et al. (1990). Mathematical achievement of children in China and the United States. *Child Development, 61*, 1053–1066.
Stevenson, J. (1986). Adaptability: Theoretical considerations. *Journal of Structural Learning, 9*, 107–117.
Stevenson, J. (1998). Performance of the cognitive holding power questionnaire in schools. *Learning and Instruction, 8*, 393–410.
Stevenson, J., & Evans, G. (1994). Conceptualisation and measurement of cognitive holding power. *Journal of Educational Measurement, 31*, 161–181.
Sun, X. (1995). An introduction of the ideas and conceptions of realistic mathematics education. *Journal of Subject Education, 8*(9), 16–18.
Van den Heuvel-Panhuizen, M. (2000). *Mathematics education in the Netherlands: A guided tour. Freudenthal Institute CD-ROM for ICME9*. Utrecht, The Netherlands: Utrecht University.
Verschaffel, L., De Corte, E., & Lasure, S. (1994). Realistic considerations in mathematical modeling of school arithmetic word problems. *Learning and Instruction, 4*, 273–294.
Verschaffel, L., De Corte, E., & Lasure, S. (1999). Children's conceptions about the role of real-world knowledge in mathematical modeling of school word problems. In W. Schnotz, S. Vosniadou & M. Carretero (Eds.), *New perspectives on conceptual change* (pp. 175–189). Oxford, UK: Elsevier.
Verschaffel, L., Greer, B., & De Corte, E. (2000). *Making sense of word problems*. Lisse, The Netherlands: Swets & Zeitlinger.
Wong, K. M. P. (1997). Do real-world situations necessarily constitute "authentic" mathematical tasks in the mathematics classroom? *Curriculum Forum, 6*(2), 1–15.
Wyndhamn, J., & Säljö, R. (1997). Word problems and mathematical reasoning: A study of children's mastery of reference and meaning in textual realities. *Learning and Instruction, 7*, 361–382.
Xin, Z. (2006). *The research of knowledge construction: From constructivism to empirical investigations*. Beijing, China: Educational Sciences Publishing House.

Xin, Z. (2008). Fourth through sixth graders' representations of area-of-rectangle problems: Influences of relational complexity and cognitive holding power. *The Journal of Psychology, 142*, 581–600.

Xin, Z., Lin, C., Zhang, L., & Yan, R. (2007). The performance of Chinese primary school students on realistic arithmetic word problems. *Educational Psychology in Practice, 23*, 145–159.

Xin, Z., Ning, L., & Chi, L. (2005). The relationship between cognitive holding power and constructivist pedagogy in mathematical education. *Psychological Science* (Shanghai), *28*, 1324–1329.

Xin, Z., & Zhang, L. (2005). Solving realistic problem and constructing realistic mathematics. *Journal of the Chinese Society of Education, 16*, 38–41.

Xin, Z., & Zhang, L. (2009). Cognitive holding power, fluid intelligence, and mathematical achievement as predictors of children's realistic problem solving. *Learning and Individual Differences, 19*, 124–129.

Xu, S. (2006). A research on pupils' realistic considerations on problematic word problems and related factors. *Psychological Development and Education, 22*(2), 76–80.

Xu, S. (2007), A study of sixth-graders' realistic consideration of word problem solving under different conditions. *Psychological Science* (Shanghai), *30*, 705–707.

Yoshida, H., Verschaffel, L., & De Corte, E. (1997). Realistic considerations in solving problematic word problems: Do Japanese and Belgian children have the same difficulties? *Learning and Instruction, 7*, 329–338.

Zhang, G. (2005). Mathematization and realistic mathematics education: An analysis of their contributions to exploratory mathematics project work. *Journal of Mathematics Education, 14*, 35–37.

Zhang, H., & Zhou, Y. (2003). The teaching of mathematics in Chinese elementary schools. *International Journal of Psychology, 38*, 286–298.

Zhao, J. (2006). From street mathematics to school mathematics: Reflections on the "construction of real-life mathematics". *Journal of the Chinese Society of Education, 17*(12), 56–58.

Ziqiang, Xin
Institute of Developmental Psychology
Beijing Normal University
China

ROGER SÄLJÖ, EVA RIESBECK, AND JAN WYNDHAMN

9. LEARNING TO MODEL: COORDINATING NATURAL LANGUAGE AND MATHEMATICAL OPERATIONS WHEN SOLVING WORD PROBLEMS

INTRODUCTION

A central element of the skills that go into what is described in modern language as "information literacy" is the ability to understand, use, and manipulate symbolic information in productive and relevant manners. Such intellectual capacities are considered necessary in order to master the increasingly complex information ecology that we live in, both at work and in other spheres of life, in present-day society. International comparisons of student achievement, such as the famous PISA-studies (www.pisa.oecd.org), increasingly tend to focus on these types of skills, which are seen as essential and generative ingredients of people's life skills in the information society.

Using symbolic systems implies learning how to represent some part of the world in symbolic form in relevant manners. Much, if not most, of our learning is of this kind. Learning the alphabet and the number system are examples of how one has to become familiar with how sounds (phonemes) are represented in writing (and thus appear as graphemes), and how objects can be counted and organised by means of the symbolic tools of numbers and specific mathematical operations. Even in cases when we learn what may at first instance be perceived as manual skills, for instance how to make an artefact (Keller & Keller, 1996), or how to pack milk cartons in an optimal manner in containers (Scribner, 1984), the activities at some stage require purposeful consideration of the relationships between symbolic representations and the physical world we are operating in.

From a sociocultural perspective, this reliance on symbolic tools in any kind of human activity testifies to the central role that semiotic resources play in mediating the world for people (Wertsch, 2007). It is language and other symbolic tools (numbers, images, graphs, etc.) that allow us to know about the world in manners that help us act in the world in flexible and relevant ways. In schooling, the appropriation of such symbolic tools of mediation plays an important, even dominant, role. Much effort is devoted to learning to define and use concepts of various kinds, formulae, algorithms, grammatical rules, and so on. Mastery of such discursive resources is part of the intellectual "tool-kit" (Wertsch, 1998) that people are expected to bring with them into society.

MATHEMATICAL REASONING AS INTRA- AND INTER-SEMIOTIC WORK

Throughout history, people have developed many different kinds of semiotic systems that are used for meaning-making. These systems have emerged as parts of the increasing division of labour in society, where different professions and academic disciplines have created their own social languages (Bakhtin, 1986), semiotic tools, and artefacts (maps, charts, tables etc.). In the educational system, vital parts of these discourses are reproduced within school subjects such as physics, mathematics, geography, and so on. A traditional element of the educational construction of disciplines and disciplinary knowledge is also that these various types of knowledge are seen as distinctively different in terms of their domains. Physics differs from chemistry and mathematics differs from the languages; they all have to be learned separately as if they were unconnected fields of knowledge.

However, from a sociocultural perspective it is obvious that in human practices the distinction between different semiotic systems or domains is often difficult to uphold in any strict sense. Anyone who reads a newspaper, uses a map or a computer, or engages in some other mediated activity, will inevitably use multiple symbolic resources: numbers, spoken and written language, and symbolic representations such as images, graphs, and tables. Even someone who engages in pure and abstract mathematical reasoning cannot avoid relying on language at some stage. Even mathematical argumentation has to be embedded in narratives to do its work.

In the study to be reported here, the problem addressed concerns how students learn to, as Freudenthal (1973) puts it, "mathematise" the world by means of elementary forms of mathematical modelling. Expressed differently, the object of study is how students learn to coordinate mathematical notations and operations with objects and events in a physical reality described in language. Modelling implies that mathematical operations and notations "touch" reality (Rommetveit, 1974), i.e., they are used as mediational means for making claims about states of affairs and relationships in the world (Verschaffel, Greer, & De Corte, 2000; Wyndhamn & Säljö, 1997).

In a sociocultural perspective, modelling implies engaging in inter-semiotic work, i.e., one has to decide about the appropriate and productive manners of coordinating linguistic categories and mathematical expressions and operations in order to come to a solution of a problem. Learning such inter-semiotic skills is clearly different from operating within the conceptual frameworks of mathematics itself. In the latter case, i.e., in intra-semiotic meaning-making, the truth value of statements and arguments is established on the basis of analytical considerations of how a particular usage of concepts fits into the universe of meaning that is mathematical discourse (O'Halloran, 2003).

One of the activities in which students encounter problems of such inter-semiotic work is when solving so-called word problems (Greer, 1997). Representing "two interwoven semiotic worlds, the story-like description of non-mathematical real-world situations and an implicit web of mathematical relations, mathematical word problems are considered to be an important part of mathematics education" (Reusser & Stebler, 1997, p. 309). The instructional argument for using such problems as exercises is precisely this; they allow for developing skills of understanding how mathematical reasoning may be "applied" to a "real" world of objects and events.

Word Problems as Semiotic Challenges

There is extensive research on the difficulties students encounter when learning to solve word problems (cf. Verschaffel et al., 2000, for an analytical summary), and we will not attempt to summarise the findings. The particular feature of learning that we are interested in here concerns details of the intra- and inter-semiotic work that students have to engage in when learning how to solve such problems. The difficulties students have in such settings, in our opinion, may tell us something interesting at a more general level about the nature of learning of symbolic reasoning in institutional settings.

A prominent finding in most of this research is that students' performance on word problems differs dramatically depending on how the problems are designed. Even in cases where the mathematical properties of the tasks in principle are identical in terms of the expected operations, the outcomes often differ. Verschaffel et al. (2000) have systematised the study of such differences by designing what they refer to as standard (S)-problems and problematic (P)-problems, respectively. Briefly, an S-item (for example, "A boat sails at a speed of 45 kilometres per hour. How long does it take this boat to sail 180 kilometres?") is formulated according to the standard expectations in mathematics teaching, and it can be solved through a straightforward operation such as a division or a multiplication. This, in our terminology, implies that an S-problem does not require any extensive inter-semiotic work; the text can be read and converted to into a mathematical operation in a fairly direct manner.

A P-item, on the other hand, requires more extensive consideration of how the situation should be modelled, and if the information provided is relevant and sufficient for solving the problem. In the literature, there are many famous examples of this kind of item, where the information is either insufficient or irrelevant to solving a problem, or where the students must consider more carefully in what manner the verbal information is to be translated into a mathematical form in order to be successful. Baruk (1985), for instance, reports on studies of the famous "age of the captain" problem in which children were asked to solve a problem of the following kind: "There are 26 sheep and 10 goats on a ship. How old is the captain?" (see Selter, this volume). Another famous such example is what Verschaffel et al. (2000, p. 19) refer to as the Runner problem: "John's best time to run 100 meters is 17 seconds. How long will it take him to run 1 kilometre?" At a general level, the results of these kinds of studies show that children tend to respond to the problems even if the information given is irrelevant to answering the question given, as in the case of the "age of the captain" problem. Another result is that P-items of the kind represented by the Runner problem tend to be solved as if they were S-problems. In this case this implies that the children simply multiply 17 seconds by 10 to find out how long it takes to run one kilometre. Furthermore, it is interesting to see that intercultural comparisons show similar results. The Runner problem, for instance, has been used in countries in different parts of the world, and the results are thought-provoking: "the percentages of students in the various countries who gave the unqualified answer 170 seconds ranged from 93% to 100%." (Verschaffel et al., 2000, p. 44). This implies that the superiority that children in Japan, for instance, show on international comparisons in mathematics (at least in comparison to European students) disappears when this kind of difficulty is introduced.

Even if all word problems imply inter-semiotic work in the sense that written statements have to be translated into mathematical operations (and back again when the answer is given), the P-problems imply that students have to do more extensive inter-semiotic work. They have to consider what is a reasonable manner of modelling the task in mathematical language, and if the information given is relevant and sufficient. It is obvious from the research that students are not prepared for these kinds of difficulties, and very few of them seem willing to answer a mathematics task by saying that the information is not sufficient or relevant, which *per se* is an interesting finding of how children accommodate to mathematics teaching. Students are obviously trained to expect the S-type of items in the classroom situation. This situated nature of children's reasoning was illustrated in a study by Säljö and Wyndhamn (1988), who presented 5th and 6th graders with one of the following kinds of problems: A) "A cow produces 18 litres of milk per day. How many liters of milk does the cow produce during one week?", and B) "Kalle goes to school and on the average he has seven lessons per day. How many lessons does he have per week?" In brief, the results show that the overall percentage of correct answer differs between 90 per cent on the first item to 70 per cent on the second. This implies that when one has to consider that a school week is five days (and not seven), the performance drops. But what is even more interesting in these findings is that the drop in performance is selective, affecting mainly the students who have been characterised by their teachers as low achievers. For the high achievers the corresponding difference in outcome between the items was small.

Problem Solving in an Ambiguous Reality

What the above studies illustrate is that problems become more difficult when the relationships between the verbal formulation and the mathematical operations are not of the standard kind. In the study reported here, the problem was designed so that it presupposes that one attends to how the situation should be modelled. Thus, it was intentionally designed so as to encourage the participants to attend to the non-trivial relationship between the story and the modelling necessary. The problem was formulated as follows:

> Two boys, Charles and Martin, are going to help Nicholas rake leaves on his plot of land. The plot is 1200 square metres. Charles rakes 700 square metres during four hours and Martin does 500 square metres during two hours. They get 180 crowns/kronor (SEK) for their work. How are the boys going to divide the money so that it is fair?
>
> Show through your calculations or in some other way how you have solved the task.

Charles should get ..... crowns
Martin should get ..... crowns

As can be seen, to handle this problem of a "fair" sharing of the money the pupils must somehow decide on what is a relevant way to model the situation. That is they must ask themselves what "fair" implies in this particular setting when two friends work together on a common task, but where their efforts seem to differ. Charles works longer and covers a larger surface, while Martin works half the time but obviously more intensively, since he, in proportional terms, covers more land. Thus, how one deals with this problem of sharing money is clearly an issue of what modelling one assumes to be relevant in order to arrive at a fair solution of a pragmatic problem.

METHOD

The problem was given to pupils in the 5th Grade (i.e., when students are 11 or 12 years of age). It was solved as group work during regular teaching hours. Twenty-six groups with three pupils in each participated. The groups were homogenised with respect to their mathematical abilities: high-, average- and low-achievers, respectively. The assignment of the children to the different groups was done by the class teacher. The group work was audio-taped and later transcribed in full. The groups worked between 9 and 20 minutes on the problem with an average of 14 minutes.

The problem was read out loud to the participants by one of the researchers (ER). The group members also received the problem in written form, so that they could read it themselves as they worked (which they also did). The researcher was present throughout the problem solving process and occasionally provided neutral comments when the groups got stuck or found it difficult to continue. She also encouraged the members to verbalise their reasoning, for instance by asking why they argued for a particular solution (see below for illustrations).

RESULTS

At a general level, the results illustrate that all groups in one way or another argued that the problem is difficult to solve, and that it is not self-evident how the money should be divided. In some implicit sense, the members of the groups therefore realised that the calculations have to be relative to some kind of reasonable assumption of what it means to divide the money in a fair manner. They perceived that there clearly is more than one way to do this. Thus, the discussions are characterised by students' engaging in "realistic considerations" (Verschaffel et al., 2000) of what it implies to share money between friends. At the same time, it is equally obvious that the reasoning is situated in the rationalities that characterise the particular context of doing word problems in the mathematics classroom. The pupils assume that there is one mathematical solution which is the best, and that all the information given should be used in the solution.

Before illustrating the argumentation that students engage in, we should like to point out that the most obvious result in this study is that none of the groups, not even among the high-achievers, concludes that it is impossible to use all the information given in the context of *one* model. Instead, the work in all groups is based on precisely this assumption: there must be one way of calculating that takes into account all the information provided and that still produces a fair split of the pay. This is an interesting finding, which no doubt must be seen as a consequence of the fact that the exercise is understood as a word problem of the kind one encounters in the school context. Thus, there is no group in which it is explicitly recognised that depending on how one defines the concept of "fairness" in this setting, the modelling will be different, and, consequently, the amount of money the two boys get will differ.

In the groups there are four different ways of modelling the task. These models, in turn, imply different calculations. Most of these four models can be found among almost all of the groups at some stage of their problem solving. This implies that the groups moved back and forth between different models. The four models, described through some clear cases, are the following[1].

Models for sharing	*Illustration*	
I. Divide equally (180/2)	Group 19 (Low)[2]	
	David	Is it Charles and Martin who are going to share the money?[3]
	R(esearcher)	What do the rest of you think? (long pause)
	R	How do you think they should go about now if they are going to divide the money in a fair way?
	David	90.
	Henrik	Then they get as much between them.
II. The amount of work carried out	Group 3 (Average)	
	R	What do you find out in the task?
	Samuel	That one rakes 700 square metres and another one 500 square metres.
	R	You are supposed to find out in this group what they are to be paid and what is fair.
	Samuel	It is fair if Charles gets 100 crowns and the other one gets 80 crowns
	Rikard	I think they should get the same.
	Samuel	Charles rakes more than Martin did.
	R	Yes, but why exactly 100 crowns and 80 crowns?
	Samuel	That's what it amounts to roughly. 200 square metres. [alludes to the difference between the boys in terms of how much land they covered]

(Continued)

III. Time used for work	Group 13 (High)	
	R	*How many are there raking?*
	Carl	*Two.*
	Anna	*One rakes for four and one for two hours.*
	R	*What do you think about him who rakes for four hours?*
	Anna	*He must get more.*
	R	*Do you think so too?*
	Gustav	*Yes, he rakes for only two hours.*
IV. Piece rate/payment by performance	Group 2 (High)	
	Jenny	*One doesn't get paid for the time. You sort of get paid for how much you do (....) It is how much they have been raking. I think we should go on how much they rake. It is the raking which is the hard part.*
	Kattis	*Charles he raked for four hours while Martin raked for two. (...) But Martin did more raking during two hours than what Charles did during four. During four hours he raked 700 while Martin during two hours raked 500. Martin raked more.*

These various models are all reasonable, and the principles behind them represent assumptions which are easy to identify. If one takes as a point of departure that Martin and Charles are friends, the modelling that follows category I above implies that equal pay is a relevant argument for sharing the money (and thus one disregards the work performed). None of the groups keeps to this mode of reasoning for very long, though, and none of them gives this as their final answer (see below). It seems reasonable to assume that the members consider this solution too easy for this task to qualify as an exercise in mathematics. The argumentation that follows from the second principle implies that the amount of work one has performed should serve as the criterion for dividing the money. Raking 700 square metres is more work than 500 and justifies a higher share of the money. The third principle implies that it is the time spent working that is relevant to consider. Charles works for four hours and Martin for two, and this should be considered. The final model implies that one should be paid by performance. Martin has worked fewer hours and only 500 square metres, but he has worked harder and more efficiently. This should be considered when dividing the money.

As pointed out, the groups moved between these four models, and most of them used all of them during some part of their discussions. The data also show that the students use quite sophisticated arguments and analogies when arguing for their particular model. There is also an awareness of the fact that the models are conflictual, and there is a rather intense argumentation about what model is the most reasonable one to use. Kattis, who is a participant in the group illustrating the pay by performance model according to which the money should be divided on the basis of how hard the boys have worked, offers a detailed and lively explanation of what the differences are between paying someone for the time they have been working or for how hard they have been working.

EXCERPT 1. GROUP 2 (HIGH).

Kattis: *Now you're (Jenny) a doctor, my father is. You work from seven sharp to five. Karin, you're also a doctor and you work from eight to four. But Karin she does seven eight operations during one day while Jenny here does five. That's a difference of three operations and she (Jenny) works less. Will their parents be paid for how many operations they perform or for how long they work? 'Cause my father says that in Germany or England, then, you get paid for how many operations you perform, here they pay you for how long you work.*

The interesting question in this context is how the students convert these principles about which they discuss so intensively into quantifications, i.e., how do they mathematise the problem after these deliberations?

Mathematising as Communicative Work

In the groups, the discussions move back and forth between these four models of reasoning. To give an overview over the outcome, Table 1 shows the models that are suggested as the first and final proposals respectively of the 26 groups.

Table 1. Models suggested for sharing money in first and final suggestion from the groups

Model for sharing	First suggestion No. of groups	Final suggestion No. of groups
I. Divide equally (180/2)	11	0
II. Amount of work	9	3
III. Time worked	6	14
IV. Piece rate/payment by performance	0	7

As can be seen, the most frequent initial suggestion is to share the money equally. This proposal however does not appear as the final option in any of the groups, which can be taken as a sign that the groups did consider the modelling aspect of the task. And, as we have already pointed out, a guess is that this particular solution is conceived as too simple by the members of the groups in order for the task to qualify as an exercise in mathematics.

When it comes to the final suggestion, the above figures must be interpreted with caution. It is sometimes difficult to see what model is being decided on at the end of the problem-solving process, and in a few cases it is also difficult to see if the calculations performed are congruent with the model suggested. However, it is clear that time is the variable most frequently considered as relevant for dividing the money, and the payment by performance model comes second. Two groups never arrive at a final decision about how to model the task. Let us take a brief look at the various models that were used and the calculations they resulted in.

Calculations Using Time as Premise

When using time as the relevant criterion for dividing the money, the most frequent solution is to calculate how many hours in all the two boys have worked, which is six. As a next step follows a division 180/6, which gives 30 SEK per hour. Following this model, the final step is to multiply 4 by 30 to get the sum for Charles and 2 by 30 for Martin. The following excerpt from one of the groups gives a clear illustration of how this model was implemented in the calculations.

EXCERPT 2. GROUP 17 (AVERAGE).

Ingrid: *It is six hours and if you divide 180 by six and then Charles will get four sixths and Martin two sixths.*

The information about the square metres that the boys rake is also introduced in many discussions without making clear that there is an inconsistency in the modelling if one tries to combine the two variables of time and square metres. Another model of reasoning that is based on time is the following.

EXCERPT 3. GROUP 24 (AVERAGE).

Kristina: *I took 180 and divided it by two that makes 90. Charles worked twice as long. That's why he should have another 45 crowns.*

Two groups use this model of giving 135 and 90 crowns to the two boys, respectively, as their final suggestion of how to solve the problem.

Calculations Using Amount of Work and/or Payment by Performance as Premises

Also in the cases in which the groups focus on the amount of work the boys have carried out, time is more or less explicitly present as a factor. This is also what makes the problem solving more complicated for the participants. Most of the reasoning that builds on models taking into account how much the boys have been raking, or how fast (or hard) they have worked, involves estimating, rather than calculating, how these factors should be handled. One approach is to divide by two and then compensate Charles for having worked more by raking 700 square metres. This results in two different answers. In one case, the amounts suggested are 100 and 80 crowns, for the two boys respectively, and in the other case 110 and 70.

EXCERPT 4. GROUP 21 (HIGH).

Nina: *If we got 90 each, then one should have less and the other should have more. The difference should be a bit bigger. One should have 70 and the other should have 110.*

The groups that attempt to consider the difference in efficiency end up in rather complicated forms of reasoning. This argumentation on how to pay by performance is sometimes difficult to translate into a principle for calculating that takes into account the information provided. Two groups end up in calculations with several decimals in their attempts to ascertain how fast the two boys manage to rake one square metre. Based on this figure, the members go on to extrapolate a way of sharing of the money that corresponds to the pace of work. In other groups, the members do not go as far as to the details of making calculations, but rather one establishes that there is a difference in the pace of work and that this should be reflected in how the money is divided. In this case this implies that one argues that the difference should be smaller than if one uses time as the decisive factor.

If one looks at what suggestions for dividing the money the 26 groups eventually end up in (and in many cases with considerable support from the researcher present), one finds that the model which implies using the time as the decisive factor for sharing the money is the most frequent one, as we have already pointed out. Fourteen groups decide on this model and this implies that one ends up in one of two answers; 120 and 60 or 135 and 45, respectively. Among the groups that use the payment by performance model, the most frequent strategy is one of roughly estimating, rather than calculating, what the difference should be. Or, alternatively, one argues that there is some kind relationship between the numbers given in the task. In these groups, one arrives at a conclusion that the money should be divided either as 110 and 70 or as 100 and 80. Two groups engage in rather complicated modes of reasoning, and the discussions do not result in any clear-cut final decisions on how to divide the money.

Reasoning and Discourse: Why is the Problem Difficult?

It is obvious from the discussions in the groups that the students are not used to or prepared for this kind of problem. At a concrete level, the problems they have seem to be different from what is generally found in the literature on word problems. In this literature, it is often emphasised that the students do not make "realistic considerations" in the sense that they do not consider seriously what is written in the text and how this relates to an external reality. Rather, they treat the word problem as any ordinary mathematics task and end up in an answer where the mathematical solution arrived at is unrealistic.

In this case, the students are continuously considering what is a reasonable and realistic manner of reasoning. That is, they are involved in inter-semiotic work moving between the verbal description, the model and the calculations. The different models I-IV are all reasonable, and they can be argued for as logical if one makes certain assumptions as premises for the problem solving. It is quite reasonable to divide the money equally among friends (and irrespective of your work effort). Time can of course also be seen as a relevant criterion when compensating for work efforts, and whether one has managed 500 or 700 square metres may very well be argued for as a decisive factor in a situation such as the one described in the problem. And, from a similar point of view, how hard you have worked can also serve as a premise for how to share money in a fair manner. In spite of the fact that all groups engage in such realistic reasoning, their analytical work is quite unsystematic. When finishing the problem, most groups also seemed uncertain if they really had managed to deal with the problem in a sensible manner. It does not seem reasonable to assume that the students lack the cognitive abilities or the skills relevant for solving a problem of this kind. Instead, we argue that the difficulties they are experiencing are of two kinds. One of them has to do with the situated nature of the practice they are engaged in; the other one is related to the fact that they do not seem to be used to making the kind of analysis that this type of problem presupposes.

The first type of difficulty implies that the students attempt to handle the problem as a mathematics exercise, or, in other words, their thinking is situated in the specific communicative context which is the mathematics class. This implies, among other things, that the participants during most of their work assume that there is one solution in which all factors can be taken into account simultaneously. Another consequence of this situatedness in mathematics learning is also that they seem to assume that all the information presented in the task must be included.

EXCERPT 5. GROUP 17 (HIGH).

Martin: *Charles is raking for four hours but if we put it like this and if Martin would have raked for two hours, then it would be solved a long time ago. But now it said about the square metres and then one must calculate how much they work per hour. That's why the square metres are mentioned.*

What Martin argues can be seen as the result of a particular kind of communicative socialisation which creates specific kinds of expectations (but not others) of what is rational when solving a problem of this kind. It could not be as simple as only using the six hours for dividing the money; that would be too simple for the problem to fit into the category of a word problem. You have to, Martin argues, take the square metres into account in order to arrive at a problem which is mathematically complex enough to qualify as an exercise in this context.

The tacit assumption behind the activities in all groups is that there has to be a mathematical solution that takes into account all the information given in the task. This is also the main reason why the problem is so difficult for the participants. More specifically, the fundamental problem for the participants is that they do not realise that one has to establish *what model to use*, and *then* temporarily continue the reasoning and the calculations *within* the framework of that model. Instead of characterising this difficulty as a problem of insufficient understanding of language (when reading the problem), or of lack of mathematical abilities in any general sense, we would like to see this as a discursive problem (Resnick, Säljö, & Pontecorvo, 1997), which has to do with an unfamiliarity with realising in what context and on what level a particular argument is relevant. What happens in the discussions, thus, is that the members continuously mix the various models used for calculating, and they come with arguments and counterarguments without taking into account on what model a particular contribution to the discussion

	Model	
Amount of work done	Time	Pay by performance
Daniel: *He did more. He [Charles] did 700 and he [Martin] did 500 ...*		
	Daniel: *One works twice as much as the other ...*	
		Daniel: *He who works two hours more should have more than 90. He who works for two hours, he should have a little more 'cause he does 500 metres. That's not very much less than 700.*
	Sofia: *It sort of depends on how long he works. One has to think of the hours as well.*	
Daniel: *Someone did 700 and someone 500 and then the difference is 200*		
		Ida: *Martin must have some more since he did it so fast (...)*
Daniel: *Yes, but he had less ...*		
		Ida: *Yes, but he did it much faster.*
Daniel: *Yes but he had much less*		
	Daniel: *Charles worked for four hours and he for two hours.* Sofia: *Yes, that's twice as much*	
Daniel: *If one takes 700 divided by two that makes it 350. And then150 is more than half [i.e., 600].Then it should be some more for that, since*		

LEARNING TO MODEL

	Model	
Amount of work done	Time	Pay by performance
one works half the time.		
How much?		
Ida:		
How much?		
Daniel:		
You don't have to worry		
about the time?		
		Ida:
		Both.
	Ida:	
	He did four hours	
	and he did more.	
	He did two hours	
	less.	
Sofia:		
Why should he get a 100		
and he 80?		
Daniel:		
How much of the work they		
did.		
Ida:		
The lot is 1200.		
Daniel:		
Yes one is to calculate		
what share of the work		
they did.		
Ida:		
Together.		

builds. Let us illustrate this by quote from Group 7 (High), where the members move between the models and calculations without noticing what premises apply in each case.

We do not have to discuss this excerpt in all its detail. Rather, the point is one of illustrating that the members in a discussion of this kind identify the various options with respect to modelling the task that are possible. But what makes the reasoning unclear – also for the participants – is that one does not distinguish between the principles and identifies when one speaks within each of them and when one moves between them. Put differently, the members do not continue the reasoning within one model so that the consequences become clear, and then continue with the next one to see where it leads to. Instead, the counterarguments against one model often come from a different model without realising that the premises for the reasoning and calculations have changed. In the first three utterances in this excerpt, we see how Daniel moves between the three models without considering that they are different in terms of their premises and implications. Sofia then comes in and argues that one has to consider the time, and Daniel responds to her comment by pointing out that one has to take the areas into account. Ida, in her first contribution, introduces the pay by performance model. And in this manner the discussion goes on.

By arguing that the problem of understanding is discursive in nature, we want to emphasise that it concerns how one argues, and how one decides what arguments are relevant within one particular model, and which arguments that imply that one moves over to another model with different, and conflicting, assumptions.

An interesting question is what role the mathematical skills of the students play in this case. We will not go deeply into this matter. There are some differences, but as far as the essential difference is concerned, the groups are quite similar. The groups that have been described as high-achievers by their teachers discuss the problem more intensively, and they go into the different models more in depth and establish what calculations have to be carried out. But, and this is important, they do not seem to be more prepared to deal with tasks of this kind. Even the high-achievers assume that there is one principle for mathematising that takes into account all the information provided. This model is what they are searching for, and this is why they end up in the same difficulties as the other groups. The students who have been characterised as low-achievers most frequently end up in the model where time is the decisive criterion, and they disregard the rest of the information. Using this model results in calculations that are manageable.

CONCLUSIONS

Word problems, which are such a central part of mathematics learning, can be seen as attempts to connect mathematical reasoning to everyday life. Thus, they are manifestations of the idea that mathematics is part of mundane practices in everyday life. The pupils are presented with short stories in writing, and they are required to discover and extract the mathematics that is relevant to solving them. The task for the students is to realise what mathematical symbols and operations are applicable. The information provided in such exercises is often organised so that the decision on how to model them is facilitated, i.e., they are S-problems in Verschaffel et al.'s (2000) terminology. After the symbol manipulation part of the exercise, the result arrived at has to be "reinterpreted" in the context of the real world practices which are described in the task, since the student is expected to decide what the answer means.

The studies which have been carried out on word-problem solving illustrate that the students are acting in a complex situation. From an analytical perspective one can describe, as the essence of this complexity, that the students have to engage in inter-semiotic work whereby a text written in natural language has to be translated into mathematical form and then back again. Or, expressed differently, from the cognitive point of view the task requires that the student oscillates between the mathematical model and the written account of a physical reality. The difficulties students experience cannot be reduced to handling the information given and combining it with whatever they know. They very clearly understand the information and they consider it from various points of view. They obviously make the information given into a figure in their reasoning, and they are searching for a suitable mathematical ground against which to interpret it.

It is therefore not surprising that the students during mathematics lessons stay within the mathematical world and let the mathematical syntax decide the solution of a practical, everyday problem. The background against which the reasoning takes place is mathematics, and this mode of reasoning is strengthened by the particular culture of school mathematics (see Bruner, 1996). The word problems are surrounded by tacit assumptions such as that every problem is possible to solve, all information given should be used, there is only one possible solution and only one correct answer. Socialisation into such a tradition for interpreting problems makes it difficult to realise what this particular problem is about.

What this study points to is an alternative perspective on human knowing and skills in which the discursive nature of our knowledge is emphasised. Such a perspective also opens up for a discussion of pedagogical considerations that extend beyond mathematics learning. Through discourses people develop systematic modes of communicating about phenomena in the world. Discourses are mechanisms for, as Östman (1995) points out, meaning making that exclude and include explanations of phenomena according to certain "rules." When talking about everyday matters, we use everyday discourse. When reasoning in mathematics, we engage in meaning making within another discourse with different rules.

As individuals we constantly move between different kinds of discourses that sometimes overlap and sometimes are mutually exclusive. As a consequence, we sometimes have to consider what discursive practices are relevant when solving problems and when arguing in a particular setting. That such moves between discourses – inter-semiotic work – is sometimes complicated is illustrated by the study about the concept of week, which we summarised at the beginning of this chapter. Most of the high-achieving students in that study managed to move between discursive boundaries without any problem; they realised that a week can be either seven days (calendar week) or five days (school week) depending on what discursive practice is relevant. The low-achieving students, on the other hand, to a much higher degree stayed within one discursive practice and kept to the "rule" that a week is seven days. Consequently, when given problems where the relevant definition of a week is five days, they run into problems in spite of the fact that they know very well that they only go to school five days a week. This observation illustrates that moving between discourses requires complex and subtle skills about how to make meaning in a world on paper (Olson, 1994).

The students participating in this study encountered a different kind of difficulty where incompatible information was given in the formulation of the problem. In order to manage this kind of problem, one has to realise when one is moving within and between specific discursive constructions. One has to perform an analysis of the following kind: if one assumes that one divides the money in accordance with the time the boys have worked, what will the result be? If we consider how much land one has raked, what will the outcome be? and so on. Following the results produced through these different models, and the calculations they result in, one can discuss what is a reasonable way of dividing the money. Thus, the argumentation has to be of a deductive and argumentative kind. A premise or a model produces a certain result, which one then has to consider in terms of its implications when it comes to dividing the money. Once the premises for the argumentation are established, the calculations follow, and one has to stick to these rules in order to be able to consider the results.

The students in our study have problems in precisely this respect; they do not manage to keep apart the various models, and the reasoning they imply. They are not able to realise what the logic of the argumentation is as it unfolds and what are productive arguments at a particular point in time. Instead, arguments, reasons and information that belong to different mathematical models are introduced without considering how these can be accounted for within a specific model.

In all groups the members engage in "realistic considerations", and they spend most of the time discussing how one can solve the problem in a manner which is reasonable from a pragmatic point of view. In all groups but a few, the members are also dissatisfied with their apparent inability to find a model for sharing the money which takes all the information given into account in a reasonable manner.

The pedagogical conclusion is that the students have to learn to consider and evaluate what can be accommodated to within one model and its logic, and what falls outside this particular model and its assumptions. At the same time as our study illustrates the obvious difficulties students have in this respect, it also documents that it most likely would be quite easy for a teacher, or a more competent peer, to use Vygotskian language, to enter into a dialogue with the students in which this nature of the problem is made clear. Thus, the students in our groups should be given insights into what it implies to use models and to engage in inter-semiotic reasoning, in order to make them able to shift between discursive positions that are productive for solving a problem in accordance with certain assumptions. Developing such skills is a central feature of what it means to learn in a complex and ambiguous world, where multiple interpretations of objects and events often occur, and where knowing is always relative to the assumptions one has to make.

ACKNOWLEDGEMENTS

The research reported here has been funded by The Swedish Research Council. This chapter was written while the first author was a Finland Distinguished Professor at the Centre for Learning Research, University of Turku.

NOTES

[1] To make the transcripts easier to read, we have edited them without changing the meaning of what is said. For the sake of facilitating the understanding of the dialogues, we have also used digits in the transcriptions when referring to the sums of money and the square metres.
[2] Low indicates that the group members had been characterised by their teacher as low-performing in mathematics. The two other groups are referred to as Average and High, respectively.
[3] Text written in this style are original data (translated from Swedish).

REFERENCES

Bakhtin, M. M. (1986). *Speech genres and other late essays*. Austin, TX: University of Texas Press.
Baruk, S. (1985). *L'âge du capitaine. De l'erreur en mathématiques* [The age of the captain. On errors in mathematics]. Paris: Seuil.

Bruner, J. S. (1996). *The culture of education*. Cambridge, MA: Harvard University Press.
Freudenthal, H. (1973). *Mathematik als pädagogische Aufgabe* [Mathematics as a pedagogical task]. Stuttgart: Klett.
Greer, B. (1997). Modelling reality in mathematics classrooms: The case of word problems. *Learning and Instruction, 7*, 293–307.
Keller, C., & Keller, J. D. (1996). *Cognition and tool use: The blacksmith at work*. New York: Cambridge University Press.
O'Halloran, K. (2003). Intersemiosis in mathematics and science. Grammatical metaphor and semiotic metaphor. In A. M. Simon-Vandenbergen, M. Taverniers & L. Ravelli (Eds.), *Grammatical metaphor* (pp. 337–366). Amsterdam: John Benjamins.
Olson, D. R. (1994). *The world on paper*. Cambridge, UK: Cambridge University Press.
Östman, L. (1995). *Socialisation och mening. No-utbildning som politiskt och miljömoraliskt problem* [Socialisation and meaning. Education in natural sciences as political and environmentally moral problem]. Uppsala, Sweden: Acta Universitatis Uppsaliensis.
Resnick, L. B., Säljö, R., & Pontecorvo, C. (1997). Discourse, tools and reasoning. In L. B. Resnick, R. Säljö, C. Pontecorvo & B. Burge (Eds.), *Discourse, tools, and reasoning* (pp. 1–20). New York: Springer.
Reusser, K., & Stebler, R. (1997). Every problem has a solution: The suspension of reality and sense making in the culture of school mathematics. *Learning and Instruction, 7*, 309–328.
Rommetveit, R. (1974). *On message structure*. London: Academic Press.
Säljö, R., & Wyndhamn, J. (1988). A week has seven days. Or does it? On bridging linguistic openness and mathematical precision. *For the Learning of Mathematics, 8*(3), 16–19.
Scribner, S. (1984). Studying working intelligence. In B. Rogoff & J. Lave (Eds.), *Everyday cognition: Its development in social context* (pp. 9–40). Cambridge, MA: Harvard University Press.
Verschaffel, L., Greer, B., & De Corte, E. (2000). *Making sense of word problems*. Lisse, The Netherlands: Swets & Zeitlinger.
Wertsch, J. V. (1998). *Mind as action*. New York: Oxford University Press.
Wertsch, J. V. (2007). Mediation. In H. Daniels, M. Cole & J. V. Wertsch (Eds.), *The Cambridge companion to Vygotsky* (pp. 178–192). New York: Cambridge University Press.
Wyndhamn, J., & Säljö, R. (1997). Word problems and mathematical reasoning – A study of children's mastery of reference and meaning in textual realities. *Learning and Instruction, 7*, 361–382.

Roger Säljö
University of Gothenburg
Sweden
and
University of Turku
Finland

Eva Riesbeck
Linköping University
Sweden

Jan Wyndhamn
Linköping University
Sweden

NORIYUKI INOUE

10. THE ISSUE OF REALITY IN WORD PROBLEM SOLVING

Learning from Students' Justifications of "Unrealistic" Solutions to Real Wor(l)d Problems

INTRODUCTION

Many researchers have investigated the tendency of students to give unrealistic answers to real wor(l)d problems without considering familiar aspects of reality (Greer, 1993, 1997; Verschaffel, De Corte, & Lasure, 1994; Wyndhamn & Säljö, 1997, etc.). However, it has been also reported that students who give unrealistic answers attempt to justify their answers when the disconnect is pointed out (see Verschaffel, Greer, & De Corte, 2000). This chapter describes a study that examined the nature of these justifications and attempts to derive meaningful educational implications from them.

Rationales Underlying "Unrealistic" Solutions

When it was first reported that school-age children have a tendency to solve real wor(l)d problems without considering familiar aspects of reality, many researchers and educators became highly concerned with the tendency. For instance, consider the widely discussed problems in the following:

12 sheep and 13 goats are on a boat. How old is the captain? (Baruk, 1985)

John's best time to run 100 m is 17 seconds. How long will it take to run 1 km? (Verschaffel et al., 1994)

In solving these problems, a majority of early grade elementary school students readily responded "25 years old" to the first problem, as if the captain's age could be determined by the number of the animals, and more than 90% of 13 and 14-year-olds responded "170 seconds" to the second problem, as if the person could maintain the best time for 1 km, failing to reflect common-sense understanding of reality in problem solving. Similar findings have been replicated for a wide variety of problems, across different age levels, and cultural settings (see Verschaffel et al., 2000).

Schoenfeld (1991) characterised this type of problem solving as "suspension of sense-making", referring to the disconnect between problem solving and the students' understanding of reality. Based on this view, the students' problem solving is reduced to a procedural, mindless activity with little sense-making beyond the quantitative procedures used in problem solving. If this is truly the case, this disconnect is highly problematic for mathematics educators and researchers who attempt to ground mathematical reasoning in students' everyday knowledge. In solving these word problems, students seem to be failing to take into account their understanding of everyday practices described in the word problems.

However, as this phenomenon has become widely recognised, new theoretical discussions on this issue have emerged. Hatano (1997) argued that these "unrealistic" solutions might not be totally unrealistic or disconnected from everyday knowledge. The student's solutions could stem from difference in the interpretations of the problem situation between the students and the researchers. For instance, answering 17 sec × 1000/100=170 sec to the above runner problem is not really unrealistic if the students assume that the runner is a well-trained super-athlete who does not experience fatigue while running 1 km.

Cooper (1994, 1998) offers a different explanation for the reason behind the "unrealistic" solutions, arguing that it stems from the socio-cultural norm of schooling that emphasises de-contextualised, calculational exercises. According to this view, students' "unrealistic" responses reflect the students' socio-cultural relationship to school mathematics and their willingness to employ the approaches emphasised in school. In fact, it is reported that students tend to give less unrealistic answers if a real wor(l)d problem is presented as a social studies problem, rather than a mathematics problem (Säljö & Wyndhamn, 1993).

These discussions imply that the "unrealistic" solutions may not simply stem from mindless or procedural problem solving, but could originate in students' diverse effort to make sense of the problem solving in terms of their personal understanding of the problem situation and the nature of the problem solving activity in the socio-cultural context. In fact, many students whose problem solving did not seem to reflect familiar aspects of reality are known to defend their answers when their attention is drawn to the issue (see Verschaffel et al., 2000). Some of the interpretations are highly creative, as exemplified by the child who suggested that the captain was given an animal on each birthday so that he could keep track of his age (Selter, 1994). Others are less far-fetched, such as the assumption about a super-fit athlete mentioned above.

Inoue (2005) used the clinical interview method to conduct a systematic study on this issue with undergraduate students, and found that some of the responses that initially looked unrealistic actually entailed sensible rationales that had stemmed from the difference in the interpretations of the problem situation or the students' willingness to conform to the socio-cultural norm of schooling. For instance, consider the following problem.

> You need to arrive at JFK international airport at 7 PM to pick up a friend. At 4 PM, you left for the airport that is 180 miles away. You drove the first 60 miles in an hour. Your friend called you and asked if you could be on time. How would you respond?

Our common-sense understanding of the traffic around a metropolitan airport is that the car cannot get to the airport at 7 PM due to traffic jams and various road conditions. Therefore, examples of what qualify as "realistic" answers could be:

– The car would arrive at the airport later than 7 PM since the car would get stuck in traffic jams.
– The car could get to the airport on time, only if there is no road construction or traffic jams on the way.
– The arrival time would depend on the traffic condition. If there is no traffic jams, the car can get to the airport at 7 PM, but if there are traffic jams, it will be late.

In this study, about 70% of the undergraduate students sampled from the greater New York area failed to reflect these "common-sense" factors in their answers, simply responding that the car will arrive at the airport at 7 PM on time. They all used simple proportional reasoning (e.g., 180/60 = 3 hours) to calculate the answer without reflecting on their experiences of driving to the urban airport and getting stuck in heavy traffic jams. On the surface, the students' problem solving seems mindless or irrational. However, in-depth clinical interviews with these students indicated that many of these responses were not totally unrealistic answers. Some of them (14%) were based on the "conformist approach" where students knew that real-life factors, such as traffic, would influence their real-life situations, but they intentionally ignored these factors in problem solving because of assuming that they were supposed to use only the numbers given in the problem. Others (24%) were based on the students' idiosyncratic interpretations of the problem situations (e.g., you can use an alternative route when there are traffic jams on the highway), of which 8% of the responses included evidence that these interpretations took place during problem solving and 16% did not entail such evidence, that is, the students could have simply calculated the numbers during the problem solving and devised sensible justifications in the interview situation. (The nature of these post-hoc justifications will be discussed later.) Excluding these cases, only 32% of the answers were found to be purely calculational answers for which the students did not provide any sensible rationale, even when the unrealistic nature of their responses was pointed out to them.

To summarise, the study evidenced that the students' seemingly calculational answers were actually based on 1) personal interpretations of the problem situation, either during of after the problem solving, which differed from the researchers' common-sense understanding of the problem situation, 2) personal interpretations of the nature of problem solving as calculation exercises that overrode their inclination to think about the real-life factors not described in the problem, or 3) purely calculational answers for which the student did not make any effort to give any justification or rationale. Inoue (2005) argues that looking into students' justifications of their seemingly unrealistic answers can inform us of the various ways in which students interpret and make sense of the problem situation as well as the nature of problem solving activity.

What is Really "Realistic"?

When research on real wor(l)d problems was initially introduced to the research and education community, the only correct responses were considered to be the ones that reflect common-sense understanding (as interpreted by the researchers) of real life practices (see Baruk, 1985; Carpenter, Lindquist, Matthews, & Silver, 1983; Davis, 1989, for instance). However, we have increasingly become aware of the need to use more refined criteria to evaluate students' responses so that we can better analyse the ways in which students solve different types of real wor(l)d problems (Inoue, 2008; Verschaffel et al., 2000). An important question is what we should employ as meaningful criteria in evaluating students' responses to real wor(l)d problems at this time. More specifically, what evidence warrants us to consider that students who solved a real wor(l)d problem engaged in the problem solving as a mindless, irrational activity disconnected from their understanding of reality?

For instance, if students employ different interpretations of the problem situation (e.g., taking alternative routes in the airport problem), this type of response should not be seen as inferior to "realistic" solutions (as judged by the researchers and educators) since both types of solutions are based on the students' *personal* understanding of reality. The only difference is in whether or not the students' personal interpretations of realistic situations match the common-sense understanding of the everyday situation. As long as the students' interpretations of their solutions are grounded in the students' understanding of reality, we cannot label such responses as irrational or mindless.

However, there is a methodological challenge here. If the students engaged in a personal interpretation of the problem solving *after* common-sense real-life factors (e.g., traffic jams, fatigue, etc.) were pointed out, one could argue that such a post-hoc creation of interpretations is a mere excuse to defend themselves. However, it could also be argued that they at least attempted to bridge mathematical problem solving to their real-life experiences, even if this might have taken place retrospectively. Put differently, the post-hoc justification of their answers could be seen as evidence that the students have not totally given up grounding the problem solving in their everyday experiences (Inoue, 2008). Even though their personal interpretation could have taken place in response to the interviewer's prompt after problem solving, it could indicate that they did not totally throw away the effort to make sense of problem solving in terms of their experiences, once they learned that the new rule of the game was that real-life factors matter in the problem solving. In this sense, this type of response is not totally unrealistic and disconnected from their understanding of reality. Rather, it could be seen as reflecting the students' attempt to associate problem solving with their personal understanding of real life practices.

Then what about problem solving in which students know that the real life factors could influence the solution, but intentionally ignore them and provide a calculational answer based on the understanding that it is what is expected in the situation? Should this be regarded as a totally "unrealistic" response? According to the socio-cultural perspective discussed before (Cooper, 1994, 1998), this is not a totally unrealistic answer, since the students made a "realistic" attempt to survive in the socio-cultural discourse of school mathematics where they are normally expected to solve the problems using only the information described in the problem. In other words, their decision not to reflect on real life factors could be seen as a "realistic" effort to assimilate their problem solving to the socio-cultural discourse shared in mathematics classrooms.

If this is the case, one could argue that the same explanation could apply to the students who gave purely calculational answers (i.e., those who simply calculated numbers without recognising that the real-life factors could influence the solution and did not justify their answers even after that possibility was pointed out). The reason why they did not recognise the influence of real life factors or justify their answers could be that the prompt was too ambiguous for them to judge that the rule of the game was different. However, if they are explicitly told that they could link problem solving with their everyday experiences, they may be able to give sensible justifications of their answers using their personal experiences. In other words, even if the students gave calculational answers, it could be the case that many of them may be capable of giving sensible justifications of their calculational responses if they are explicitly asked to make sense of the problem solving in terms of their everyday knowledge. If this is the case, even the "purely calculational answers" may not serve as evidence that the students are mindless, irrational, and mechanistic problem solvers.

RESEARCH QUESTIONS

Based on the above discussions, a study was conducted to seek answers to the following questions. If students provide calculational answers and do not justify their answers, to what extent are they capable of providing rationales for their answers when they are explicitly asked to justify them? What is the nature of the rationales that they use for justifying their answers?

METHOD

In this study, 20 undergraduate students were recruited from an introductory-level psychology class in Southern California. Most of the existing research has used school-aged children for studying this issue, but this study employed undergraduate students since 1) they have more prior knowledge of everyday practices 2) and they are better at explaining their thoughts and justifications verbally.

In the study, the students were given two word problems whose solutions depended on realistic factors associated with the problem situation. The first problem was the airport problem discussed above in which the airport name was changed to Los Angeles International Airport, considering the fact that all the students lived in Southern California. For the second problem, half of the students were given the runner problem, and the other half of the students were given the reading problem adopted from Verschaffel et al. (1994) and Inoue (2005).

First problem

You need to arrive at Los Angeles International Airport at 7 PM to pick up a friend. At 4 PM, you left for the airport that is 180 miles away. You drove the first 60 miles in an hour. Your friend called you and asked if you could be on time. How would you respond?

Second problem

John's best time to run 100 meters is 17 seconds. How long will it take him to run 1 kilometre?

or

There are 240 pages of reading assignment. It usually takes 30 minutes to finish 20 pages. If the reading is started at 10 AM, can it be finished by 4 PM?

These problems have a similar mathematical structure and relationship to real- life factors, that is, the solution depends on the rate of progress influenced by factors such as fatigue and hunger. However, these problems differ in the ways that the students could answer them. The airport and reading problems elicit yes-or-no answers, while the runner problem requires a numerical answer. The analysis of the impact of this difference on the students' responses will be discussed later. In this study, only two problems were given to the students to avoid possible learning effects (the impact of which in solving two real wor(l)d problems was reported by Inoue (2005) to be trivial).

In the study, each student met with the experimenter individually. First, they were given the test form and asked to solve the two word problems by showing their work. No time limit was given to them. All the students seemed highly engaged in the problem-solving activity. After they solved the word problems, their written responses were examined. *If their responses did not seem to reflect the common-sense understanding of everyday situations, clinical interviews were conducted.* For each of their answers, the following questions were asked, based on the interview protocol developed by Inoue (2005):

1) If the same thing happens to you, would you respond in the same way in real life as you did in solving the problem? Why?

The students' answers to this question could show whether they intentionally ignored the real-life factors even though they were aware of their influence in the everyday situation. In other words, the answers to this question indicate whether or not the students solved the problem considering the real-life meaningfulness of the solution. If the students responded that their answers would work in real-life situations, the following question was asked. (If not, they were asked the third question.)

2) Your solution may not work in real life because of (real life factors). Why did you answer that way?

The students' responses to this question could demonstrate whether the students could justify their responses in terms of their idiosyncratic interpretations of the problem situation when confronted with the irrationality of their responses. If the students justified their answers with idiosyncratic interpretations of the problem situations, it implies they had formulated the interpretations either during or after the problem solving in response to this interview question. As discussed before, distinguishing these two types of responses poses a methodological challenge, but since the main focus of this study is on whether students who gave calculational answers (i.e., those who did not justify their answers) could justify their answers when they were explicitly prompted to do so, these two types of answer were not distinguished. (See Inoue (2005) and Verschaffel (2002) for more detailed discussions on distinguishing these two types of responses). In response to this interview question, if the students gave no justification of their responses and admitted that they simply calculated the numbers or intentionally ignored real-life factors, the following question was asked:

3) Please think about on what condition your answer could become realistic. Could you come up with any assumptions or explanations that can make your answers justifiable?

This question was asked to see if the students who admitted that they simply calculated numbers could make post-hoc justifications of their calculational answers when they were explicitly asked to do so. This question was also given as a prompt to make the assumption that the nature of problem solving is not a calculation exercise, but to find a solution that makes sense in terms of their everyday knowledge. It is possible that the students provide post-hoc justifications by being prompted by the first and second interview questions, but this question was asked to explicitly request the students who did not justify their answers up to this point to devise post-hoc justifications.

During the clinical interview, the interviewer probed unclear responses to gain an in-depth understanding of the students' interpretation, as suggested by Ginsburg (1997).

RESULTS

First, all the students' responses were classified into three categories based on their written answers and their responses to the first and second clinical interview questions. If a written response reflected the common-sense understanding of everyday practice (e.g., "the arrival time will be after 7 PM depending on the traffic condition"), then it was categorised as "solution based on common-sense understanding of everyday practice". If not, it was categorised into one of two further categories, depending on what happened during the interviews. If the students indicated that they would respond in the same way in real life in response to the first interview question and justified their seemingly calculational answer with a sensible rationale in response to the second interview question (e.g., "the arrival time can be 7 PM since there are no traffic jams on Sunday"), then it was categorised as "'unrealistic' solution that the student justified spontaneously". If the student intentionally ignored real-life factors or gave no justification for the response admitting that they simply calculated the numbers, then the response was categorised as "'unrealistic' solution that the student did not justify spontaneously".

Table 1 shows the distribution of responses to this portion of the clinical interview based on the above three categories. There were a total of 18 responses (45%) where the students did not give justifications of their solutions spontaneously, even after being alerted by the second interview question that their answers would not work in real-life situations. These 18 responses were given by 12 students, 5 who did not give justifications to either of the problems, and 7 who gave justifications to only one of the problems. The 18 cases included 2 cases (given by 2 different students) where they recognised the significance of the real-life factors in everyday situations, but intentionally ignored the real-life factors. For instance, one of the students who solved the airport problem indicated that he was aware that traffic jams could change the arrival time, but he ignored possible traffic jams in solving the problem since he thought that the purpose of the problem solving was to calculate the numbers provided in the problem and give the answer. Note that each student solved two problems, and, therefore, each student contributed twice to Table 1.

Table 1. Students' responses to the real wor(l)d problems based on the first and second interview questions

Types of responses	Overall Percentage	Airport	Reading	Runner
Solutions based on common-sense understanding of everyday practice	43 % (17/40)	60% (12/20)	50% (5/10)	0% (0/10)
"Unrealistic" solutions that the students justified spontaneously	13 % (5/40)	5% (1/20)	30% (3/10)	10% (1/10)
"Unrealistic" solutions that the students did not justify spontaneously	45% (18/40)	35% (7/20)	20% (2/10)	90% (9/10)
Sensible justifications were given after being prompted explicitly	76% (14/18)	57% (4/7)	100% (2/2)	89% (8/9)

Out of the 18 cases where the students did not give justifications of their solutions even when it was pointed out in the second interview question that their answers would not work in real-life situations, there were 14 cases when the students were able to provide sensible explanations when prompted to do so by the third interview question, confirming the hypothesis that a large majority of the students can justify their calculational answers when they are explicitly asked to do so.

As can be seen in Table 1, there were large differences in the ways students responded to the three questions used, possibly because of the difference in content characteristics of the wor(l)d problems such as whether the problem was asking for yes-or-no or a numerical answer and the degrees of creativity required to give sensible justifications, as discussed before. The differences in these content characteristics seem to have made a difference in the ways that the students perceived the problem requirements.

THE ISSUE OF REALITY IN MATHEMATICAL MODELLING

Table 2. Students' sample justifications of seemingly "unrealistic" solutions

	Airport Problem	Reading Problem	Runner Problem
Spontaneous justifications	– You can make up the time by increasing speed in the second hour.	– If I need to cram, I will put off eating and other things. – If a person is forced and not distracted, it is possible.	– He is a professional athlete. He can make his average time approach the best time.
Justifications after being prompted explicitly	– If it was on a national holiday and no one is on the highway, it is possible. It is possible, but not probable. – If it is on Sunday, the car would not be stuck in any traffic jam. – You can speed up before you get stuck in the traffic and compensate the delay.	– If you really care about the reading, it is possible. You can bring the book to the restroom and continue to read. You can also starve yourself if reading is important. – You can read faster in the beginning by expecting you would be tired later.	– The problem does not say that John runs 1 kilometer continuously. If he runs 100 meters separately, it is possible. – If he trains himself to run at the best time, he can always keep the pace. You can push yourself to that direction. – If John is a professional athlete, he is conditioned to run his best time for 1 kilometers. This would be possible only for a high functioning professional athlete practicing 365 days. – If a person is a marathon runner or in a track team, it would be possible. They are trained to maintain the speed. – It is possible, if John is a robot or superhero in a movie. – It is possible to sustain his speed since he went through a lot of training on this.

Table 2 lists a sample of post-hoc justifications that the students presented after they were prompted to do so in the third interview question (justifications after being prompted explicitly) as well as a sample of justifications that the students gave in response to the second interview questions (spontaneous justifications). As can be seen in Table 2, most of the students' justifications were based on the claim that common-sense real life factors do not necessarily apply to a particular real life situation. In other words, the most common strategy to justify their calculational answers was to designate a special situation and assumptions that could make their answers appear reasonable.

There were 4 out of 18 cases where the students could not justify their calculational answers even after being asked to justify their answers in the third interview question. Out of the 4 cases, 3 cases were from the airport problem and 1 case was from the runner problem. For the airport problem, the students who failed to give justifications inferred that it would be possible to get to the airport in the morning time, but they reasoned driving to the airport around 7 PM would definitely make them encounter a traffic jam. For the runner problem, the student simply stated that it would not be possible to run 1 kilometer with the best time to run 100 meters in any situation. In all of these cases, the students were able to give sensible justifications of the other problem that they solved.

DISCUSSION

In this study, a large majority of the students who gave calculational answers were able to give sensible rationales for those answers when asked to do so. Even if they did not justify their answers initially, they could provide sensible justifications of their calculational answers when explicitly prompted. It appears that the only thing that they needed was simply to be asked to do so. As discussed before, it has been suggested that "unrealistic" responses to real wor(l)d problems could largely stem from an "educational contract", that is, the students' relationship to the socio-mathematical norms of the problem-solving situation. The above finding indicates that the students can readily nullify this contract and make sense of their answers with their own interpretations of the problem situation if they clearly see that "the rules of the game" have changed.

Since the population of this study was undergraduate students, it is possible that this tendency may differ among school-age children because of the difference in their metacognitive capacity and sensitivity to the socio-mathematical norms. However, this study points to the possibility that school-aged children may also possess similar abilities to make sense of the calculational answers in terms of everyday experiences, possibly to different degrees.

What is Really Wrong with Calculational Answers?

These findings raise an important question. If the students who provided calculational answers could readily justify these answers when prompted to do so, what is really problematic about the students who such answers? On the surface, the students who gave calculational answers may appear mindless, irrational, or mechanistic. However, since most of the students who gave such answers possessed the ability to bridge the calculational answers and their everyday knowledge, what is really problematic seems to be the lack of the opportunity (or assurance) for the students to freely do so.

According to Lave (1992), word problem solving describes stylised representations of hypothetical experiences separated from the learners' experiences. In word problem solving, students' minds could be torn between two types of knowledge systems that the word problem activates – one developed in the traditional mathematics classroom and the other developed through real-world experiences (Inoue, 2005). In solving word problems, they could make a choice in this double-bind situation, with some of assuming that problem solving is an arena for sense-making in terms of their everyday experiences, and others that it is a school-based, calculation exercise disconnected from their understanding of real-life practices. In this study, 56% (i.e., 43% + 13% = 56% See Table 1.) of the problem solving reflected the former assumption and 45% did the latter assumption. However, once the students who had employed the latter assumption were prompted to employ the former assumption, almost all were able to function under this assumption and make sense of their calculational answers in terms of their everyday knowledge. What was needed was simply to be asked to make the assumption that problem solving is an arena for finding a solution that would make sense in real-life practices. This indicates that the students' tendency to disconnect problem solving and their everyday experiences is dependent on the way they interpret the nature of the problem-solving activity as well as whether they were given the opportunity to interpret problem solving in terms of their everyday experience.

The Nature of Justifications

Looking into the students' strategies to justify their answers, most of the students rationalised their solutions by referring to special cases where common-sense factors could become irrelevant. In a way, this reflects an epistemological shift in their interpretation of the problem solving from being asked to provide an answer that does not depend on a specific situation toward being asked to find a real life case where their calculational answers would appear realistic. For instance, the justification "the car will get there at 7 PM since there is no traffic on Sunday" incorporates this strategy to justify the problem solving in terms of a specific case, after examining a variety of situational assumptions and choosing an appropriate assumption among them, namely that the driving is taking place on Sunday. In a way, this is a highly intellectual endeavour.

Obviously, in traditional schooling, students are not asked to examine different sets of assumptions for solving mathematical word problems. Word problem solving in school contexts serves as a game under "tacitly agreed rules of interpretation" (Greer, 1997, p. 297). These rules are internalised in the students' minds through the socio-mathematical norm, or "hidden curriculum" of traditional schooling that could influence many aspects of the intellectual activities in schools (Gatto, 1992; Waller, 1932). For instance, consider the following assumptions about word problem solving that could be shared in traditional settings:
- You are not supposed to use the information not presented in the problem description.
- You need to perform at least one mathematical operation to generate the answer.
- You are not allowed to say that the answer really depends on unknown factors.
- You are supposed to give an answer that is expressed in a numerical form.
- You are not supposed to justify your answer once it is determined to be wrong.

Although these possible assumptions are not derived from the data collected in this study, what underlies students' calculational answers could be the tendency to follow these types of rules that have been reinforced and internalised through their previous schooling. Similarly, there are many implicitly shared assumptions that need to be employed in using mathematical operations in school mathematics. For instance, consider the following examples violating one of the assumptions, in which equal signs that do not represent mathematical equivalence, but represent action-related changes or transformations from the initial states (the left side) to the resulting states (the right side), one possible assumption or interpretation that children could possess about equal signs (Ginsburg, 1996; Seo & Ginsburg, 2003):

$3 + 1 = 1$	Three wrestlers appeared on a computer screen followed by a fourth wrestler, and upon defeat, wrestlers disappear. Only one wrestler, who defeated all the others, remained.
$3 \times 4 = 13$	3 million dollars were deposited at four different times, and 1 million dollars of interest gradually accumulated during that period.
$12 \div 3 = 1$	12 hamburgers were shared by three persons, but each person wanted to eat only one.

What these examples highlight is the fact that employing different assumptions could create very different descriptions of real life events. These examples also illustrate that the complexity of real life situations could be described with different sets of assumptions from the ones employed in school mathematics. As a result, word problem solving imposes a cognitive challenge to the students. On the one hand, they feel the need to fit the basic mathematical assumptions and representations that they learn in schools in real life situations described in the problem. On the other hand, they feel that the real life practices described in the word problems are so complex and dynamic that simply applying the basic mathematical assumptions and representations that they learn in schools to the situations may not be feasible. This conflict could serve as one of the largest hurdles in grounding mathematical learning in students' everyday knowledge. (See Davis & Hersh (1981), Usiskin (2006), and Verschaffel et al. (2000, Chap. 7) for more detailed discussions on this issue).

This issue could also be seen as a manifestation of a form of tension between the theoretical and the applied approaches that exist in the field of mathematics. If one employs the theoretical approach, it is important to pursue a solution based on clear and pre-set assumptions shared by the theoreticians in the field. However, if one employs the applied approach, it is important to explore essential assumptions and conditions in the specific context and find the solutions that actually work and are suitable in that context. Obviously, mathematical problem solving skills that are taught in traditional schools reflect a narrow type of discourse heavily biased toward the theoretical, de-contextualised approach to problem solving (Nunes, Schliemann, & Carraher, 1993). The students' calculational answers could be seen to originate in such a bias in the traditional instruction of mathematics. In mathematics classrooms, word problems are often used with the intention of overcoming such a bias, but simply giving word problems that describe real-life situations to students will not resolve this issue. The real challenge for educators is to present students with "authentic dilemmas" (Lave, 1992, p. 85) that could engage their intentions to seek out authentic solutions.

Rich Educational Opportunity

An important question, then, is how educators could incorporate such authentic dilemmas in classroom activities. In this study, the students who were asked to justify their answers actually considered complex factors (e.g., days of the week, the purpose of reading, the training level of the runner, etc.) and made sense of the problem solving in terms of particular real-life situations. It could be argued that this is an important, authentic activity for students to engage in. One could list many examples from our real life practices where failing to do this could lead to a variety of disasters. For instance:
- Failing to take account of track patterns in drawing up a train operation schedule leads to derailing of a train at a curve.
- Failing to incorporate a possible sampling error leads to an erroneous prediction of an election result.
- Failing to incorporate annual changes in mortgage rates leads to bankruptcy.

Similarly, in mathematical modelling of real-life phenomena, the true challenge lies in determining an appropriate set of assumptions and conditions as well as effectively communicating the factors that would influence the model (Pollak, 1997). Without careful examination of the situational assumptions, word problem solving cannot be an authentic endeavour.

In this sense, asking students to examine the validity of various calculational answers to real wor(l)d problems has a large potential in bringing more authentic problem-solving activities into classrooms, especially in secondary schools where students have already established their understanding of basic mathematical operations. For instance, educators could initiate the following activities:
- Discussing a wide variety of problem solving situations where pure calculations do not provide solutions that would actually work in real life situations.
- Having students create their own justifications of calculational answers to real wor(l)d problems.
- Having students evaluate different solutions to real wor(l)d problems by listing the assumptions that make the solutions acceptable.
- Having students develop and represent mathematical models that incorporate a wide variety of real life factors using nested conditional statements or other meaningful representations.
- Having students discuss appropriate assumptions that could be used in specific contexts.

Through these activities, students could learn to go beyond school mathematics and develop their understanding of mathematical modelling practices. Attempts of this nature can be found in Verschaffel et al. (2000) where a series of design experiments that furnish some of these features is described. If this type of intervention is effectively implemented in mathematics classrooms, it would help students consider problem solving under different sets of assumptions and restructure mathematical problem solving towards a more meaningful, "realistic" activity relevant to their lives.

CONCLUSION

To conclude, this study suggests that examining a variety of "unrealistic" responses in mathematics classrooms could serve as an invaluable opportunity for us to discover effective ways of filling the gap between the theoretical and applied approaches to mathematical problem solving. Instead of dismissing students' calculational answers as simply irrational responses, considering different justifications of the calculational answers and examining different sets of assumptions for solving word problems can provide rich opportunities for students to learn how to use their mathematical knowledge beyond school-based problem solving. This could help the students conceptualise word problem solving in terms of meaningful assumptions and conditions for modelling reality, rather than the assumptions imposed by textbooks, teachers, or other authority figures. This is definitely an important agenda for educators who are preparing students for an increasingly complex world.

REFERENCES

Baruk, S. (1985). L'âge du capitaine. De l'erreur en mathématiques [The age of the captain. On errors in mathematics]. Paris: Seuil.

Carpenter, T. P., Lindquist, M. M., Matthews, W., & Silver, E. A. (1983). Results of the third NAEP mathematics assessment: Secondary school. Mathematics Teacher, 76, 652–659.

Cooper, B. (1994). Authentic testing in mathematics? The boundary between everyday and mathematical knowledge in national curriculum testing in English schools. Assessment in Education: Principles, Policy & Practice, 11, 143–166.

Cooper, B. (1998). Using Bernstein and Bourdieu to understand children's difficulties with "realistic" mathematics testing: An exploratory study. International Journal of Qualitative Studies in Education, 11, 511–532.

Davis, P. J., & Hersh, R. (1981). The mathematical experience. Boston: Birkhauser.

Davis, R. B. (1989). The culture of mathematics and the culture of schools. Journal of Mathematical Behavior, 8, 143–160.

Gatto, J. M. (1992). Dumbing us down: The hidden curriculum of compulsory schooling. St. Paul, MN: New Society Publishers.

Ginsburg, H. P. (1996). Toby's Math. In R. Sternberg & T. Ben-Zeev (Eds.), The nature of mathematical thinking. Mahwah, NJ: Erlbaum.

Ginsburg, H. P. (1997). Entering the child's mind: The clinical interview in psychological research and practice. New York: Cambridge University Press.

Greer, B. (1993). The mathematical modeling perspective on wor(l)d problems. Journal of Mathematical Behavior, 12, 239–250.

Greer, B. (1997). Modelling reality in mathematics classrooms: The case of word problems. Learning and Instruction, 7, 293–307.

Hatano, G. (1997). Cost and benefit of modeling activity. Commentary. Learning and Instruction, 7, 383–387.

Inoue, N. (2005). The realistic reasons behind unrealistic solutions: The role of interpretive activity in word problem solving. Learning and Instruction, 15, 69–83.

Inoue, N. (2008). Minimalism as a guiding principle: Linking mathematical learning to everyday knowledge. Mathematical Thinking and Learning, 10, 1–32.

Lave, J. (1992). Word problems: A microcosm of theories of learning. In P. Light & G. Butterworth (Eds.), Context and cognition: Ways of learning and knowing (pp. 74–99). Hillsdale, NJ: Erlbaum.

Nunes, T., Schliemann, A., & Carraher, D. (1993). Street mathematics and school mathematics. New York: Cambridge University Press.

Pollak, H. (1997). Solving problems in the real world. In L. Steen (Ed.), *Why numbers count: Quantitative literacy for tomorrow's America* (pp. 91–105). New York: College Board.
Säljö, R., & Wyndhamn, J. (1993). Solving everyday problems in the formal setting: An empirical study of the school as context for thought. In S. Chaiklin & J. Lave (Eds.), *Understanding practice: Perspectives on activity and context* (pp. 327–342). New York: Cambridge University Press.
Schoenfeld, A. (1991). On mathematics as sense-making: An informal attack on the unfortunate divorce of formal and informal mathematics. In J. Voss, D. Perkins, & J. Segal (Eds.), *Informal reasoning and education* (pp. 311–343). Hillsdale, NJ: Erlbaum.
Selter, C. (1994). How old is the captain? *Strategies, 5*, 34–37.
Seo, K.-H., & Ginsburg, H. P. (2003). "You've god to carefully read the math sentence…": Classroom context and children's interpretations of the equal sign. In A. J. Baroody & A. Dowker (Eds.), *The development of arithmetic concepts and skills* (pp. 161–188). Mahwah, NJ: Erlbaum.
Usiskin, Z. (2006). The arithmetic operations as mathematical models. In W. Blum, P. L. Galbraith, H.-W. Henn & M. Niss (Eds.), *ICMI study 14: Applications and modeling in mathematics education* (pp. 257–264). New York: Springer.
Verschaffel, L. (2002). Taking the modeling perspective seriously at the elementary school level: Promises and pitfalls (Plenary lecture). In A. Cockburn & E. Nardi (Eds.), *Proceedings of the 26th annual conference of the International Group for the Psychology of Mathematics Education* (Vol. 1, pp. 64–82). School of Education and Professional Development, University of East Anglia, U.K.
Verschaffel, L., De Corte, E., & Lasure, S. (1994). Realistic considerations in mathematical modeling of school arithmetic word problems. *Learning and Instruction, 4*, 273–294.
Verschaffel, L., Greer, B., & De Corte, E. (2000). *Making sense of word problems*. Lisse, The Netherlands: Swets & Zeitlinger.
Waller, W. W. (1932). *The sociology of teaching*. New York: Russell & Russell.
Wyndhamn, J., & Säljö, R. (1997). Word problems and mathematical reasoning – A study of children's mastery of reference and meaning in textual realities. *Learning and Instruction, 17*, 361–382.

Noriyuki Inoue
School of Leadership and Education Sciences
University of San Diego
San Diego, CA
U.S.A.

SHUK-KWAN S. LEUNG

RESEARCH EFFORTS ON PROBING STUDENTS' CONCEPTIONS IN MATHEMATICS AND IN REALITY: STRUCTURING PROBLEMS, SOLVING PROBLEMS, AND JUSTIFYING SOLUTIONS

Discussion of Part III: Probing Students' Conceptions

INTRODUCTION

I begin with some general points on this section and then summarise the main points from the four chapters, with particular attention to the significance of findings, limitations of the studies, and recommendations for extending research and applying its lessons in schools. I close with suggestions on how to learn about students' understanding in solving word problems and propose an elaboration of the model of problem solving created by Polya (1945). In explaining the model, I revisit tasks that were investigated in the studies reported in this section, and also refer to some of my prior results on mathematical problem posing.

After the first two sections of the book, on theoretical issues and socio-cultural factors, two sections on probing conceptions follow that build on the theoretical analyses and consideration of socio-cultural factors of the first two sections. In the third section the focus is on students while the fourth section targets teachers.

An important part of building a theory of mathematical cognition, and of teaching effectively, is to find ways to "enter the child's mind" (Ginsburg, 1997). A range of methodologies have been developed with this end in view (Ginsburg, 2009). Of course, inferring what another person is thinking is a complex process. In the present context, we are trying to get an understanding of how students, individually and collectively, think about the "real world" in relation to mathematics. Thus, students may learn that if a problem about ages in the "real world" (RW) leads to a quadratic equation in the "mathematical world" (MW) that has one positive and one negative solution (in MW), then only the positive solution is accepted (RW).

The attempt to probe the student's understanding is complicated by the fact that the student's thinking is affected by the conventions of mathematics and mathematics instruction and by their experiences in mathematics classrooms. For this reason, probing children's understanding is a necessary beginning, but it needs to be supplemented by studying the instructional history of the students, and in particular teachers' understanding, how that influences their teaching and how that, in turn, influences the behaviour of the students (as in the fourth section of this book).

In probing students' conceptions, task and subject variables have been promising guides for various research agendas in the history of research on mathematical problem solving and problem posing (Leung & Silver, 1997). In this section, the effects of a variety of such variables have been examined, based on various theoretical frameworks that have guided the design of tasks. In the following, particular attention will be given to the innovative aspects of the studies.

COMMENTS ON THE CHAPTERS

Within the four chapters three major themes regarding students' performances can be identified: structuring a problem (problem formulation or problem reformulation), problem solving, and justifying solutions.

The chapter by Verschaffel, Van Dooren, Chen, and Stessens introduces problem posing as a new methodology in the context of understanding children's construal of P-problems. Unlike standard word problems, in which the situation has been pre-packaged to the point that very superficial aspects can cue the response, the word problems investigated in this section involve judgments in deciding what appropriate models of the described situations might be.

The authors build on two existing bodies of research, namely: (a) that concerns with problem posing, including, in particular, its relationship to problem solving, and (b) the work on "problematic" word problems, or P-problems (Verschaffel, Greer, & De Corte, 2000), in which direct mapping on to one or more arithmetic operations is not appropriate when real-world considerations are taken into account. They point out that, hitherto, the research on problem posing and word problems has been limited to standard textbook problems (S-problems). In this study, the particular class of word problems considered, on which there exists a very considerable body of research, involves division with remainder (DWR). For such problems, many researchers have pointed out that children's responses often appear not to make sense, as in the case of the now infamous "buses" problem from the third National Assessment of Educational Progress in the U.S. (Carpenter, Lindquist, Matthews, & Silver, 1983).

Verschaffel et al. presented both problem solving and problem posing to the same students, looked for relationships between the performances, and established that DWR problems offer a fruitful context for such investigations. For the problem posing aspect of the study, they began from a suggestion by Streefland (1988) that children be asked to construct different word problems for which the "core calculation", a division of a positive integer by another, with remainder, is the same but the precise form of the answer depends on the context; in this case, three variants were used. In the parallel activity on problem solving, children were given three word problems for which the appropriate form of the answer differed depending on the situation described. Verschaffel et al. found a correlation between the performances on problem solving and problem posing, though, on the whole, students performed much better on problem solving than on problem posing. With respect to subject variables, age and ability level had the expected results, whereas gender differences were not statistically significant.

In this study, we can see the limitations of a one-shot data collection on both problem posing and solving. In my experience, with students and teachers in Taiwan and Hong Kong, children did not perform well in problem posing when we collected data only once. But after working with teachers, who acted as problem posers in teacher-training sessions, then studying how teachers used and designed problem-posing tasks in systematic action research relating to different mathematical content areas and at different grades, students improved in problem posing and a strong relationship to problem solving resulted (Leung, 2001). There is at least a "lag time" for children to become familiar with tasks like problem posing. In an earlier study, teachers reported that children became familiarised with problem posing task from the third week on (Leung, 1997). Gradually, after several weeks or so, they began to pose and solve their own tasks and modify friends' tasks, and, finally, were competent enough to critique and find "errors" in textbook or test items. My point is that the part on how teachers teach is missing in this chapter, and my suggestion, accordingly, is to consider collecting data again, from other students who have been taught real-world problem solving and are familiar with problem posing.

A number of suggestions may be made for alternative task variables. For example, one could try asking students to pose one easy and one difficult problem (Van den Heuvel-Panhuizen, Middleton, & Streefland, 1995). This method will enable a researcher to probe students' ranges of perceived difficulty, and their conceptions of easy and difficult will become apparent (see Silver, 1994, for other examples of this approach). Another variation would be to invite students to consider tasks matching situations with discrete or continuous quantities. For example, in RW, squeezing a few remaining students into 12 buses instead of finding 13 will save the cost of one bus. By contrast, when we divide milk into cartons, we need one more carton otherwise milk will be spilt!

The chapter by Xin is about constructing representations for "problematic" word problems, where it is necessary to refine a simplistic mapping of the solution described in the word problem on to arithmetic structures. The ten P-problems from Verschaffel, De Corte, and Lasure (1994) were translated (with appropriate adjustments) and investigated in China (as they have been in many countries). It could reasonably be argued that in many of these problems the presuppositions (Dillon, 1988) are unclear. In situations in which clarifications can be sought and given, or the interpretations can be negotiated, it would be natural to ask questions such as:
- In calculating the distance between two students' homes are the homes on opposite sides, or the same side, of the school?
- In tying two pieces of rope together, do we assume (e.g., as a simplifying assumption) that a knot takes up zero length of rope?
- In mixing hot liquids, should losing temperature to the surroundings be taken into account?

For comparison purposes, as in Verschaffel et al. (1994) and numerous replications, ten parallel "standard problems" (S-problems) were also included, where the straightforward mapping of the problems onto arithmetic operations is reasonable (at least as judged by the researchers). In all the many replications that have been reported, students have always achieved very high scores on the S-problems, and complications of interpretation have never been reported (perhaps because it has been assumed they don't occur).

Though performances by Chinese students on the P-items, in a number of studies, were higher than those reported in other countries, the general finding was also a lack of ability for Chinese students in solving P-problems appropriately. Performance improved with age, which Xin suggests could be due to increasing knowledge about the RW aspects of some of the problems (for example, the physics of mixing liquids of different temperatures). As with other replications, the nature of the problems, which are not homogeneous, can be implicated in the large range in difficulty level across the ten P-items. In particular, it has been suggested that problems like the buses or the balloon problem, for which RW considerations should come into play at the stage of interpreting the answer, are relatively easier because of that aspect.

As other researchers have done, Xin et al. checked the effects of interventions with written instructions printed on test papers, drawing students' attention to the need to consider that the problem might be not as easy as it seems, and asking them to consider the real-life situations behind the problem statements, then asking directly if it is appropriate to solve these problems by using straightforward arithmetic operations. As has generally been the case, they found rather small improvements, indicating that the tendency to respond without paying attention to RW is deep-seated and not just a matter of being alerted to the possibility.

A new theoretical element introduced in this chapter is the construct of cognitive holding power conceptualised by Stevenson (Stevenson & Evans, 1994), distinguishing between first order cognitive holding power (FOCHP) and second order (SOCHP). First order procedures are automated procedures that enable the achievement of specific goals, while second order procedures aim at more general purposes, draw on interpretation of new situations, apply existing knowledge in new ways, and enable transfer. This distinction is rather similar to that drawn by Hatano (2003, p. xi), defining routine expertise as: "Simply being able to complete school exercises quickly and accurately without understanding", whereas adaptive expertise means "the ability to apply meaningfully learned procedures flexibly and creatively". The application of this theoretical construct goes quite naturally with the methodological device (standard since Greer (1993) and Verschaffel et al. (1994)) of presenting matched pairs of S- and P-items, since the former, plausibly, require only FOCHP, and similarly routine expertise, whereas the latter require also SOCHP, and adaptive expertise.

From the data, Xin concludes that FOCHP is necessary but not sufficient for successfully solving P-problems. In his interpretation, FOCHP (as measured by a paper-and-pencil test) did not facilitate children to consider the realistic context, but offered basic knowledge required to solve P-problems. Three recommendations are made which accord with what many others have suggested. First, students should be confronted with more P-problems in their daily lessons and examinations. Second, teachers should apply more effective instructional approaches. Third, learning settings with high second order cognitive holding power should be created.

DISCUSSION PART III

Another original aspect is the careful distinction between showing indications of taking realistic considerations into account, and actually offering answers that are "correct", that is to say, appropriate as judged by the researcher. For example, an appropriate answer to the problem about the birthday party is that there would be at most 11 friends at the party.

It is clear from Xin's description of the educational environment that examinations in mainland China constitute a powerful socio-cultural factor in shaping teachers' teaching and students' learning. Such effects are well-known worldwide. For example, the effects on schools, teachers, and students of standardised testing in the United States have been documented by Nichols and Berliner (2007). If examinations are timed and there is not enough time, a way to score well is not to spend time addressing real life considerations (more generally, students are often advised not to think very much, but to answer quickly).

Xin makes positive suggestions about changing the nature of instruction. Finding out conditions for "can" is a natural next step after researching on "cannot". There should be more research on exploring possible innovations and improvements in instructions and setting, beyond merely reporting on what students cannot do. For example, in one study, knowing the fact that children fail to solve word problems, the researchers invited the more able students to convert word problems to versions they preferred and then used such problems in subsequent teaching (Cohen & Stover, 1981), finding that children improved in solving those problems. Once children are guided to do so, they perform better in attending to aspects of RW. It is left for us to study how and whether or not teachers and students can be changed over time (see Section 4 of this book). Perhaps, given the powerful effects of examinations, one way is to add test items like P-problems, or to include test items on first and second order cognitive power in assessing teachers.

The study by Säljö, Riesbeck, and Wyndhamn revolves around a word problem with no clear answer, given as a probe to Grade 5 students. The problem is about two boys being paid an amount of money for raking leaves. One rakes 700 square metres in 4 hours and the other 500 metres in 2 hours, and the question is how should they divide the money. The problem is interesting in many respects. It is reminiscent of the historic "Luca's problem" from the early days of probability theory, which is about the fair way of dividing stakes when a gambling game is terminated before the result becomes known. Davis and Hersh (1986, p. 24) show how complex the judgment is, and how dependent on the assumptions put into any model.

One can imagine that if the scenario described actually took place, the boys would take into account many other considerations. There are relevant aspects of the work done, such as whether the conditions were similar in the two areas worked on, and whether one boy did a more thorough job. There are also aspects relating to the boys, such as their interpersonal relationship, their individual economic circumstances, and so on. Thus, by being limited to a closed description, in which the only information available is that provided, it is signalled to the students that they must operate according to the rules of the "Word Problem game". On the other hand, there was the opportunity to discuss the problem in groups, and with the researcher, circumstances in which it is known that deeper thinking about RW aspects can take place (e.g., Wyndhamn & Säljö, 1997). Indeed, the students' suggested solutions evolved and deepened over time.

Central to the investigators' concerns is how the students negotiated the discursive boundaries within and between MW and RW, between mathematical and everyday discourses, a topic that is increasingly being researched in mathematics classrooms, including those with bilingual students (Adler, 2001). They concluded that the students did not grasp a fundamental aspect of modelling, namely that a model has a conditional aspect – if you make such and such assumptions, it implies such and such. As Säljö et al. put it (p. 187), "the fundamental problem for the participants is that they do not realise that one has to establish *what model to use*, and *then* temporarily continue the reasoning and the calculations *within* the framework of that model." However, on the basis of the study, they do suggest that it would be possible, with appropriate teaching, to provide students with this insight.

Säljö et al. concluded that there is a tacit assumption for all the students that there has to be a mathematical solution that takes into account all the information given in the task. Although there are multiple models, each with some justification, it is assumed to be a proportion problem and the general principle applied is direct proportion (the more you make an effort or produce work the more you get as pay). We can remember tasks with extraneous data in the inventory of problems on mathematical abilities in a Soviet study (Krutetskii, 1976). In this sense, if one uses data on number of hours only and ignores the area of land or vice versa then the other data are being treated as extraneous. Often, even if one direct proportion or the other was the basic principle put forward, the students attempted rough adjustments to take account of the other data.

The argumentation among the students does show awareness that different models are possible, and incompatible. There is even an interesting comment showing awareness that the appropriate model could be defined relative to different societal conventions, when one of the students points out that a doctor in some countries is paid by the number of operations performed, in another by the amount of time worked.

As with the study by Verschaffel et al., a major limitation is that there is only one task. Säljö et al. comment that it is obvious that the students are not used to this kind of problem. Accordingly, for further research efforts it would be appropriate to carry out an extension of this study with students who had experience in arguing about, and comparing models for, such problems. Säljö et al. (p. 192) conclude with the statement that: "Developing such skills is a central feature of what it means to learn in a complex and ambiguous world, where multiple interpretations of objects and events often occur, and where knowing is always relative to the assumptions one has to make."

Inoue's study has a different focus, namely using interviews to get a clearer view of what, at first sight, may be interpreted as "suspension of sense making" in responses to items on pencil-and-paper tests. He makes the important point that, in much of the research (e.g., Verschaffel et al., 2000) the researchers rely on their intuitions about what makes a response "realistic" or "non-realistic". These judgments may be queried in terms of students having different interpretations, perhaps idiosyncratic or whimsical. This point has been made previously by Selter (1994, this volume).

Inoue's study is different from most of the other research in this tradition in that college students were interviewed. That has certain advantages, but raises some questions about the "experimental contract", namely how did the students construe the experimental setting? Unfortunately, Inoue does not report what the students were told about the nature of the task they were being asked to work on and what the researcher's agenda was.

Besides two problems derived from earlier research, Inoue used another about figuring out whether one could get to the airport in time, in order to inform a friend one is planning to meet. This scenario is a situation with which presumably at least most of the students could identify. But, as with the fair division of pay problem posed by Säljö et al., it is one where, if the equivalent situation happened to the student, there would be more information either known or obtainable (see also Palm, this volume). So again, we may conjecture that the very form of the question, and the setting in which it is presented, cue the rules of the Word Problem game.

All tasks used by Inoue involved rate in some sense, and a reasonable approach to each would be to carry out a corresponding "core calculation" and then consider how it might be revised in the light of RW considerations. What Inoue focused on were cases in which the latter revision was not made initially on a pencil-and-paper test, and on students' justifications for responding in this way. The key strength of this study, as with Selter's work, is that it does not make assumptions about the students' rationale for their responses. By follow-up interviews, and a carefully arranged sequence of questions, Inoue aimed to tease apart cases where the students had reasonable, personal (maybe idiosyncratic) justifications for their "unrealistic" written answers, from cases where they could retrospectively provide such a justification. Inoue argues that, even in the latter case, there is an indication of ability to relate MW and RW aspects.

Thus, his methodology supplements findings in the other three chapters. Asking a person to solve a structured problem (like the Airport problem), and provide an answer is not sufficient. We also care how they provide justifications and whether the answers are reasonable. One alternative methodology is to ask undergraduates to respond to solutions and justifications made by others. This is one of three particular features in mathematics teaching in Taiwan, in accordance with the most recent curriculum standards. First, an introduction starts with a problem in realistic context. Second, children solve individually and freely. No one correct model solution can be found in the textbook. Teachers attend to original thinking of the children – correct or incorrect. Third, there is a high emphasis on reflections and on communicating one's thinking: "Tell your friend how you solve the problem", or "Is this answer correct?" or "Are there other solutions?". After instruction, teacher and students collate ideas, check each others' reasoning, decide on the acceptance/ rejection of ideas, and come up with a set of ideas belonging to every one in the class. This approach is widely implemented, at least at elementary school level.

BEYOND POLYA'S MODEL OF PROBLEM-SOLVING

Polya (1945) famously formulated a phase description of problem solving, which I extend in two aspects that reflect on the contributions in this section. The extensions begin from the observation that Polya almost exclusively focused on well-structured problems within "pure mathematics". So, first, while the initial understanding of the problem, relative to the solver, may be far from straightforward, the statement of the problem does lead unambiguously to a clear characterisation of the problem that is the starting point for the mathematical analysis. Secondly, in Polya's analysis of a very large number of examples, there is very limited need for discussion of whether, at different points in the process, there is need to take RW considerations into account.

The description of problem solving in information-processing terms is that there is a initial given state, a goal state, and a set of allowable operations; the problem then is to navigate from the goal state by using allowable operations, through the problem space, to get to the goal state. Traditional well-known problems such as the Tower of Hanoi, or Missionaries and Cannibals and its variants, lend themselves very readily to this way of thinking about problems (and, one may reasonably suggest, have received a great deal of attention for this reason).

Thus, a problem is well-structured if the objects, operators, and goals are well defined (Reitman, 1965). Reitman identified four categories of problems according to whether each of the given and goal states are undefined or well-defined (a similar distinction might be added for the operators). Based on the above specifications, only problems for which both given and goal states are well-defined are well-structured. The other three types are ill-structured problems which open up opportunities for problem posing, problem re-formulation/representation or, simply, structuring problems. A relationship between ill-structured problems and problem finding was found by Voss (1990). Indeed, "problem finding, that is, how individuals formulate and identify a problem ... in itself is an ill-structured problem" (Voss, 1990, p. 12). The reasons Voss suggested were two. First, the representation of the problem can vary according to how the person perceives the situation. Second, there are no generally agreed upon solutions (in this case, solutions are actually problems). Reitman's classification and Voss' discussion suggested that ill-structured problem solving includes problem posing, in terms of defining the given, the goal, or both.

Jonassen (2004) points out that "a problem with problem solving is that *problem* has many meanings", in particular spanning well-structured problems such as those typically used in mathematics classes, and the ill-structured problems that dominate people's lives:

> ... most of these problems that people face in their everyday lives are ill structured. They are not the well-structured problems that students at every level of schooling, from kindergarten through graduate school, attempt to solve at the back of every textbook chapter. (p. 1).

Indeed, Jonassen (p. 2) argues that "the only legitimate goal of education and training should be problem solving" because "no one in the everyday world gets paid

DISCUSSION PART III

for memorising facts and taking exams. Most people get paid for solving problems." Compare to Schank (2004, p. 22): "Education should be about preparation for real life" and the statement that ends the chapter by Säljö et al., quoted earlier. Jonassen (p. 4) goes on to question, with experimental evidence, the conventional wisdom that "in general, the processes used to solve ill-structured problems are the same as those used to solve well structured problems (Simon, 1978, p. 287) and to conclude that "it seems reasonable to predict that different intellectual skills are required to solve well-structured than ill-structured problems (p. 4)." Jonassen's characterisation of story problems places them squarely in the category of well-structured problems:

> ... these problems are usually, though not most effectively, solved by learners by identifying key words in the story, selecting the appropriate algorithm and sequence for solving the problem, applying the algorithm, and checking their responses...

> Story problem solving requires not only calculation accuracy but also the comprehension of textual information, the capacity to visualize the data, the capacity to recognize the semantic structure of the problem, the capacity to sequence their solution activities correctly, and the capacity and willingness to evaluate the procedure that they used to solve the problem (pp. 10-11).

The main theme of the work summarised in Verschaffel et al. (2000) is that feeding children a diet of word problems that match this description has detrimental effects, particularly when children conform to the implicit message that RW considerations need not be taken into account in mathematics classes. Of course, word problems do not have to be like that. They can present scenarios, to quote Freudenthal (1991, p. 30), that are "rich and to be structured" as opposed to "[semantically] poor and structured."

While problems classified as P-problems are generally, to a greater or lesser extent ill-structured, the problem presented by Säljö et al. is most fundamentally ill-structured among the studies in this section. In terms of Reitman's four-way classification, there is a well-defined given state, the operators are well-defined but the goal state is undefined. Arguably, it is a problem without a "right answer" and therein may lie the reason the students found it difficult to deal with. The only way to handle it is perhaps, as Voss suggested, to take a contingent modelling approach expressed as "If the given problem is X, then my solution is Y."

I now consider how Polya's description of phases in problem solving might be elaborated to take into account RW considerations at various points. According to Polya (1945), there are four phases in problem solving: understanding the problem, devising a plan, carrying out the plan, and, looking back. Indeed, these phases map rather closely onto the characterisation of word problems by Jonassen, cited above. However, problem solving means more than a straightforward execution of a standard procedure and going through each phase only once and not back and forth. In following steps in recipes, once a cookery step is done one cannot go back to the previous phase. In problem solving, however, going back and forth is common and each switch to a different phase signals a person's evaluation of what he or she did in the current phase. These aspects may be shown schematically as in Figure 1, with the "forward" (clockwise) arrows representing what happens in the simplest case, when the solver passes through the understand/ plan/ carry out/ look back phases without any need to backtrack, and the inclusion of the "backward" (anti-clockwise) arrows representing (possibly repeated) backtracking at various stages. Schoenfeld (e.g., Schoenfeld, 1992) produced a representational elaboration in which a particular problem solver's movement through phases (classified as Read, Analyse, Explore, Plan, Implement, or Verify) are plotted on a time line, showing the degree of backtracking. The layout of Figure 1 is reminiscent of standard schematic representations of the modelling process, and the distinction between modelling and problem solving is not so clear, especially in the work of Lesh (Lesh & Caylor, this volume; see also English, this volume). Indeed, in relation to word problems, the distinction is annulled by the characterisation of word problems as exercises in mathematical modelling (Verschaffel et al., 2000).

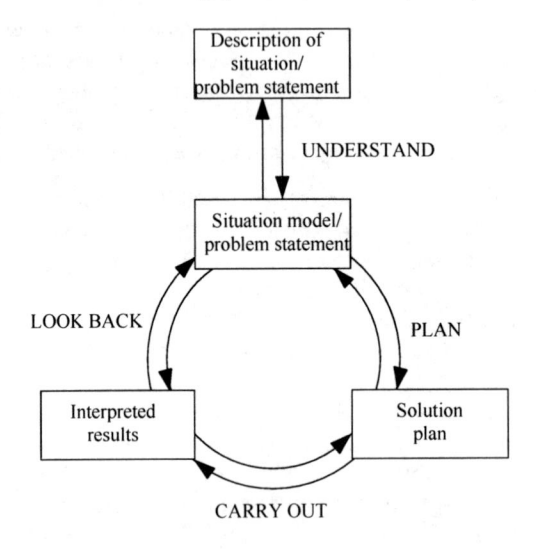

Figure 1. Phases in problem solving (after Polya, 1945)

First, let me indicate how problem posing fits within the general schematic description of Figure 1. Problem posing, broadly interpreted, can occur at many points in the total process (Silver, 1994). For example, when a problem has been successfully solved, the solver may consider generalisations or variants of the problem. One general form of problem posing is when the initial text includes a description of a scenario, but not specification of a problem. The student is then asked to generate problems meaningful in relation to the described scenario. In the study by Verschaffel et al., a rather different form of problem posing was used, in which the interpreted results of calculations were stipulated (e.g., a "core calculation" of 100 ÷ 8, with result modified to 13, 12, or 12.5), and the task was to reconstruct possible elements within the structure of Figure 1 so that those interpreted results would be appropriate.

My next point is to consider Figure 1 in terms of places in the process where, when P-problems are presented, RW considerations come into play, triggering a need to backtrack to a different phase. DWR problems, as used by Verschaffel et al., have the property that they cue a "core calculation" namely division; most students recognise that is appropriate, but many fail to make the necessary adjustment to the specific scenario. Here the main phase at which, potentially, the student should be alerted to something needing attention is at the stage of interpreted results and looking back.

Many of the other P-problems share this aspect of failure to modify the result of a core calculation. In the problems studied by Inoue carrying out the core calculation is a reasonable move. It tells one, for example, that if you can maintain the same speed, you will be at the airport on time, and you can then begin to consider what might upset that calculation. A major problem is when, as pointed out by Säljö et al., solvers treat P-problems as if they are S-problems. Thus, they carry out the core calculation, but do not reflect on the interpretation of its result. Indeed, it has often been observed that students asked to check their solution only check the accuracy of the calculation.

Sometimes, what students do might even be described as not even trying to understand the problem but choosing a plan mindlessly based on superficial cues, as in Nesher's (1980) research and analysis of the water mixture problem. In other cases, the student might not have the requisite knowledge e.g., that adding liquids of different temperatures will result in a mixture with an intermediate temperature (though one might expect even young children to have experience of mixing hot and cold water to get a moderate temperature). In other cases, the concept of "inert knowledge" (Whitehead, 1929) may be invoked. It is hardly unreasonable to assume, for example, that most students know that an athlete cannot maintain the pace achievable over a short distance for a much longer distance.

In summary, if Polya's model is to be applicable to the solution of the kinds of P-problem studied in this section, then it must be supplemented by consideration of the key points at which RW considerations will trigger a perceived need to backtrack (as given in figure).

FINAL COMMENTS: CONCEPTIONS IN MATHEMATICS AND IN REALITY

The activation of real-life knowledge is an important goal in research and practice (Verschaffel et al., 2000). One purpose of mathematics education is the application of mathematical techniques to solve problems in the real world. As Inoue (p. 207) points out, severe consequences can follow from failure to take account of reality.

A student may learn algorithms well in school and score exceedingly well on S-problems in tests but forget or fail to act upon knowledge gained through real-life experiences. Teachers see answers such as " -25" as the age of a person, or "12.5" as the number of buses, from students from all over the world. This is because they have become accustomed to answering such problems presented in school settings that are de-contextualised. Similarly, in problem posing, an elementary school child may pose a height problem like "John was 20 cm tall when he was 5 years old. He was 20 cm taller after one year. What is his height when he was 6 years old?" In reality, how many children are 20 cm tall? In reality, how many children grows 20 cm from their fifth to their sixth year?

I admire the multiple efforts of the investigators reported in this section and agree that the four research designs in structuring problems, solving, and justifying solutions are promising windows for probing students' conceptions in mathematical understanding and their consideration of real-world constraints.

Let me conclude with some encouraging remarks. It is possible to improve methodologies for studying students' conceptions, and also feasible to work with practitioners so that they implement the tasks designed in research, to result in the vision that mathematics educators aim for, of meaningfully linking MW and RW. Instead of collecting one-shot data and reporting that "teachers do not use problem posing tasks nor use P-problems in instructions" or "children did not perform well…" we can improve the training of pre-service teachers (Leung, 1996), or work on action research projects with in-service teachers and trace growth in teaching and learning from data collected over time (Leung, 1999, 2002).

REFERENCES

Adler, J. (2001). *Teaching mathematics in multicultural classrooms*. Dordrecht, The Netherlands: Kluwer.

Carpenter, T. P., Lindquist, M. M., Matthews, W., & Silver, E. A. (1983). Results of the third NAEP mathematics assessment: Secondary school. *Mathematics Teacher, 76*, 652–659.

Cohen, S. A., & Stover, G. (1981). Effects of teaching sixth-grade students to modify format variables of math word problems. *Reading Research Quarterly, 16*, 175–200.

Davis, P. J., & Hersh, R. (1986). *Descartes' dream: The world according to mathematics*. Sussex, UK: Harvester.

Dillon, J. T. (1988). Levels of problem finding vs problem solving. *Questioning Exchange, 2*, 105–115.

Freudenthal, H. (1991). *Revisiting mathematics education*. Dordrecht, The Netherlands: Kluwer.

Ginsburg, H. (1997). *Entering the child's mind*. Cambridge, UK: Cambridge University Press.

Ginsburg, H. (2009). The challenge of formative assessment in mathematics education: Children's minds, teachers' minds. *Human Development, 52*, 109–128.

Greer, B. (1993). The modeling perspective on wor(l)d problems. *Journal of Mathematical Behavior, 12*, 239–250.

Hatano, G. (2003). Foreword. In A. J. Baroody & A. Dowker (Eds.), *The development of arithmetic concepts and skills: Constructing adaptive expertise* (pp. xi–xiii). Mahwah, NJ: Erlbaum.

Jonassen, D. H. (2004). *Learning to solve problems: An instructional design guide*. San Francisco: Pfeiffer.

Krutetskii, V. A. (1976). *The psychology of mathematical abilities in school children*. Chicago: University of Chicago Press.

Leung, S. S. (1996). Problem posing as assessment: Reflections and reconstructions. *The Mathematics Educator, 1*, 159–171.

Leung, S. S. (1997). On the role of creative thinking in problem posing. *Zentralblatt für Didaktik der Mathematik, 97*(3), 81–85.

Leung, S. S. (1999). A change in focus: Problem posing and professional development. In J. Truran & K. Truran (Eds.), *Making a difference. Proceedings of the 22nd annual conference of the Mathematics Education Research Group of Australasia, Adelaide* (p. 574). Sydney, Australia: MERGA.

Leung, S. S. (2001). Integrating problem posing into mathematics teaching: Case of prospective and practicing teachers. In F.-L. Lin (Ed.), *Common sense in mathematics education. Proceedings of the 2001 Netherlands and Taiwan Conference on Mathematics Education, Taipei, Taiwan* (pp. 273–284). Taipei, Taiwan: National Taiwan Normal University.

Leung, S. S., & Silver, E. A. (1997). The role of task format, mathematics knowledge, and creative thinking on the arithmetic problem posing of prospective elementary school teachers. *Mathematics Education Research Journal, 9*, 5–24.

Nesher, P. (1980). The stereotyped nature of school word problems. *For the Learning of Mathematics, 1*(1), 41–48.

Nichols, S. L., & Berliner, D. C. (2007). *Collateral damage: How high-stakes testing corrupts America's schools*. Cambridge, MA: Harvard University Press.

Polya, G. (1945). *How to solve it* (2nd ed.). New York: Doubleday.

Reitman, W. (1965). *Cognition and thought*. New York: Wiley.

Schank, R. (2004). *Making minds less well educated than our own*. Mahwah, NJ: Erlbaum.

Schoenfeld, A. H. (1992). Learning to think mathematically: Problem solving, metacognition, and sense making in mathematics. In D. A. Grouws (Ed.), *Handbook of research on mathematics teaching and learning* (pp. 334–370). New York: Macmillan.

Selter, C. (1994). How old is the captain? *Strategies, 5*(1), 34–37.

Silver, E. A. (1994). On mathematical problem posing. *For the Learning of Mathematics, 1*(1), 19–28.

Simon, H. A. (1978). Information-processing theory of human problem solving. In W. K. Estes (Ed.), *Handbook of learning and cognitive processes* (Vol. 5, pp. 271–295). Hillsdale, NJ: Erlbaum.

Stevenson, J., & Evans, G. (1994). Conceptualisation and measurement of cognitive holding power. *Journal of Educational Measurement, 31*, 161–181.

Streefland, L. (1988). Reconstructive learning. In A. Borbas (Ed.), *Proceedings of the twelfth international conference for the Psychology of Mathematics Education* (Vol. 1, pp. 75–91). Oxford, UK: Elsevier.

Van den Heuvel-Panhuizen, I. M., Middleton, J. A., & Streefland, L. (1995). Student-generated problems: Easy and difficult problems on percentage. *For the Learning of Mathematics, 15*(3), 21–27.

Verschaffel, L., De Corte, E., & Lasure, S. (1994). Realistic considerations in mathematical modeling of school arithmetic word problems. *Learning and Instruction, 4*, 273–294.

Verschaffel, L., Greer, B., & de Corte, E. (2000). *Making sense of word problems*. Lisse, The Netherlands: Swets & Zeitlinger.

Voss, J. F. (1990). Das Lösen schlecht strukturierter Probleme – Ein Überblick [On the solving of ill-structured problems: A review]. *Unterrichtswissenschaft, 18*, 313–337.

Whitehead, A. N. (1929). *The aims of education*. New York: Macmillan.

Wyndhamn, J., & Säljö, R. (1997). Word problems and mathematical reasoning: A study of children's mastery of reference and meaning in textual realities. *Learning and Instruction, 7*, 361–382.

Shuk-Kwan S. Leung
National Sun Yat-sen University
Taiwan

PART IV: PROBING TEACHERS' CONCEPTIONS

OLIVE CHAPMAN

11. TEACHERS' CONCEPTIONS AND USE OF MATHEMATICAL CONTEXTUAL PROBLEMS IN CANADA

INTRODUCTION

In recent years, the mathematics teacher has received much attention in studies in mathematics education aimed at understanding his or her mathematically related conceptions, beliefs, knowledge, or practice. However, there is little available on experienced mathematics teachers and their conceptions and use of mathematical contextual problems (CPs) in their teaching. CPs can play a significant role in the teaching and learning of school mathematics with meaning and understanding. "The opportunity for students to experience mathematics in a context is important" (NCTM, 2000, p. 66). This importance is associated with making connections and applications outside of mathematics. CPs can be used as a basis for application and integrating the real world in mathematics education, motivating students to understand the importance of mathematical concepts, and helping students to develop their creative, critical, and problem-solving abilities. As Verschaffel (2002) noted, CPs can "bring reality into the mathematics classroom [and] create occasions for learning and practicing the different aspects of applied problem solving, without the practical ... inconveniences of direct contact with the real world situation (p. 64)." But whether these ways of thinking about CPs get implemented in the mathematics classroom will depend on the teacher. Thus, studying how teachers conceptualise CPs could offer a basis to understand how they are likely to impact the use of CPs in their teaching.

This chapter focuses on such a study to address teachers' conceptions and use of CPs in their teaching. It is based on a research project that investigated prospective and practicing teachers' perspectives of making sense of CPs. The focus here is on the practicing elementary and secondary school teachers. In particular, the chapter discusses the teachers' conceptions of CPs, the teaching models used with CPs, and connections between teachers, conceptions, and teaching models. The label "contextual problem (CP)" is being used to refer to word problems in the broadest sense, i.e., to include algorithmic/routine and non-algorithmic/non-routine word problems. This is intended to capture the range of conceptions the participants held of word problems. The following are examples of these CPs from some of the participating secondary teachers' practice.

Algorithmic: *A car rental agency charges $200 per week plus $0.15 per mile to rent a car. How many miles can you travel in one week for $320?*

Non-algorithmic: *(a) When eggs in a basket are removed 2, 3, 4, 5, and 6 at a time, 1, 2, 3, 4, and 5 eggs remain, respectively. When they are taken out 7 at a time, none are left over. Find the smallest number of eggs that could be in the basket.*
(b) Find the volume of a doughnut (actual doughnuts are used).

RELATED RESEARCH LITERATURE

Mathematics teachers have received less attention than students in studies of CPs. In addition, despite the large number of studies on mathematics teachers that now exists, there is little focus explicitly on CPs, in particular, their thinking about CPs or their teaching of problem solving through CPs. When teachers were researched in studies involving CPs, a trend similar to that for students was followed, i.e., they were studied from the perspective of the learner or problem solver. These studies used CPs to investigate mathematics teachers' knowledge of arithmetic concepts, their solution processes for arithmetic and algebraic word problems, or their problem-solving strategies. The studies involved mainly prospective elementary teachers. The findings of these studies generally highlighted the difficulties these teachers had with CPs.

Very few studies involving the mathematics teacher and CPs were found prior to the 1990's. These studies identified deficiencies in the teachers' understanding of arithmetic operations through the use of word problems. For example, Tirosh, Graeber and Glover (1986) investigated whether 129 prospective elementary teachers had the same misconceptions noted among students in their choice of operation for multiplication and division word problems based on previous studies. They found that the participants were influenced by the same primitive, behavioural models (e.g., repeated addition and partitive division) for multiplication and division. Greer and Mangan (1986) reported on a similar study involving choice of operations for single-operation word problems involving multiplication and division for a sample that included 50 preservice elementary teachers. They found that primitive operations continued to affect the interpretation of the situations even after extensive formal training.

Studies published on the teacher and CPs increased in the 1990's, but not significantly. Their focus also expanded to include different aspects of problem solving. For example, Leung (1994) analysed problem-posing processes of eight prospective elementary teachers with differing levels of mathematical knowledge. Findings showed that those with high mathematical knowledge systematically manipulated given conditions to make problems and used solutions to prior posed problems as new pieces of information to pose subsequent problems. Those with low mathematics knowledge posed problems that might not be solved mathematically and the mathematics problems posed were not necessarily related in structure. Taplin (1996) explored the approaches to problem solving used by 40 prospective elementary teachers in her education course and found that they preferred to work with a narrow range of strategies. They tended to select a method of approach and not change from that through the course. Studies by Contreras and Martínez-Cruz (2001, 2003) also examined prospective teachers' solution processes, focusing on arithmetic word problems. In the 2001 study, the 68 participants did not always base their responses on realistic considerations of the context situation. In the 2003 study, most of the responses of the 139 participants contained incorrect solutions to the problems that were due to failure to interpret correctly the solution produced by addition or subtraction of the two numbers given in each word problem.

Some of these studies on problem solving included both elementary and secondary prospective teachers. For example, Schmidt and Bednarz (1995) examined modes of problem solving that 131 prospective elementary and secondary teachers used in arithmetical and algebraic contexts to identify the resistance and eventual difficulties that arose in the shift from one type of approach to the other. They found that dissociation of algebra and arithmetic existed among many of the participants. The majority of them confined themselves to algebra even when dealing with arithmetical problems. The prospective elementary teachers appeared to be the best prepared to use arithmetic for arithmetic problems and algebra for algebra problems. Van Dooren, Verschaffel, and Onghena (2003) also investigated the arithmetic and algebraic word problem-solving skills and strategies for 97 prospective elementary and secondary teachers, both at the beginning and end of their teacher training, and ways in which they evaluated students' algebraic and arithmetical solutions. The authors found that the prospective secondary teachers clearly preferred algebra even for solving very easy problems for which arithmetic was more appropriate. About half of the prospective elementary teachers adaptively switched between arithmetic and algebra while the other half experienced serious difficulties with algebra. Their problem-solving behaviour was strongly related to their evaluations of students' solutions.

Some studies focused on teachers' perspectives, conceptions, beliefs, practice or development in relation to problem solving (e.g., Chapman, 1997; Fernandes, 1994; Grouws, Good, & Dougherty, 1990; Ponte, 1994) but not explicitly regarding CPs. One exception to this is Verschaffel, De Corte, and Borghart (1997) who investigated prospective teachers' conceptions and beliefs about the role of real-world knowledge in arithmetic word-problem solving. Overall, then, studies on mathematics teachers have not explicitly focused on their teaching with CPs by systematically studying their thinking and practice. But knowing about their basis for making sense of CPs and the nature of their behaviours in the classroom could have meaningful implications regarding learning opportunities for both prospective and practicing mathematics teachers.

THEORETICAL PERSPECTIVE

"Conception" as a theoretical construct has played a prominent role in framing studies on the mathematics teacher. Several recent studies continue to adopt it as a basis of understanding mathematics teachers' thinking and knowledge (e.g., Barrantes & Blanco, 2006; Brendefur & Frykholm, 2000; Brown, Hanley, Darby, & Calder, 2007; Knuth, 2002). In these studies, teacher thinking is valued as a basis for understanding his or her classroom behaviours, in particular, and teaching, in general. The importance of researching the teacher is associated with the view that teachers are the determining factor of how the mathematics curriculum is interpreted and taught. Some research supports this view by providing evidence or justification of the relationship between mathematics teachers' conceptions or beliefs and their instructional practices and the role of their beliefs in supporting or restricting change to those practices (Ernest, 1989, 1991; Fennema & Franke, 1992; Thompson, 1992).

The meaning of "conception" has varied in studies in mathematics education, particularly in terms of scope, but is generally located within a cognitive framework. In Ponte (1994), it is described as the underlying organising frame of concepts having essentially a cognitive nature. Thompson (1992) described it as a mental structure of a general nature that includes "a teacher's conscious or subconscious beliefs, concepts, meanings, rules, mental images and preferences concerning the disciplines of mathematics" (p. 132). In the present study, a similar view of conception is adopted. Specifically, conceptions are viewed as the categories of meanings underlying different teachers' descriptions of how they make sense of and experience CPs in their teaching and in relation to their students' learning. They embody the teachers' intentions, what they value and their personal meanings regarding CPs. Conceptions are also being associated with the teachers' practical knowledge, that is, knowledge that arises out of action or experience (Elbaz, 1983; Fensternmacher, 1994). This focus includes knowledge of what are CPs and how to use CPs that the teachers accumulated and developed from participating in, and reflecting on, their students' and their own experiences with CPs in the classroom. In general, these conceptions are related to "pedagogical content knowledge" (Shulman, 1986), that is, for example, the teachers' understanding of the ways of representing and formulating CPs and the solutions of CPs in order to make them comprehensible to students, what makes the learning of problem-solving with CPs easy or difficult, and students' thinking about CPs.

In this chapter, then, researching teachers' conceptions of CPs is investigating practicing teachers' conceptual understanding of CPs in relation to their experiences as teachers, that is, their conceptions associated with their practical knowledge. This means that their conceptions of CPs will be different or similar based on their individual situations. The goal in this study, however, is not to treat each teacher as a case in terms of describing his or her conceptions and teaching, but to identify from the data collected all of the possible conceptions of CPs and models of teaching with CPs held by the teachers as a group. The study also identifies dominant orientations among the teachers toward particular conceptions of CPs and models of teaching.

RESEARCH PROCESS OF STUDY

The participants in this portion of a larger study on teachers' sense making of CPs were eleven practicing secondary and four practicing elementary school teachers with 16 to 30 years of teaching experience. They were from different local schools. They were teachers I was acquainted with and invited to participate based on their openness in talking about their teaching and thinking. Six of the secondary teachers were considered in their school systems to be excellent mathematics teachers, in general. They had received teaching awards and/or were involved in co-authoring or reviewing mathematics textbooks and in leading professional development for other mathematics teachers. These teachers will be referred to as exemplary teachers. This combination of teachers turned out to represent a broad range of teaching approaches in regard to their teaching of mathematics in general.

The main sources of data for the larger study were open-ended interviews and classroom observations. The interviews explored the participants' thinking and experiences with CPs in three contexts: past experiences as students and teachers, current practice, and future practice (i.e., expectations). In addition to focusing on their explicit conceptions of CPs and teaching, the interviews also addressed implicit conceptions by considering the relevant prior knowledge, abilities, and expectations they brought to their experiences with CPs in their teaching; task features, classroom processes and contextual conditions relating to CPs; and planning and intentions for CPs in their teaching. The interviews did not suggest particular attributes of CPs to talk about or any definition of CPs. Actually, the term "word problems" was used in the interviews. Interview questions were framed in both a cognitive context to allow the teachers to share *their* way of thinking by providing theoretical responses (e.g., explicit conceptions) and a phenomenological context to allow them to describe their teaching behaviours as lived experiences (i.e., stories of actual events that embodied implicit conceptions). For example, some questions were of the form: How do you view word problems? What do word problems mean to you? What do you think is the role of word problems in mathematics/curriculum/ your teaching? How do you think word problems should be taught? Other questions were in the form of open situations to address, e.g., telling stories of memorable, liked and disliked mathematics classes involving CPs that they taught; role-play giving a presentation on CPs at a teacher conference; role-play having a conversation with a prospective teacher about CPs; and analysing a list of CPs prepared by the researcher. The interviews were audiotaped and transcribed. Classroom observations and field notes focused on the teachers' actual instructional behaviours during lessons involving CPs. Eight to ten lessons (60 to 85 minutes each) were observed and audiotaped for each teacher. Post-observation discussions, when necessary, focused on clarifying the teachers' thinking in relation to their actions.

Data analysis involved the researcher and two research assistants working independently to thoroughly review the data and identify attributes of the teachers' thinking and actions that were characteristic of their conceptions of CPs and teaching with CPs. Transcripts were read, initially to gain a general impression of the participants' thinking and then significant statements and behaviours were identified. The open-ended coding focused on statements and actions that reflected judgments, intentions, expectations, and values of the teachers regarding CPs that occurred on several occasions in different contexts of the data. The coded information was validated through an iterative process of identification and constant comparison and grouped under broad themes of the teachers' thinking. The emerging conceptions of CPs were analysed by comparing significant statements for points of variation and agreement around which they could be grouped to form categories of description.

TEACHERS' CONCEPTIONS OF CONTEXTUAL PROBLEMS

This section draws the findings together, presenting the dimensions of variation in the teachers' understanding of CPs as a set of six conceptions. All of the conceptions represent differing but interrelated facets of CPs. It is important to remember that the characteristics of CPs are flexible and the conceptual boundaries themselves are not rigid but have a degree of overlap among them. Although some teachers tended to emphasise particular characteristics of CPs, most individuals presented several different conceptions. Descriptions of the six conceptions follow with quotes from the teachers used as illustrations of them.

(i) *CP as computation*: This is associated with what one teacher described as "verbal computations," another as "worded exercises" and another as "hidden math concepts". These CPs have transparent or obvious semantic structures and obvious solutions, i.e., they have language or clue words that explicitly suggest the mathematics concepts involved or the solutions to the CPs.

(ii) *CP as text*: This considers CPs as conveyors of information and/or knowledge about mathematical situations. For example, they are: "[a way] to transfer information to somebody else;" "a way to share mathematical experience with another;" "stories from which you can extract mathematics;" and "written statements in which mathematics will emerge."

(iii) *CP as object*: This treats CPs as consisting of fixed, universal or pre-determined properties that are independent of the student. These CPs can be generalised, for example, by: "concept taught, e.g., systems of equations," a pre-determined algorithm, and "type of problem [context], e.g., coin, age, distance, number." They "have clear language, no extraneous information, clear about what they want, not ambiguous."

(iv) *CP as experience*: This treats CPs as lived realities for the students. The nature of the CPs depends on how they are experienced by the student – the particular association, emotions or images they excite, what they call forth in the mind of the student. The experience and thus the CPs could be positive and worthwhile or negative and unrewarding. For example, they (CPs) are positive experience for students when they, "capture their attention," "invite them, intrigue them, and prod them to want to solve it," "[involve] a discussion or conversation in which something is unknown about the world of mathematics in which you are trying to invite the students to become a participant," "[involve] the students' story," "help them experience the world," "[involve] a situation that has interest and appeal to student," or "have a context that's relevant to the students."

Without these characteristics, the CPs become negative experiences or enigmas and erode students' confidence. These CPs involve situations students cannot relate to contextually and this mathematically. For example:

> Students don't understand where they're coming from. ... They can't make sense of them.

When they see these word problems ... they don't seem to be something that invite them to apply their skills or to use their knowledge of something, but more threaten them.

(v) *CP as problem*: This emerged from the teachers' thinking in three ways depending on the teacher involved.

First, a CP is a problem for a student based on the relationship between it and the student. For example:

> All word problems are real problems if students have not encountered them before. ... I don't think there's anything in the problem that makes it necessarily routine or non-routine. ... No problem is routine if you've never seen it before.

> Students don't have a predetermined solution process.

> It's a problem you want to have the answer to, that is, something that is needed, is practical, is worthwhile, that has some kind of relevance.

> It's like anything else that you don't know what the outcome will be and you're kind of game for anything else, so you just take your chances and you try and use the tools that are available to you, see what happens.

Second, a CP is a problem based on the nature of it or its solution, in particular, whether the CP is algorithmic or non-algorithmic. In the case of algorithmic CPs, for which "you can type the problem" based on its structure, they are problems because the solutions or structure of the solutions have to be deduced initially from the problem situations. They are "problems for which students must deduce a structure to determine a solution." In the case of non-algorithmic CPs for which "you cannot type the problem, categorise it so that you can read it and do it" they are problems because they are:

> the ones where they [students] have to bring quite a few different tools to solve them ... and think on a lot of levels and have to bring a lot of things into play.

> Students must impose a structure on the problem to create a solution.

> They allow you to think and come up with a solution that may use different areas, techniques that you know about but combine it in different ways.

> They make you see things differently; take you down different paths.
> They initiate discussion ... promote dialogue.

Third, a CP is a problem based on the teaching approach or the teacher's intent, i.e., when and how it is introduced to students by the teacher. For example, a teacher could take a potentially routine problem and problematise it by presenting it before the routine approach is determined. As some teachers explained:

> If they [routine CPs] are given to students at the right stages as something beyond their level of experience at this time... [they] could be used to practice their problem-solving skills.

If you want it to be a problem-solving type of question, it's all in how you present the question.

(vi) *CP as tool*: Thus emerged in the teachers' thinking as being associated with the following three types of CPs.

Type 1 consists of situations that are generally tailor-made to illustrate a mathematical concept or skill. As some teachers explained, these CPs are:

A means to apply concept or practice a skill they [students] have seen most recently in class.

Instances of applications of mathematical concepts ... the whole point of them is to give the students experience in practicing that concept, similar application of that particular concept.

They can be used to demonstrate, or as an example, or simple application of a formula that students have been working with.

Type 2 CPs provide a means for dealing with new situations and fostering mathematical thinking. For example:

They are intended to get at some in-depth thinking ... serve to enhance and understand a topic or depth of thought.

They are [used] to get the kids to handle a new situation where it does not seem like anything that we've done before.

They're another way of asking you how to do math and they're designed to encourage thinking, analytical skills, logical skills, reading skills. They can be applications of math concepts, and therefore they can be used to reinforce math skills learned to develop understanding, and they have infinite variations. ... They're open-ended. They just keep going.

Type 3 CPs are a way to frame and present mathematics for learning. Thus CPs: "should not be seen as a separate topic;" "should be done with every topic;" "should not [be at the] end of a unit" and "should not [be] a separate unit." The CPs should form the "basis for presenting each concept" and be intertwined with other concepts.

You always introduce a new concept or idea in a context of a word problem. I come to realise that everything about mathematics is framed within word problems. It should be something that is integrated throughout the year and throughout each of the lessons.

The preceding set of conceptions reflects the combined thinking of all of the teachers based on their explicitly and implicitly espoused views associated with their practical knowledge. Thus it provides a spectrum of possible conceptions practicing teachers could hold about CPs. These conceptions are not all distinct and could be grouped based on how they are connected conceptually. One way of doing thus that provides a model for understanding the teachers' use of CPs in their teaching is based on three views summarised in Table 1: the objectivist view, the utilitarian view and the humanistic view.

Table 1. Categories of conceptions of CP

Objectivist View	Utilitarian View	Humanistic View
Computations	Text	Experience
Objects	Tools:	Problems:
Problems: algorithmic	– illustrate concept – promote thinking – frame teaching	– relationship with student – non-algorithmic – meaningful algorithmic – teacher intent

The objectivist view represents the conceptions that consider the CPs to have independent existence or being about mathematical facts. It focuses on the structure or properties of the problems and treats the problems as ends in themselves. It is oriented towards computational-algorithmic CPs and a problem-centred approach of dealing with them, i.e., it treats the problem situation and solution as existing independent of students. The utilitarian view represents the conceptions that consider the CPs in terms of their worth based on their contributions to maximising students' learning. It focuses on the applied property of the problems and treats the problems as means to an end. It is oriented towards both algorithmic and non-algorithmic CPs with a focus on how to use or apply them based on their level of meaningfulness to students' learning. Finally, the humanistic view represents the conceptions that consider the CPs in relation to people. It focuses on the personal aspect of the students' experience: their interests, meanings, creativity, choices, and self-awareness. It values the social context of the problem with preference to problem situations that have "realistic value for the students." It is oriented towards student-centred CPs, i.e., the problem situation and solution are connected to students, thus, there is a focus on the relationship between students and the CP and students are encouraged to make sense of CPs through reason, experience and shared ideas. It values students' solutions as their stories, their experiences, and their mathematical thinking.

Collectively, then, the teachers held conceptions that covered three philosophical perspectives of knowledge. These three views will be discussed later in terms of comparing the teachers, after considering the conceptions of teaching emerging from their practice.

TEACHERS' CONCEPTIONS OF TEACHING WITH CONTEXTUAL PROBLEMS

The teachers' conceptions of teaching with CPs emerged as four models of teaching: imposition, abandonment, directed-inquiry and dialogic-inquiry. These labels are selected to reflect the relationship between teacher, students, and a CP during instruction. The factors considered in describing these models are the learning goal; relationship between a CP, teacher and students; problem-solving process; choice of CPs; and placement of CPs in a course. Table 2 summarises some of the key features for each model, followed by a brief elaboration of each.

Table 2. Teaching models

Model	Goal	Key Relationship	Solution Process	Problems	Placement
Imposition	The correct solution	Teacher imposes CP interpretation and algorithm	Fragmented steps	Computational-algorithmic	Separate topic or end of unit
Abandonment	The correct solution	Teacher abandons CP interpretation and students' process	Identify nonverbal exercise	Computational-algorithmic	With nonverbal exercises, end of topic
Directed-Inquiry	Understanding process	Teacher directs CP interpretation and students' process	Specific heuristics	Computational and meaningful applied algorithmic	Separate topic and end of unit
Dialogic-Inquiry	Understanding process; problem-solving and mathematical thinking	Teacher facilitates students' CP interpretation and process	General heuristics; strategies	Non-algorithmic and meaningful applied algorithmic	Integrated throughout course

Imposition Model: In this teaching approach, the goal is for students to be able to obtain a correct solution to a CP. The relationship between CP, teacher and student is centred on the teacher as the agent of the correct solution. The following is a schema of this relationship:

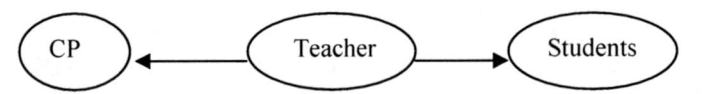

CP ← Teacher → Students

In this relationship, the teacher determines the interpretation and algorithm for the CP and imposes them on the students as passive recipients. Thus, the arrow from teacher to CP represents the teacher determining what the problem is about and how to solve it. This unidirectional arrow indicates that only one interpretation and solution are considered even if others are possible. The unidirectional arrow from the teacher to students represents the teacher imposing how the problem should be interpreted and what steps should be used to arrive at a solution, i.e., students initially have no active role in interacting with the problem or teacher. The problem-solving process is presented as a linear set of fragmented steps. The problem is treated as a collection of verbal statements or key words to be translated to mathematics symbols, concept, or procedure. Mainly computational-algorithmic CPs are used, i.e., there is no consideration of their meaningfulness to students. The CPs are treated as a separate topic or placed at the end of a unit in the course.

Abandonment Model: In this teaching approach, the goal is also for students to be able to obtain a correct answer to a CP, but the relationship between the CP, teacher and student now is centred on the CP as follows:

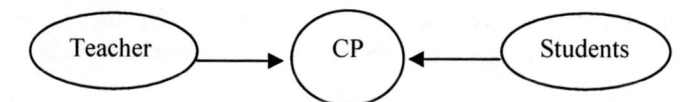

```
  Teacher  ──────▶   CP   ◀──────  Students
```

In this relationship, the teacher and students independently interact with the problem to solve it. The effect is the teacher abandoning any direct basis of helping the students to solve the problem and thus abandoning the students to deal with the problem on their own. They are assigned the CP along with non-contextual exercises, e.g., solving quadratic equations, to practice the mathematics concept after the teacher modeled it in its decontextualised form only, i.e., the CPs are treated as a different form of the nonverbal exercises. The problem-solving process, while not explicitly stated or modeled for students, was deduced from the teacher's thinking as involving a linear sequence of steps, i.e., read problem, apply mathematics concept previously illustrated, compute. Only computational-algorithmic CPs are used, generally as part of the set of nonverbal exercises at the end of a curriculum topic.

Directed-Inquiry Model: In this teaching approach, the goal is students' understanding of the process of arriving at the solution to the CP. The relationship between CP, teacher and student forms a triad as follows.

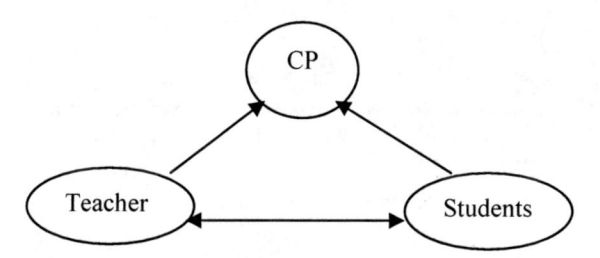

```
              CP
             ▲  ▲
            ╱    ╲
           ╱      ╲
       Teacher ◀──▶ Students
```

In this relationship, the teacher determines a process then students interact with the problem under the direction of the teacher to understand the process. The unidirectional arrows indicate only one interpretation and solution is considered even if others are possible. There is now a two-directional arrow between the teacher and students to indicate a two-way interaction in which the teacher helps students to understand how to interpret and solve the CP based on the process predetermined by the teacher. In this directed inquiry, the teacher poses questions and uses prompts to get students actively involved in unpacking the problems and to notice the connections between problem and solution. In some situations, the process is then summarised into an algorithm or specific set of heuristics (e.g., Table 3) and used to reinforce students' understanding of it. The problem-solving process is of the following form: think of unknowns or variables; focus on semantic context of problem to interpret and translate it mathematically, make conclusion about the value of the variables or unknowns and whether they satisfy the relationships among them. Table 3 provides examples of what one teacher wrote on the chalkboard to summarise the process for solving CPs on systems of equations in a Grade 10 class and quadratic equations in a Grade 11 class. In this model of teaching, the CPs are treated as a separate topic within a unit dealing with problem solving and application of the mathematics concepts taught in that unit. Both computational and meaningful applied algorithmic CPs are used.

Table 3. A teacher's problem solving algorithms

Grade 10 Class
Problem Solving
1. Read the question and define the unknowns with a variable
2. Translate the English words into a mathematical equation
3. Solve for the variable
4. Write a complete sentence to show the answer to the question
Grade 11 class
Problem Solving
1. Read question. Define variables.
2. Translate words into mathematical symbols and equation noting any restriction on the variables
3. Solve for the quadratic equation (use any method) Check answer.
4. Write a concluding statement which answers the question

Dialogic-Inquiry Model: In this teaching approach, the goals are students' understanding of the solution process for CPs and development of mathematical and problem-solving thinking. Similar to the directed-inquiry model, the relationship between CP, teacher, and student forms a triad but with different depth and scope of connections among these three components of the triad as follows.

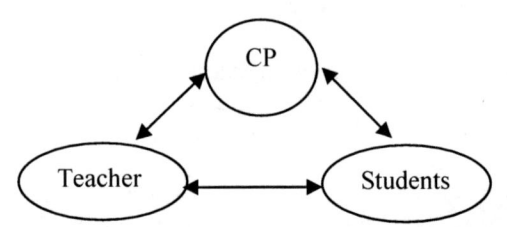

The two-directional arrows between teacher and CP and students and CP indicate that the teacher is open to multiple interpretations and solutions of the CP for him/herself and for the students. This allows students to dialogue with the problems, usually in small groups, to interpret and try to solve it. The two-directional arrow between the teacher and students indicate a two-way interaction in which the teacher helps students to evaluate and understand their solution processes and problem-solving thinking and to arrive at problem-solving approaches/heuristics that made sense to them. In this dialogical inquiry, students first inquire into the problem-solving process by trying to make sense of the CPs based on what they know and are able to do. The teacher facilitates and extends the inquiry by posing questions and using prompts to get the students to unpack and justify their thinking and processes and to notice alternative possibilities. Students are also encouraged to pose questions to the teacher and each other during their small-group or whole-class inquiry discussions. In general, students are given opportunities to develop their versions or understanding of problem-solving heuristics under the guidance of the teacher.

The problem-solving process for this model embodies general heuristics and strategies dealing with understanding the problem, planning, trying a strategy, reflecting, evaluating, and extending. A humanistic component of the process allows for treatment of the problem as a phenomenon related to the students' experiences. Thus, students could make sense of the problem by critiquing and revising the problem situation. Students could also create their own problems about things or situations that they consider to be interesting to solve and share with each other. Both non-algorithmic and meaningfully applied algorithmic CPs are used, with the latter being problematised and initially approached from the perspective of general heuristics or strategies. The CPs are generally integrated throughout the course; treated as ongoing. Thus, they are used to start, develop, and end a mathematics topic in the curriculum.

The preceding summaries of the four models do not capture their complexities, in particular, for the inquiry-based approaches. But these simplified versions are intended to highlight some of the key factors that characterise each model. At the core of these models are the problem-solving processes students are taught, directly or indirectly, for dealing with CPs. These processes range from what has been considered superficial to genuine problem solving (e.g., Polya, 1954) or modelling (Verschaffel, Greer, & De Corte, 2000). For example, in relation to models discussed in Verschaffel et al. (2000), the imposition and abandonment approaches contain a process with similar features to their superficial and artificial solution process that goes from problem text to a mathematical model to a derivation from the model to a report (p. 13). The directed-inquiry approach contains a process with some similar features to their modelling process, which is cyclic and consists of understanding problem situation, modelling, mathematical analysis, interpretation, evaluation, and communication (p. xii). Finally, the dialogic-inquiry approach contains a process similar to their elaborated view of the modelling process (p. 168), that requires more student involvement in the process.

COMPARING TEACHERS, CONCEPTIONS, AND TEACHING

There were some clear differences between the group of exemplary teachers and the other teachers. Thus, they will be discussed as two distinct groups and, from hereon, will be referred to as Group X for the six exemplary teachers and Group NX for the nine others, i.e., non-exemplary.

Group X

These teachers differed in terms of the specifics of their teaching but were similar in terms of their orientation to particular conceptions and teaching models. They all articulated the objectivist view of CPs, but, for the most part, they ranked it the lowest in terms of its contribution to students' learning. So, for example, they minimised the use of computational-algorithmic CPs associated with this view. As one explained, "They're extra, they're not necessary, they're trivial and they do little most of the time to enhance a topic." Another noted, "They aren't all that important, so if you have to cut corners some place and you don't have a lot of time ... they can be dismissed."

Group X also held the utilitarian view. Compared to Group NX, they held this view with more depth, in particular, focusing on CPs as a basis of conveying mathematical and social knowledge, of meaningful illustration or application of mathematical concepts, of promoting thinking, and of framing teaching. In addition, these teachers also held the humanistic view with more depth than any of those in Group NX, emphasising the importance of associating CPs with experience and their relationship to students. They ranked this view the highest in terms of its contribution to students' learning.

The dialogic-inquiry teaching model was the dominant one for Group X. However, these teachers also used the directed-inquiry model, but their focus was always student-centred. As one explained:

> They won't see the point of it if there's no discussion. ... For example, why are we doing it this way, and why does it work, when we do this, and what is it about the mathematics that makes this an adequate model for that kind of problem? ... If the students aren't in there creating it, they don't get it.

In general, Group X teachers were more flexible in their teaching and more successful in motivating students to work with CPs and helping them to learn to solve CPs. Their teaching was also different from that of Group NX teachers in terms of integration of CP throughout their courses, consistent use of relevant or interesting CPs, and students' participation in developing problem-solving heuristics or their own solution processes.

Group NX

This group is more heterogeneous than Group X in orientation to the conceptions and teaching models. Like Group X, this group held the objectivist view of CPs. However, unlike Group X, for over half of this group, it was their primary or dominant view. This produced two sub-groups for Group NX. The first sub-group (2 elementary and 3 secondary teachers) made no distinction between superficial-computational and meaningful applied algorithmic CPs, thus holding a strict objectivist view. They focused on one aspect of the utilitarian view, i.e., illustration or application of mathematics concept. They did not hold the humanistic view. For most of these teachers, the imposition model was dominant, but they occasionally used the abandonment model. For only one (secondary), the abandonment model was dominant, but he often resorted to the imposition model when students were not able to solve the problem.

The second sub-group (2 elementary and 2 secondary), in contrast to the first, made a distinction between superficial/computational and meaningful applied algorithmic CPs in their objectivist view and did not prioritise a strict version of this view. They also held a more extended utilitarian view, but not to the same depth as Group X. They focused on illustration or application of mathematics concepts and promoting thinking in a directed way. In addition, they held a partial humanistic view, focusing on the relationship between the CPs and students and teacher intent. For these teachers, the directed-inquiry model was dominant, with occasional use of the dialogic-inquiry.

Conceptions versus Teaching

The relationship between conceptions and teaching is not straightforward since other factors such as context (Ernest, 1991) play a role in how conceptions may be enacted in the classroom. However, dominant orientations in the teachers' thinking and teaching suggest particular relationships between conception and models of teaching. While focusing on such orientations strips away any anomalies of these relationships, the intent is to highlight core connections that likely exist in spite of such anomalies. These core relationships, based on the preceding comparison of the teachers, are summarised in Table 4.

Table 4. Connections between conceptions and teaching

Model of Teaching	Model of Conceptions
Imposition	Objectivist + partial utilitarian
Abandonment	Objectivist + partial utilitarian
Directed-inquiry	Partial humanistic + partial utilitarian
Dialogic-inquiry	Humanistic + utilitarian

The objectivist view is strongly connected to the imposition and abandonment models. The utilitarian view is connected to all of the models but not to the same degree. It increases in depth with imposition and abandonment models at the lower end, direct-inquiry in the middle, and dialogic-inquiry at the upper end. The humanistic view is connected with the two inquiry models but with different depth, the dialogic-inquiry having much greater depth. The objectivist view, thus, is aligned with a problem-centred, teacher-oriented focus while the humanistic view is aligned with a student-oriented, context-situated focus for dealing with CPs in students' learning. The abandonment view on the surface gives the appearance of allowing for students' autonomy as in the dialogic-inquiry model, but this is not necessarily so because the intent is for students to mimic the approaches demonstrated by the teacher in the nonverbal exercises.

Another aspect of the relationships involving the conceptions and teaching that is of relevance is the connection to conceptions of mathematics. One way in which this can be represented is viewing a conception of teaching as being nested in a conception of CPs and nested in a conception of mathematics as follows:

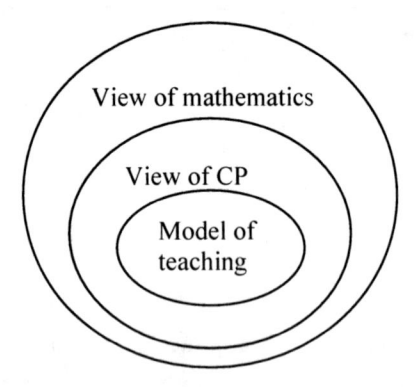

Although not discussed here, the teachers held conceptions of mathematics that paralleled their dominant views of CPs and teaching models. Thus this added component is important for future investigation to understand the connections.

CONCLUSIONS AND IMPLICATIONS FOR TEACHER EDUCATION

The conceptions discussed in this chapter offer a possible range of ways of thinking about CPs that teachers could hold and models of teaching associated with CPs that have the potential to limit or enhance how problem solving with CPs are likely to be perceived, experienced, and learnt by students. These conceptions have scope and depth from a pedagogical context. A teacher can hold several of these conceptions, but the combination and depth involved are important in relation to teaching. For example, it is unlikely for one to be able to conceptualise and use an inquiry approach with a dominant objectivist view. Based on the findings, for meaningful teaching with CPs, teachers should hold knowledge that includes depth in a humanistic and utilitarian view of CPs and an inquiry-based pedagogy that requires: understanding of relationship between CPs, students, and teacher; understanding of the role of problem context in problem solving or modelling and learning; and understanding of problem-solving thinking or process.

A key implication of this study in terms of teachers' development in teaching with CPs and in problem solving is the explicit consideration of teachers' conceptions of CPs in learning opportunities for them and not simply a focus on solving CPs. For example, they should develop awareness and understanding of: (i) their conceptions currently in place, (ii) viable alternatives, e.g., practiced-based versus theory-based conceptions, and (iii) connections of conceptions to teaching. The conceptions discussed here offer particular structures against which other teachers could examine their own conceptions and assumptions in order to gain understanding of their current thinking and teaching. These conceptions can provide a basis to interpret what the teachers do, to pose questions to facilitate depth in their reflection and to allow them to become aware of alternative ways of thinking of and teaching with CPs that are potentially more meaningful for students. Such awareness can provide or lead to development of useful knowledge for dealing with CPs. However, it is not being suggested that this by itself is a basis for change in teaching. But it seems to be an important component of teacher education or professional development to help in enabling progress in reforming teaching of mathematics. In addition, this proposed need for awareness can be made for other areas of mathematics, but CPs are unique because of their contextual situations that give them a more obvious orientation to humanistic qualities, leading to conceptions with some distinct qualities and the need for special attention to make them and their impact on students' learning explicit for teachers.

ACKNOWLEDGEMENT

This paper is based on a research project funded by the Social Sciences and Humanities Research Council of Canada.

REFERENCES

Barrantes, M., & Blanco, L. J. (2006). A study of prospective primary teachers' conceptions of teaching and learning school geometry. *Journal of Mathematics Teacher Education, 9*, 411–436.

Brendefur, J., & Frykholm, J. (2000). Promoting mathematical communication in the classroom: Two preservice teachers' conceptions and practices. *Journal of Mathematics Teacher Education, 3*, 125–153.

Brown, T., Hanley, U., Darby, S., & Calder, N. (2007). Teachers' conceptions of learning philosophies: Discussing context and contextualising discussion. *Journal of Mathematics Teacher Education, 10*, 183–200.

Chapman, O. (1997). Metaphors in the teaching of mathematical problem solving. *Educational Studies in Mathematics, 32*, 201–228.

Contreras, J. N., & Martínez-Cruz, A. M. (2001). An investigation of preservice elementary teachers' solution processes to problematic story problems with division of fractions. In M. Van den Heuvel-Panhuizen (Ed.), *Proceedings of the 25th conference of the International Group for the Psychology of Mathematics Education* (Vol. 2, pp. 289–296). Utrecht, The Netherlands: Utrecht University.

Contreras, J. N., & Martinez-Cruz, A. M. (2003). Preservice elementary teachers' solution processes to problematic addition and subtraction word problem. In N. Pateman, B. Dougherty & J. Zilliox (Eds.), *Proceedings of the 27th conference of the International Group for the Psychology of Mathematics Education* (Vol. 2, pp. 237–244). Honolulu, HI: University of Hawaii.

Elbaz, F. (1983). *Teacher thinking: A study of practical knowledge*. London: Croom Helm.

Ernest, P. (1989). The knowledge, beliefs and attitudes of the mathematics teacher: A model. *Journal of Education for Teaching, 15*, 13–33.

Ernest, P. (1991). *The philosophy of mathematics education*. London: Falmer.

Fennema, E., & Franke, M. L. (1992). Teachers' knowledge and its impact. In D. Grouws (Ed.), *Handbook of research on mathematics teaching and learning* (pp. 147–164). New York: Macmillan.

Fenstermacher, G. D. (1994). The knower and the known: The nature of knowledge in research on teaching. *Review of Research in Education, 20*, 3–56.

Fernandes, D. (1994). Two teachers' conceptions and practices about problem solving. In J. P. Ponte & J. F. Matos (Eds.), *Proceedings of the 18th conference of the International Group for the Psychology of Mathematics Education* (Vol. 2, pp. 328–335). Lisbon, Portugal: University of Lisbon.

Greer, B., & Mangan, C. (1986). Choice of operations: From 10-year-olds to student teachers. In C. Hoyles & R. Noss (Eds.), *Proceedings of the 10th conference of the International Group for the Psychology of Mathematics Education* (Vol. 1, pp. 25–30). London: University of London.

Grouws, D. A., Good, T. A., & Dougherty, B. J. (1990). Teacher conceptions about problem solving and problem solving instruction. In G. Booker, P. Cobb & T. N. de Meridicutti (Eds.), *Proceedings of the 14th conference of the International Group for the Psychology of Mathematics Education* (Vol. 1, pp. 135–142). Oaxtepex, Mexico: Consejo Nacional de Ciencia y Technologia.

Knuth, E. J. (2002). Teachers' conceptions of proof in the context of secondary school mathematics. *Journal of Mathematics Teacher Education, 5*, 61–88.

Leung, S. S. (1994). On analysing problem-posing processes: A study of prospective elementary teachers differing in mathematics knowledge. In J. P. Ponte & J. F. Matos (Eds.), *Proceedings of the 18th conference of the International Group for the Psychology of Mathematics Education* (Vol. 3, pp. 168–175). Lisbon, Portugal: University of Lisbon.

National Council of Teachers of Mathematics. (2000). *Principles and standards for school mathematics*. Reston, VA: Author.

Polya, G. (1954). *How to solve it*. New York: Anchor Books.

Ponte, J. P. (1994). Mathematics teachers' professional knowledge. In J. P. Ponte & J. F. Matos (Eds.), *Proceedings of the 18th conference of the International Group for the Psychology of Mathematics Education* (Vol. 1, pp. 195–210). Lisbon, Portugal: University of Lisbon.

Schmidt, S., & Bednarz, N. (1995). The gap between arithmetical and algebraic reasonings in problem-solving among pre-service teachers. In L. Meira & D. Carraher (Eds.), *Proceedings of the 19th conference of the International Group for the Psychology of Mathematics Education* (Vol. 2, pp. 82–89). Recife, Brazil: Universidade Federal de Pernambuco.

Shulman, L. S. (1986). Those who understand: Knowledge growth in teaching. *Educational Researcher, 15*(2), 4–14.

Taplin, M. (1996). Pre-service teachers' problem solving strategies. In L. Puig & A. Gutiérrez (Eds.), *Proceedings of the 20th conference of the International Group for the Psychology of Mathematics Education* (Vol. 4, pp. 299–306). Valencia, Spain: University of Valencia.

Thompson, A. G. (1992). Teachers' beliefs and conceptions: A synthesis of the research. In D. Grouws (Ed.), *Handbook of research on mathematics teaching and learning* (pp. 127–146). New York: Macmillan.

Tirosh, D., Graeber, A., & Glover, R. (1986). Pre-service teachers' choice of operation for multiplication and division word problems. In University of London Institute of Education (Eds.), *Proceedings of the 10th conference of the International Group for the Psychology of Mathematics Education* (Vol. 1, pp. 57–62). London: University of London.

Van Dooren, W., Verschaffel, L., & Onghena, P. (2003). Preservice teachers' preferred strategies for solving arithmetic and algebra word problems. *Journal of Mathematics Teacher Education, 6*, 27–52.

Verschaffel, L., Greer, B., & De Corte, E. (2000). *Making sense of word problems*. Lisse, The Netherlands: Swets and Zeitlinger.

Verschaffel, L. (2002). Taking the modeling perspective seriously at the elementary level: Promises and pitfalls. In A. D. Cockburn & E. Nardi (Eds.), *Proceedings of the 26th annual conference of the International Group for the Psychology of Mathematics Education* (Vol. 1, pp. 64–80). Norwich, UK: University of East Anglia.

Verschaffel, L., De Corte, E., & Borghart, I. (1997). Pre-service teachers' conceptions and beliefs about the role of real-world knowledge in mathematical modeling of school word problems. *Learning and Instruction, 4*, 339–359.

Olive Chapman
Faculty of Education
University of Calgary
Canada

FIEN DEPAEPE, ERIK DE CORTE, AND LIEVEN VERSCHAFFEL

12. ANALYSIS OF THE REALISTIC NATURE OF WORD PROBLEMS IN UPPER ELEMENTARY MATHEMATICS EDUCATION IN FLANDERS

INTRODUCTION

An in-depth analysis of the word problems in a widely used textbook series, *Eurobasis*, was conducted. Moreover, based on a seven-month observation period we investigated which problems from the textbook were used by two teachers during that period and which self-generated problems they added. The first section situates the investigation within the research on (realistic) mathematical modelling and introduces the framework for analysing the realistic nature of word problems on which we have heavily relied. Next, the objectives and methodology of the study are described. The results of the study are then presented and the chapter concludes with some methodological and content-related remarks.

THEORETICAL FRAMEWORK

One of the major justifications for the important role of mathematics in the elementary school curriculum is its usefulness for understanding the world around us, coping with everyday problems, and for future professions (Blum & Niss, 1991). In particular, the inclusion of application and modelling problems – typically in the form of so-called word problems – is intended to convince students of this usefulness and to develop in them the skills of knowing when and how to apply their mathematics effectively in situations encountered in everyday life.

However, during the last decades, scholars have shown more and more awareness of the bridging problem between school and everyday mathematics, and the risks involved. Empirical studies have revealed that, after several years of schooling, many students demonstrate a very strong tendency to exclude real-world knowledge and realistic considerations when confronted with problems that require – at least from the authors' point of view – the application of judgment based on real-world knowledge and assumptions rather than the routine application of superficial solution strategies (Greer, 1993; Verschaffel, De Corte, & Lasure, 1994). Following Schoenfeld (1991), these scholars suggested that students who produced unrealistic answers were not "senseless" or "irrational". They argued that this *suspension of sense-making* in word problem solving was mainly caused by two aspects of the instructional practice, namely (1) the stereotyped and unrealistic nature of the problems given, and (2) the way in which these problems are conceived by teachers (Verschaffel, Greer, & De Corte, 2000).

L. Verschaffel et al. (eds.), Words and Worlds: Modelling Verbal Descriptions of Situations, 245–263.
© *2009 Sense Publishers. All rights reserved.*

Starting from the above criticisms on the traditional teaching of word problems, new learning environments have been developed, implemented, and evaluated, aimed at the enhancement of students' genuine mathematical modelling. In these studies students are confronted with complex problems wherein the context plays a pivotal role. Besides, the teacher is stimulated to create a classroom culture that is conducive to the development of the skills, conceptions, and attitudes that are characteristic for genuine mathematical modelling (see e.g., Cognition and Technology Group at Vanderbilt, 1997; Gravemeijer, 1997; Mason & Scrivani, 2004; Verschaffel et al., 1999). In these intervention studies positive outcomes have been obtained in terms of performance, underlying solution processes, and mathematics-related beliefs.

This genuine modelling approach is beginning to be implemented in mathematics educational policy in many countries. For instance, in Flanders new standards and curricula for primary mathematics education have been formulated, aiming at establishing in students a modelling disposition (i.e., a focus on mathematical reasoning and problem-solving skills and their application to real-life situations) (Ministerie van de Vlaamse Gemeenschap, 2001). However, according to Niss (2001), it is still the case generally that genuine modelling perspectives and activities continue to be scarce in everyday practice of mathematics education. This is not a big surprise, since the actual implementation of such a perspective is not without major challenges, such as: how much reference to the complexity of reality is possible and appropriate in the everyday classroom context? Does the adoption of a genuine modelling perspective result in the complete exclusion of traditional word problems? Is a genuine modelling perspective feasible and valuable for all children, including the (mathematically) weaker ones? (Verschaffel, 2002).

At the moment, little is known about how teachers determine whether, when, and how students are exposed to such realistic modelling experiences. In an attempt to fill this gap, Palm (2002, this volume) developed a fine-grained conceptual framework for analysing the realistic nature of word problems. The basic idea of his framework lies in the notion of *simulation*: a word problem is considered to be realistic if the important aspects of the word problem are taken into account under conditions representative for that out-of-school situation. The operationalisation of the framework includes a number of such aspects that play an important role in the extent to which students may engage in similar mathematical activities in the school task as in the out-of-school situation (for an overview, see Palm, this volume). Palm and Burman (2004) applied a number of these aspects in an analysis of the quality of real life simulations in Finnish and Swedish national assessment tasks. Their results indicated that, in relation to the aspects "event", "realism of data", "language use", "guidance", "availability of solution strategies", and "solution requirements", the proportion of assessment tasks simulating corresponding situations in real life beyond school was fairly high. But, substantial differences were found between Finland and Sweden in the proportion of assessment tasks simulating the distinguished aspects well.

A second contribution to fill the gap referred to above, also represented in this book, is Chapman's (2006) recent analysis of how teachers conceptualise and deal with the context of mathematics word problems in their teaching. Chapman distinguishes between two modes of conceiving word problems: a paradigmatic (i.e., a focus on mathematical models or structures that are universal and context-free) versus a narrative mode (i.e., a focus on the situational aspects of the problem).

Inspired by the work of Palm and Chapman, we designed a study in which we investigated both the nature of the word problems and the ways in which teachers approach these problems in two regular sixth-grade classrooms in Flanders. In the present chapter we will only report the analysis of the nature of the problems provided by the mathematical textbook and those that were actually used in the mathematics lessons. We wonder whether the new standards for primary school mathematics in Flanders have resulted in an increase of "realism" of mathematical problems in textbooks and mathematics lessons. As already mentioned, these new standards demand a modelling approach in order to foster in students meaningful mathematics learning (e.g., Ministerie van de Vlaamse Gemeenschap, 2001). The ways in which teachers treat these problems in their lessons is beyond the scope of this chapter (but see Verschaffel, Depaepe, & De Corte, 2007).

METHODOLOGY

Data Collection

The study is framed within a broader research project in which we conducted an in-depth analysis of the current teaching of word problem solving in upper primary school based on the videorecording of lessons over a seven-month period. The focus of the analysis was on explicitly and implicitly negotiated classroom norms and their relationship to individual's beliefs and problem-solving capabilities. A broad range of data was collected: videotapes of all mathematics lessons of the first two weeks and of all problem-solving lessons during the whole observation period, teachers' interviews, students' interviews, students' beliefs questionnaires, students' problem-solving tests, and a general mathematics achievement test. The dataset used for this contribution comprised all problem-solving lessons of the seven-month observation period. This selection resulted in 17 regular problem-solving lessons (each of about 60 minutes) and 3 lessons during which a problem-solving test was administered. Assessment problems were included in our analysis since it is widely accepted that they have a big impact on students' conceptions of the kind of tasks that they are supposed to solve in a mathematics classroom (Greer, 1997). We distinguished between an analysis of tasks provided by the textbook[1], and tasks actually used in the mathematics lessons. Within the tasks that were actually used in the mathematics lessons, we further distinguished between textbook and teacher-generated problems.

The two teachers, Peter and Anna (which are pseudonyms) were selected on the basis of a pilot study showing substantial differences in their instructional approaches towards mathematical problem solving. For instance, the pilot study revealed that Anna emphasised heuristics and metacognitive skills much more strongly than Peter did. Whereas Peter never used group work, a substantial amount of the total lesson time was spent on group work in Anna's classroom. Based on these preliminary findings, we expected that the two teachers would reveal a different approach in selecting and handling word problems. Otherwise, they were both well qualified, motivated teachers, and their students did not encounter major learning difficulties.

Both teachers used the same mathematical textbook *Eurobasis* (Boone, D'haveloose, Muylle, & Van Maele, n.d.). Criteria for selecting this textbook were the frequency with which it is used (i.e., it is the most frequently used textbook in Flanders) and its representativeness for the standards and curricula for primary mathematics education in Flanders. For instance, the introductory part of that textbook explicitly refers to a practically oriented version of Verschaffel et al.'s intervention study (1999) and accordingly states that the problem contexts should be adapted to students' experiential worlds. Moreover, the textbook word problems deal with topics typical for sixth-grade mathematics: gross/net/tare, distance/speed/time, percentages, unequal division, direct/indirect proportionality, mixing different amounts, reading and interpreting graphs, etc.

Data Analysis

The textbook tasks as well as those implemented by the teachers were classified in terms of the framework of Palm and Burman (2004), the aspects of which are listed in Table 1. All tasks[2] that were presented either by the textbook or by the teacher were considered to be mathematical problems. Two classification levels were distinguished for all but one aspect. The two levels relate to whether a task was judged as simulating the aspects of a corresponding out-of-school situation to a reasonable degree (1) or not (0). For the aspect "specificity of data" three levels were distinguished: A task was coded as "2" when it is simulated to a considerable degree, "1" when it is simulated to some degree, and "0" when it is judged as not being simulated. In line with Palm and Burman (2004) the classification procedure stopped if criteria marked in Table 1 with an asterisk (*) were coded as not being reasonably simulated, "since it was only low fidelity simulations of these aspects that caused fundamentally different mathematical requirements between the assessment tasks and the corresponding situations beyond school" (Palm & Burman, 2004, p. 8). However, in this respect we did not entirely follow Palm and Burman. Contrary to these authors, we believe that the latter argument does not count for the aspect "external tools". Therefore, we decided to code "guidance" and "solution requirements", even if we scored "0" for "external tools".

If a textbook problem was implemented by the teacher, we used the same level for all but one aspect in the analysis of the textbook tasks and in the analysis of the tasks implemented by the teacher. With regard to the aspect "external tools" a different coding might occur, if there is a discrepancy in being allowed to use the calculator between the textbook authors and the teachers.

The operationalisation of the different aspects of the framework is presented in Table 1. While we relied heavily on Palm and Burman's (2004) definitions, at some points we added some specifications (in italics). To check the degree of reliability the classification of all textbook problems was carried out by two independent coders, which resulted in a very good interrater reliability ($\kappa = .88$[3]).

Table 1. Framework for analysing the realism of word problems (Palm & Burman, 2004)

Aspect	Description
Event*	1 = The event in the school task could be encountered in real life outside school. 0 = The school task is about an imaginary event[4]; the event includes objects from the real world, but is still a fictitious event; *or the school task is a pure mathematical task which is not embedded in a context.*
Question*	1 = The question in the school task has been asked, or might be asked, in the simulated event. The answer to the question is of practical value or of interest for others than just the people very interested in mathematics. 0 = The question in the school task is judged not to have been asked, and would not be asked, in the event described in the task.
Purpose in the figurative context	1 = The purpose of solving the task is *explicitly mentioned* in the school task *and in concordance with* the purpose of solving the task in the simulated situation. 0 = The purpose of solving the task in the simulated situation is unclear. The school context could be generally described, not pointing to a specific situation, resulting in many possible situations and purposes of solving the task. In other tasks, the situation described in the task is more specific but still open for more than one purpose.
Existence of data*	1 = The relevant data that are important for the solution in the simulated situation coincide with the accessible data in the school task. 0 = The data that are important for the solution in the simulated situation are not the same as the accessible data in the school situation and/or this information is accessible only by applying other competencies that are different from those required in the simulated situation.
Realism of data	1 = Numbers and values given are identical to or very close to the corresponding numbers and values in the simulated situation. 0 = Numbers and values given are not realistic.
Specificity of data	2 = The text of the task describes a specific situation in which the subjects, objects, and places in the school context are specific. *If graphs are used, the source is mentioned.* 1 = The situation in the school task is not specific, but at a minimum the objects that are the foci of mathematical treatment are specific. 0 = The situation in the school context is a general situation in which the subjects and objects are not specified.
Language use	1 = The task is linguistically similar to the corresponding simulated situation. *Specific mathematical concepts which are not used in daily language are avoided.* 0 = The terminology, sentence structure, or amount of text in the school task is judged to affect more than an insignificant proportion of students in such a way that the possibility to use the same mathematics in the school task and in the simulated situation is greatly impaired.

(Continued)

Availability of solution strategies	1 = The students' available solution strategies allow them to solve the task in the same way as the taken character in the simulated situation would have done. *The textbook is not directing the students in a specific direction in order to solve the problem.* 0 = The students' available solution strategies to solve the task are different than in the simulated situation. *The textbook is directing the students into a specific solution strategy, which the problem solver would not necessary have used while solving a similar problem in real life.*
External tools	1 = The availability of external tools (i.e., concrete tools outside the mind: calculator, map, ruler…), important for the solution of a task is similar in the school task, to the availability in the simulated real situation. 0 = There is a discrepancy between these tools in the two corresponding situations.
Guidance	1 = The same guidance is provided in the school task and in the corresponding out-of-school situation. 0 = The task does not match in the guidance given between the school task and the corresponding out-of-school situation.
Solution requirements	1 = The explicit or implicit requirements on the solution to a task are considered to be similar to the corresponding situation in real life. 0 = The explicit or implicit requirements on the solution to a school task are not considered to be similar to the corresponding real-life situation.

The way in which we classified mathematical problems according to the above-mentioned aspects is illustrated for four textbook problems. These four problems are presented in Figure 1 and Table 2 shows how they were classified.

Problem 1. Kim would like to buy inline-skates. From today on, she wants to save money for at most ten weeks. Each week she saves €4. Each two weeks she receives €5 from her grandmother, since Kim always does some shopping and pieces of work for her. She has €43.55 in her money-box. Which pair of inline-skates can Kim buy?

€ 163,59   € 198,29   € 69,39   € 89,49

Problem 2. Jens saves €1 coins in order to make a trip. He counts the money he has saved. If he puts the coins out in twos, 1 coin is left over; if he puts them out in fours, likewise; and if he puts them out in fives, there also is 1 coin left over. How many coins could Jens have saved?

THE REALISTIC NATURE OF WORD PROBLEMS

Problem 3. You can read about the amounts of donations in the section <u>support Greenpeace</u>. Here you can find how the money is spent:
  18% goes to Greenpeace International
  25 to 30% goes to campaigns in Belgium
  18% is spent on communication and information to support the campaigns
  About 10% goes to administration and location
  About 30% is spent on the recruitment of funds and the service for sympathisers
  www.greenpeace.be

1. The organisation received 3433000 euro in 2001. At least how much was spent on campaigns in Belgium?
2. Which part was given to Greenpeace International? Indicate on the bar.

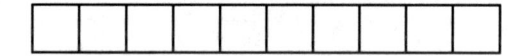

Problem 4. A jeweller makes a gold ring of 11 grams pure gold (12 euro per gram) and 4 grams silver (2.50 euro per gram)

Q [5] How much does the alloy cost?

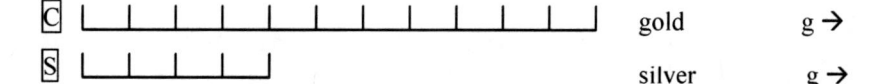

C |___|___|___|___|___|___|___|___|___|___|___| gold   g →
S |___|___|___|___|___| silver g →

                                                         OK

Figure 1. Illustrations from the textbook

Table 2. The classification of the problems according to the framework for analysing the realism of word problems

Aspect	Problem 1	Problem 2	Problem 3 3.1	Problem 3 3.2	Problem 4
Event	1	1	1	1	1
Question	1	0	1	1	1
Purpose	1		0	0	0
Existence	1		1	1	1
Realism	1		1	1	1
Specificity	2		2	2	1
Language use	1		1	1	1
Solution strategies	1		1	0	1
External tools	0		1	1	0
Guidance	1		1	1	0
Solution requirements	1		1	0	1

RESULTS

Table 3 represents the analysis according to Palm and Burman's (2004) framework of all mathematical tasks involved in the study. As mentioned earlier, we distinguished between a textbook-analysis (228 problems) and an analysis of the problems implemented in Peter's (180 problems) and Anna's problem-solving lessons (166 problems). With regard to the problems implemented by each teacher we made a distinction between textbook- and teacher-generated problems.

Table 3. The absolute numbers (N) and percentages (%) yielded by the analysis of the simulation of each aspect of the framework for the textbook problems and for the textbook- (TB) and teacher-generated (TE) word problems implemented in the problem-solving lessons

Aspect	Level		Text book	Peter TB	Peter TE	Peter TOT	Anna TB	Anna TE	Anna TOT
Event	0	N	12	11	0	11	4	0	4
		%	5	7	0	6	3	0	2
	1	N	216	156	13	169	115	47	162
		%	95	93	100	94	97	100	98
Question	0	N	65	45	1	46	26	10	36
		%	30	29	8	27	23	21	22
	1	N	151	110	12	122	88	37	125
		%	70	71	92	73	77	79	78
Purpose	0	N	129	91	8	99	79	35	114
		%	85	83	67	81	90	95	91
	1	N	22	19	4	23	9	2	11
		%	15	17	33	19	10	5	9
Existence	0	N	19	16	2	18	10	3	13
		%	13	15	17	15	11	8	10
	1	N	132	94	10	104	78	34	112
		%	87	85	83	85	89	92	90
Realism	0	N	1	1	2	3	1	0	1
		%	1	1	20	3	1	0	1
	1	N	131	93	8	101	77	34	11
		%	99	99	80	97	99	100	99
Specificity	0	N	4	2	0	2	4	3	7
		%	3	2	0	2	5	9	6
	1	N	77	51	7	58	45	16	61
		%	58	54	70	56	58	47	54
	2	N	51	41	3	44	29	15	44
		%	39	44	30	42	37	44	39
Language use	0	N	0	0	0	0	0	0	0
		%	0	0	0	0	0	0	0
	1	N	132	94	10	104	78	34	112
		%	100	100	100	100	100	100	100
Solution strategies	0	N	14	9	0	9	8	0	8
		%	11	10	0	9	10	0	7
	1	N	118	85	10	95	70	34	104
		%	89	90	100	91	90	100	93

External tools	0	N	81	8	1	9	0	0	0
		%	61	9	10	9	0	0	0
	1	N	51	86	9	95	78	34	112
		%	39	91	90	91	100	100	100
Guidance	0	N	91	74	0	74	53	0	53
		%	69	79	0	71	68	0	47
	1	N	41	20	10	30	25	34	59
		%	31	21	100	29	32	100	53
Solution requirements	0	N	11	10	0	10	11	2	13
		%	8	11	0	10	14	6	12
	1	N	121	84	10	94	67	32	99
		%	92	89	100	90	86	94	88

The following sections give – separately for each aspect of the framework – an overview of the results for the tasks as initially set up by the textbook, and those that were selected by the teacher for implementation in the observed problem-solving lessons. The problems referred to in Figure 1 will be used to illustrate the results.

Event

Almost all problems presented by the textbook (95%) and in both teachers' lessons (Peter: 94%; Anna: 98%) referred to events that could, in principle, be encountered in real life outside school. For instance, problem 1 is a typical example of such a textbook problem, and was selected by both participating teachers. One of the major challenges in developing tasks is probably to make them interesting for *all* students (or as many as possible). For instance, with regard to this inline-skate problem, some students might be interested, whereas others not. Besides, although the majority of the contexts are realistic, only a part of them are closely related to *students'* experiential worlds. Some students, and both teachers, even complained in the interviews about the non-interesting character of some of the textbook problems. To quote one of Anna's students: "Those problems concerning gross, tare and net, some are about trucks and such. Actually, we do not really need these kinds of things in real life." Nonetheless, both the teachers and the textbook authors have succeeded in framing a lot of tasks that fit closely with students' interests and prior knowledge.

Only a few tasks belonged to the abstract world of mathematics; some others did include objects of the real world, but were still fictitious events (e.g., different people throwing dice while waiting until the doors of a shop open).

Question

About 30% of the textbook problems based on a realistic event involved a question which would actually not be posed in life outside school. Problem 2 presents an event that could occur in real life (i.e., a child who is saving money in his money-box to make a trip); but the task takes the format of a "mathematics puzzle or riddle"

(Swetz, this volume). By contrast, problem 1 involves a question that may be posed in a corresponding real-life situation. The questions in the word problems implemented by Anna were to some extent more realistic (78%) than those in Peter's lessons (73%).

Analysing the word problems in relation to this aspect raised a shrewd suspicion that the results were partially mediated by the topic of the word problem. For instance, word problems about unequal division (e.g., "During the school party there is a playback competition for students. 26 students are participating, two more girls than boys. How many girls and how many boys appear?") typically involved a question that would actually not be posed in real life.

Purpose

Tasks that were composed of a well-simulated event and question could be related to more than one purpose for 85% of the textbook problems and in about 81% and 91% of the problems implemented by Peter and Anna, respectively. For instance, in problem 3 it is not clear from the problem text for what reason the problem solver has to calculate the money that was spent on campaigns in Belgium. However, in many cases, the purpose for solving the problem in the simulated situation is implicitly clear from the question in the problem statement. As an illustration, in problem 4, the jeweller probably wants to know the cost of the ring in order to define its selling price. A nice example wherein the (social) goal of the problem-solving activity is articulated is problem 1. The textbook authors do not ask students to merely calculate Kim's pocket-money, but to determine which pair of inline-skates she can buy with the money she has saved.

Existence

In only about 13% of the textbook problems consisting of a realistic context and question were different data given to solve the problem compared to the situation wherein one would encounter the problem in real life. Similar findings were observed in Peter's (15%) and Anna's (11%) problem-solving lessons. For instance, in one of the textbook problems the speed at which a fuel pump fills a tank is given, data which you usually do not have while filling a car tank.

Realism

In all but one problem from the textbook – consisting of a realistic event, question and containing similar data – the values given in the school task were very similar to those in real life. The problem which was scored as 0 on this particular aspect dealt with fuel prices (€0.70 per litre). It should be admitted, however, that the exceptional increase in price of fuel over the past years is the explanation for the current mismatch in values between this school task and reality. The problem that prices of objects involved in the task automatically become out-of-date is inherently connected to textbook tasks that are still used in a classroom years after their design.

The same problem is discussed in Anna's and Peter's lessons, and two additional problems in Peter's lessons also consisted of non-realistic values (e.g., an interest of 10% on a bank account).

Specificity

In only 3% of the textbook problems was the information about the subject and objects involved in the problem context abstract (score 0). For instance: "Four plats du jour cost €48. And seven?". Anna additionally discussed some non-specific problems (6% of her tasks), such as "*one* is having 2.5% interest on *a* bank account". The majority of the tasks were scored as 1 because they are partly specific (see problem 4).

Language Use

We did not encounter examples in which the terminology in the school task was significantly more complex or specialised as compared with that used in corresponding real-life situations.

Solution Strategies

In about 10% of the word problems – consisting of a realistic event and question, and containing similar data – in the textbook as well as in both teachers' lessons, students' available solution strategies did not allow them to solve the problem in the same way as in the corresponding real-life situation. For instance, in problem 1 similar solution strategies to solve the problem are available to the problem solver in sixth grade as to Kim in the real life situation. By contrast, problem 3.2 is directing the student into a specific solution strategy (i.e., indicating the part on a bar), whereas the problem solver in a corresponding real life setting probably would compute 18% of €3433000 in order to answer the question "Which part was given to Greenpeace International?"

External Tools

The aspect "availability of external tools" related mostly to students being allowed to use the calculator and whether this was realistic in the simulated situation too. Other external tools are timetables, tables of postal rates, etc.

In order to make clear that a calculator was allowed, the textbook authors added a symbol (see problem 3.1) or made reference to its use in the problem text (e.g., "compute by means of the calculator"). However, in most of the textbook problems it was not explicitly mentioned that students were allowed to use the calculator, although in a corresponding real life situation its use would be of great help. In some problems students were not urged to use the calculator, but neither would the problem solver make use of it in a real life situation. This is, for instance, the case for tasks that involve the interpretation of tables and graphs.

Our analysis revealed that less than half of the textbook word problems (39%) simulated well the availability of external tools. With respect to the implementation of the word problems by both teachers, we recoded the tasks for this aspect based on the observation in the classroom whether or not the students were allowed to use similar external tools as they would do in reality. This resulted in a higher score for the aspect "external tools" (100% for Anna's and 91% for Peter's classroom).

Guidance

Most textbook problems (69%) do not simulate well the guidance – in the form of implicit and explicit hints – that would normally be provided in a corresponding real life situation. The main cause for this observation is – maybe paradoxically – the intention of the textbook authors to foster in students a modelling disposition. Indeed, to do so, the textbook *Eurobasis* provides hints (in the format of letters that refer to the different stages of the modelling cycle, or to heuristics that are especially useful in the first two phases of that cycle) for the majority of the problems in order to stimulate and engage students to perform certain steps of the modelling process (e.g., "OK" for evaluating the solution) or to use certain heuristics (e.g., "S" for scheme). As an example, we refer to problem 4. Such hints do normally not occur in real life situations. Other hints that are sometimes provided by the problem are representations (see also problem 4), which would actually not be given in everyday life.

In Anna's case the teacher-developed tasks revealed a 100% match, which increased substantially her overall percentage (53%). She used such tasks frequently, and as they were often presented orally, the kind of textbook hints (e.g., letters to refer to phases of the modelling cycle, representations …) almost inevitably disappeared. As Peter did not frequently complement the textbook problems with self-developed tasks, this did not result in a substantial improvement of the percentage of tasks in which the (absence of) guidance was well simulated (29%).

However, the teacher's implementation of each problem included to some extent "guiding" students in a specific direction, for instance, by the nature of the teacher's questions, the way in which the questions succeeded each other, the way in which the teacher reacted on students' responses, etc.

Solution Requirements

The solution requirements of the large majority of all textbook problems (92%) and of those implemented by the teachers (Peter 90%; Anna 88%) could be considered to be similar to the corresponding situations in real life. Referring again to problem 1 in which students are asked which inline-skates Kim could buy, similar requirements would be expected in the corresponding real life situation. However, classifying the word problems in relation to this aspect was not always easy due to the restricted knowledge concerning the purpose of solving the problem, and consequently which requirements the solution would have in real life. For instance, one textbook problem asks the students to interpret a table by computing the difference in the number of visitors to museums between 1990 and 1995. In this example, we actually do not know whether – in a corresponding out-of-school situation – such a precise answer is needed, since we do not know much about that corresponding situation (e.g., a precise answer may be needed if the government wants to compute the grants to be paid to museums; a rough estimation may be sufficient if the government is interested whether people's interest in museums increases or decreases).

Conclusion

Overall, both textbook-developed and teacher-developed materials seem to simulate quite well a number of aspects that are assumed to be important in designing realistic tasks. More specifically, the majority of the word problems involved in this study are embedded in a situation that possibly could occur in life outside school; in many cases similar data is provided; the language used is not too far from everyday semantics; students have similar solution strategies at their disposal as the problem solver would have in real life; and the solution of the school task is characterised by similar requirements as in the corresponding situation in reality. The simulation of some other aspects was to some degree more problematic, such as the specificity of the data; the clarity of the purpose of solving the task; the realistic nature of the question; and the guidance provided. These findings were strikingly consistent with the study of Palm and Burman (2004) about the nature of Finnish and Swedish assessment tasks (see section 1).

However, the rather positive results need to be toned down when considering the scores of the problems on the aspects of the framework where the classification stops, namely event, question, and existence of data. Indeed, only 132 out of 228 (58%) textbook problems and respectively 104 out of 180 (58%) and 112 out of 166 (67%) problems in Peter's and Anna's classroom were classified as involving jointly a realistic event, a realistic question, and similar data to solve the problem as would be the case in life outside school. So, actually, if also these problems in which a realistic "event", "question", or "set of data" was missing were included in the analysis of all aspects, this would substantially decrease the percentage of tasks that were simulating well these particular aspects.

The findings also show that the nature of the problems set up by the textbook, and those implemented by the teachers are to a high degree similar. First, teachers usually followed the sequence of problems presented in the textbook and discussed those that were feasible within the time constraints of their lesson. Besides, teacher-generated tasks were similar to those provided by the textbook. This finding is in line with Gerofsky's (1997; this volume) view that word problems are designed as a simulation of other word problems rather than of real life. Moreover, despite our observations from the pilot study (Depaepe, De Corte, & Verschaffel, 2007) revealing teachers' differences in approaching word problems, the two participating teachers implemented quite similar tasks.

DISCUSSION

More and more scholars have pointed to substantial differences between school word problems and problems encountered in real life, and have argued that, therefore, the current teaching of (standard) word problems does not at all foster in students a modelling disposition (e.g., Gerofsky, 1997; Nesher, 1980; Verschaffel et al., 2000). Palm's (2002, this volume; Palm & Burman, 2004) framework for analysing the realistic nature of mathematical word problems allows for a fine-grained judgment about the extent to which school word problems refer to and represent reality. A major advantage is that this framework goes beyond a mere general judgment of the realism of tasks based on vague criteria, which was sometimes the case in previous research, but allows a systematic analysis of each aspect of realism starting from an operational definition. Despite these merits of the framework, we experienced also some methodological and content-related limitations while using this system.

In applying their conceptual framework to assessment tasks, Palm and Burman (2004) already pointed to the difficulty of determining the most appropriate classification level for each task. We tried to reduce this scoring difficulty by adding some additional specifications in the operationalisation of the levels of some aspects. Nevertheless, it remained often difficult to decide which level of a certain aspect was most appropriate. Refining the operationalisations of the aspects distinguished in the framework for analysing the realism of word problems may offer a challenging agenda for further research.

Moreover – and in line with the latter suggestion – one could question the theoretical grounding of distinguishing three levels of categorisation for the aspect "specificity of data" versus only two levels for all other aspects of the framework, for which a more fine-grained three-level graduation may also be more appropriate. For instance, with respect to "event" a threefold distinction could be conceptualised as follows: (0) the event described in the problem does not occur in life outside school *whatsoever*; (1) the event described in the problem could be encountered in real life by *people in general*; and (2) the event described in the problem is closely related to *students'* experiential worlds.

Furthermore, Palm and Burman (2004) suggest that the more aspects of school problems are simulated well relative to a corresponding real life situation the better the problems are from a realistic point of view, as "they could facilitate an experience of school mathematics as useful and powerful for solving meaningful task situations in real life beyond school" (p. 2). However, some critical remarks should be made with regard to this assumption.

First of all, not simulating all aspects of a corresponding real world situation can sometimes make sense. For instance, the intention of the textbook authors of *Eurobasis* to make students aware of the different stages of the modelling cycle throughout the problems causes a "0" score on the "guidance" aspect of the framework, but may be useful in view of fostering in students the acquisition of the heuristics and metacognitive skills that underlie a genuine modelling disposition.

Second, most problems which one encounters in real life beyond school are modelling problems in which the translation of the situational model into a mathematical model is neither straightforward nor simple. Some scholars (e.g., Cognition and Technology Group at Vanderbilt, 1997; Greer, 1993; Verschaffel et al., 1994, 2000) devoted considerable effort to develop what they called "problematic" word problems, which simulated well the complex relation between the situational and mathematical model if one takes into account the realistic constraints of the situation. However, Palm and Burman's framework for analysing realistic tasks does not contain an aspect which focuses on this sometimes complex relationship between the situational and mathematical model of a problem. If one really wants students to become competent problem solvers in real life, one should integrate such problematic problems into the mathematics curriculum, the more so as our textbook analysis revealed that only a few of the problems appealed to this non-direct translation of the situational model into a mathematical model. Moreover, the textbook authors and both participating teachers sometimes even seemed to neglect realistic considerations about the problem context. For example, one of the tasks of a problem-solving test was the following:

> Corinne composes assortments of sweets for her birthday party. She chooses 250g cola sweets (€0.75/100g), one box of chocolates (€3.25/500g) and 250g acid drops (€0.90/100g). There are four friends at her party. How much does this mixture of sweets cost for each child?

The textbook authors propose a solution to this problem, in which they calculate the price of the total composite of sweets (i.e., €7.38/1kg), and divide that price by four (i.e., the price for each friend equals €1.85). However, they do not take into account that Corinne will also take part in her own birthday party and will have an assortment of sweets. So, in fact, the price has to be divided by five (i.e. €1.48). Surprisingly, the teachers followed the proposed solution in the evaluation of students' responses. Moreover, only a few students took into account this realistic consideration in the solution of this problem (3 out of 19 students in Peter's classroom and only 1 out of 24 students in Anna's classroom). Strikingly, contrary to Peter, Anna did not value this realistic consideration.

Third, some word problems do not at all well simulate a real world situation, but have nevertheless an important function in the mathematics curriculum, because they foster mathematical thought and/or intellectual play. For instance, mathematical puzzles and riddles do not meet the requirements of Palm's (2002) framework, but can challenge students in a mathematical, intellectual, and recreational way that transcends the realism of everyday life (Swetz, this volume). These problems are characterised by "an intrinsic consistency and interesting mathematical structure rather than consistency with or importance for everyday life. These problems are intended implicitly to introduce children into substantial mathematics" (Toom, 1999, p. 37). In this respect, Palm and Burman (2004) state:

> there can be several purposes for including tasks comprising non-mathematical objects in their figurative contexts in mathematics education, and not all of these purposes require emulation of certain aspects of a real life task situation to be attained. (...) For example, it [the simulation of the aspects] does not

say anything about which mathematical competencies are important and required in life beyond school (p. 25).

Fourth, one should be aware of the fact that the context of schooling and the real world context are fundamentally different. Therefore, word problems as a reflection of real world events and situations is rather a utopia than a feasible goal. In line with Wyndhamn and Säljö (1997) we agree that "in school even so-called realistic problems are presented under very specific communicative conditions – the realism of the realistic word problems is not identical to the realism we would perceive if acting in a different context" (p. 369). Or, following Reusser and Stebler (1997) "authenticity in problem solving – in principle – is hard to achieve in schools, which are, by definition, artificial institutions with an inevitable bias to mediate reality by the symbolic codes of abstract language" (p. 324). According to Gravemeijer (1997) "the question for the students, however, is what level of reduction is expected" (p. 392). Consequently, with regard to the framework of Palm (2002, this volume), even if a problem is simulating well all aspects to a reasonable degree, it remains a *simulation* of another reality, which will inevitably be accompanied by other intentions, conventions, implications, and emotions than the corresponding problem encountered out of school.

Finally, at least as important as the nature of the word problems is the way in which these problems are implemented and treated in the classroom. Hiebert et al. (1996) argue "given a different culture, even large-scale real-life situations can be drained of their problematic possibilities. Tasks are inherently neither problematic nor routine. Whether they become problematic depends on how teachers and students treat them" (p. 16). The same counts for the "realistic nature" of tasks – tasks are inherently neither realistic nor purely mathematical. Moreover, whether they become realistic depends on how the context is attended to during instruction. We assume that a similar task can be treated in quite different ways, on a continuum varying from enriching to narrowing the situational context of a problem. For instance, regarding to the example of Corinne's birthday party, mentioned above, the teacher plays an important role in stimulating or discouraging students to take into account realistic considerations when mathematising the problem. However, according to Chapman (2006)

> a review of the literature suggests that there has been little attention given explicitly to the teaching of word problems and, in particular, no focus on how context is dealt with from the perspective of the teacher or the classroom (p. 214).

Analysing the way in which the teacher treats these problems moves beyond the scope of Palm's (2002) framework. In this regard, the distinction made by Chapman between teachers' paradigmatic-oriented and narrative-oriented perspectives offers some promising perspectives. We explored this issue in the context of a broader research project concerning the current teaching of word problem solving in upper primary schools (Depaepe, De Corte, & Verschaffel, in press).

ACKNOWLEDGEMENTS

This research was partially supported by Grant GOA 2006/01 "Developing adaptive expertise in mathematics education" from the Research Fund KULeuven, Belgium. The authors would like to thank Geraldine Clarebout for her help in the analysis of the textbook tasks.

NOTES

[1] We do not separately discuss the assessment tasks, as a first analysis did not reveal substantial differences between the nature of the textbook tasks and the problem-solving test.

[2] Problem-posing tasks, in which students were invited to formulate a question in a given situation (n=8) were not involved in the study. In line with Palm and Burman (2004) each subtask or different question of the word problem was considered as a separate task.

[3] The global interrater reliability was computed by reducing the three levels of "specificity" to two (only one textbook task was labelled 0 by coder 1, and none by coder 2; this task was removed from the dataset).
The interrater reliability for the distinct aspects was also high: "event" ($\kappa = 1$), "question" ($\kappa = .78$), "purpose" ($\kappa = .52$), "existence" ($\kappa = .75$), "specificity" ($\kappa = .80$), "solution strategies" ($\kappa = .84$), "external tools" ($\kappa = .79$), "guidance" ($\kappa = 1$), and "solution requirements" ($\kappa = .75$). The interrater reliability of the aspects "realism" and "language use" were not calculated since not all coders had labelled a task 0. However, a comparison of the data for "realism" and "language use" revealed respectively only one 0 for coder 1 and two 0's for coder 2.

[4] Within the Dutch tradition of realistic mathematics education "realistic event" is differently conceptualized; i.e., the emphasis is not restricted to its possible occurrence in real life, rather it is on situations which students can imagine (e.g., the fantasy world of fairy tales is also considered to be realistic, as long as they are real in students' minds). We followed Palm and Burman's operationalization since an analysis of the tasks presented by the textbook and those implemented by the teachers revealed that none of these tasks were embedded in a fantasy-like context.

[5] The textbook authors explicitly refer to (parts of) the problem-solving process by means of letters which symbolize certain heuristics (S = scheme) and phases (Q = question; C = computation; OK = checking and interpreting the outcome).

REFERENCES

Blum, W., & Niss, M. (1991). Applied mathematical problem solving, modelling, applications, and links to other subjects – state, trends, and issues in mathematics education. *Educational Studies in Mathematics, 22,* 37–68.

Boone, M., D'haveloose, W., Muylle, H., & Van Maele, K. (s.d.). *Eurobasis 6.* Brugge, Belgium: Die Keure.

Chapman, O. (2006). Classroom practices for context of mathematics word problems. *Educational Studies in Mathematics, 62,* 211–230.

Cognition and Technology Group at Vanderbilt. (1997). *The Jasper Project: Lessons in curriculum, instruction, assessment, and professional development.* Mahwah, NJ: Erlbaum.

Depaepe, F., De Corte, E., & Verschaffel, L. (2007). Unraveling the culture of the mathematics classroom: A video-based study in sixth grade. *International Journal of Educational Research, 46,* 266–279.

Depaepe, F., De Corte, E., & Verschaffel, L. (in press). Teachers' approaches towards word problem solving: Elaborating or restricting the problem context. *Teaching and Teacher Education.*

Gerofsky, S. (1997). An exchange about word problems. *For the Learning of Mathematics, 17*(2), 22–23.

Gravemeijer, K. (1997). Commentary. Solving word problems: A case of modelling? *Learning and Instruction, 7,* 389–397.

Greer, B. (1993). The modelling perspective on wor(l)d problems. *Journal of Mathematical Behavior, 12*, 239–250.
Greer, B. (1997). Modelling reality in mathematics classrooms. *Learning and Instruction, 7*, 293–307.
Hiebert, J., Carpenter, T. P., Fennema, E., Fuson, K., Human, P., Olivier, A., et al. (1996). Problem solving as a basis for reform in curriculum and instruction: The case of mathematics. *Educational Researcher, 25*(4), 12–21.
Mason, L., & Scrivani, L. (2004). Enhancing students' mathematical beliefs: An intervention study. *Learning and Instruction, 14*, 153–176.
Ministerie van de Vlaamse Gemeenschap. (2001). *Ontwikkelingsdoelen en eindtermen. Informatiemap voor de onderwijspraktijk, gewoon basisonderwijs* [Educational standards for the elementary school. Information folder for the educational practice]. Brussels, Belgium: Departement Onderwijs.
Nesher, P. (1980). The stereotyped nature of school word problems. *For the Learning of Mathematics, 1*, 41–48.
Niss, M. (2001). Issues and problems of research on the teaching and learning of applications and modelling. In J. F. Matos, W. Blum, S. K. Houston & S. P. Carreira (Eds.), *Modelling and mathematics education. ICTMA 9: Applications in science and technology* (pp. 72–89). Chichester, UK: Horwood.
Palm, T. (2002). *The realism of mathematical school tasks. Features and consequences.* Unpublished Doctoral Dissertation, University of Umea, Sweden.
Palm, T., & Burman, L. (2004). Reality in mathematics assessment: An analysis of task-reality concordance in Finnish and Swedish national assessments. *Nordic Studies in Mathematics Education, 9*(3), 1–33.
Reusser, K., & Stebler, R. (1997). Every word problem has a solution: The social rationality of mathematical modeling in schools. *Learning and Instruction, 7*, 309–327.
Schoenfeld, A. (1991). On mathematics as sense-making: An informal attack on the unfortunate divorce of formal and informal mathematics. In J. F. Voss, D. N. Perkins & J. W. Segal (Eds.), *Informal reasoning and education* (pp. 311–343). Hillsdale, NJ: Erlbaum.
Toom, A. (1999). Word problems: Applications or mental manipulatives. *For the Learning of Mathematics, 19*, 36–38.
Verschaffel, L. (2002). Taking the modeling perspective seriously at the elementary school level: Promises and pitfalls (Plenary lecture). In A. Cockburn & E. Nardi (Eds.), *Proceedings of the 26th annual conference of the International Group for the Psychology of Mathematics Education* (Vol. 1, pp. 64–82). School of Education and Professional Development, University of East Anglia, U.K.
Verschaffel, L., De Corte, E., & Lasure, S. (1994). Realistic considerations in mathematical modelling of school arithmetic word problems. *Learning and Instruction, 4*, 273–294.
Verschaffel, L., De Corte, E., Lasure, S., Van Vaerenbergh, G., Bogaerts, H., & Ratinckx, E. (1999). Learning to solve mathematical application problems: A design experiment with fifth graders. *Mathematical Thinking and Learning, 1*, 195–229.
Verschaffel, L., Depaepe, F., & De Corte, E. (2007, November 11–16). *Upper elementary school teachers' conceptions about and approaches towards mathematical modelling and problem solving: How do they cope with reality?* Paper presented at a conference on "Professional Development of Mathematics Teachers Research and Practice from an International Perspective" held at the Mathematische Forschungsinstitut Oberwolfach (Germany).
Verschaffel, L., Greer, B., & De Corte, E. (2000). *Making sense of word problems.* Lisse, The Netherlands: Swets & Zeitlinger.
Wyndhamn, J., & Säljö, R. (1997). Word problems and mathematical reasoning: A study of children's mastery of reference and meaning in textual realities. *Learning and Instruction, 7*, 361–382.

Fien Depaepe
Research Assistant Research Foundation – Flanders
Center for Instructional Psychology and Technology
Katholieke Universiteit Leuven
Belgium

Erik De Corte
Center for Instructional Psychology and Technology
Katholieke Universiteit Leuven
Belgium

Lieven Verschaffel
Center for Instructional Psychology and Technology
Katholieke Universiteit Leuven
Belgium

JULIE GAINSBURG

13. HOW AND WHY SECONDARY MATHEMATICS TEACHERS MAKE (OR DON'T MAKE) REAL-WORLD CONNECTIONS IN TEACHING

INTRODUCTION

Much research has examined the nature of word problems in published mathematics curriculum and student responses to word problems as well as to more complex, authentic mathematical modelling problems. Less attention has been paid to how teachers think about and implement connections between school mathematics and the real world. Attention to teachers is crucial, however, because what teachers think and do essentially governs whether and how students will encounter real-world connections for the mathematics they learn in school. In this chapter, I report on a study investigating mathematics teachers' decisions about real-world connections in their teaching – how they use connections, why, and the factors that influence that use. While many chapters in this book deal particularly with word problems, my interest was in the range of ways teachers connect mathematics to the real world.

Broadening the scope to investigate a range of real-world connections is complicated by the lack of an established definition of a real-world connection in the literature and among practitioners. In a prior, exploratory study (Gainsburg, 2008), I investigated how mathematics teachers conceptualise this phenomenon – what teaching practices they considered real-world connections (RWCs), what they believed to be the purposes of RWCs, and what constituted an effective RWC – as well as how often and why they used RWCs in class, and what factors supported and constrained that use. For that study, I designed my instruments to avoid imposing particular, a priori interpretations of "real-world connection" and to invite teachers to determine what practices constituted RWCs. I even carefully chose the term connection for neutrality, not implying a particular direction or purpose (as might the terms example, model, or application). The study reported in this chapter used categories of RWCs that emerged from teachers' responses in that earlier study, to more specifically investigate teachers' practices and decisions regarding RWCs. Even with the advantage of categories, this new study should be considered exploratory, because each category still required some degree of teacher interpretation.

FRAMEWORK

Clark and Peterson (1986) offer a comprehensive framework for research about teachers' thought and action, delineating important variables and relationships among them. A subset of those relationships were particularly salient for my study:
1) Teachers' plans largely determine what occurs in the classroom.
2) Teachers' theories and beliefs impact planning (see also Calderhead, 1996; Ernest, 1989; Thompson, 1992).
3) Student behaviour (both prior to a planned activity and in response to it) impacts teachers' beliefs and plans.
4) Other factors external to the teacher, including resources, general student characteristics, and expectations from school and other communities, shape teacher beliefs, planning decisions, and student responses.

Reflecting the "drawing on" perspective articulated by Remillard (2005), I viewed the teacher as an active designer of the "enacted curriculum," who draws not only on the textbook but multiple resources, and I sought to understand the influences on those design decisions. Within this perspective, my "interpretivist" stance (Calderhead, 1996; Remillard, 2005) presumed that the beliefs and meanings that guide teachers' practice are context dependent and necessary to understand in order to interpret teachers' decisions. I further assumed that teachers' planning decisions and rationales were important targets for study, because they largely determine students' mathematical opportunities and, at the same time, reveal teacher beliefs.

Specifically, my research questions were:
1) How and how often do high school mathematics teachers use RWCs in teaching?
2) What are teachers' rationales for making and not making RWCs?
3) What constrains teachers' use of RWCs? What resources support it?
4) How and why do teachers differentiate the use of RWCs among classes or kinds of students?

I designed a written questionnaire that inquired about the frequency of teachers' use of various types of RWCs in teaching: purposes, constraints, and resources for using RWCs; differences in teachers' use of RWCs among classes; and how teachers viewed the efficacy of RWCs to teach new mathematics. The response options reflected existing literature and the results of my exploratory study. For example, scholars cite several purposes for connecting classroom mathematics to the real world, including enhancing students' understanding of mathematical concepts (De Lange, 1996; Steen & Forman, 1995), motivating learning (National Academy of Sciences, 2003), helping students apply mathematics to real problems, particularly those arising in the workplace (National Research Council, 1998), and enhancing students' understanding of nonmathematical phenomena (Lehrer, Schauble, Strom, & Pligge, 2001; National Council of Teachers of Mathematics, 2000). I incorporated these into the response options to the question about purpose. With the response options regarding constraints, I tried to span the range of cognitive and cultural aspects theorised to influence mathematics teachers' practice: knowledge and beliefs about mathematics, pedagogy, and particular students; school structural elements (resources and time); and external accountability measures and curricular mandates (Borko & Putnam, 1996; Ernest, 1989; Greer, 1997; Schoenfeld, 1998; Thompson, 1992). Other questions targeted two areas of beliefs, discussed next, that the exploratory study unearthed as potentially relevant but did not systematically examine.

The Efficacy of RWCs to Teach New Mathematics

Peterson, Fennema, Carpenter, and Loef (1989) found that first-grade teachers ranged widely in their assumptions about whether mathematics instruction should build from students' naturalistic ideas or whether number facts should be first taught as discrete, formal, abstract components. Similarly, some teachers in my exploratory study indicated a belief that students should have a good grasp of a (decontextualised) mathematical concept or procedure before applying it to the real world; they considered real-world situations or models ineffective ways to teach new mathematics. Other teachers agreed with mathematics reformers (e.g., De Lange, 1996; Steen & Forman, 1995) that real contexts could be powerful supports for developing new mathematical concepts. I presumed that these personal theories about the pedagogical potential of RWCs would influence whether and how teachers used RWCs.

Differentiation

The results of the earlier study suggested that some teachers differentiated their use of RWCs among groups of students. Prior research (e.g., Desmoine, Smith, Baker, & Ueno, 2005; Jackson, 1986) has demonstrated teachers' tendency to use more "conceptual" (or reform) teaching – emphasising real-world and open-ended problems, student reflection and investigation, and alternative hypotheses (Desmoine et al., 2005) – with high-performing students, and more computational instruction with low-performing or economically disadvantaged students, at least till they master the basics (Spillane, 2001). This tendency reflects not only intellectual but also behavioural considerations. Teachers believe that low-SES and low-achieving students need more tightly controlled classrooms and that control is more easily achieved through traditional, didactic teaching (Spillane, 2001) and reduced expectations (Metz, 1988). Relatedly, teachers define their goals according to the futures they anticipate for their students. Thus, teachers in low-SES schools tend to focus on practical skills while teachers in high-SES schools aim at college preparation (Hemmings, 1988). These findings predict that teachers would use more, and more substantive, RWCs with more advanced classes and higher-SES students than in classes with low-SES or mathematically struggling students.

METHODS

Ninety-two mathematics teachers, in six high schools in multiple California districts, completed the questionnaire. I calculated descriptive statistics for the entire sample. Because experience can influence teachers' practice and beliefs (Richardson, 1996), I also disaggregated the data for two sub-samples: teachers with fewer and more than the median years of experience (10), henceforward called "newer" and "experienced" or "veteran" teachers.

Teachers were invited to identify themselves on the questionnaire to indicate their willingness to be observed or interviewed, and 35 of the 92 did so. From these, I selected five teachers for observation and interview and six additional teachers for interview only. I did not intend this sub-sample to represent the entire group (although it spanned all six schools). Instead, I targeted teachers whose questionnaires indicated the most significant or differentiated use of RWCs. The goal of the observations and interviews was a richer picture of the conditions and rationales behind the use of RWCs. Choosing teachers at the "high-end" of the use or differentiation spectrum decreased the probability of interviewing or observing teachers with little to say or demonstrate regarding either phenomenon.

I observed two lessons on the same day in each of the five teachers' classrooms. The teachers determined the dates and times, per my request to see two classes that differed in the way RWCs were used. After the observations, I interviewed the teacher to learn about her planning decisions – for the lessons I observed and in general – and her ideas about RWCs. The primary purpose of the observations was to ground the interview in practice – to allow teachers to respond to specific events and decisions rather than only speak generally about their actions and beliefs (Brown, Collins, & Duguid, 1989; Calderhead, 1996). For the six interview-only teachers, my questions were identical except that I first asked for examples of RWCs they had recently made – again, to ground their responses in specific events and classes. Observation and interview data were analysed for common themes and used to illuminate the results of the questionnaire.

FINDINGS

Frequency and Types of RWC

The questionnaire asked teachers to indicate the frequency with which they made each of four types of RWC. These types were generated through the exploratory study from teachers' open-ended descriptions of RWCs they had made. Table 1 shows the types as worded on the questionnaire and the percent of teachers selecting each frequency.

Apparently, most teachers make RWCs at least weekly, mainly by assigning word problems or mentioning examples. Yet, in many classes, students are only exposed to these types of connections monthly or less. Extended projects or labs are rarer: only about 13% of the teachers use these types at least weekly and about 19% never use them. Teachers also infrequently ask students to generate their own RWCs. These findings caution against a common association between reform methods and connecting mathematics to the real world. Reformers (e.g., NCTM, 2000) emphasise RWCs in the forms of mathematical modelling tasks and open-ended investigations about real situations. Yet teachers can and do make RWCs via traditional, didactic teaching. These data suggest that many students' primary exposure to RWCs comes via traditional textbook word problems and "teacher talk."

Experience only minimally impacted the overall frequency of teachers' use of RWCs. To measure overall frequency, I used an equally weighted composite score for the frequency of the four types of RWCs, assigning a 4 for each "daily" response, 3 for each "weekly" response, etc., with 16 as the highest possible score and 0 as the lowest. Newer teachers (with less than the median years of experience) had a mean combined frequency score of 9.77, while experienced teachers had a mean combined frequency score of 8.70, a difference that a one-way ANOVA test showed was not significant, $t(79) = 1.75$, $p = 0.083$. Any experience effect would appear to be in the use of the more reform-oriented types of RWCs. Experience did not impact the frequency of use of either of the first two types (word problems or mentioned examples). Newer teachers, however, used projects or labs more frequently that experienced teachers, with frequency means of 1.60 and 1.16, respectively; $t(78) = 2.03$, $p = 0.046$. Newer teachers also used student-generated RWCs more frequently than experienced teachers, although this difference did not reach significance. Frequency means were 1.95 and 1.43, respectively, $t(78) = 1.94$, $p = 0.056$.

Table 1. Frequencies of types of RWCs

Type of Real-World Connection	Daily	Weekly	Monthly	1-2 times a year	Never
a) Assigning "word problems" with realistic contexts	26%	49%	22%	3%	0%
b) Mentioning real-world examples as I teach a math concept or skill	39%	49%	11%	1%	0%
c) Having students do extended projects or labs (30+ minutes) involving real situations or objects	3%	10%	29%	40%	19%
d) Asking students to come up with their own real-world examples or uses for math concepts	8%	23%	22%	29%	19%

The interviews and observations underscored the importance of activity type in the matter of how and how often teachers use RWCs. One interviewed teacher, Karen (teacher names are pseudonyms), reported making frequent RWCs but usually via direct instruction. Indeed, the interviews indicated that decisions about activity type are independent of, and more salient to, teachers than the decision to make a RWC or not. For Nora, who used a published reform curriculum that developed all of the mathematics in context, her most pressing instructional decisions involved not whether to make RWCs but the format of activities. She often found her first-year algebra students lacking the necessary persistence and skill for the curriculum's extensive problems, designed to be solved in collaborative groups. This forced her back on traditional methods, such as individually completed worksheets, which, consequently, reduced or trivialised the RWCs her students encountered. For Nora and others, the format of the RWC was more critical for planning than the fact that it made a connection. The teachers apparently saw textbook exercises, contextualised and not, to have more in common with each other than did a textbook exercise and project that both involved applications. My questions at times seemed to confront teachers with an unfamiliar or irrelevant dichotomy – "real world" or not – and I often felt I was forcing teachers to verbalise ideas they had not completely thought through before. The salience for teachers of activity type and the wide range of activities they considered RWCs warrant some scepticism about their responses to questions that treated RWCs as a unitary phenomenon.

Providing types of RWCs in the first question may also have expanded or restricted what teachers would otherwise have considered RWCs for the remainder of the questionnaire. The observations and interviews were more open ended, as I did not specify a definition of RWC when scheduling observations or in my interview questions. As a group, these teachers demonstrated or mentioned RWCs that fit all four given types and others, including teachers using real-world models (present or imagined) to illustrate mathematical concepts, teachers or students creating or interpreting mathematical models of real situations, a teacher showing a popular movie about a topic that could be analysed statistically, and teachers using real-world metaphors for metacognitive issues (study habits or mathematical ways of thinking). The meaning of "real" was also left open, and two interviewed teachers named RWCs whose realness they questioned, namely geometric constructions and references to the physics concept of wormholes, and the mathematical figure Gabriel's Horn. (Teacher uncertainty about what makes a connection real, or real enough, is discussed in Gainsburg [2008]).

Purposes and Efficacy Beliefs

The questionnaire asked teachers to select their main purpose for making RWCs. Fairly equal numbers of teachers selected each of the first three options, as seen in Table 2.

Table 2. Percent of teachers selecting purposes for RWCs

Purpose response options as stated in questionnaire	All teachers (Mean overall frequency score)	Newer teachers	Experienced teachers
To motivate students or grab their interest	26% (9.39/16)	21%	28%
To make a math concept easier for students to understand	32% (9.28/16)	33%	28%
To convince students that math is relevant to their lives	38% (9.06/16)	43%	39%
To educate students about non-math issues (e.g., careers, scientific or social phenomena, art)	3% (10.00/16)	2%	6%
Other	1% (10.00/16)	0%	0%

Experience did not appear to affect teachers' primary purpose, nor did teachers' primary purpose affect their overall frequency of RWCs, $\chi^2(3) = 1.10$, $p = .78$. The interviews, however, revealed the complexity of this issue (and limitations of a forced-choice questionnaire). Most interviewees each mentioned multiple purposes for RWCs, including ones not offered on the questionnaire, such as test preparation, visualisation, everyday (student) survival, skill recall, illustration of the limits of mathematics, and a way for teachers to share their lives. Nevertheless, the interviews echoed the trend in the questionnaire data towards "affective" purposes – to convince students that math is relevant to their lives, motivate them, or grab their interest (64% of surveyed teachers) – rather than the "conceptual" purpose (32%). Relatedly, the interviewed teachers barely mentioned mathematical richness as a criterion for a strong RWC. Asked to evaluate particular RWCs they had made, only one of the 11 teachers cited as a strength that a RWC had deepened students' understanding of a mathematical concept, while two other teachers said they valued RWCs that required high-level thinking in general. Virtually all other criteria given by interviewees for strong RWCs concerned the real-world context, especially its relevance or interest to students.

Related to purpose, another questionnaire item addressed the teachers' faith in the efficacy of RWCs to teach new mathematics. Teachers were asked to rate their belief on a 1-5 continuum, with the 1 endpoint indicating agreement with the statement, "A student must completely master a math concept or skill before connecting it to the real world can be effective," and the 5 endpoint with "Connecting to the real world is a highly effective way to teach a new concept or skill."

The mean response was 3.97 and the median 4. Only three teachers selected 1 or 2, while 3, 4, and 5 were nearly equally selected. Thus, as a group, the teachers tended to believe that RWCs could help students learn new mathematics but were not completely convinced of the efficacy of RWCs to do so or saw situations where RWCs failed in this regard. New and experienced teachers rated themselves similarly on this item (their mean scores were 4.00 and 4.02, respectively).

The interviews demonstrated that this efficacy belief is not an absolute principle for an individual teacher but can depend on the context or students. Vera's efficacy belief varied by mathematical topic:

> It depends on the subject . . . The reason I put myself in the middle [of the continuum] is because in calculus you really need to have mastered everything before you can even look at those connections. In geometry, though, the connection – I mean, you have a lawn in the front of your house and it's the shape of a circle. You see it everyday . . . These are things that they deal with every day that they don't have to have mastered through proofs to be able to do this.

Ann's belief in the efficacy of RWCs varied by level of student. She described the frequency with which she made RWCs:

> Anywhere from weekly down to daily, depending on the level of the class. Some classes it might be, for a while, almost every day, you know? But some classes, you have to – it takes a while to get the skills in, so you don't dare try

an application if they don't have enough skills because they'll get frustrated and there's no sense in frustration.

Teachers who placed themselves higher on the RWC-efficacy continuum used RWCs only slightly more frequently than those who placed themselves lower. Those below the median (selecting 3, 2, or 1), that is, more sceptical about the efficacy of RWCs to teach new mathematics, had a mean overall composite frequency score of 8.3 (out of a possible 16). Those at the median (4) had a mean frequency score of 9.6, and those selecting a 5 – the highest level of confidence in the efficacy of RWCs to teach new mathematics – had a mean frequency score of 10.6. A one-way ANOVA showed that the differences in RWC frequency among these three efficacy groups (below, at, and above the median) were statistically significant, $F(2, 89) = 5.004$, $p = .008$. In a Tukey HSD post hoc means comparison, the frequency means for teachers below and above the efficacy median were significantly different at the .05 level. Comparing the mean combined frequency scores only for the two reform types of RWCs (projects/labs and student-generated RWCs), the pattern held. A one-way ANOVA showed that the differences among the three efficacy groups were statistically significant, $F(2, 89) = 3.519$, $p = .034$, with greater frequency associated with higher continuum scores. Again, in a Tukey HSD post hoc means comparison, the frequency means for the teachers below and above the efficacy median were significantly different at the .05 level.

Although statistically significant, the impact of the belief in the efficacy of RWCs to teach new mathematics on decisions about how often to use RWCs is small, underscoring that teachers see other benefits of RWCs besides concept development. Counterintuitively, teachers who rated themselves 3 or lower on the efficacy continuum were likelier to cite the "conceptual" purpose for using RWCs (50% did) than those who self-rated at a 5 (19% cited the "conceptual" purpose). The latter group, despite its apparent confidence in RWCs to develop mathematical understanding, more often (41%) cited "motivate students or grab their interest" as their main purpose for using RWCs.

A limitation of the questionnaire emerged during the interviews, when some teachers explained that their decisions aimed at a broader purpose than teaching particular mathematical topics. These teachers were driven by the goal of raising healthy, productive adolescents, sometimes using their own lives as a model. Some of these teachers employed RWCs for non-mathematical purposes, but Lily shared personal stories to illustrate the role of mathematics in responsible adulthood:

> The main thing is I tell them, yeah, I'm a working single parent; I'm always worried about money, and budgeting. . . . I tell them that it's so important to keep track of your money, and planning for retirement is a big headache for me [*laughing*], and raising my daughter. So I say all this [mathematics] you can apply in your personal lives. 'Cause this is something I've discovered: A lot of the girls, even in – we're in the 21st century, and some of the girls are still thinking that they can rely on their own husbands and they don't need to know any of this math, and why do girls need to go in to math and science? And I try to brainwash them all the time! I tell them, okay, even if you

believe in that, and you just want to get rich through your husband and rely on your husband, you're still going to manage your family. . . . Just as a homemaker you need the math because it's complicated: your investments, your taxes, everything.

Resources and Constraints

Confirming a finding of my exploratory study, most teachers (67% in this study) get their ideas for RWCs mainly from their heads or past experience. Course textbooks are the primary RWC resource for only 25% of the teachers, including 31% of the newer teachers and 17% of experienced teachers. That newer teachers depend more than veterans on textbooks may reflect their lesser ability to independently generate RWCs, or the textbooks for the kinds of courses assigned to newer teachers may contain more RWCs. Other resource options on the questionnaire – other curriculum resources, professional development workshops or meetings, and colleagues – are used far less. Still, the interviewed teachers cited a host of sources for RWCs, including books about teaching mathematics, TV news and other programs, the Internet, professional conferences, university education or mathematics courses, released AP Exam items, colleagues, family members, and students.

On the questionnaire, only seven teachers indicated satisfaction with the amount of RWCs they made. The remaining 85 rated the significance of each item on a list of possible constraints on their use of RWCs. Table 3 shows the constraints and the percent of teachers giving each response, as well as the percents for newer and experienced teachers.

The most significant perceived constraints on the use of RWCs were limited class time, mandated curricula or tests, the extra time required to plan RWCs, and a lack of ideas or resources. The 11 interviewed teachers echoed these results, despite their more frequent use of RWCs than the typical questionnaire respondent. Two of the 11 cited no constraints during their interview; they made RWCs daily and were satisfied with this amount. Of the nine who cited (usually multiple) constraints, eight mentioned limited class time (to cover required topics), two mentioned limited planning time, and five mentioned a lack of ideas or resources (sometimes only for a particular course). Two interviewed teachers also mentioned student-related constraints, one observing that her younger students were reluctant to participate in labs or speak up, and the other citing a failure to transfer, specifically that her students did not connect the mathematics they learned in real-world projects to exam problems. Finally, one interviewed teacher felt constrained by her department's lack of commitment to RWCs.

On the questionnaire, newer teachers were likelier than veterans to cite a lack of ideas or resources as a constraint. The extra time to plan lessons with RWCs also deterred more new teachers than experienced. But experienced teachers were likelier to feel highly constrained because RWCs were not emphasised by required curricula and standardised tests. Relatedly, experienced teachers were likelier to cite limited in-class time as a highly significant constraint. Experienced teachers were also likelier to limit their use of RWCs because they believed students should be learning to think abstractly, not relying on concrete examples. These findings could result from course differences, if the more experienced teachers taught more advanced courses, such as AP Calculus or Honors Geometry, which demand rapid content coverage, for which the curricula and exams may de-emphasise RWCs, and in which teachers may see abstraction as central.

Table 3. Constraints on RWCs

Possible reasons you DON'T make more real-world connections	Percent of all teachers, and teachers below (<) and above (>) the median experience level, selecting each rating		
	Not a significant reason	Partly or sometimes a reason	A highly significant reason
Real-world connections tend to take more class time than I feel I can spend on most math topics	39% (<38%) (>40%)	39% (<46%) (>29%)	23% (<16%) (>31%)
Real-world connections usually don't seem to be all that effective	70% (<75%) (>71%)	26% (<19%) (>27%)	4% (<6%) (>3%)
Real-world connections aren't stressed in the required curriculum or on the standardised tests my students take	46% (<50%) (>41%)	41% (<42%) (>35%)	14% (<8%) (>24%)
I'd need more resources, ideas, or training about what connections to make or how to make them	30% (<16%) (>38%)	50% (<68%) (>35%)	20% (<16%) (>27%)
It takes too much time to plan lessons with real-world connections	39% (<30%) (>49%)	48% (<54%) (>40%)	13% (<16%) (>11%)
The classroom is more difficult to manage when I use real-world connections	73% (<78%) (>68%)	18% (<19%) (>18%)	9% (<3%) (>15%)
Students at the level I teach should be learning to think abstractly, not relying on concrete examples	75% (<86%) (>65%)	23% (<14%) (>32%)	1% (<0%) (>3%)
My students don't have sufficient math skills for real-world connections to be helpful	65% (<73%) (>61%)	27% (<24%) (>30%)	7% (<3%) (>9%)
My students don't have sufficient English skills to adequately access or benefit from real-world connections	70% (<68%) (>77%)	26% (<27%) (>24%)	4% (<5%) (>0%)

Differentiation

On the questionnaire, 54 teachers (59%) claimed to differentiate significantly how frequently they used RWCs across classes. Those 54 "differentiating teachers" were asked to select their main reasons for differentiating. Table 4 shows the percents of differentiating teachers who chose each explanation for their high- and low-RWC class.

Table 4. Reasons for differentiated frequencies of RWCs

[Choose] the **one** characteristic of this class that best explains **why** you make more real-world connections in this class than in other classes:	% of the 54 who differentiated	[Choose] the **one** characteristic of this class that best explains **why** you make fewer real-world connections in this class than in other classes:	% of the 54 who differentiated
a) Students' high mathematical ability level	11.1	a) Students' high mathematical ability level	3.7
b) Students' low mathematical ability level	3.7	b) Students' low mathematical ability level	13.0
c) Students' good behavior or high level of motivation	3.7	c) Students' good behavior or high level of motivation	3.7
d) Students' poor behavior or lack of motivation	3.7	d) Students' poor behavior or lack of motivation	1.9
e) Students' good English language skills	0	e) Students' good English language skills	0
f) Students' poor English language skills	0	f) Students' poor English language skills	3.7
g) It is easy to find real-world connections for math content in this course	37.0	g) It is hard to find real-world connections for the math content in this course	7.4
h) Less time pressure to cover material in this course	3.7	h) More time pressure to cover material in this course	31.4
i) Real-world connections seem to enhance these students' learning better than they do for students some other classes	14.8	i) Real-world connections don't seem to enhance these students' learning as well as they do for students in some other classes	11.1
j) It's more important to help these students see real-world connections than it is for students some other classes	3.7	j) It's less important to help these students see real-world connections than it is for students in some other classes	0
k) These students need a real challenge, which I can provide through real-world activities	0	k) These students are not prepared for the challenge that real-world activities typically pose	5.6
j) Other (please write in)	9.3	j) Other (please write in)	11.1

Course content. Supporting the hypothesis in the prior section, Table 4 shows that course content was the most popular explanation for why differentiating teachers made more RWCs in the class where they did so most frequently. Thirty-seven percent chose "It is easy to find real-world connections for math content in this course," and some comments written for the "Other" option explained that the curriculum for this high-frequency course had RWCs built in. To explain why they made RWCs least frequently in another class, 31% of differentiating teachers chose the most popular explanation: "More time pressure to cover material in this course."

Several interviewed teachers also implicated course content as a major reason for differentiating RWC frequency. Fran felt RWCs became complicated as course content advanced:

> When I [taught] middle school, I made a whole lot more connections, because the math was at a – I don't know if I want to really say a simpler level, but at a more realistic level. . . . For me, it's easier to make the connections with the Introduction to Algebra [course] because the math is not as complicated and the standards are not as well defined. And if the math is not as complicated, then the example from the real world doesn't have to be that complicated.

There was little evidence of a directional trend in the impact of course level. For 28 of the differentiating teachers, their highest RWC-frequency class was higher level than their lowest frequency class, while 22 made more RWCs in their lower-level course. A trend could be masked by the relative nature of these data. I did not ask teachers to list every course they taught, so I could not compare course levels in absolute terms across teachers.

Statistics teachers portrayed that course as exceptional because RWCs were built in. For Mike, the many RWCs provided in his statistics textbook drove his frequent use of RWCs:

> [In statistics], almost everything you end up doing, especially as the semester goes on, ends up being a word problem. The book's pretty good about supplying them. . . . In algebra and geometry, it's definitely harder and so usually I'll make [RWCs] myself, and I would say it probably happens maybe monthly.

For Carrie, the impetus was the relative importance of RWCs on the AP Statistics exam versus in the state algebra standards:

> The [state] algebra 1 standards are very process driven. [Students] must be able to factor this; they must be able to graph this; they must be able to solve this. Very few of the standards are focused on they must be able to apply this or understand this. . . . Whereas the AP [Statistics] test, they need to know how to apply this and how to analyse this. So I think the standards, in a lot of ways, dictate do you still try to make the connections for the buy-in and to actually give them useful problem solving tools in life?

Motivating productive student behaviour. On the questionnaire, only 27% of the teachers cited difficulty managing the classroom as a constraint on their use of

RWCs, and only six teachers indicated that behaviour or motivation level was their primary reason for differentiating RWC frequency across courses. (Interestingly, as a group, these six teachers gave both good and poor behaviour as reasons for both high and low frequency.) Yet four interviewed teachers made explicit that their decisions about RWCs were shaped by their need to motivate and maintain productive behaviour – a need that could both inspire and inhibit their use of RWCs. I observed Tom teaching the same lesson during the first and last periods of the day. Despite his stated commitment to RWCs, in his rambunctious afternoon class Tom omitted a connection he had made first period, surrendering the time to students to begin their homework. He explained to me, "I've lowered my expectations for sixth period because my energy level isn't up to combating all the noise levels constantly."

On the other hand, motivating good behaviour was a reason Barbara connected to her students' lives, even in non-mathematical and informal ways: "When you also can connect to students on a real – when they see you as a real person and they're comfortable . . . I don't have to yell and scream at them to get them to cooperate."

Teachers' notions about the differing motivational needs of their students were not generally guided by fixed principles relating abstract student qualities to pedagogy (e.g., "Struggling students need hands-on tasks"). Instead, the interviewed teachers interpreted motivational needs class by class, according to experience-based characterisations of particular student groups (e.g., "My period four class is more open to discussion than period five"). These characterisations took into account not only mathematical and language ability but also time of day, group chemistry, attitudes, maturity, and the futures the teacher anticipated for the students. Still, there were a few discernable patterns. Teachers tended to characterise students in advanced classes as self-motivated for schoolwork and therefore less in need of motivational interventions (e.g., RWCs) than low-level or struggling students. Mike saw a greater need for RWCs in his non-AP statistics class than his AP version:

> The AP statistics students, at least a good half of them, will sort of do whatever you tell them. They'll do their work. Whether they're interested or not, I don't know. But they'll do it! They'll do what they're supposed to, whereas the non-AP class there's more of a motivational problem. There's a lot of students who have not had success in math classes and so one of my goals is to get them motivated, have them have experience of success at this stage.

Further, teachers made judgments about the *kind* of RWCs their students needed. The prevailing view was that students in low-level classes, at-risk or struggling students, and students outside the mainstream culture (e.g., recent immigrants) benefited from RWCs that featured everyday, concrete, consumer-related contexts, while more advanced (college-bound) students should be exposed to, or were naturally interested in, more sophisticated, abstract, academic contexts. Ann described the RWCs she made in her diploma-exam-prep class:

It's more on a fundamental level. You have to balance your checkbook. You have to go to the grocery store and buy this food. You're making change from your paycheck . . . I try to make it very personal. Not so much of you're at a job, they're asking you to do something. Whereas with the higher-level class and the calculus, it's your job to figure this out. You're the guy in charge. With the [diploma-prep] kids, you have to carpet the floor and you don't want to get gypped, so you figure out your square footage yourself.

Implicit in Ann's comment is an anticipation of students' future statuses in the workplace, with students in higher-level classes headed for managerial roles and those in low-level classes for more subservient positions. (Hemmings [1988] also noted this phenomenon in teachers).

Thus, there is evidence of a tendency to view students in low-level classes or struggling students as needing more RWCs for motivation, especially RWCs related to everyday, concrete contexts. This tendency partly contradicts the prediction that teachers would use RWCs less often with low-level students, because of the association between RWCs and reform methods – an association this study shows to be inappropriate. Of course, the belief that RWCs are more important for struggling students may not mean those students actually encounter more RWCs. Interpreted motivational needs may conflict with interpreted behavioural needs, producing the apparent contradiction of teachers claiming to value RWCs especially for struggling students, then withholding RWCs from such students for management reasons.

DISCUSSION

Several findings of this study inform future research and teacher-education efforts concerning real-world connections in mathematics teaching.

First, the hypothetical decision I explored – whether to connect mathematics to the real world – appears of relatively little salience to teachers, raising doubts as to whether a "real-world connection" is, for teachers, even a discrete construct and subject of deliberation per se. On the other hand, the format in which a connection is made matters greatly to teachers, who more frequently make RWCs in formats that can fit comfortably into traditional teaching styles than in formats that align with reform teaching. Isolating RWCs as a focus of decisions should be recognised as a research strategy and not necessarily how teachers organise their thinking about lessons. When communicating with teachers, policy makers and teacher educators should avoid portraying RWCs as a unitary phenomenon and explicate the format in which students should engage in the connection.

Teachers range in their purposes for using RWCs and the degree to which they find RWCs effective for teaching new mathematics, but these sentiments hardly affect how often teachers use RWCs. (Further studies could investigate whether they affect the *manner* in which teachers use RWCs.) More teachers cited an affective purpose than a conceptual one. Even the interviewed teachers, selected for their higher frequency of RWC use, rarely justified their assessment of a "strong" RWC on the basis of mathematical richness or potential to deepen mathematical understanding. If RWCs are primarily viewed as motivational, they would seem more expendable in an overscheduled curriculum (time pressures being a main constraint on the use of RWCs) that privileges math-concept mastery than they would if viewed as powerful aids to concept development. The statistics course offers a vision of the possible, in that with textbooks rich in RWCs and accountability measures requiring realistic problem solving, teachers have made RWCs central to their statistics courses. These findings suggest that to encourage RWCs, teacher educators must convince teachers of their value for developing mathematical understanding and demonstrate how to leverage them for this purpose. Additionally, increasing teachers' access to professional development and resources that promote RWCs may be effective ways to encourage their use, but the RWCs they feature should be mathematically rich.

Teachers' perceptions of student characteristics affect how often teachers use RWCs, but the direction only vaguely echoes the pattern noted in reform teaching, namely greater occurrence in high-SES and high-achieving classes. The slight trend of more RWCs in courses with more advanced topics seems to reflect teachers' perception that low-level classes are more poorly behaved, with RWCs exacerbating the problem. This trend apparently does not result from a perception that low-achieving students need RWCs less; indeed, teachers tend to see low-achieving students in greater need of RWCs, mainly for motivation. A stronger influence on the differential use of RWCs is the ease with which they can be found for course content, with no evidence that either more or less advanced course topics are easier in this regard. Overall, the interview and observation data support the idea (Calderhead, 1996) that general teacher theories, while they exist, are weaker determinants of how teachers actually plan and implement lessons than situation-specific knowledge or predictions about what will work for a particular class on a particular day.

Finally, this study supports calls for research on teaching that steps outside the narrow subject-specific focus of recent popularity (Borko & Putnam, 1996). Theoretical frameworks should be broad enough to register the tremendous influence of teachers' need to control student behaviour (highlighted by Doyle, 1986; Romberg & Carpenter, 1986) and of teachers' broader, more transformative goals (Jackson, 1986), such as apprenticing students into adulthood. A current research emphasis is teachers' understanding of mathematical concepts, including facility with various forms of representations (e.g., Thompson & Thompson, 1996). I did not evaluate teachers' knowledge of mathematical connections, although teacher knowledge surely impacts how and how effectively teachers contextualise mathematics. Yet, the results of this study suggest that a host of other constraints arise first to determine whether teachers will make RWCs at all, and what kind. Further study would be needed to ascertain the impact of teacher knowledge about RWCs on their use, and whether different levels of knowledge, or different judgments about what constitutes "effective" RWCs, differently enable or motivate teachers to hurdle environmental constraints to RWCs. For example, is a teacher who is familiar with engineering applications less hobbled by the lack of RWCs in her course textbook?

REFERENCES

Borko, H., & Putnam, R. T. (1996). Learning to teach. In D. C. Berliner & R. C. Calfee (Eds.), *Handbook of educational psychology* (pp. 673–708). New York: Macmillan.
Brown, J. S., Collins, A., & Duguid, P. (1989). Situated cognition and the culture of learning. *Educational Researcher, 18*(1), 32–42.
Calderhead, J. (1996). Teachers: Beliefs and knowledge. In D. C. Berliner & R. C. Calfee (Eds.), *Handbook of educational psychology* (pp. 709–725). New York: Macmillan.
Clark, C. M., & Peterson, P. L. (1986). Teachers' thought processes. In M. C. Wittrock (Ed.), *Handbook of research on teaching* (3rd ed., pp. 255–296). New York: Macmillan.
De Lange, J. (1996). Using and applying mathematics in education. In A. J. Bishop, K. Clements, C. Keitel, J. Kilpatrick & C. Laborde (Eds.), *International handbook of mathematics education* (pp. 49–97). Boston: Kluwer.
Desmoine, L. M., Smith, T., Baker, D., & Ueno, K. (2005). Assessing barriers to the reform of U.S. mathematics instruction from an international perspective. *American Educational Research Journal, 42*, 501–535.
Doyle, W. (1986). Classroom organization and management. In M. C. Wittrock (Ed.), *Handbook of research on teaching* (3rd ed., pp. 392–431). New York: Macmillan.
Ernest, P. (1989). The knowledge, beliefs, and attitudes of the mathematics teacher: A model. *Journal of Education for Teaching, 15*, 13–33.
Gainsburg, J. (2008). Real-world connections in secondary math teaching. *Journal of Mathematics Teacher Education, 11*, 199–219.
Greer, B. (1997). Modeling reality in mathematics classrooms: The case of word problems. *Learning and Instruction, 7*, 293–307.
Hemmings, A. (1988). "Real" teaching: How high school teachers negotiate national, community, and student pressures when they define their work. In M. H. Metz (Ed.), *Field study on teachers' engagement: Project on the effects of the school as a workplace on teacher' engagement—Phase one. Final report.* Madison, WI: National Center on Effective Secondary Schools.
Jackson, P. W. (1986). *The practice of teaching.* New York: Teachers College Press.
Lehrer, R., Schauble, L., Strom, D., & Pligge, M. (2001). Similarity of form and substance: From inscriptions to models. In D. Klahr & S. Carver (Eds.), *Cognition and instruction: 25 years of progress* (pp. 39–74). Mahwah, NJ: Erlbaum.
Metz, M. H. (1988). Teachers' ultimate dependence on their students. In M. H. Metz (Ed.), *Field study on teachers' engagement: Project on the effects of the school as a workplace on teachers' engagement—Phase one. Final report.* Madison, WI: National Center on Effective Secondary Schools.
National Academy of Sciences. (2003). *Engaging schools: Fostering high school students' motivation to learn.* Washington, DC: National Academy Press.
National Council of Teachers of Mathematics (NCTM). (2000). *Principles and standards for school mathematics.* Reston, VA: NCTM.
National Research Council (NRC). (1998). *High school mathematics at work: Essays and examples for the education of all students.* Washington, DC: National Academy Press.
Peterson, P. L., Fennema, E., Carpenter, T. P., & Loef, M. (1989). Teachers' pedagogical content beliefs in mathematics. *Cognition and Instruction, 6*, 1–40.
Remillard, J. T. (2005). Examining key concepts in research on teachers' use of mathematics curricula. *Review of Educational Research, 75*, 211–246.
Richardson, V. (1996). The role of attitudes and beliefs in learning to teach. In J. Sikula, T.J. Buttery & E. Guyton (Eds.), *Handbook of research on teacher education* (2nd ed., pp. 102–119). New York: Simon & Schuster Macmillan.
Romberg, T. A., & Carpenter, T. P. (1986). Research on teaching and learning mathematics: Two disciplines of scientific inquiry. In M. C. Wittrock (Ed.), *Handbook of research on teaching* (3rd ed., pp. 850–873). New York: Macmillan.

Schoenfeld, A. S. (1998). Toward a theory of teaching-in-context. *Issues in Education, 4*, 1–94.
Spillane, J. P. (2001). Challenging instruction for "all students": Policy, practitioners, and practice. In S. Furhman (Ed.), *From the capital to the classroom: Standards-based reform in the states, One-hundredth yearbook of the National Society for the Study of Education* (Part II, pp. 217–241). Chicago: The University of Chicago Press.
Steen, L. A., & Forman, S. L. (1995). Mathematics for work and life. In I. M. Carl (Ed.), *Prospectus for school mathematics* (pp. 219–241). Reston, VA: NCTM.
Thompson, A. G. (1992). Teachers' beliefs and conceptions: A synthesis of the research. In D. A. Grouws (Ed.), *National Council of Teachers of Mathematics Handbook of Research on Mathematics Teaching and Learning* (pp. 127–146). New York: Macmillan.
Thompson, A. G., & Thompson, P. W. (1996). Talking about rates conceptually, Part II: Mathematical knowledge for teaching. *Journal for Research in Mathematics Education, 27*, 2–24.

Julie Gainsburg
California State University, Northridge
U.S.A.

JOÃO PEDRO DA PONTE

TEACHERS' KNOWLEDGE AND PRACTICES REGARDING CONTEXTUAL PROBLEMS AND REAL WORLD CONNECTIONS

Discussion of Part IV: Probing Teachers' Conceptions

INTRODUCTION

A discussion of the ways mathematics teachers deal with contextual problems must necessarily be based on views of teachers' knowledge, beliefs, conceptions, and practices, with special attention to classroom teaching. Therefore, I begin this chapter with some remarks on these issues, addressing two particular elements – learning tasks and classroom communication. Then, I look at how the authors of the three chapters from this section address how teachers view and use contextual word problems and real world connections in their teaching practice, giving particular attention to the role that teachers assign to realistic contexts and the factors that seem to influence their views and practices. Finally, I consider the implications of these studies for further research, curriculum development, and teacher education.

A FRAMEWORK TO STUDY TEACHERS' KNOWLEDGE AND PRACTICES

Mathematics teachers make decisions in their professional practice when they select tasks, plan teaching strategies, and choose materials appropriate to what they see as the curriculum objectives for mathematics teaching. In such process they take into account the characteristics of their students, their working conditions and the features of the social and educational environments, and adjust their decisions as they evaluate their students' learning and reflect on their practices. The choices and constraints that teachers face may be rather different at elementary, secondary, and university levels, depending also on the nature of the educational system, public policies, and social organisation. However, nowadays, all mathematics teachers face new challenges in their practice, such as the cultural diversity of the student population that makes the classroom into a very complex setting, and the recommendations for fundamental changes in the role of the teacher, from that of a deliverer of knowledge to that of a facilitator of learning (Brooks & Suydam, 1993; Ponte, 2008).

Teachers' practice is largely framed by two main elements: (1) the tasks that they select to propose to their students and the way these tasks evolve during teaching (Arbaugh & Brown, 2005; Stein & Smith, 1998), and (2) the way teachers manage classroom communication (Bishop & Goffree, 1986; Brendefur & Frykholm, 2000; Sierpinska, 1998). The tasks proposed by the teacher may be exercises that are homogeneous and at a rather low level of cognitive demand (Stein & Smith, 1998). However, they also may be quite diversified, including challenges at high levels of cognitive demand, such as problems, investigations, projects, and modelling situations (NCTM, 1991; Ponte, 2008; Smith & Stein, 1998). Furthermore, tasks may be framed in many contexts – from strictly mathematical to strongly dependent on situational elements – requiring rather different cognitive processes and promoting different learning objectives (Skvosmose, 2001). In their daily classroom practice, teachers organise sequences of tasks in order to support the development of students' learning trajectories (Simon & Tzur, 2006), so that they may grasp connections between concepts and consolidate their learning.

Communication is a social process within which participants interact, sharing information and mutually constraining their activity and evolution. Univocal and dialogic classroom communication support rather different teaching practices (Alrø & Skovsmose, 2004; Brendefur & Frykholm, 2000). In fact, teachers play a critical role in enabling or limiting the communicative processes in the classroom (Lappan & Theule-Lubienski, 1989). When teachers select rich and challenging tasks, they create opportunities for students to express and argue their own views (Lampert & Cobb, 2003; Ponte & Santos, 1998). Especially important, in terms of classroom communication, are the moments in which the students present to the whole class the strategies that they used to solve problems and justify their results. Such moments promote argumentation and allow the institutionalisation of knowledge for all students in the class (Christiansen & Walther, 1986).

Teachers' practices are framed by their knowledge, beliefs, and conceptions regarding mathematics and mathematics teaching, and also by the ways in which they interpret and value the different elements of their working context – students' abilities, interests and expectations, curriculum guidelines, resources available, the school's professional culture, external assessments, parents' concerns, etc. In their practice, teachers use their "craft knowledge", which may be regarded "as action-oriented knowledge which is not generally made explicit by teachers, which they may indeed find difficult to articulate, or which they may even be unaware of using" (Ruthven & Goodchild, 2008, p. 573). Craft knowledge arises from what teachers do and, in turn, informs it. Teachers develop such knowledge through the processes of reflecting and practical problem solving that they engage in carrying out their jobs. This knowledge is, therefore, closely related to professional practice and is oriented towards practice. It may be more or less principled, depending on the professional culture and the teacher's previous reflective and professional development experiences. Teachers' beliefs and conceptions are important structuring elements of their craft knowledge. But this knowledge is much deeper than what the teacher is able to make explicit verbally – it is embedded in what the teacher does in his/her professional practice (Ponte, Matos, Guimarães, Canavarro, & Leal,

1994). Craft knowledge may be elicited in a number of ways, especially by observing and reflecting jointly with teachers about their practices or by stimulating teachers to reflect deeply or to research their practices.

STUDIES OF TEACHERS WORKING WITH WORD PROBLEMS AND REAL WORLD CONNECTIONS

Let us consider, then, what the different studies suggest about the roles that teachers assign to real world contexts, particularly in word problems. In their chapter, Depaepe, De Corte, and Verschaffel address the way teachers relate to the "genuine modelling approach", in which students tackle "complex problems wherein the context plays a pivotal role" (p. 246). In this approach the teacher is encouraged to create a classroom culture that is conducive to the development of some characteristic skills, conceptions, and attitudes. Their analysis draws on Palm's (this volume) framework concerning the realistic nature of word problems, a framework based on the notion of "simulation" – that is, "a word problem is considered to be realistic if the important aspects of the word problem are taken into account under conditions representative for that out-of-school situation" (p. 246). They also draw on Chapman's (2006) discussion about the way word problem contexts are conceptualised and dealt with in their teaching – with a major distinction between a "paradigmatic" mode that focuses on universal and context-free mathematical models or structures and a "narrative mode" that focuses on the situational features of the problem. Specifically, the authors address the nature of the problems presented in a widely used Flemish mathematics grade 6 textbook and the problems that were actually used by two teachers of this grade level.

The authors show that, overall, both textbook and teacher-developed problems involve a high number of realistic characteristics. However, more than one third of the problems proposed by the textbook or used by the teachers lacked at least one of the essential features of realistic problems – involving a realistic event, posing a realistic question, and providing data similar to the data available in the contextual situation. The authors also show that the problems that the teachers propose in class tend to be quite similar to those of the textbook. In fact, they indicate that the teachers tended to follow the sequence of problems of the textbook, selecting those that they felt could be handled in the time available and when the teachers generated new problems these tended to be similar to the textbook problems.

In her study, Chapman notes that there is very little previous research on teachers' using contextual problems and looks at teachers' conceptions and practical knowledge on this issue. She describes several conceptions teachers may have of contextual problems and presents empirical illustrations of them in four elementary and eleven secondary Canadian school teachers. The main sources of data were open-ended interviews and observations in the classroom.

The author presents three philosophical perspectives of knowledge – objectivist, utilitarian, and humanistic – and indicates how contextual problems are regarded in each of them. The objectivist view tends to regard the problem situation and the solution as existing independently of the students and is oriented towards computation-algorithmic problems. The utilitarian view regards the value of contextual problems as dependent on their potential to promote students' learning and is oriented towards both algorithmic and non-algorithmic problems. And, finally, the humanistic view looks at contextual problems in relation to people, focusing on the personal aspects of the students' experience. It values students' stories, experiences and mathematical thinking. Chapman states that collectively "the teachers held conceptions that covered three philosophical perspectives of knowledge" (p. 235). There is a strong parallel between this framework and that of the Depaepe et al. chapter, as the narrative and humanistic constructs seem very similar and the same happens with the paradigmatic and objectivist views.

The chapter also presents four major teaching models of teaching with contextual problems that emerged from teachers' conceptions: imposition, abandonment, directed-inquiry, and dialogic-inquiry. Whereas in the imposition and abandonment models the goal is to find the correct solution and the emphasis is on computational-algorithmic problems, in directed and dialogic-inquiry the goal is in understanding the process and meaningfully applied algorithmic problems have a prominent place. Whereas in imposition and directed inquiry the teacher imposes or directs students' interpretations and processes, in abandonment and dialogic-inquiry the teacher provides students with the opportunity to make their own interpretations of the problem and choice of strategies. The way communication is handled in the classroom bears a close relationship to these models.

The study by Gainsburg does not address teachers' use of word problems but, in a more general way, how teachers use real-world connections, putting the emphasis on what they think and do – their practices, decisions, thoughts, and actions. The author is concerned with the way the teachers "use connections, why, and the factors that influence that use" (p. 265). In her view, teachers' classroom practice is largely determined by teachers' plans, these are influenced by teachers' theories and beliefs that, in turn, are influenced by student behaviour; and all these elements are influenced by several factors external to the teacher, such as resources, students' characteristics, and social and school expectations. The author assumes that teachers' beliefs frame their practices and are dependent on the teachers' work context – including student behaviour. That is, the relation between student behaviour and teachers' beliefs and practices goes both ways – both influencing each other.

This study involves 92 California high school teachers (who responded to a questionnaire) and 11 teachers (who were interviewed and, in some cases, observed). The results suggest that to connect mathematics to the real world appears to be not a unitary construct but a multifaceted idea. They also suggest that connecting mathematics to the real world is not so important to high school teachers as one could expect. About one half of the teachers who responded to the questionnaire indicate that they assign world problems with realistic contexts to students weekly; one fourth do it daily and another fourth only monthly or 1-2 times a year. This suggests that teachers do not regard this kind of task as very important in their teaching. In addition, these teachers more often use real-world connections within a "direct" teaching style than within "reform" teaching. For example, one of the teachers interviewed, based in her assessment of low persistence and skill of her students, decided not to follow the reform-oriented guidelines of the textbook, which emphasised real-world connections, and resorted to "traditional methods" that strongly impoverished the real-world connections that students had opportunity to meet. In the view of Gainsburg, the consideration of the degree of structure of the task and the style of organisation of students' work are more important for the decision of the teacher about what to do in the classroom than the option of emphasising or not real-world connections.

The studies by Depaepe et al. and by Chapman draw on similar frameworks and underline similar aspects. They consider an objectivist/paradigmatic view and, in one way or another, relate it to "traditional" teaching approaches and they also consider a humanistic/narrative view that they relate to "reform" mathematics teaching. They also suggest that it is not merely the real-world connection that matters, but also the *way in which* this is done. Furthermore, the two teachers of the Depaepe et al. study and several if not most of the teachers in Chapman's study seem to give an important place to word problems, valuing their role to support student learning. The paper of Gainsburg also echoes the distinction between traditional and reform teaching but, in contrast, the teachers in this study seem to pay, overall, little attention to real-world connections. These differences may result from a number of factors. First, the methodology of the Depaepe et al., and the Chapman studies involved long-term interactions of the researchers with the teachers, which was not the case in the Gainsburg study. Such extended work addressing one single topic naturally promotes teacher attention to that topic and may induce a higher value of it. A second possibility for the strong differences in teachers' perspectives may be related to the fact that Depaepe et al. and Chapman address specifically word problems whereas Gainsburg addresses real world connections more broadly. Word problems represent a well known kind of task but real-world connections may mean several different things, as Gainsburg herself recognises – ranging from exercises that make reference to some contextual situations or an example that is provided during instruction, to a complex modelling task or an extended project. The more diffuse nature of the construct "real world connection" may be the reason why teachers appear to give less importance to it. A third possibility for the differences in the orientation of the teachers' responses may be that the two participants in the Depaepe et al. study were elementary school teachers and the participants in the Chapman were a mixed group of elementary and secondary school teachers, whereas the participants in the Gainsburg study were all secondary school teachers. It may be that elementary school teachers tend to put more value on contextual elements than secondary school teachers. And, finally, a fourth reason for the differences may have its origin in the fact that the studies were done in different countries (Belgium, Canada, USA) with different cultures, social and economic conditions, and more importantly, with different educational regimes and, perhaps, different curricula and traditions in school mathematics. That is, the differences found in the studies may be related to the design of the studies or to the specific characteristics of the participants and of the professional and school contexts from which they were drawn.

FACTORS THAT INFLUENCE TEACHERS' PRACTICES WITH CONTEXTUAL PROBLEMS AND REAL WORLD CONNECTIONS

Let us turn now our attention to the factors that seem to influence teachers' conceptions and practices. The investigations take also rather different orientations in this regard. The study by Chapman addresses the conceptions of teachers concerning knowledge in general and their models of teaching which are framed as a description of teachers' practices. The author indicates that meaningful teaching with contextual problems tends to occur with exemplary teachers that hold the humanistic view of such problems in a dominant way (albeit holding also to some degree the objectivist and utilitarian views). Besides, these exemplary teachers hold dominantly the dialogic-inquiry model, although they also sometimes use the directed-inquiry model. These teachers are, in general, more flexible in their teaching. They also achieve a better integration of contextual problems in their courses. The author also makes a relationship between models of teaching and models of conceptions of knowledge, showing connections between dialogic-inquiry and humanistic and utilitarian views, between direct-inquiry and partial humanistic and partial utilitarian, and between imposition and abandonment with objectivist and partial utilitarian. Therefore, the models presented by the author – concerning views of knowledge (objectivist, utilitarian, humanistic) and concerning teaching with contextual problems (imposition, abandonment, directed- and dialogic-inquiry) – seem to provide a powerful framework to explain how teachers deal with contextual problem in their classroom practice.

The chapter by Gainsburg also looks at teachers' conceptions. However, it pays more attention to the way teachers reflect on external constraints in carrying out their jobs. The author suggests that, for teachers, there are two main reasons to use real-world connections. The first is an affective purpose – to motivate students, attracting their interest and convincing them that mathematics is relevant for their lives – and appears quite strongly in teachers' responses. The second is a cognitive purpose – to make a math concept easier to understand – but has a less clear status in the teachers' priorities. The author suggests that "as a group, the teachers tend to believe that RWCs [real-world connections] could help students learn new mathematics but were not completely convinced of the efficacy of RWCs to do so or saw situations where RWCs failed in this regard" (p. 271). Whereas for some teachers the belief in the efficacy of connections depends on the topic (e.g., low in calculus but high in geometry), for other teachers it depends on the level of the students. The author indicates that teachers who value more the efficacy of making real-world connections to promote students' learning used them in their practice slightly more frequently than the others. In her view, this is also an indicator that, besides students' conceptual development, teachers see other benefits in working with real-world connections. Statistics is a very special case of a topic in which real-world connections tend to play quite an important role.

According to Gainsburg, two thirds of the teachers in her study report getting their ideas for real-world connections from their personal experience and only one fourth report drawing on textbooks. The constraints on the use of such connections most commonly cited by teachers were scarcity of class time, mandated curricula and external assessment, shortage of time for planning, and lack of resources. Two teachers who were interviewed also cited constraints related to the students, indicating that their uneasiness in participating in the classroom and difficulties in connecting the mathematics learned in contextual situations with the more formal mathematics of the exam. One teacher mentioned the lack of interest on this approach of her school department. The main reasons indicated by teachers for not using real-world connections are: (1) time pressure to cover the course material, (2) students low mathematical ability, and (3) such connections seem to not very helpful in enhance students' learning in this class.

It is interesting to note that more than a half of the teachers who responded to the questionnaire indicated that they differentiate significantly the use of real-world connections in different classes. That is, teachers' perceptions of student characteristics affect how often teachers use real-world connections. They tend to view low ability students as needing more real-world connections, especially those related to real word contexts, for their motivation. But teachers also indicate that the classes with such students are more difficult to manage, precluding them to use real-world connections. And Gainsburg notes that teachers' situation specific knowledge or predictions about what may happen in this or that scenario are a stronger determinant of what teachers do than their general theories.

Finally, the two teachers of the Depaepe et al., study tend to rely very much on the mathematics textbook to select the problems for their students. Teacher created problems are very similar to textbook problems, suggesting that, as an educational resource, the textbook constitutes indeed an important instrument that has a major influence on teachers' practices. The authors indicate that the two teachers had different instructional approaches but at the end appear to use word problems of a rather similar nature. That is, this study signals out one single factor, external to the teachers – the textbook – as the main influence on teachers practice. It is puzzling, however, that this result is in apparent contradiction with the results of the Gainsburg study that downplay the importance of textbooks. These different results may be due to the fact that this latter study addressed a different and more diffuse notion ("real world connections") and approached teachers with a very different methodology. It may also suggest differences in teachers' professional practices or in their educational contexts.

Whereas the model of Chapman seems include variables that are quite important in describing teachers' conceptions and craft knowledge directly related to their practices of using contextual problems, we do not have similar models to address the external factors related to the school, social and political contexts that play in significant role on this issue. Gainsburg shows that the way teachers perceive the students (low/high ability, motivated/not motivated) plays a significant role in teachers' decisions and suggests the influence of several other factors such as time constraints, curriculum resources, external assessment and school conditions. Also, Depaepe et al. clearly indicate the prominent role that the textbook may play. However, we are lacking refined models that account for the relations of contextual variables and teachers' conceptions and practices.

IMPLICATIONS FOR RESEARCH, CURRICULUM DEVELOPMENT AND TEACHER EDUCATION

Let us now consider the implications of the three chapters for further research, for curriculum development and for teacher education. For example, Depaepe et al. discuss at length methodological issues concerning classification levels. Furthermore, the authors discuss the assumption of Palm that, to be educationally effective, word problems should simulate as accurately as possible the real life situation. They indicate several arguments why this may not be the case: (1) sometimes it makes sense not simulating all aspects of a given situation; (2) the most interesting word problems are the "problematic" ones; (3) some problems do not intend to simulate real life situations but are nevertheless important from a pedagogical point of view; (4) the context of schooling and real world are fundamentally different; and (5) at least as important as the nature of word problems is the way these problems are treated in the classroom. It may seem that the only the last argument (5) is really related to teachers' knowledge and practices. However, the way teachers act in their planning and in their teaching is highly dependent on how they regard the educational features of world problems and how they may relate to the classroom activity.

In fact, the issue of the relationship between word problems and real life contexts is important both for researchers and for teachers. A high degree of realism may be essential to enable students to draw on their knowledge of the context to learn the concepts, representations, and processes, and to provide them with the ability to use such knowledge in future situations. At the same time, some degree of simplification may also be necessary to have sensible and productive learning paths. Where to draw the fine line between realism and simplification is a matter for further research and for informed judgment. Besides "genuine modelling" we also need to learn about establishing learning paths that lead students through successive levels of abstraction and mastery of conceptual and procedural tools. The reflection of the authors about the importance of the way word problems are treated in the classroom reinforces the need to probe further into the issues that teachers face in selecting and organising tasks for instruction and in conducting classroom practice. Teachers that are sensitive to these issues have important craft knowledge in this regard, and collaborative projects involving teachers and researchers may be fruitful settings to study further on this field.

Chapman indicates that future investigations should study the connections between teachers' conceptions of mathematics, their views of contextual problems, and their teaching models. Such research may provide a deeper understanding of the teachers' conceptions that relate to their practices in teaching these problems. However, as I indicated above, other factors related to the teachers' working conditions and professional culture may also be important issues to address.

Gainsburg indicates that "teachers range in their purposes for using RWCs and the degree to which they find RWCs effective for teaching new mathematics" (p. 280). She also indicates that "these sentiments hardly affect how often teachers use RCWs" but "further studies could investigate whether they affect the *manner* in which teachers use RWCs" (p. 278, italics in the original). Therefore, she suggests that researchers may have a closer look to the relations between these variables. This author concludes that teachers do not take real-world connections as very important and researchers should pay attention to other issues that teachers find more problematic, such as dealing with students. She considers that research on teaching must look outside the "narrow subject-specific focus" and pay attention to the wider concerns of teachers, notably, controlling student behaviour and promoting "teachers' broader, more transformative goals" (p. 279). However, I would suggest that the two kinds of research are necessary and that it is important to integrate their results. For school systems in which behavioural problems are overwhelming, research with a broad focus on students' behaviour and teachers' strategies for handing classes is certainly very urgent but for school systems in which there are productive working conditions in classrooms research with a subject-specific focus on mathematics education may provide more useful information.

Given the scarcity of research on the use of contextual problems by teachers documented by Chapman, there is much to be done in this field. For example, researchers need to pay more attention to the way teachers perceive word problems as a particular kind of task that they include in their planning. Word problems are commonly used to apply known concepts, representations, and procedures. What does it take in order that teachers use word problems to introduce or to develop new mathematics ideas? What particular kinds of word problems may they see as most suited to this effect? How do teacher regard the balance realistic features with other didactical properties? Do they see word problems playing a similar role for every topic? Another issue has to do with the way word problems are tackled in the classroom, the way strategies and solutions are presented and discussed, and the way the results are further extended and generalised by students. What may be the roles of teachers and students during this work and what kind of communication processes may support fruitful explorations? In my view, the study by Chapman provides an entry point into many of these issues but they need to be tackled in a more specific way, taking into account grade levels, topics, school systems, and social and professional conditions.

The studies also have suggestions for teacher development. For example, Gainsburg considers that "to encourage RWCs, teacher educators must convince teachers of their value for developing mathematical understanding" (p. 279). In fact, this seems to be a reasonable recommendation, given the mixed views that the teachers have on this issue. Chapman indicates that for "meaningful teaching with contextual problems teachers should hold knowledge that includes depth in a humanistic and utilitarian view of contextual problems and an inquiry-based pedagogy" (p. 242). Therefore, in her view, teacher development opportunities should make "explicit consideration of teachers' conceptions of CPs [contextual problems] in learning opportunities for them" (p. 245). Reflecting on their teaching with the constructs provided in her study, the teachers may then "become aware of alternative ways of thinking and teaching" (p. 243) with contextual problems. The author indicates that this is not by itself a sufficient condition for change in teaching, but, nevertheless, it may be an important component of teacher education. In her perspective, professional development may help teachers to reflect in order to become aware of alternative ways of thinking and teaching with contextualised problems.

These studies offer valuable suggestions for teachers' professional development, indicating points that may be addressed in teacher education programs and even suggesting reflective activities that may support the evolution of teachers' conceptions and practices. However, there is some danger in organising teacher education programs based on very specific findings and concerns. Therefore, attention needs also to be given to ways of organising such teacher education in actual teachers' inservice working conditions or in pre-service teacher education settings that take into account the integrated nature of teachers' craft knowledge and the actual processes of conducting classroom practice in the teachers' working conditions. Studying such issues constitutes an important matter for future research.

REFERENCES

Alrø, H., & Skovsmose, O. (2004). Dialogic learning in collaborative investigation. *Nordisk Matematikdidaktikk, 9*(2), 39–62.

Arbaugh, F., & Brown, C. (2005). Analysing mathematical tasks: A catalyst for change? *Journal of Mathematics Teacher Education*, 499–536.

Bishop, A., & Goffree, F. (1986). Classroom organization and dynamics. In B. Christiansen, A. G. Howson, & M. Otte (Eds.), *Perspectives on mathematics education* (pp. 309–365). Dordrecht, The Netherlands: D. Reidel.

Brendefur, J., & Frykholm, J. (2000). Promoting mathematical communication in the classroom: Two preservice teachers' conceptions and practices. *Journal of Mathematics Teacher Education, 3*, 125–153.

Brooks, K., & Suydam, M. (1993). Planning and organizing curriculum. In P. S. Wilson (Ed.), *Research ideas for the classroom: High school mathematics* (pp. 232–244). Reston, VA: NCTM.

Chapman, O. (2006). Classroom practices for context of mathematics word problems. *Educational Studies in Mathematics, 62*, 211–230.

Christiansen, B., & Walther, G. (1986). Task and activity. In B. Christiansen, A. G. Howson & M. Otte (Eds.), *Perspectives on mathematics education* (pp. 243–307). Dordrecht, The Netherlands: D. Reidel.

Lampert, M., & Cobb, P. (2003). Communication and language. In J. Kilpatrick, W. G. Martin & D. Shifter (Eds.), *A research companion to principles and standards for school mathematics* (pp. 237–249). Reston, VA: NCTM.

Lappan, G., & Theule-Lubienski, S. (1994). Training teachers or educating professionals? What are the issues and how are they being resolved? In D. Robitaille, D. Wheeler, & C. Kieran (Eds.), *Selected Lectures from the 7th International Congress on Mathematical Education* (pp. 249–261). Sainte-Foy, Canada: Les Presses de l'Université Laval.

NCTM. (1991). *Professional standards for teaching mathematics*. Reston, VA: NCTM.

Ponte, J. P. (2005). Gestão curricular em Matemática. In GTI (Ed.), *O professor e o desenvolvimento curricular* (pp. 11–34). Lisboa: APM.

Ponte, J. P. (2008). Investigating mathematics: A challenge for students, teachers, and mathemaricas education reseachers. In B. Maj, M. Pytlak, & E. Swoboda (Eds.), *Supporting independent thinking through mathematical education* (pp. 122–137). Rzeszow: Wydawnictwo Uniwersytetu Rzeszowskiego.

Ponte, J. P., Matos, J. F., Guimarães, H., Canavarro, P., & Leal, L. C. (1994). Teachers' and students' views and attitudes towards a new mathematics curriculum. *Educational Studies in Mathematics, 26*, 347–365.

Ponte, J. P., & Santos, L. (1998). Práticas lectivas num contexto de reforma curricular. *Quadrante, 7*(1), 3–33.

Ruthven, K., & Goodchild, S. (2008). Linking research with teaching: Towards synergy of scholarly and craft knowledge. In L. English (Ed.), *Handbook of international research in mathematics education* (2nd ed., pp. 565–592). New York: Routledge.

Sierpinska, A. (1998). Three epistemologies, three views of classroom communication: Constructivism, sociocultural approaches, interactionism. In H. Steinbring, M. G. B. Bussi, & A. Sierpinska (Eds.), *Language and communication in the mathematics classroom* (pp. 30–62). Reston, VA: NCTM.

Simon, M. A., & Tzur, R. (2006). Explicating the role of mathematical tasks in conceptual learning: An elaboration of the hypothetical learning trajectory. *Educational Studies in Mathematics, 62,* 91–104.

Smith, M. S., & Stein, M. K. (1998). Selecting and creating mathematical tasks: From research to practice. *Mathematics Teaching in the Middle School, 3,* 344–350.

Stein, M. K., & Smith, M. S. (1998). Mathematical tasks as a framework for reflection: From research to practice. *Mathematics Teaching in the Middle School, 3,* 268–275.

João Pedro da Ponte
Instituto de Educação
Universidade de Lisboa
Portugal

PART V: CHANGING CLASSROOMS

CINZIA BONOTTO

14. WORKING TOWARDS TEACHING REALISTIC MATHEMATICAL MODELLING AND PROBLEM POSING IN ITALIAN CLASSROOMS

INTRODUCTION

During recent decades, a growing body of empirical research has documented that the practice of word problem solving in school mathematics promotes in students the exclusion of realistic considerations and a "suspension of sense-making" (Schoenfeld, 1991), and rarely reaches the idea of mathematical modelling. Primary and secondary school students tend to exclude relevant and plausible familiar aspects of reality from their observation and reasoning (for a comprehensive overview of these studies see Verschaffel, Greer, & De Corte, 2000). Recent Italian research (Bonotto & Wilczewski, 2007) confirms these results.

There are several reasons for this lack of use of everyday-life knowledge: textual factors relating to the stereotypical nature of the most frequently used textbook problems (see e.g., Wyndhamn & Säljö, 1997), presentational or contextual factors associated with practices and environments, and expectations related to the classroom culture of mathematical problem solving (see e.g., Gravemeijer, 1997; Palm, 2008).

Furthermore, it has been noted that the use of stereotyped problems and the accompanying classroom climate relate to teachers' beliefs about the goals of mathematics education. In the researches of Verschaffel, De Corte, and Borghart (1997) and Bonotto and Wilczewski (2007), student-teachers were asked to judge realistic and non-realistic answers to problematic word problems. The research shows that the student-teachers' overall evaluation of the stereotyped, non-realistic answers to these items was considerably more positive than for the realistic answers grounded in context-based considerations. The teachers seem to believe that the activation of realistic context-based considerations should not be stimulated but rather discouraged in elementary-school mathematics.

Finally, in my opinion, another reason for the abstention from using realistic considerations is that the practice of word problem solving is relegated to classroom activities, having meaning and location, in terms of time and space, only within the school; rarely will students encounter these activities in this form outside of school (Bonotto, 2005).

This analysis indicates a difference in views on the function of word problems in mathematics education. Researchers relate word problems to problem solving and applications of mathematics, while student-teachers (and probably teachers in general) see word problems as nothing more, and nothing less, than exercises in the four basic operations. Those exercises also have a justification and suitable place within the teaching of mathematics, though certainly not that of favouring mathematical modelling, and especially realistic mathematical modelling, i.e. "both real-world based and quantitatively constrained sense-making" (Reusser & Stebler, 1997).

To implement an early introduction in elementary schools of fundamental ideas about mathematical modelling, in particular realistic mathematical modelling, and to lay the foundations of a mathematisation disposition, some changes are necessary. In particular the type of activity used to create interplay between mathematics classroom activities and everyday-life experience, primarily word problems, must be replaced with more realistic and less stereotyped problem situations.

In this chapter, based on results obtained in several teaching experiments, we discuss how these changes can be brought about at primary school level through classroom activities that are more easily related to the experiential world of the student and consistent with a sense-making disposition. As we shall see in our examples, the activities make extensive use of suitable artifacts that, with their incorporated mathematics, can play a fundamental role in bringing students' out-of-school reasoning experiences into play, by creating a new tension between school mathematics and everyday-life knowledge (Bonotto, 2007).

The classroom activities are also based on the use of a variety of complementary, integrated, and interactive teaching methods, and on the introduction of new socio-mathematical norms (Yackel & Cobb, 1996), in an attempt to create a substantially modified teaching/learning environment. This environment is focused on fostering a mindful approach toward realistic mathematical modelling and a problem-posing attitude, as encouraged by recent Italian document for new curricula (see Boero & Daupeto, 2007, for a discussion).

THEORETICAL AND EMPIRICAL BACKGROUND

About Modelling

Various views of the modelling process co-exist within educational circles. These have to do both with perceptions of the modelling process, and constraints and opportunities perceived to exist within particular educational settings.

> The term mathematical modelling is not only used to refer to a process whereby a situation has to be problematised and understood, translated into mathematics, worked out mathematically, translated back into the original (real-world) situation, evaluated and communicated. Besides this type of modelling, which requires that the student has already at his disposal at least some mathematical models and tools to mathematise, there is another kind of modelling, wherein model-eliciting activities are used as a vehicle for *the development* (rather than the application) of mathematical concepts (Greer, Verschaffel, & Mukhopadhyay, 2007, p. 90).

A particularly sustained and theoretically highly developed program on model-eliciting activities has been carried out by Lesh and his colleagues (Lesh & Doerr, 2003; Lesh & Lehrer, 2003; Lesh & Zawojewski, 2007).

The "emergent modelling approach" of Gravemeijer taps into the same potential but with a focus on long-term learning processes, in which a model develops from an informal, situated model ("a model of") into a generalisable mathematical structure ("a model for").

These emergent models are seen as originating from activity in, and reasoning about situations. From this perspective, the process of constructing models is one of progressive reorganizing situations. The model and the situation being modeled co-evolve and are mutually constituted in the course of modelling activity (Gravemeijer, 2007, p. 138).

Although it is very difficult, if not impossible, to make a sharp distinction between the two aspects of mathematical modelling, it is clear that they are associated with different phases in the teaching/learning process and with different kinds of instructional activities (Greer et al., 2007).

An early introduction in schools of fundamental ideas about modelling is not only possible but also indeed desirable even at the primary school level (see also Usiskin (2007) for some suggestions of ways to reconsider, for example, arithmetic operations as mathematical models).

It might be appropriate to introduce the modelling perspective much earlier in the child's education ... in order to prevent – rather than remedy – routine behaviour and to continue this preventive effort throughout the mathematics curriculum (De Bock, Van Dooren, & Janssens, 2007, p. 247).

Further, the modelling can be seen as a means of recognising the potential of mathematics as a critical tool to interpret and understand reality, the communities children live in, or society in general. Teaching students to interpret critically the reality they live in and to understand its codes and messages so as not to be excluded or misled, should be an important goal for compulsory education (Bonotto, 2005; Greer et al., 2007).

About Problem Posing

Problem posing is an important companion to problem solving and lies at the heart of mathematical activity. Kilpatrick (1987) and Silver (1994) are among many mathematics educators who have suggested that the incorporation of problem solving and problem-posing situations into mathematics classrooms could have a positive impact on students' mathematical thinking.

From a teaching perspective, problem-posing activities reveal much about the understandings, skills and attitudes the problem poser brings to a given situation and thus become a powerful assessment tool (English, 1997; Leung, 1996; Lowrie, 2002). Not surprisingly, reports such as those produced by the National Council of Teachers of Mathematics (1989, 1991, 2000) have called for an increased emphasis on problem-posing activities in the mathematics classroom.

Problem posing and problem solving are closely related. As Silver (1995) suggested, problem posing could occur prior to problem solving when problems were being generated from a particular situation or after solving a problem when experiences from the problem-solving context are modified or applied to new situations. In addition, problem posing could occur during problem solving when the individual intentionally changes goals while in the process of solving the problem. Such metacognitive processes underlie mathematical power and autonomy and it is not surprising that "more able" students are more successful in generating problems (English, 1997).

Several studies have reported approaches to incorporate problem posing in instruction. These studies provided evidence that problem posing has a positive influence on students' thinking, problem-solving skills, attitudes, and confidence in mathematics and mathematical problem solving (English, 1997, 1998, 2003; Leung, 1996; Silver, 1994).

Recently Mestre (2002), using problem posing as a tool for studying cognitive processes, asserted that problem posing can be used to investigate the transfer of concepts across contexts, and to identify students' knowledge, reasoning, and conceptual development. Furthermore, children's expression of mathematical ideas through the creation of their own mathematics problems demonstrates not only their understanding and level of concept development, but also their perception of the nature of mathematics and their attitude towards this discipline (Ellerton & Clarkson, 1996).

Nevertheless, despite the importance of problem posing and its contribution to conceptual understanding of mathematical ideas, little is known about the nature of the underlying thinking processes that constitute problem posing, and the schemes through which students' mathematical problem posing can be analysed and assessed (Christou, Mousoulides, Pittalis, Pitta-Pantazi, & Sriraman, 2005).

Problem posing has been defined by researchers from different perspectives (see Silver & Cai, 1996). In this contribution I consider mathematical problem posing as the process by which, on the basis of mathematical experience, students construct personal interpretations of concrete situations and formulate them as meaningful mathematical problems. It, therefore, becomes an opportunity for interpretation and critical analysis of reality in different ways: i) they have to distinguish significant data from irrelevant data; ii) they must discover the relations between the facts; iii) they must decide whether the information in their possession is sufficient to solve the problem; and iv) they must investigate if numerical data involved is numerically and/or contextually coherent. These activities are typical of the modelling process and are similar to situations to be mathematised that students have encountered or will encounter outside school. According to English (1998):

> ...we need to broaden the types of problem experiences we present to children ... and, in so doing, help children "connect" with school mathematics by encouraging everyday problem posing ... We can capitalize on the informal activities situated in children's daily lives and get children in the habit of recognizing mathematical situations wherever they might be (p. 100).

About Artifacts

Cole (1995) points out that an essential property of artifacts is their being ideal (in that they contain in coded form the interactions of which they were previously a part and which they mediate in the present) and material (in that they exist only insofar as they are embodied in concrete objects). This aspect supports their bilateral influence and offers common bases to culture and discourse. Furthermore artifacts, besides embodying the intellectual history of a culture, also incorporate many theories the users accept, albeit unconsciously. "Artifact and conventions are cultural forms that have been created over the course of social history which also figure into the goals that emerge in cultural practices" (Saxe, Dawson, Fall, & Howard, 1996, p. 125). The use of artifacts mediates intellectual activities, and – at the same time – enables and constrains human thinking. Through these subtle processes social history is brought into any individual act of cognition.

The artifacts we introduced into classroom activities, for example supermarket bills, bottle and can labels, a weekly TV guide, the weather forecast from a newspaper, some menus of restaurants and pizzerias (see e.g., Bonotto 2001, 2003a, 2003b, 2005 and 2006), are materials, real or reproduced, which children typically meet in real-life situations. In this way we can offer the opportunity of making connections between the mathematics incorporated in real-life situations and school mathematics, which although closely related, are governed by different laws and principles. These artifacts are relevant and meaningful to children because they are part of their real life experience, offering significant references to concrete, or more concrete, situations. In this way, we can enable children to keep their reasoning processes meaningful and to monitor their inferences. As a consequence, they can offload their cognitive space and free cognitive resources to develop more knowledge (Arcavi, 1994).

The use of artifacts in our classroom activities has been articulated in various stages, with different educational and content objectives (Bonotto, 2005).

First, they can constitute a didactic interface between in- and out-of-school experience and knowledge and can become tools of mediation and integration between in- and out-of-school mathematics, by facilitating students' out-of-school reasoning experiences to come into play. The double nature of the artifacts, that is belonging to the world of everyday life and to the world of symbols, to use Freudenthal's (1991) expression, makes possible the movement from the situations in which the mathematics is usually utilised to the underlying mathematical structure and vice versa, from mathematical concepts to real-world situations, by favoring "horizontal mathematisation".

Second, the artifacts may also become, through some modifications – for instance removing some data present in the artifacts – real mathematising tools, able on the one hand to create new mathematical goals, and on the other to provide pupils and students with a basic sense experience in mathematisation and in realistic mathematical modelling (Bonotto, 2005). In this case, although the artifacts lose their fixed structure and no longer faithfully represent out-of-school reality, they remain strongly linked to real world situations. In this new role, the artifact can be used to introduce new mathematical knowledge through the particular learning process that Freudenthal (1991) defined as "prospective learning" or "anticipatory learning"; it thus also becomes a mathematising tool that preserves the focus on meaning found in everyday situations. We think that the prospective learning is better enhanced by a "rich context" as outlined by Freudenthal, that is, a context which not only serves as the application area but also as source for learning mathematics, and in particular for the emergence of a mathematical modelling disposition. The classroom activities present in the teaching experiments we have conducted fall under this type of context. These experiences can also favor the type of "retrospective" learning that occurs when old notions are recalled in order to be considered at a higher level and within a broader context, a process typical of adult mathematicians (Freudenthal, 1991).

This different use of the artifacts made it possible to carry out, also, compatibly with the grade level, "vertical mathematisation", from concepts to concepts, that may be described as the process of reorganisation within the mathematical system itself. This occurs when symbols, i.e. embedded mathematical facts, become objects to be put in relationship, modified, manipulated, and reflected upon by the children through property noticing, conjecturing, problem solving, and problem posing.

The following are some examples of artifacts introduced into classroom activities with, briefly specified, the content learning goal:
- some supermarket bills to introduce some aspects of multiplicative structure of decimal numbers (Bonotto, 2005)
- some menus of restaurants and pizzerias to enhance the understanding of decimal numbers (Bonotto, 2006), in particular of what Hiebert (1985), calls site 1 ("symbols and their referents"), and site 3 ("solutions and their reasonableness in light of other knowledge")
- a ruler to enhance the construction of a comprehensive numerical structure, which integrates the natural and decimal number systems (Bonotto, 2001)
- a cover of a ring binder to introduce the concept of surface area (Bonotto, 2003a)
- a weekly TV guide to develop the concept of equivalence between time intervals expressed in different ways (Bonotto, 2003b)
- an informational booklet issued by "Poste Italiane" to estimate and discover area and length dimensions of some envelopes (Bonotto & Ceroni, 2003).

The use of suitable artifacts allows the teacher to propose many questions, remarks, and culturally and scientifically interesting inquiries. The activities and connections that can be made depend, of course, on the students' scholastic level. These artifacts may contain different codes, percentages, numerical expressions, and different quantities with their related units of measure, and hence are connected with other mathematical concepts and also other disciplines (chemistry, biology, geography, astronomy, etc.). In the case of the weekly TV guide, for example, the teaching experiment favoured a link with the linguistic and anthropological areas too (see Bonotto 2003b). It could be said that the artifacts are related to mathematics (and other disciplines) as far as one is able to find these relationships.

From our experience, children confronted with this kind of activity also show flexibility in their reasoning processes by exploring, comparing, and selecting among different strategies. These strategies are often sensitive to the context and number quantities involved, and closer to the procedures emerging from out-of-school mathematics practice (Bonotto, 2005).

To summarise, the artifacts can be used i) as tools to apply old knowledge to new contexts, thus becoming good material for meaningful exercises, ii) to reinforce mathematical knowledge already possessed, or to review it at a higher level, and iii) as motivating stepping-stones to launch, at a first stage, new mathematical knowledge.

Furthermore by asking children:
- to select other artifacts from their everyday life
- to identify the embedded mathematical facts
- to look for analogies and differences (e.g., different number representations)
- to generate problems (e.g., discover relationships between quantities).

The children should be encouraged to recognise a great variety of situations as mathematical situations, or more precisely mathematisable situations, since a great deal of mathematics is embedded in everyday life. A "re-mathematisation" process is thereby favored, wherein students are invited to unpack from artifacts the mathematics that has been "hidden" in them, in contrast with the demathematisation process in which the need to understand mathematics that becomes embodies in artifacts disappears (see Gellert & Jablonka, 2007). In this way we can multiply the occasions when students encounter mathematics outside of the school context, "everydaying" the mathematics (Bonotto, 2005).

This approach can enable students to become involved with mathematics, to break down their conceptions of mathematics as a remote body of knowledge, and to develop a positive attitude towards school mathematics.

Discussion and Open Problems

I believe that immersing students in situations which can be related to their own direct experience, and are more consistent with a sense-making disposition, allows them to deepen and broaden their understanding of the scope and usefulness of mathematics as well as learning ways of thinking mathematically that are supported by mathematising situations (Bonotto, 2005).

Using appropriate artifacts that students can understand, analyse and interpret, and favouring modelling processes, we can present mathematics as a means of interpreting and understanding reality and increase the opportunities of observing mathematics outside the school context. The usefulness and pervasive character of mathematics are merely two of its many facets and cannot by themselves capture its very special character, relevance, and cultural value. Nonetheless, these two elements can be usefully exploited from a teaching point of view because they can change students' common behaviour and attitude (Bonotto, 2007).

But is there a reverse of the coin, if the word "reverse" can be used? The use of these artifacts is not easy or, in any case, is not easy to implement for the teacher. These tools differ from those usually mastered by the teacher that are typically highly structured, rigid, and not really suitable to develop alternative processes deriving from circumstantial solicitations, unforeseen interests, particular classroom situations.

The teacher has to be ready to create and manage open situations that are continuously transforming, that can be mastered only after long experimentation, and of which he/she cannot foresee the final evolution or result. As a matter of fact, these situations are sensitive to the social interactions that are established, to the students' reactions, their ability to ask questions, to find links between school and extra-school knowledge; hence the teacher has to be able to modify in real time the contents objectives of the lesson. The teacher has to be, and to feel, very strong and qualified both on the mathematical contents and on the educational objectives that are potentially contained in these artifacts (Bonotto, 2007). In this way the class cannot be prepared in advance in all of its aspects, nor from above; it should rather plan for various "branches" to be then drawn together through a process whose management is quite hard.

Furthermore, the teacher must not forget the moment of the institutionalisation of knowledge being constructed together with the pupils, which has to be a shared moment so that these potentially interesting, stimulating, and involving activities can be duly finalised. Mainly in the higher degrees of education, the teacher has to try to overcome the limits of the simplification of mathematics that is embedded in reality to grasp the special features of this discipline (abstraction, generalisation, formalisation...). An appreciation and understanding of the potential to generalise what is learned and its application to future problems are important. This appreciation can only come from examining and reflecting on the underlying structures and processes (Boaler, 1993).

Finally, for a real possibility to implement such an approach, the teachers have to try: 1) to modify their attitude to mathematics, which is influenced by the way they have learned it; 2) to revise their beliefs about the role of everyday knowledge in mathematical problem solving; 3) to see mathematics incorporated in the real world as a starting point for mathematical modelling activities in the classroom, thus revising their current classroom practice; 4) to know much more about the everyday lives of their students to offer them significant references to familiar and concrete situations belonging to the sociocultural environment of the pupils. Only in these ways can a different classroom culture be attained.

TEACHING/LEARNING ENVIRONMENT

Basic Characteristics

Besides the use of suitable artifacts, as discussed above, the teaching/learning environment designed and implemented in the classroom, and present in all the studies we have conducted, is characterised by:
- the application of a variety of complementary, integrated, and interactive instructional techniques (involving children's own written descriptions of the methods they use, whole-class discussion, and the drafting of a text by the whole class)

– an attempt to establish a new classroom culture through new socio-mathematical norms, in the sense of Yackel and Cobb (1996).

As far as the first point is concerned, most of the lessons follow an instructional model consisting of the following sequence of classroom activities: a) a short introduction to the class as a whole; b) an individual written assignment whereby students explain the reasoning followed and strategy applied; c) a final whole-class discussion (comprising the clearer and more convincing explanations emerging from the whole-class discussion) aimed at socialisation of the knowledge acquired. At the end of the teaching experiment the whole class contributes to producing a collective text. We consider that the interactivity of these instructional techniques is essential because of the opportunities to induce reflection as well as cognitive and metacognitive changes in students. This process may be very important for teachers also, since it enables them to recognise and analyse individual reasoning processes that are not always explicit (in the first phase, corresponding to the written report). In the second phase (corresponding to the collective discussion), comparing the different answers and strategies, children's first attempts at generalising, and further remarks made during the discussion, lead to collectively drawing up a collective text. This text, which completes the activity, is necessary to systematise the mathematical structures underlying the classroom activity; it is the phase of institutionalisation of the mathematical concepts and processes shared by the whole class (Bonotto, 2005).

Concerning the second point, i.e. establishing a new classroom culture through new socio-mathematical norms, the students are expect to approach an unfamiliar problem as a situation to be mathematised, not primarily to apply ready-made solution procedures, as in the RME perspective. This does not mean that knowledge of solution procedures does not play a role, but the primary objective is to make sense of the problem. In practice, it will often be a matter of shuttling back and forth between the interpretation of the problem and a review of possible suitable procedures, models, or results.

At the same time, the teacher is expected to encourage students to use their own methods, exploring their usefulness and soundness with regard to the problem. He/she is supposed to stimulate students to articulate and reflect on their personal beliefs, misconceptions, and informal problem-solving strategies or models. By questioning assumptions and debating the relative merits of alternative strategies or models, the teacher and students negotiate and establish taken-as-shared meanings about the results that are more or less acceptable according to the situation (Bonotto, 2005). In other words, new norms about what counts as a good or acceptable response, or as a good or acceptable solution procedure are debated, in order to undermine some deeply rooted and counterproductive beliefs and attitudes such as that: a) mathematics problems have only one right answer, b) there is only one correct way to solve any mathematical problem (see Verschaffel et al., 1999).

According to the socio-constructivist perspective, these norms are not predetermined criteria introduced into the classroom from outside. Instead, the understandings are constructed and continually modified through the interaction between teacher and pupils, as well as by the artifact, whose introduction into the classroom setting brings from the outside world potential norms and ways of reflection that open lines of cultural conceptual development to the children. According to Yackel and Cobb (1996, p. 460) "the development of individuals' reasoning and sense-making processes cannot be separated from their participation in the interactive constitution of taken-as-shared mathematical meanings".

SOME RESULTS

In our teaching experiments, contrary to the practice of traditional word problem solving, children did not ignore the relevant and plausible, familiar aspects of reality from their observation and reasoning. Furthermore, the use of the artifacts brought about the evocation of situations that are in fact experienced, activating the ability both to pose and solve problems. For example, in a study in which the artifact used was a weekly TV guide (Bonotto 2003b), one child tackled a spontaneous dilemma concerning a film whose review was next to the one assigned and whose viewing time partially overlapped. He posed a new type of question: "Once the first film is over, how much of the second film can I watch?".

During the teaching experiment described in Bonotto (2005), using market receipts that establish the net price given the weight and the unit price provides, for example, an introduction to multiplication of decimal numbers that leads students to reflect on and to see numbers as possible representations of weights or prices, referring to everyday elements while reasoning. Thus, the students make reference to the real world with remarks such as, "If you buy less than a kilo you will spend less than the kilo price; if you buy more than a kilo the price will be higher." The link with the real world, besides favouring a sense-making disposition, supported a bi-directional process between the interpretation of the problem and a review of possible results (horizontal mathematisation). For example when the children found that a kilo of bread could cost 2000000 Lira they immediately commented "I must have been wrong, it's too much." In this way, in this teaching experiment we also laid the basis for overcoming some conceptual obstacles in the development of understanding multiplication (particularly when extended beyond the integers). In particular, we addressed the misconception that multiplication always produces a larger result than the factors, an overgeneralisation of a rule valid for integers (see e.g., Greer (1994) for a analysis of this misconception in relation to the solution of word problems involving decimal numbers smaller than 1). When, at the end of the experiment, it was asked during a whole-class discussion whether multiplication always produces results larger than the factors, the answer was, "It depends on the numbers", followed by the reason for that (see Bonotto (2005) for the whole-class discussion). These observations support the hypothesis that these kinds of classroom activities can give support for accessing more formal mathematical knowledge and promote a process of "abstraction-as-construction", in accordance with the "emergent" modelling perspective (Gravemeijer, 2007).

```
                    BONED PARMA HAM
         kg          lire/kg          Lire
        0.210         38,900           ....
```
1) Without doing exact calculations can you work out the approximate cost?
2) Now try to calculate the exact cost.

Chiara's protocol

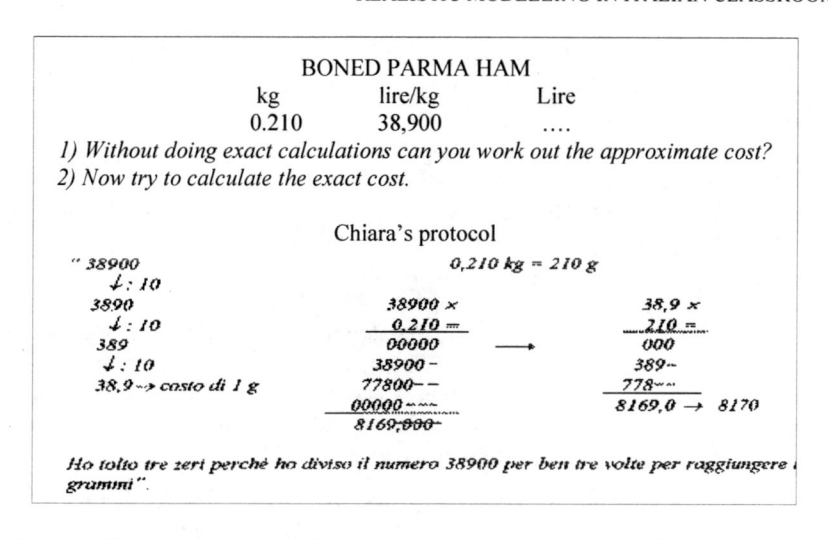

```
" 38900                    0,210 kg = 210 g
  ↓: 10
  3890                     38900 ×              38,9 ×
  ↓: 10                     0,210 =              210 =
   389                       00000                000
  ↓: 10                     38900 -              389--
  38,9 → costo di 1 g      77800- -              778-··
                           00000 ---          8169,0 → 8170
                           8169,000-
```

Ho tolto tre zeri perché ho diviso il numero 38900 per ben tre volte per raggiungere i grammi".

Figure 1. Receipt used in a teaching experiment, related tasks, and Chiara's protocol

Chiara's protocol, reported in Figure 1, refers to the second task related to the receipt reproduced there. It should be emphasised that the class involved had not yet been taught the algorithm of multiplying decimal numbers. Chiara first found the prices corresponding to the various units of measurement, then carried out the operation in two different ways and indicated their connection with an arrow. The two operations support each other in that each confirms the result of the other. She also gave a further explanation of how she placed the decimal point using the relationship between kilograms and grams. She managed to apply the rules in situations she had never met before, without uncertainty, and using them easily to find the results. This protocol is also a good example of prospective and retrospective learning (0.210 kg = 210 g). Chiara also progressed from horizontal to vertical mathematisation. The procedures were placed in relation to each other, and she verified that they were equivalent, therefore becoming objects of study and reflection. She also knew the result obtained was a valid mathematical result, but in the real world 8,170 lire would be more likely written as the exact cost, showing that in the two contexts (in- and out-of-school mathematics) different numbers are used.

During all our teaching experiments there were occasions that allowed us to emphasise the fact that in- and out-of-school mathematics are different worlds. Frequently, it was noted that, for example, the students' results and those present in the receipts differed, a fact that underlines the deep contrasts between out-of-school mathematics and in-school mathematics. These differences are deeply intertwined but governed by different laws and principles. Although mathematics lends its language and symbolism to reality, these manifest themselves in different ways according to the context. The children were aware that when they go to the bakery they never ask for "0.478 kilos of bread", but rather "half a kilo of bread." Indeed, as in one of the discussions reported in Bonotto (2005), a student remarked, "That would be too much mathematics!".

Children confronted with this kind of activity also exhibit flexibility in their reasoning processes by exploring, comparing, and selecting among different strategies or models. The following excerpt from a classroom discussion is an example of how these strategies are sensitive to the context and number quantities involved, and are better mastered and controlled from the metacognitive point of view (see Bonotto [2005, 2006] for other examples). They are therefore closer to the procedures that emerge from out-of-school mathematics practice. In the sixth session of the teaching experiment (described in Bonotto, 2006), the children first had to complete the bill shown in Figure 2, using the data on a menu provided by the teacher. In that bill, two items were deliberately deleted (one dish and one drink). After completion, the children were asked to answer the following questions: "How many people were eating together?" and iii) "If they decide to pay equally (independently of the precise cost of the individual meals, this is a frequent Italian custom for paying), how much would each person pay?"

> Paolo: *I think three people were eating because there are three things to eat and three things to drink. But there's a problem. I tried to do the division like this: 20.50 : 3 = 6 .83333* [he shows the whole algorithm], *that still makes 3.... So I thought that perhaps since 3 is a small number I could round it up and have everyone pay € 6.83.*
>
> [Like Paolo, all the other children reached the same solution]: *The number is infinite but the money has to be counted down to the cents and so you have to round it up.*
>
> T(eacher): *So... we have seen that when you divide a decimal number, you sometimes get a recurring decimal number. Would anyone like to try and explain what this means?*
>
> Paolo. *Does it mean that the result is never-ending?*
>
> T: *OK. You're right... but there's something else... what about the part that never ends?*
>
> Chiara: *It's always the same.... 3 for example!*
>
> T: *What do you think? Where can we place this number in the line of numbers?*
>
> Marco: *I think that we can put 6.83333333333 here, between the 6 and the 7 but nearer the seven.*
>
> T: *OK Let's try and be a little more precise... Between the unit 6 and the unit 7... How about the decimal?*
>
> Marco: *It's 83 cents of a euro and so 8 tenths and 3 hundredths...*
>
> T: *Very good... but we saw that it has infinite numbers ... so we have to try and continue... There's another 3 after that. Do you remember what that indicates?*
>
> Chiara: *It means a little bit of a thousand parts.*
>
> T: *Good... it's called a thousandth... How did we draw a thousandth before? Do you remember?*
>
> Anna: *We divided the hundredth into 10 parts.*
>
> T: *But we said that if we wanted to we could carry on... How can we do that? Do you remember?*

Anna: *I think we can make a bigger drawing... a gigantic one... so we can divide the thousandths into 10 parts...*
T: *Very good... Do you realise we've now reached the fourth number after the decimal point... if we carry on we can divide again and again...*
Anna: *If we had an enormous piece of paper, we could divide and divide to infinity!*
T: *What do you think we should do with these recurring numbers... in our case for example?* [referring to the question "*If each person pays equally, how much would each one pay?*"].
Paolo: *I rounded it up and so everyone had to pay € 6.83...*
Anna: *But if each of them pays € 6.83 it comes to € 20.49 and the bill is for € 20. 50... So I think one of them has to put in an extra cent.*
Giulia: *I don't think that's right... they all have to put in the same amount of money and so they all put in € 6.84 and that makes € 20.52. There are two cents extra and in restaurants the change is usually left as a tip.*
Matteo: *I think that's the best way too and if they don't want to leave the extra two cents as a tip they can put it away for the next time they eat together.*

```
          RISTORANTE
          "QUARTA C"
          Via Mazzini, 26
       Desenzano del Garda (BS)
            18/04/2005

                              €euro
1  Cheyenne Chicken           6, 8 0
1  Apache                     6, 0 0
1.................................
2 Acqua minerale (0,50)       2, 4 0
.................................

TOTALE.................   € 2 0, 5 0
GRAZIE E ARRIVEDERCI
```

Figure 2. Bill used in a session of a teaching experiment

This discussion shows the emergence of "prospective" learning (in this case regarding the concept of recurring decimal numbers), and confirms how the children have by no means excluded real-world knowledge from their observations and reasoning. In this session, and others, they showed a great deal of originality in the solutions they proposed. If this problem had been given in the traditional form using only words and within a more traditional teaching/learning environment the children would almost certainly have given the solution as € 6.833333333.... without any concern for the plausibility of the solution, as confirmed by the results obtained in the research of Bonotto and Wilczewski (2007) using similar problems. What is more, by upsetting the rule that says that every mathematical problem has only one solution, the children came closer to the more complex reality of everyday life where, for example, there are problems that have a number of different solutions.

The experience of our studies proved a fruitful one not only from the cognitive viewpoint but also from the metacognitive one. Presenting the students with activities that are meaningful because they involve the use of material familiar to them increased their motivation to learn, even among the less able ones. A good example is the case of an immigrant child with learning difficulties related mainly to linguistic problems. For her, as for many others, being confronted with a well-known everyday object with "few words and lots of numbers" acted as a stimulus. Indeed, when working with pricelists and menus of restaurants and of pizza shops (Bonotto, 2006), it led her to say "It's easier than the problems in the book because we already know how things work at a restaurant!". This confirms that "Using a receipt, which is poor in words but rich in implicit meanings, overturns the usual buying and selling problem situation, which is often rich in words but poor in meaningful references" (Bonotto, 2005, p. 321).

The positive results obtained in this kind of teaching experiments (for quantitative results, see e.g., Bonotto [2003b, 2006]) can be attributed to a combination of closely linked factors:
- an extensive use of suitable artifacts that, with their incorporated mathematics, played a fundamental role in bringing students' out-of-school reasoning and experiences into play, and allowed a good control of inferences and results;
- the application of a variety of complementary, integrated, and interactive instructional techniques;
- the introduction of particular socio-mathematical norms that played an important role in giving meaning to new mathematical knowledge, in reinforcing previous knowledge and in paying systematic attention to the nature of the problems and the classroom culture;
- an adequate balance between problem-posing and problem-solving activities, in order to promote also a mathematical modelling disposition.

CONCLUSIONS

In this chapter, I have discussed the results of some teaching experiences based on the use of suitable cultural artifacts, interactive teaching methods, and the introduction of new socio-mathematical norms. An effort was made to create a substantially modified teaching/learning environment that focused on fostering a mindful approach towards realistic mathematical modelling and problem posing.

As in other studies (e.g., Verschaffel et al., 1999), the effective establishment of a learning environment like the one described here makes very high demands on the teacher, and therefore requires revision and change in teacher training, both initially and through in-service programs.

We do not suggest that the classroom activities described here are a prototype for all classroom activities related to mathematics, although we think that the presence of realistic mathematical modelling activity, as well as of problem posing activity, should not emanate from a specific part of the curriculum but should permeate the entire curriculum.

REFERENCES

Arcavi, A. (1994). Symbol sense: Informal sense-making in formal mathematics. *For the Learning of Mathematics, 14*(3), 24–35.
Boaler, J. (1993). The role of contexts in the mathematics classroom: Do they make mathematics more "real"? *For the Learning of Mathematics, 13*(2), 12–17.
Boero, P., & Daupeto, C. (2007). Problem solving in mathematics education in Italy: Dreams and reality. *ZDM – The International Journal on Mathematics Education, 39*(5–6), 383–393.
Bonotto, C. (2001). From the decimal number as a measure to the decimal number as a mental object. In M. van den Heuvel-Panhuizen (Ed.), *Proceedings of the 25th conference of the International Group for the Psychology of Mathematics Education* (Vol. 2, pp. 193–200). Utrecht, The Netherlands: Utrecht University.
Bonotto, C. (2003a). About students' understanding and learning of the concept of surface area. In D. H. Clements & G. Bright (Eds.), *Learning and teaching measurement, 2003 NCTM Yearbook* (pp. 157–167). Reston, VA: National Council of Teachers of Mathematics.
Bonotto, C. (2003b). Investigating the mathematics incorporated in the real world as a starting point for mathematics classroom activities. In N. A. Pateman, B. J. Dougherty & J. Zilliox (Eds.), *Proceedings of the 27th conference of the International Group for the Psychology of Mathematics Education* (Vol. 2, pp.129–136). Honolulu, HI: Hawaii University.
Bonotto, C. (2005). How informal out-of-school mathematics can help students make sense of formal in-school mathematics: The case of multiplying by decimal numbers. *Mathematical Thinking and Learning. An International Journal, 7*, 313–344.
Bonotto, C. (2006). Extending students' understanding of decimal numbers via realistic mathematical modeling and problem posing. In J. Novotná, H. Moraová, M. Krátká, & N. Stehlíková (Eds.), *Proceedings of the 30th conference of the International Group for the Psychology of Mathematics Education* (Vol. 2, pp. 193–200). Prague, Czech Republic: Prague Charles University.
Bonotto, C. (2007). How to replace the word problems with activities of realistic mathematical modeling. In W. Blum, P. Galbraith, M. Niss & H. W. Henn (Eds.), *Modelling and applications in mathematics education* (New ICMI Studies Series no. 10, pp. 185–192). New York: Springer.
Bonotto, C., & Ceroni, G. (2003, July 22–28). How can the use of suitable cultural artifacts as didactic materials facilitate and make more effective mathematics learning? *CIEAEM 55*, Plock (Poland), 45–47.
Bonotto, C., & Wilczewski, E. (2007). I problemi di matematica nella scuola primaria: Sull'attivazione o meno di conoscenze di tipo realistico. In C. Bonotto (Ed.), *Quotidianizzare la matematica* (pp. 101–134). Lecce, Italy: La Biblioteca Pensa Multimedia.
Christou, C., Mousoulides, N., Pittalis, M., Pitta-Pantazi, D., & Sriraman, B. (2005). An empirical taxonomy of problem posing processes. *Zentralblatt für Didaktik der Mathematik, 37*, 149–158.
Cole, M. (1995). Culture and cognitive development: From cross-cultural research to creating systems of cultural mediation. *Culture & Psychology, 1*(1), 25–54.
De Bock, D., Van Dooren, W., & Janssens, D. (2007). Studying and remedying students' modelling competencies: Routine, behaviour or adaptive expertise. In W. Blum, P. Galbraith, M. Niss, H. W. Henn (Eds.), *Modelling and applications in mathematics education* (New ICMI Studies Series no. 10, pp. 241–248). New York: Springer.
Ellerton, N. F., & Clarkson, P. C. (1996). Language factors in mathematics teaching. In A. J. Bishop et al. (Eds.), *International handbook of mathematics education* (pp. 83–87). Dordrecht, The Netherlands: Kluwer.
English, L. D. (1997). The development of fifth-grade children's problem-posing abilities. *Educational Studies in Mathematics, 34*, 183–217.
English, L. D. (1998). Children's problem posing within formal and informal contexts. *Journal for Research in Mathematics Education, 29*, 83–106.

English, L. D. (2003). Engaging students in problem posing in an inquiry-oriented mathematics classroom. In F. Lester & R. Charles (Eds.), *Teaching mathematics through problem solving* (pp. 187–198). Reston, VA: National Council of Teachers of Mathematics.

Freudenthal, H. (1991). *Revisiting mathematics education. China lectures.* Dordrecht, The Netherlands: Kluwer.

Gellert, U., & Jablonka, E. (2007). Mathematization – Demathematization. In U. Gellert & E. Jablonka (Eds.), *Mathematization and demathematization: Social, philosophical and educational ramifications* (pp. 1–18). Rotterdam, The Netherlands: Sense Publishers.

Gravemeijer, K. (1997). Commentary solving word problems: A case of modelling. *Learning and Instruction, 7,* 389–397.

Gravemeijer, K. (2007). Emergent modeling as a precursor to mathematical modeling. In W. Blum, P. Galbraith, M. Niss & H. W. Henn (Eds.), *Modelling and applications in mathematics education* (New ICMI Studies Series no. 10, pp. 137–144). New York: Springer.

Greer, B. (1994). Extending the meaning of multiplication and division. In G. Harel & J. Confrey (Eds.), *The development of multiplicative reasoning in the learning of mathematics* (pp. 61–85). Albany, NY: SUNY Press.

Greer, B., Verschaffel, L., & Mukhopadhyay, S. (2007). Modelling for life: Mathematics and children's experience. In W. Blum, P. Galbraith, M. Niss & H. W. Henn (Eds.), *Modelling and applications in mathematics education* (New ICMI Studies Series no. 10, pp. 89–98). New York: Springer.

Hiebert, J. (1985). Children's knowledge of common and decimal fractions. *Education and Urban Society, 17,* 427–437.

Kilpatrick, J. (1987). Problem formulating: Where do good problems come from? In A. H. Schoenfeld (Ed.), *Cognitive science and mathematics education* (pp. 123–147). Hillsdale, NJ: Erlbaum.

Lesh, R., & Doerr, H. (2003). *Beyond constructivism: Models and modelling perspectives on mathematics problem solving, learning and teaching.* Mahwah, NJ: Erlbaum.

Lesh, R., & Lehrer, R. (2003). Models and modeling perspectives on the development of students and teachers. *Mathematical Thinking and Learning, 5,* 109–129.

Lesh, R., & Zawojewski, J. (2007). Problem solving and modeling. In F. K. Lester, Jr. (Ed.), *Second handbook of research on mathematics teaching and learning* (pp. 763–804). Charlotte, NC: Information Age Publishing.

Leung, S. K. (1996). Problem posing as assessment: Reflections and reconstructions. *The Mathematics Educator, 1,* 159–171.

Lowrie, T. (2002). Designing a framework for problem posing: Young children generating open-ended tasks. *Contemporary Issues in Early Childhood, 3,* 354–364.

Palm, T. (2008). Impact of authenticity on sense making in word problem solving. *Educational Studies in Mathematics, 67,* 37–58.

Reusser, K., & Stebler, R. (1997). Every word problem has a solution: The suspension of reality and sense-making in the culture of school mathematics. *Learning and Instruction, 7,* 309–328.

Saxe, B. G., Dawson, V., Fall, R., & Howard, S. (1996). Culture and children's mathematical thinking. In R. J. Sternberg & T. Ben-Zeev (Eds.), *The nature of mathematical thinking* (pp. 119–144). Mahwah, NJ: Erlbaum.

Schoenfeld, A. H. (1991). On mathematics as sense-making: An informal attack on the unfortunate divorce of formal and informal mathematics. In J. F. Voss, D. N. Perkins & J. W. Segal (Eds.), *Informal reasoning and education* (pp. 311–343). Hillsdale, NJ: Erlbaum.

Silver, E. A. (1994). On mathematical problem solving. *For the Learning of Mathematics, 14*(1), 19–28.

Silver, E. A. (1995). The nature and use of open problems in mathematics education: Mathematical and pedagogical perspectives. *International Reviews on Mathematical Education, 27*(2), 67–72.

Silver, E. A., & Cai, J. (1996). An analysis of arithmetic problem posing by middle school students. *Journal for Research in Mathematics Education, 27,* 521–539.

Usiskin, Z. (2007). The arithmetic operations as mathematical models. In W. Blum, P. Galbraith, M. Niss & H. W. Henn (Eds.), *Modelling and applications in mathematics education* (New ICMI Studies Series no. 10, pp. 257–264). New York: Springer.

Verschaffel, L., De Corte, E., & Borghart, I. (1997). Pre-service teacher's conceptions and beliefs about the role of real-world knowledge in mathematical modeling of school word problems. *Learning and Instruction, 7,* 339–359.

Verschaffel, L., De Corte, E., Lasure, S., Van Vaerenbergh, G., Bogaerts, H., & Ratinckx, E. (1999). Learning to solve mathematical application problems: A design experiment with fifth graders. *Mathematical Thinking and Learning. An International Journal, 1,* 195–229.

Verschaffel, L., Greer, B., & De Corte, E. (2000). *Making sense of word problems.* Lisse, The Netherlands: Swets & Zeitlinger.

Wyndhamn, J., & Säljö, R. (1997). Word problems and mathematical reasoning – A study of children's mastery of reference and meaning in textual realities. *Learning and Instruction, 7,* 361–382.

Yackel, E., & Cobb, P. (1996). Classroom sociomathematical norms and intellectual autonomy. *Journal for Research in Mathematics Education, 27,* 458–477.

Cinzia Bonotto
Dipartimento di Matematica Pura ed Applicata
Università di Padova
Italy

CHRISTOPH SELTER

15. STIMULATING REFLECTION ON WORD PROBLEMS BY MEANS OF STUDENTS' OWN PRODUCTIONS

INTRODUCTION

Like several papers and books on the topic of word problems this contribution also starts off with a piece of research dealing with the so-called age-of-the-captain problems (Baruk, 1985; Verschaffel, Greer, & De Corte, 2000). The experiment described here made use of an interesting variation.

Two Swiss researchers gave students from grades 2 to 6 the following picture (see Figure 1) at the beginning of a lesson on German, arts, or history – not on mathematics (Keller & Brandenberg, 1999). The short text in the bottom right can be translated as "How old is the captain?".

Wie alt ist der Kapitän?

Figure 1. How old is the captain? (Keller & Brandenberg, 1999)

The students were just given the information: "Here is a problem for you." 53 out of 77 students looked for numbers in the picture and combined them, 46 put down "28 years". The students were also asked to write down what they had thought and how they had arrived at their solution. Two further questions were posed: "What do you think about the problem? How did you like working on it?"

Those students arriving at the answer 28, as a rule, explained this by statements like "I counted sheep and goats." In some cases the numbers were dealt with slightly differently: "The captain is 56 years old. First I counted the animals, and

L. Verschaffel et al. (eds.), Words and Worlds: Modelling Verbal Descriptions of Situations, 315–331.
© 2009 Sense Publishers. All rights reserved.

then I multiplied the result by 2. I came to the conclusion that, if there are 28 animals, the captain must be twice as old."

Eighteen children gave answers that led to the assumption that they did not make use of the number of animals in the picture, like for instance ...
- "100.000 years. You do not know the age. Hence, you can write down what you like."
- "I think the captain is about 42 years old."
- "69 years. Usually, a captain is that old. But you cannot see him."

Four students indicated that the problem could not be solved from their point of view: "I did not see any captain. How should I know, whether there is a captain at all and how old he is." Two students gave the answer: "I don't know."

For the moment, I will leave any interpretation to the reader. I will come back to this study later on. First another "transportation problem" will be tackled.

MAKING SENSE OF DWR PROBLEMS

The "army bus problem" is well known as an instructive example for students' difficulties solving *division with remainder* (DWR) problems. Carpenter, Lindquist, Mathews, and Silver (1983) analysed the following problem given to thirteen-year-olds in the United States in the National Assessment of Educational Performance (NAEP): "An army bus holds 36 soldiers. If 1128 soldiers are being bussed to their training site, how many buses are needed?" 70% of the students solved "1128÷36" numerically correct.
- 23% (of the total number of students) gave the answer "32 buses",
- 18% answered "31 buses" and
- 29% put down "31 remainder 12".

Similar results were obtained by other researchers (Curcio & DeFranco, 1989; Silver, 1988) – even if slight variations of the design were undertaken. Silver, Shapiro, and Deutsch (1993), for example, started their research with 195 U.S. students (grade 6 through 8) from the hypothesis that the number of "left-overs" might have influenced students' interpretations of the situation and the final solution. Thus, they used smaller numbers. Three versions of the bus problem were employed with the following numerical data: 532÷40, 540÷40 and 552÷40.

The written responses of the students showed no direct evidence of students being influenced by the size of the remainder in interpreting their solutions or arriving at their final numerical answer. Thus, the study provided considerable evidence that computational requirements were not the major obstacle to arriving at correct solutions, but, rather, students' difficulties in making sense of their numerical result.

The original "army bus problem" item was used with appropriate modifications in several other countries, e.g., China, Belgium, Japan, and Ireland (Cai & Silver, 1995; Greer, 1993; Verschaffel, De Corte, & Lasure, 1994). Overall the results were comparable. Students are liable to answer DWR problems by more or less uncritically carrying out division with the given numbers, apparently without making sense of the textual representation of the context.

This result is not restricted to the particularity of DWR problems, as further research clearly showed. Not later than the end of primary school, students seem to have acquired a set of assumptions whereby solving word problems is reduced to the selection and execution of arithmetical operations without serious consideration of the reality of the problem context (see e. g., Davis, 1989; Nesher, 1980; Reusser, 1988; Schoenfeld, 1991).

However, one important question remained unanswered, namely, are students' answers rooted in resistant beliefs about the nature of word problems or can they be explained, at least partly, by specific circumstances of the experiments (Donaldson, 1978)?

In this context, Verschaffel et al. (2000) describe several studies where (slight) variations of the design led to different results, e. g. by alerting students about problematic word problems (see e.g., Reusser & Stebler, 1997; Verschaffel et al., 1999; Yoshida, Verschaffel, & De Corte, 1997) which, however, caused only weak effects if not specifically attached to certain problems (Reusser & Stebler, 1997).

Another variation was to increase the authenticity of the experimental setting. For example, DeFranco and Curcio (1997) embedded DWR problems in two different contexts. First, 20 sixth-graders were interviewed about a typical bus problem (involving 328÷40). Then, the same 20 students were asked to make a phone call to order minivans (5 children per van) to take 32 children to a party. The information was given on a fact sheet.

Whereas two out of the 20 children gave the appropriate answer in the typical word problem setting, 16 of them gave an appropriate response in the more realistic situation: Thirteen students ordered seven minivans, and three were able to justify their answer 6 e. g. by stating that they did not need a minivan, but a smaller car would be sufficient for the two children left over.

Possibly the easier numbers of the minivan context facilitated the problem a little bit compared to the 328÷40 problem. Nevertheless, the results support the idea of embedding such problems in more realistic contexts in order to reduce the probability that students solve them in a stereotyped way.

This tendency could also be observed in other studies (see e. g., Wyndhamn & Saljö, 1997). The "experimental contract" (Greer, 1997, p. 305) or as Hundeide (1988) called it "the metacontract for the situational definition" makes it either more or less likely that the students take realistic considerations into account. Inoue (2005, p. 71) uncovers "the realistic reasons behind unrealistic solutions":

> Students' "unrealistic" answers may not be so unrealistic at all, but may stem from a "realistic" effort to adapt to the socio-cultural norm of schooling. ...
> In other words, their "unrealistic solutions" may not stem from their understanding of mathematics, but from their belief in school mathematics. ...
> Other researchers explain that students' unrealistic responses could stem from their unique interpretation of problem situations, rather than their belief system that suspends sense-making. For instance, "37.6 buses" may not be a totally irrational answer if it is intended to indicate the possibility that the 38th bus could be discounted or the auxiliary seats could be used (Hatano, 1997).

In this context, Selter (2001) conducted a study with 24 fourth-graders. One of the problems was the "army bus problem" in a football context: "820 supporters of Borussia Dortmund want to go to an away game by bus. In each bus 40 supporters can be seated. How many buses are needed?" The written solutions were classified as follows:
- Seven students gave the answer 21 buses.
- Eight students answered 20 buses.
- Six children gave answers like "20 ½ buses" or "20 remainder 20 buses".
- Three children had difficulties with the arithmetical operation, two of them dealt correctly with the (wrong) remainder.

So, the general trend of the other studies was confirmed, if the distribution of the answers with respect to the three main categories of answers is taken into account. In order to better understand the students' thinking, interviews with twelve children were conducted one week later. Boris' solution (see Figure 2) provides some anecdotal evidence.

At the beginning of the interview he worked out the division problem correctly and put down the answer: "20 buses have to drive." He continued to think about the problem and added ½ to the answer. The interviewer asked him what he had put down. He answered: "Well, 20 buses, plus ½ … not really ½, actually one bus, … one bus with half of the places occupied … plus one bus, thus 21 is the answer."

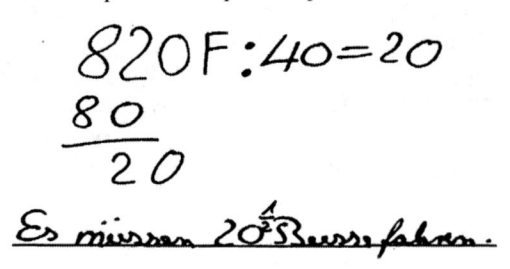

$$820 F : 40 = 20$$
$$\underline{80}$$
$$20$$

Es müssen 20 Busse fahren.

Figure 2. Boris' solution to the bus problem

The first interpretation of Boris' answer 20 ½ can be seen as a typical example of the fact that adults sometimes go wrong in understanding children's thinking processes. His written answer would haven fallen in the third category. Without the interview information it would have been classified as an example of suspension of sense making. But he did not mean half a bus, but a bus half full. He deeply thought things through, and his interpretation of the remainder is more informative than the result 21. In addition, two other children from the third category justified their answers in similar ways.

Thus, a closer look at students' thinking often revealed more rationality than observed at first (Silver et al., 1993). In this context, another study should be mentioned wherein several word problems, including age-of-the captain problems, were given to third graders (Selter, 1994b). For example: "A shepherd owns 19 sheep and 13 goats. How old is the shepherd?" or "There are 13 boys and 15 girls sitting in a classroom. How old is the teacher?"

An analysis of the videos revealed that quite a lot of the children who "solved" the problems by adding the two given numbers showed some slight irritation at the moment they were given the problems (a short laugh or any other sign of astonishment), but then immediately devoted themselves to a kind of seemingly thoughtless automatism, stating, for example "Actually, our result cannot be really right ... Shall we write it down anyway? ... Let's put it down here." These children knew that they actually could not combine the numbers in order to get the result, but they had the feeling that the solution must have been hidden somewhere. Freudenthal (1991, p. 71-72) observed this phenomenon as well and pointed out that children often try to uncover a kind of "magical context":

> To solve a problem, they look for secret marks, for signals hidden by accident or intention, and, in particular, for numbers to put them on the right track. ... How old is the captain? The 26 sheep and the 10 goats on board are like the data used by the astrologer to foretell the future.

Thus, several children tried to see the problems from a different perspective that allowed them to somehow connect the given numbers with the arithmetical operation carried out, at least after being asked how they arrived at their solution. Some examples of their creative constructions follow:
- "The shepherd was given a sheep or a goat on each of his birthdays."
- "He bought one animal for each year of his life; so he always knows his age."
- "This class is a special one because there are just as many children in it as the teacher is old. This problem would not work in our class."

In other words, it is not always a "suspension of sense-making", but in at least some cases students' *diverse sense-making activities* (Inoue, 2005, p. 80) that were underlying these seemingly "unrealistic" responses (Verschaffel, Van Dooren, & Stessens, this volume).

DIFFERENT DIDACTICAL CONTRACTS

The studies reported so far show that students' behaviour cannot primarily be explained by cognitive deficits. Their attitude towards word problem solving in school seems to be quite decisive for the high degree of non-realistic responses. The students play the "word problem game" (De Corte & Verschaffel, 1985) and follow some sort of "hidden curriculum" (Jackson, 1990).

> Students not only know from their school mathematical experience that all problems are undoubtedly solvable, but also that everything numerical included in a problem is relevant to its solution, and everything that is relevant is included in the problem text (confinement to relevance and non-ambiguity). Following this authoring script, many problem statements degenerate to badly disguised equations (Reusser & Stebler, 1997, p. 323).

Brousseau (1997) introduced the notion "didactical contract" and defined it as the system of reciprocal expectancies between teacher and pupils, which guides the actions of both. The didactical contract is necessary, on the one hand, as teaching without established routines would be an exhausting adventure for all participants. But, on the other hand, the didactical contract can – at least partly – lead to undesirable outcomes. In this connection, Reusser and Stebler (1997, p. 317) quote a student's response to the researcher's question as to why he answered a problem in a "non-realistic" way:

> I did think about the difficulty, but then I just calculated it the usual way. (Why?) Because I just had to find some sort of solution to the problem, and that was the only way it worked. I've got to have a solution, haven't I?

Children gradually seem to learn to behave "rationally" in the sense that they fulfill the requirements they have to observe as partners in the didactical contract for solving word problems.

> Within the mathematics classroom ... students do not only learn mathematical concepts and procedures; they learn how to interact in the classroom; they learn particular sets of beliefs and practices and they learn the appropriate way to behave in the mathematics classroom (Boaler, 1999, pp. 264-265).

Thus, the way word problems are typically embedded in the classroom culture offers explanations for students' behaviour. In this context Radatz (1983) conducted an interesting experiment. He mixed "normal" word problems and age-of-the-captain problems like the following: "Katja invites 8 friends to her birthday party. The party will be in 4 days." Altogether 333 children from kindergarten (5-year-olds) through grade 5 participated. The size of the numbers differed depending on the grade the children were in.

Less than 10% of the children from kindergarten and grade one tried to solve the captain problems, whereas 30% of the second graders and 60% of the forth and fifth graders did so. In grade 5 the percentage dropped to 45%. (Radatz does not explain the latter, but, for a similar result with an explanation, see Van Dooren, De Bock, Hessels, Janssens, & Verschaffel, 2005). Unfortunately, Radatz' study was not a longitudinal one, but, the results give some support for the hypothesis that students' behaviour while being confronted with captain-problems is learned in school.

> As a result of schooling, students' behaviour is pragmatically functional if they take into account any information they can draw from both problem texts and contexts. That is, their mathematical sense-making is functional if they actively and continuously construct a mental representation not only of the specific task (problem model ...), but also of the socio-contextual situation which they are in (construction of a social context model). As a consequence, to neglect "realistic" interpretations of word problems, in the first sense, is often functional because it leads to correct and expected solutions ... Why should students abandon strategies apparently perceived successful in the past? (Reusser & Stebler, 1997, pp. 325-326).

Coming back to the Swiss study using the picture of goats and sheep (Keller & Brandenberg, 1999), two important findings of the studies discussed so far can be found there:

- The creativity of a non-negligible number of students' who find intelligent justifications for their solutions and who take realistic considerations into account, although initially this does not seem to be the case, but also
- the tendency to behave according to the didactical contract and to play the "word problem game" (De Corte & Verschaffel, 1985), even if the word problems are not presented in the usual textual style.

How to overcome the latter by making use of the former? Verschaffel et al. (2000) describe three design experiments which led to promising results with respect to students' performance, their thinking processes, beliefs, and attitudes. The common characteristics of these studies were as follows (for detailed information, see Verschaffel & De Corte, 1997):
- more realistic and less stereotyped problem situations,
- a variety of teaching styles aiming at activating learners' reflection and communication and
- establishing new social and socio-mathematical norms (Yackel & Cobb, 1996).

Boaler's earlier statement about students' learning outcomes can thus be formulated positively. It seems possible to change students' beliefs and their behaviour when confronted with word problems (Niss, 2001). In this context, I want to describe the idea of using children's own productions as powerful tools for stimulating reflection.

CHILDREN'S OWN PRODUCTIONS

Children's own productions (Selter, 1994a) can be defined as their free oral or written expressions. Hereafter, I will concentrate on written productions, which can be texts, drawings, informal notations, and mixtures of them.

It is not a necessary condition that students' own productions are productions of a single individual. They also can be created cooperatively: The decisive criterion is that the students are encouraged to influence the teaching/learning process productively. Ideally, four different types can be identified, wherein the students are encouraged to
- generate problems themselves (*inventions*, see Ellerton, 1986; Maguire, 1999; Wheeler, 1967),
- solve problems with their own *strategies*,
- explore and describe mathematical *patterns*, or
- write about the teaching-learning process (*journal entries*).

The notion of children's own productions is thus not restricted to student-generated problems (see Streefland, 1990; Treffers, 1987), but is used in a broader sense for all kind of problems in which students have freedom with respect to (a) their solution method, or (b) the way in which they present their solutions. From the teacher's perspective children's own productions offer several advantages:
- They give authentic information about each student,
- the results of their analysis can be used for reflecting on preceding teaching and planning forthcoming teaching,

- the students' own productions (e. g. solution strategies) can be used as material for teaching, and
- they can support forms of authentic and open assessment.

From the students' perspective their own productions can:
- encourage active learning and reflection on their own thinking and doing,
- further processes of interaction and cooperation,
- train the ability to express their own thinking and to understand the thinking of others and
- contribute to a productive organisation of the teaching-learning process.

In the following subsection several learning environments are described, in which two particular types of children's own productions were used to stimulate forth graders' reflection on (their solutions of) word problems:
- type 1: producing word problems themselves, and
- type 4: writing texts about (their solutions of) word problems.

EXAMPLES OF LEARNING ENVIRONMENTS

Before describing how we worked on these issues with fourth graders, I should mention that we did not conduct a controlled teaching experiment with pre-, post- and retention-test. What I can offer is the description of several learning environments developed in cooperation with teachers and tried out in several classes (fourth grade).

Word problems – easy ones and difficult ones. At first, several word problems with different degrees of complexity and difficulty were given to the children on worksheets.

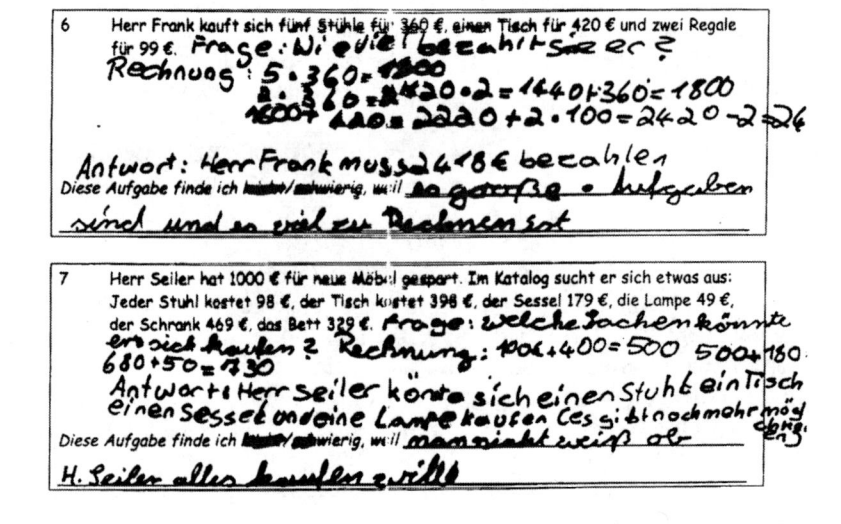

Figure 3. Lili's solutions to problems 6 and 7

STIMULATING REFLECTION ON WORD PROBLEMS

They were asked to work on problems like "Mr. Frank buys five chairs for 360€ each, one table for 420€ and two bookshelves for 99€ each." or "Mr. Seiler has saved 1000€. He takes a look at a catalogue: Each chair costs 98€, a table 398€, an arm-chair 179€, a lamp 49€, a cupboard 469€ and a bed 329€". After solving the particular problem, they were asked individually to indicate whether it was an easy or a difficult problem for them and to justify their answer.

Lili commented on problem 6 (see Figure 3) "It is difficult, because it is multiplication with big numbers and you have to do a lot of calculations." After answering problem 7 with "He could buy a chair, a table, an armchair, and a lamp (there are some more possibilities)", she also labelled it as difficult, because "one does not know whether Mr. Seiler is planning to buy everything."

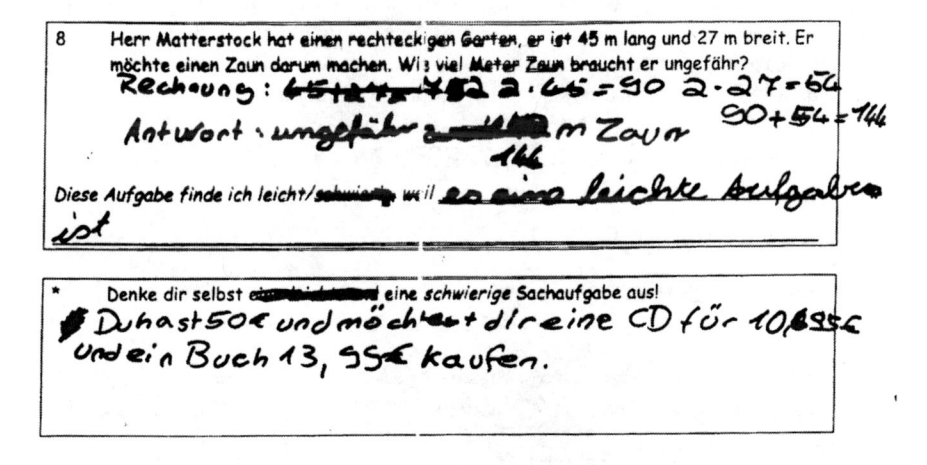

Figure 4. Lili's solutions to problems 8 and *

Other problems were characterised as easy ones by Lili, like "Mr. Matterstock has a rectangular garden, 45m long and 27m wide. He wants to surround it with a fence. How many meters of fence does he need?" In contrast to her justifications to problems 6 and 7, which were informative, she just put down: "The problem is easy for me, because it is an easy problem." (see Figure 4).

After completing their worksheets the children gathered together in groups of three and compared their solutions and their comments in small-group work. Afterwards selected problems were discussed in the classroom. Criteria were developed cooperatively which indicated whether a problem could be regarded as an easy or as a difficult one, like amount of text, size of the numbers, degree of difficulty of the operation, familiarity with the context, openness of the problem, existence of missing or superfluous data and so forth. It was also clarified that justifications given by the children should refer to at least one of these criteria.

In problem * the children were asked to invent easy and difficult problems (see also Verschaffel et al.'s chapter on problem posing in this volume). Lili went for a difficult one "You have got 50€ and you want to buy a CD for 10.95€ and a book for 13.99€". Once again, the children had to make up their mind about what makes a word problem easy, or respectively difficult. The problems were given to the classmates in small-group work. Some of them were discussed in the classroom, especially with respect to the degree of difficulty.

In the following lessons, the children were given several opportunities to invent easy and difficult problems for their classmates, and the regular discussions led to a constant improvement in not only formulating easy and difficult problems, but also in clearly justifying one's own judgment with respect to the degree of difficulty.

Word problems – solvable or unsolvable? The next learning environment dealt with solvable and unsolvable word problems like "Ms. Abels buys four balloon packages with seven balloons in each. How many balloons does she buy" or "There are 13 girls and 15 boys in a classroom. How old is the teacher?"

The children were asked to justify their answers to given problems and to discuss their justifications whether a problem was solvable or not. Also, they were asked to modify unsolvable word problems in order to make them solvable.

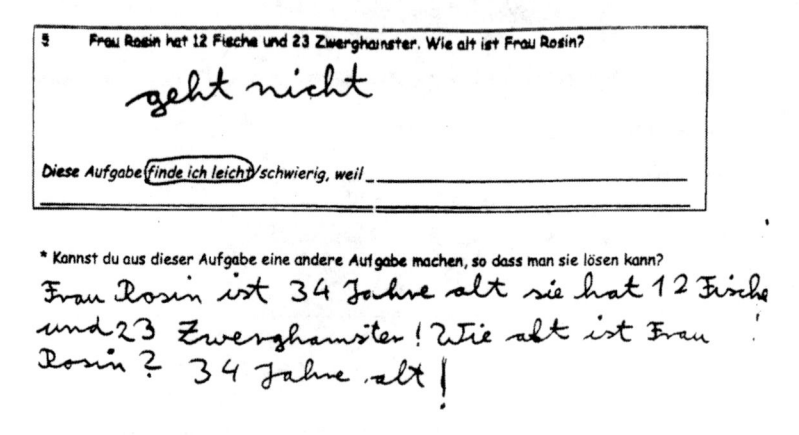

Figure 5. Natalie's solutions to the fish and hamsters problem

Natalie, for instance, put down "geht nicht" which can be translated as "doesn't work" after thinking about the problem "Ms. Rosin has got 12 fish and 23 miniature hamsters. How old is Ms. Rosin?" (see Figure 5). Then she was asked to make the problem solvable. She wrote down: "Ms. Rosin is 34 years old. She has got 12 fish and 23 miniature hamsters. How old is Ms. Rosin? She is 34 years old." (see Figure 5). This is an interesting modification. At first sight, it seems to be a rather simple problem, as it does not require any calculation at all. However, as research with the age-of-the-captain problems showed (Selter, 1994b; see also this chapter, section 2), quite a lot of the German children being interviewed added the three numbers given in the problem "A 27-year-old shepherd owns 25 sheep and 10 goats. How old is the shepherd?", arriving at the answer "62". However, here Natalie did not end up with the answer "Ms. Rosin is 69 years old."

STIMULATING REFLECTION ON WORD PROBLEMS

Once again, children's productions were used as a basis for small-group and classroom discussion. In addition, one activity for children consisted in generating an unsolvable problem and modifying it in order to make it solvable.

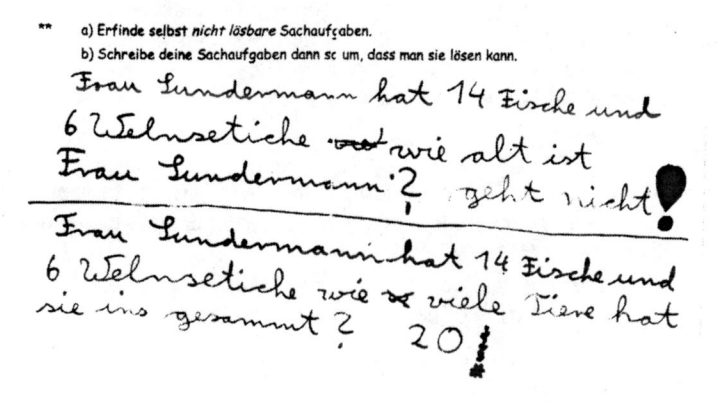

Figure 6. Natalie's own production

Natalie put down (see Figure 6): "Ms. Sundermann has 14 fish and 6 budgerigars. How old is Ms. Sundermann? – Doesn't work." Then she modified it as follows: "Ms. Sundermann has 14 fish and 6 budgerigars. How many animals does she have in total? – 20."

Some children modified the general question into "which questions can be posed?", like for instance Benni who invented the following problem "I am ten years old. My granddad is 92 years old. My aunt is 54 years old. All three persons buy a glass of lemonade, which costs 0.48€ each. Which questions can be posed?"

Think about it! After alerting students with respect to important, missing or superfluous data by means of reflecting on different problems, the attitude of having a critical look at given information was extended to different types of texts, e. g. newspaper clippings (see Figure 7).

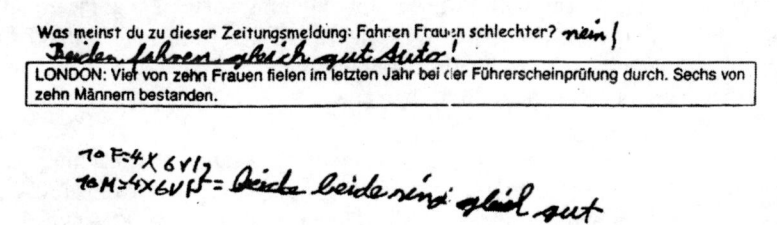

Figure 7. The driving licence problem

The clipping reads as follows: "LONDON: Four out of ten women failed their driving test last year. Six out of ten men passed it." The children were asked: "What do you think about this newspaper clipping: Do women drive worse?" Tim answered 'No. Both are doing equally well.' He explained his answer by indicating 10 F (women) = 4 (fail) 6 (pass) and 10 M (men) = 4 (fail) 6 (pass). Other statements which were discussed in the classroom read as follows:
- No. Women do not drive worse, because 10-4=6 women got a pass. And 6 men passed; 4 men failed.
- No, because 4 women and 4 men did not pass.
- It depends on how much the women learn during their driving lessons.
- You'll never know, as each human being has different driving capabilities.

Can this be true? In problems of this kind the children were explicitly asked to comment on the degree of truth of newspaper clippings (see Figure 8).

Figure 8. The class size problem

The class size problem (borrowed from van den Heuvel-Panhuizen, 2001, p. 196) was a typical problem dealt with. A newspaper clipping stated that at the end of the holidays 4000 children in the city of Gevelsberg will return to school and form 48 classes. Ayse made a clever estimation (4000÷50) and put down that this cannot be true, as there cannot be 80 children in each class.

Incomplete newspaper clippings. Another activity used in the teaching experiment was the so-called incomplete newspaper clippings. Here, numerical data were taken out of the text and put underneath it. The children have to reflect on the text and the given data and fill in the numbers in the right place. The following self-generated example from Vicky (see Figure 9) illustrates the principle very nicely: "Lovely baby born! On ____. July _____ Michelle was born. She weighed _____ g and was ____ cm tall. The circumference of her head was ____ cm."

STIMULATING REFLECTION ON WORD PROBLEMS

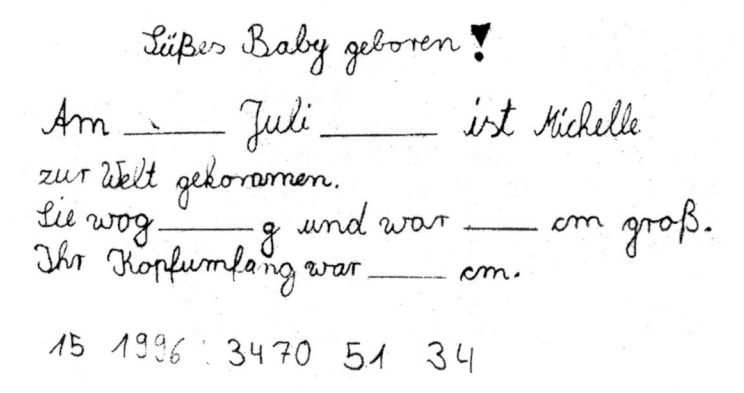

Süßes Baby geboren!

Am ___ Juli ___ ist Michelle zur Welt gekommen.
Sie wog ___ g und war ___ cm groß.
Ihr Kopfumfang war ___ cm.

15   1996   3470   51   34

Figure 9. An incomplete newspaper clipping

Our own work sheet. Several word problems which were self-generated by the students were put together for a worksheet by the teacher. At the end of the teaching experiment, this sheet was given to the students. Each student contributed one problem and had to decide beforehand which problem was selected. This task required the students' reflection once again about what they considered as an appropriate and interesting problem. Each child's name was listed beside the problem. Michelle put down: "A child needs 28 minutes per day for dressing and washing. How long does it approximately need in one week?" (see Figure 10).

Sachaufgaben für Expertenkinder

Wenn du eine Aufgabe nicht sofort lösen kannst, denke an unsere Tipps und Tricks!

1 Sachaufgaben aus der 4a

Michelle: Ein Kind braucht jeden Tag 28 Minuten zum Waschen und Anziehen.
Frage: Wie lange braucht es ungefähr in einer Woche?
Rechnung: 7·20 = 140 + 7·8 = 196
Antwort: 196 Minuten.

Figure 10. Word problems for word problem experts

After solving the problems the students asked the child who invented the problem to have a look at the correctness of the solution. The experts used smilies as icons here (☺,☻,☹), and fruitful discussions about the solutions and the solution strategies were the consequence of the steadily increasing autonomy the children were experiencing. On the top of the worksheet, the information was given: "If you do not know how to solve the problem, have a look at our list of hints and tricks". This leads us to the last activity.

Guidelines for solving word problems. At the end of almost each lesson some time was reserved for reflection on "Which hints and which tricks do we know that help us solving word problems?" Gradually a list of 16 aspects was put together. A big display hanging in the classroom was used for solving problems, but also for discussion in small-group work and class discussion. The children also made entries in the mathematics journal (see Figure 11).

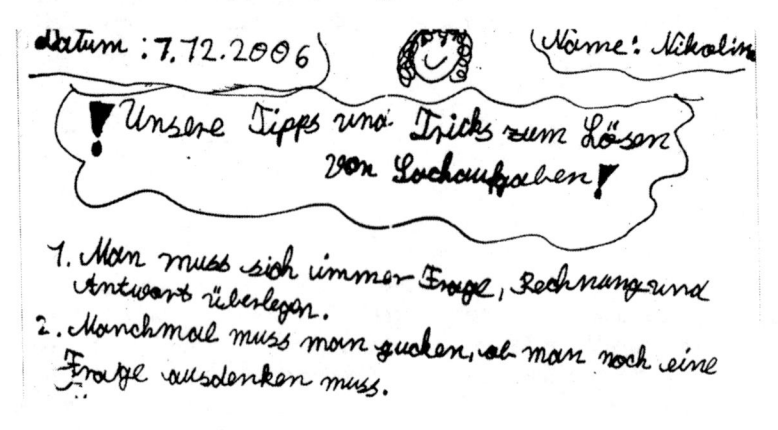

Figure 11. Nikolina's list of hints and tricks

Some hints and tricks that Nikolina included in her list may serve as representative examples.
- First you have to read the problem slowly and very carefully in order to find out whether all numbers are important.
- Sometimes you have to find out whether you have to find a question yourself.
- You must think the problem through and decide whether it is logical or not. Some problems cannot be solved.
- Sometimes it is clever to make a drawing or to tell the problem to someone else in your own words.
- …

Note that these 'rules' were not given to the children in advance, but the result of intensive reflection and communication about solving word problems.

CONCLUDING REMARKS

As mentioned earlier on, this is not a research report on a controlled and carefully evaluated teaching experiment. It is a theoretically founded description of several activities that we developed in order to encourage students to reflect on (solving) word problems.

It is the main goal of the approach to teaching described in this chapter to give children more responsibility and to see them as experts for their own learning. By constantly using their own productions, their reflection on word problems

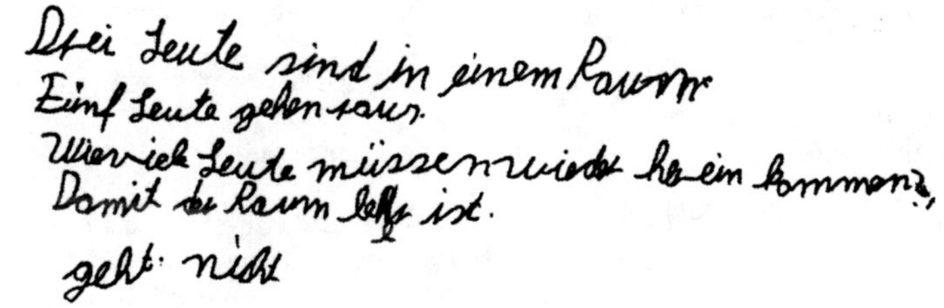

Drei Leute sind in einem Raum.
Einf Leute gehen raus.
Wieviel Leute müssen wieder he-ein kommen?,
Damit der Raum leer ist.
geht· nicht

Figure 12. Luca's room problem

was encouraged in classroom discourse and small-group work – more and more independently from the teacher, and not always as expected.

Luca for example (see Figure 12) generated the following word problem in the context of the aforementioned activity, where the children also had to indicate whether the problem was solvable or unsolvable. "There are three persons in one room. Five persons leave the room. How many persons have to return in order to have an empty room? – Unsolvable."

Our experiences lead us to the conclusion that it is a realistic option to gradually give children freedom that they can use effectively, even if a difficult topic such as word problems has to be tackled – sometimes with surprising results ...

REFERENCES

Baruk, S. (1985). *L'âge du capitaine. De l'erreur en mathématiques.* Paris: Seuil.
Boaler, J. (1999). Participation, knowledge, and beliefs: A community perspective on mathematics learning. *Educational Studies in Mathematics, 40,* 259–281.
Brousseau, G. (1997). *Theory of didactical situations in mathematics.* Dordrecht, The Netherlands: Kluwer.
Cai, J., & Silver, E. (1995). Solution processes and interpretations of solutions in solving division-with-remainder story problems: Do Chinese and U.S. students have similar difficulties? *Journal for Research in Mathematics Education, 26,* 491–497.
Carpenter, Th. P., Lindquist, M., Mathews, W., & Silver, E. A. (1983). Results of the third NAEP mathematics assessment: Secondary school. *Mathematics Teacher, 76,* 652–659.
Curcio, F. R., & DeFranco, T. C. (1989). Children's metacognitive knowledge about mathematics and mathematical problem solving. In C. A. Maher, G. A. Goldin & R. B. Davis (Eds.), *Proceedings of the eleventh annual meeting of PME, NA* (pp. 243–284). New Brunswick, NJ: Rutgers University.
Davis, R. B. (1989). The culture of mathematics and the culture of schools. *Journal of Mathematical Behavior, 8,* 143–160.
De Corte, E., & Verschaffel, L. (1985). Beginning first graders' initial representation of arithmetic word problems. *Journal of Mathematical Behavior, 4,* 3–21.
DeFranco, T. C., & Curcio, F. R. (1997). A division problem with a remainder embedded across two contexts: Children's solutions in restrictive vs. real-world setting. *Focus on Learning Problems in Mathematics, 19*(2), 58–72.
Donaldson, M. (1978). *Children's minds.* London: Fontana.
Ellerton, N. F. (1986). Children's made up mathematical problems – A new perspective on talented mathematicians. *Educational Studies in Mathematics, 17,* 261–271.
Freudenthal, H. (1991). *Revisiting mathematics education. The China lectures.* Dordrecht, The Netherlands: Kluwer.

Greer, B. (1993). The modelling perspective on wor(l)d problems. *Journal of Mathematical Behavior, 12,* 239–250.

Greer, B. (1997). Modelling reality in mathematics classrooms: The case of word problems. *Learning and Instruction, 7,* 293–307.

Hatano, G. (1997). Cost and benefit of modelling activity. Commentary. *Learning and Instruction, 7,* 383–387.

Heuvel-Panhuizen, M. van den (2001). Estimation. In M. van den Heuvel-Panhuizen (Ed.), *Children learn mathematics* (pp. 173–201). Utrecht, The Netherlands: Freudenthal Institute.

Hundeide, K. (1988). Metacontracts for situational definitions and for the presentation of cognitive skills. *The Quarterly Newsletter of the Laboratory of Comparative Human Cognition, 10,* 85–91.

Inoue, N. (2005). The realistic reasons behind unrealistic solutions: The role of interpretive activity in word problem solving. *Learning and Instruction, 15,* 69–83.

Jackson, P. (1990). *Life in classrooms.* New York: Teachers College Press.

Keller, B., & Brandenberg, M. (1999). Kapitänsaufgaben in Bildern [Captain-problems in pictures]. *Die Grundschulzeitschrift,* (126), 54–55.

Maguire, K. J. (1999). Children's generated word problems: A case study. In J. M. Truran (Ed.), *Making the difference* (pp. 336–342). Melbourne, Australia: Mathematics Education Research Group of Australasia.

Nesher, P. (1980). The stereotyped nature of school word problems. *For the Learning of Mathematics, 1*(1), 41–48.

Niss, M. (2001). Issues and problems of research on the teaching and learning of applications and modelling. In J. F. Matos, W. Blum, S. K. Houston & S. P. Carreira (Eds.), *Modelling and mathematics education* (pp. 72–89). Chichester, UK: Horwood.

Radatz, H. (1983). Untersuchungen zum Lösen eingekleideter Aufgaben [Research on solving word problems]. *Journal für Mathematik-Didaktik, 3,* 205–217.

Reusser, K. (1988). Problem solving beyond the logic of things: Contextual effects on understanding and solving word problems. *Instructional Science, 17,* 309–338.

Reusser, K., & Stebler, R. (1997). Every word problem has a solution – the social rationality of mathematical modelling in schools. *Learning and Instruction, 7,* 309–327.

Schoenfeld, A. (1991). On mathematics as sense-making. An informal attack on the unfortunate divorce of formal and informal mathematics. In J. F. Voss, et al. (Eds.), *Informal reasoning and education* (pp. 311–343). Hillsdale, NJ: Erlbaum.

Selter, Ch. (1994a). *Eigenproduktionen im Arithmetikunterricht der Grundschule* [Children's own productions in elementary school arithmetic]. Wiesbaden, Germany: Deutscher Universitätsverlag.

Selter, Ch. (1994b). How old is the captain? *Strategies, 5*(1), 34–37.

Selter, Ch. (2001). "1/2 Busses heißt: ein halbvoller Bus!" – Zu Vorgehensweisen von Grundschülern bei einer Textaufgabe mit Rest ["1/2 bus means a bus half-full!" – Solution strategies of elementary school children for DWR problems]. In C. Selter & G. Walther (Eds.), *Mathematik lernen und gesunder Menschenverstand* (pp. 162–173). Leipzig, Germany: Klett.

Silver, E. A. (1988). Solving story problems involving division with remainders: The importance of semantic processing and referential mapping. In M. J. Behr, C. B. Lacampagne, & M. M. Wheeler (Eds.), *Proceedings of the tenth annual meeting of PME-NA* (pp. 127–133). DeKalb, IL: Northern Illinois University.

Silver, E. A., Shapiro, L. J., & Deutsch, A. (1993). Sense making and the solution of division problems involving remainder: An examination of middle school students' solution processes and their interpretations of solutions. *Journal for Research in Mathematics Education, 24,* 117–135.

Streefland, L. (1990). Free productions in teaching and learning mathematics. In K. Gravemeijer, M. van den Heuvel-Panhuizen, & L. Streefland (Eds.), *Contexts, free productions, tests, and geometry in realistic mathematics education* (pp. 33–52). Utrecht, The Netherlands: OW & OC.

Treffers, A. (1987). *Three dimensions. A model of goal and theory description in mathematics instruction – The Wiskobas project.* Dordrecht, The Netherlands: Reidel.

Van Dooren, W., De Bock, D., Hessels, A., Janssens, D., & Verschaffel, L. (2005). Not everything is proportional: Effects of age and problem type on propensities for overgeneralization. *Cognition and Instruction, 23*, 57–86.

Verschaffel, L., & De Corte, E. (1997). Teaching realistic mathematical modelling in the elementary school: A teaching experiment with fifth graders. *Journal for Research in Mathematics Education, 28*, 577–601.

Verschaffel, L., De Corte, E., & Lasure, S. (1994). Realistic considerations in mathematical modelling of school arithmetic problems. *Learning and Instruction, 4*, 273–294.

Verschaffel, L., De Corte, E., Lasure, S., Van Vaerenbergh, G., Bogaerts, H., & Ratinckx, E. (1999). Design and evaluation of a learning environment for mathematical modelling and problem solving in upper elementary school children. *Mathematical Thinking and Learning, 1*, 195–229.

Verschaffel, L., Greer, B., & De Corte, E. (2000). *Making sense of word problems*. Lisse, The Netherlands: Swets & Zeitlinger.

Wheeler, D. H. (Ed.). (1967). *Notes on mathematics in primary schools*. London: Cambridge University Press.

Wyndhamn, J., & Säljo, R. (1997). Word problems and mathematical reasoning: A study of children's mastery of reference and meaning in textual realities. *Learning and Instruction, 7*, 361–382.

Yackel, E., & Cobb, P. (1996). Sociomathematical norms, argumentation, and autonomy in mathematics. *Journal for Research in Mathematics Education, 27*, 458–477.

Yoshida, H., Verschaffel, L., & De Corte, E. (1997): Realistic considerations in solving problematic word problems: Do Japanese and Belgian children have the same difficulties? *Learning and Instruction, 7*, 329–338.

Christoph Selter
Faculty of Mathematics
IEEM
TU Dortmund
Germany

RICHARD LESH AND BETH CAYLOR

16. DIFFERING CONCEPTIONS OF PROBLEM SOLVING IN MATHEMATICS EDUCATION, SCIENCE EDUCATION, AND PROFESSIONAL SCHOOLS

INTRODUCTION

The goal of this chapter is to clarify similarities and differences among four types of problem solving activities: (a) *word problems* in mathematics education, (b) *inquiry activities* in science education, (c) *case studies* or *problem-based learning activities* (PBL) in professional schools that are heavy users of mathematics, science, and technology, and (d) *model-eliciting activities* (MEA's) in our own research. Such comparisons often are difficult because *model-eliciting activities* are the only one of these four that were designed especially for the purposes of research. So, MEA's are the only one of these activities for which explicit design principles have been specified – so that it is possible to determine whether or not a given activity qualifies as being such an activity. In spite of these difficulties, however, it is productive to try to tease out distinctions, not in order to criticise one type of activity compared with another, but to identify testable hypotheses that may advance thinking about each.

WORD PROBLEMS IN MATHEMATICS EDUCATION

In the mathematics education literature, "problem solving" usually has been defined to be a situation that involves getting from givens to goals when the path is not immediately obvious (Schoenfeld, 1992). Consequently, if the givens occur in forms that have been pre-mathematicised (e.g., quantified), and if the goals also are expected to be mathematical objects, then it should be no surprise if traditional textbook word problems rarely emphasise more than a quarter of the kind of cycles (see Figure 1) that are needed in many of the kind of everyday situations where some type of mathematical thinking is needed (Lesh, Hamilton, & Kaput, 2007).

Because word problems are characterised and critiqued in most other chapters in this book, the main point that we emphasise here is that, in general, for the kind of word problems that are emphasised in mathematics textbooks and tests both the givens and the goals are mathematical quantities – rather than being (for example) objects whose relevant characteristics need to be measured or quantified. So, students never need to leave the world of mathematics, and the acceptability of answers depends on correctness rather than sensibility. Yet, even though many everyday situations where some type of mathematical thinking is needed involve

Mathematization

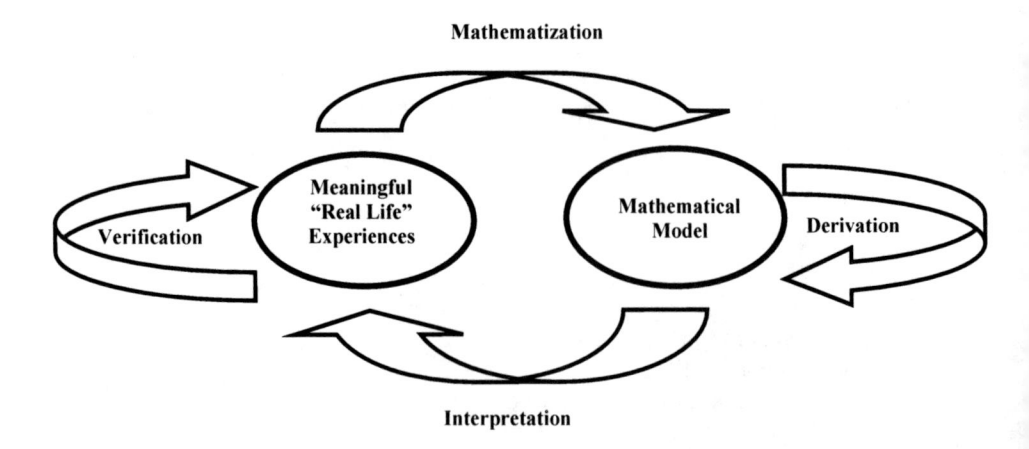

Figure 1. Solutions to modelling problems involve multiple modelling cycles

all four of the processes that are shown in Figure 1, most word problems require only minimal amounts of mathematisation, interpretation, or verification.

Outside of school, many problem solving situations not only involve decisions which require additional mathematical thinking that goes beyond the results from relevant computations, and information that is not given in pre-mathematised forms, but solutions also often involve going through several cycles of "expressing→testing→revising" alternative ways of thinking about relationship among pieces of information that are available. So, solutions tend to involve much more than proceeding along a path from initial conceptions of givens to initial conceptions of goals (Lesh & Doerr, 2003).

In the chapter on problem solving and modelling in the National Council of Teachers of Mathematics' Second Handbook of Research in Mathematics Teaching and Learning, Lesh and Zawojewski (2007) characterise mathematical problem-solving situations as goal directed situations that require students to make significant adaptations to their early interpretations of the situations (givens, goals, and possible solution processes). Moreover, interpretations (descriptions, explanations) often evolve through several interpretation cycles – which are like "drafts" of a paper. That is, in different "drafts", givens and goals often are thought about in quite different ways. So, final interpretations often develop in ways that involve sorting out, integrating, revising, and reorganising ways of thinking that are traceable to a variety of conceptual ancestors – for this reason, progress does not occur along a single path.

There are two other observations that we want to emphasise about traditional conceptions of problem solving in mathematics education. First, it tends to be assumed that learning to solve "real life" problems involves transfer from learning from "simpler" situations (where realistically complex factors related to context have been minimised) – and consequently that messy "real life" problems should therefore be more difficult than their counterparts in textbooks and tests (Lester & Kehle, 2003). Second, the literature on traditional conceptions of problem solving have been quite pessimistic about the possibility that, without providing significant amounts of guidance, average ability students will be able to create powerful forms of nearly any "big idea" in the K-16 mathematics curriculum (Silver, 1985). Sceptics say: "If it took years for history's most brilliant mathematicians to develop such concepts, how can average ability children be expected to develop such concepts during much more brief periods of time!!!"

INQUIRY ACTIVITIES IN SCIENCE EDUCATION

Science educators generally emphasise "hands-on experiences" for students (National Research Council, 1996), they emphasise teaching "fundamental abilities of inquiry" (American Association for the Advancement of Science, 1990, 1993), and they emphasise knowledge about the "nature of science" (Lederman, Abd-El-Khalick, Bell, & Schwartz, 2002) For example, Lederman and his colleagues developed a list of 7 tenets of the "Nature of Science" based on the history of scientific discoveries and science philosophy, and, in the USA, science educators are now advocating the explicit teaching of those tenets along with teaching the scientific process (Deboer, 1991). Similarly, echoing perspectives long ago associated with American Pragmatists (Dewey, 1938), Hurd's book about *Scientific Literacy: New Minds for a Changing World* (Hurd, 1998) reviewed the history of scientific literacy and called for the science curriculum to be in harmony with the contemporary ethos and practice of science. However, it is one thing to teach via inquiry and quite another to teach inquiry itself; and, in spite of the importance of "learning to learn" (Bruner, 1960) it is one thing to learn via inquiry and quite another to learn inquiry itself. The difficulties that arise are similar to those that have confounded mathematics education research on heuristics and metacognitive processes (Lester & Kehle, 2003). In reviews of the literature from Begle (1979), to Kilpatrick (1985), to Silver (1985), to Schoenfeld (1992), to Lester and Kehle (2003), to Lesh and Zawojewski (2007), the conclusions have been consistent. Although each reviewer, in their turn, offered advise about directions for future research, Lester and Kehle observed that nothing much has changed since Begel concluded that:

> (N)o clear cut directions for mathematics education are provided by the findings of these studies. In fact, there are enough indications that problem-solving strategies are both problem- and student-specific often enough to suggest that hopes of finding one (or a few strategies) which should be taught to all (or most students) are far too simplistic (Begel, 1979, p. 145).

There is little evidence that general processes that experts use to describe their past problem-solving behaviours also serve well as prescriptions to guide novices' next steps during ongoing problem solving sessions. Short lists of descriptive processes tend to be too general to be useful (Schoenfeld, 1985), yet long lists of prescriptive processes tend to become so numerous that knowing when to use them becomes the heart of understanding them (Lester & Kehle, 2003). Silver (1985) noted that, even in those few studies where some successful learning has been reported, transfer of learning has been undocumented or unimpressive. Successes generally occurred only when world-class teachers taught lengthy and complex courses where the complexity of the "treatment" makes it unclear *why* performance improved. Perhaps the students simply learned some mathematics concepts – rather than learning problem-solving strategies, heuristics, or metacognitive processes!

Problem-solving heuristics and metacognitive processes clearly have "face validity" among most mathematicians and mathematics educators. That is, they are useful for giving after-the-fact descriptions of what many mathematicians and others have done when they solve problems. But, there is a significant difference between after-the-fact descriptions of past performances by experts, and prescriptions for next steps for novices. For example, when math educators tried to go beyond using Polya-style heuristics (1957) as descriptions of what experts *have done* to also use them as prescriptions for what students *should do, it* became clear that rules-of-thumb like *clearly identifying givens and goals*, *working backwards*, or *drawing diagrams* are really only names for much longer lists of more specific rules that tell precisely what kind of pictures to draw – or what kind of actions to take when identifying givens and goals, or when working backwards (Schoenfeld, 1992). Yet, when longer lists of prescriptive rules were generated, this raised new difficulties – because new and higher-level meta-rules were needed to determine when, why, or whether to use any given rule on these long lists. Then, the cycle begins again. Short lists of rules have descriptive but not prescriptive power whereas longer lists required even higher-order rules to determine when, why, and whether to use each prescription (Schoenfeld, 2007).

So, in general, in science education, the state of research on inquiry is similar to the state of mathematics education research on metacognition.

– "Habits of mind" such as carefully monitoring and assessing your work are often counterproductive at some stages in the solution of complex problems. For example, it is well known that short periods of brainstorming sometimes are highly productive during some stages of trying to solve complex problems and that, during brainstorming sessions, "wild ideas" are generated rapidly and without critique, analysis, or assessment. So, even though habits of mind have been shown to transfer beyond the situations in which they develop, they often are counterproductive unless they are engaged at the right times and for the right purposes.

– Beliefs such as "mathematics is useful", or attitudes such as "I enjoy problem solving", or dispositions such as "trusting your intuitions" are often hopelessly naïve. For example, problem solving usually involves some periods of frustration which are not any more enjoyable than the hours of hard work that go into the development of expertise in nearly any complex activity. And, in mathematics just as in other kinds of complex activities, few people are uniformly good across all types of mathematics and mathematical activities.

Recently, our own research on heuristics and metacognition has focused on developmental studies similar to those that have investigated the development of students' understandings of early number concepts, or rational numbers and proportional reasoning, or foundation level concepts in algebra, calculus, geometry, or statistics. These studies have been showing that: (a) even in instances when the use of metacognitive processes can be observed in students' thinking, they tend to be used tacitly and implicitly rather than formally and analytically, and (b) the meanings of many metacognitive processes depend on frameworks that are more like "windows" that students look through than being "objects of reflection" that problem solvers look at to make sense of their problem solving experiences (Hamilton, Lesh, Lester, & Yoon, 2007). Consequently, to encourage the development of these frameworks, our own research has been developing "reflection tools" to help students develop more powerful language and imagery to think about what they are doing when they work on problem solving or inquiry activities. Results are showing that: (a) higher-order processes often focus on helping students develop more powerful ways to *see* (or interpret) inquiry activities, more than they focus on telling students what to *do* next, (b) they often function intuitively or tacitly rather than formally or analytically, and (c) the meanings of isolated beliefs, principles, or processes often depend on the development of holistic systems of beliefs, principles, and processes (Lesh & Zawojewski, 2007).

PROBLEM-BASED LEARNING IN FIELDS THAT ARE HEAVY USERS OF MATHEMATICS, SCIENCE, AND TECHNOLOGY

In the learning sciences, outside of the communities that think of themselves as mathematics or science educators, we have been surprised to learn that, when we speak of research on problem solving, most people assume that we are referring to research on problem-based learning (PBL). And we have been further surprised to learn that PBL activities usually are not activities in which problem solving is the means for developing concepts and abilities. Instead, students generally learn things (often in quite traditional ways) in the course of working on a problem. ... But the thing that has been most surprising of all is how little PBL research seems to be aware of the results of problem-solving research in mathematics education (Lesh & Zawojewski, 2007).

So, in some PBL *case studies* that are used in graduate schools of business, medicine, or engineering, the goal is to provide experiences where students develop the preceding kinds of frameworks. However, in the research literature, PBL activities are not defined in terms of the types of understandings students are intended to develop, they are defined in terms of task variables or things that students are expected to do – such as formulate questions (because the task was "ill defined"), explore a variety of solution paths (because the task was "open ended"), or integrate ideas from a variety of practical or theoretical perspectives (because the task was "multi-disciplinary").

Problem-based learning and project-based learning (PBL) developed first in medical schools, and they are often used as "case studies" in graduate schools of business, medicine, or engineering (Zawojewski, Diefes-Dux, & Bowman, in press). So, they usually are intended to be "realistic" in the sense that they are the kinds of situations that students are expected to encounter beyond school. Students often work in groups or teams where realistic technological tools are available. Alternative solutions are assessed according to their practical usefulness – not according to their theoretical correctness.

Similar to inquiry-based activities in science education, there does not exist a single typical prototype for PBL activities. For example, PBL activities may range from relatively brief problems which can be completed in a few minutes to larger projects which require several days or weeks of work.

Savery and Duffy (1995) list eight instructional principles of PBL curriculum based on constructivist philosophy, namely:
- Anchor all learning activities to a larger task or problem,
- Support the learner in developing ownership for the overall problem or task,
- Design an authentic task,
- Design the task and the learning environment to reflect the complexity of the environment they should be able to function in at the end of learning,
- Give the learner ownership of the process used to develop a solution,
- Design the learning environment to support and challenge the learners thinking,
- Encourage testing ideas against alternative views and alternative contexts, and
- Provide opportunity for and support reflection on both the content learned and the learning process.

A review of PBL was summarised by Albanese and Mitchell in *Academic Medicine* in 1993. They concluded that PBL is more nurturing and enjoyable, and that it motivates more individuals to enter family practice. They also found that faculty enjoyed teaching PBL. However, studies reported some lower scores on basic science assessments, gaps in knowledge, and more backwards reasoning rather than the forward reasoning attributed to experts.

In a later review of the effectiveness of PBL in medical education, Colliver (2000) emphasised many of the same problems with PBL that were identified by Albanese and Mitchell. They concluded that the ties between educational theory and research (on PBL) are loose at best, and that there is insufficient evidence in the PBL literature to support that the claim that it works (improves learning and clinical performance) – although it does seem to have measurable positive impacts on affect and attitude. However, many activities that claimed to be PBL activities were identified as being more like peer-teaching or learning-in-context situations rather than being situations that fit the notion of problem-based learning. Learners themselves seldom developed new ideas through problem solving, nor did teams of problem solvers develop any ideas that were not already known by some individuals within the group. Furthermore, what got learned usually appeared to be only a principle, or rule, or procedure, or list of facts that most instructors are likely to decide can be taught more efficiently using direct instruction – and this outcome is especially likely to happen if teachers have no way to measure the kinds of deeper or higher-order objectives that advocates of PBL claim that they emphasise.

MODEL-ELICITING ACTIVITIES

Model-eliciting activities (MEA's) are activities that require students to explicitly develop a *model* (or an explicit mathematical or scientific description or explanation) of a personally meaningful situation where some important type of mathematical or scientific thinking is needed to achieve some clearly recognised goal (Lesh & Zawojewski, 2007). At its simplest, then, a model can be thought of a being a system that is used to describe or design some other system for some purpose. The distinguishing characteristic of mathematical models is that they focus on structural characteristics of the system that is being described or designed. Similarly, because these descriptions or designs are generated for specific purposes, models also can be thought of as purposeful conceptual tools whose design typically involves a series of development cycles in which current descriptions are iteratively expressed, tested, and revised.

Principles for designing MEA's have been described in a number of recent publications (Hjalmarson & Lesh, 2008; Lesh et al., 2000, and, a brief summary of these principles is given at the end of this section. In general however, they have the following characteristics:
– They are simulations of problem-solving or decision-making situations where some significant type of mathematical or scientific thinking is needed beyond school.
– Solutions generally require at lest 45-90 minutes to construct, and they provide powerful prototypes for dealing with issues that are important to the students or others they would like to impress.
– Issues fit the interests and experiences of targeted students, and they encourage students to engage their personal knowledge, experience, and sense-making abilities.
– Solution procedures encourage students to use realistic tools and resources, including calculators, computers, consultants, colleagues, and "how to" manuals.
– Evaluation procedures recognise more than a single type and level of correct response.
– Overall activities should be able to contribute to both learning and assessment ... because students simultaneously learn and document what they are learning.
For this reason, MEA's sometimes have been called thought-revealing activities.

Before given more details about MEA's, it is important to emphasise that our original purpose for creating such activities was not to study problem solving per se. Nor were we trying to develop effective learning activities. Instead, our main goal was to investigate what it means for students to "understand" specific concepts in the K-16 mathematics or science curriculum and we also wanted to understand how these "understandings" develop in ways that are useful beyond school (Lesh, Hoover, Hole, Kelly, & Post, 2000). In particular, our research on MEA's evolved out of Piaget-inspired research on concept development – plus out of Pragmatist-inspired theories about how students make meaning out of real life experiences. As such, MEA's often involve simulations of students' everyday experiences beyond school – with the caveat that one person's conception of "reality" in not necessarily another's. Moreover, they also often turn out to be remarkably effective learning activities – because, when students develop models, these interpretation systems tend to involve Piaget-like conceptual systems related to important "big ideas" in the K-16 curriculum.

Another factor that significantly shaped the development of MEA's was our belief that mathematics is the study of structure – plus the observation that, in virtually every field where researchers have investigated similarities and differences between effective and relatively ineffective thinkers, it has been clear that effective thinkers not only *do* things differently but they also *see* (or interpret) things differently. So, effective people not only do things right, but they also do the right things at the right times, and they are able to do this because they see or interpret things differently than their less effective counterparts. So, research on MEA's begins with the assumption that students' interpretation abilities should be treated as being at least as important as their computation or deduction abilities. For these reasons, in MEA's, the products that students are asked to produce are not simply mathematical "answers" to pre-mathematised questions. Instead, MEA's require students to express their interpretations in the form of artifacts or conceptual tools which can be used to achieve some clearly recognised purpose in a "real life" situation. For example, instead of telling me how much I owe in taxes this year, problem solvers would be asked to give me (and others) a spreadsheet with graphs that will make it easy for any of us to calculate our own taxes – next year and in years thereafter. Furthermore, because our goal is to investigate more than specific solutions to specific situations, MEA's usually ask students to produce conceptual tools that are not only useful (in a specific situation) but also sharable (with other people) and reuseable (in other situations). This means that MEA's are instances of situated cognition, yet the conceptual tools and artifacts embody conceptual systems that are transferable and generalisable.

Another factor that significantly influenced the design of MEA's was the observation that the most straightforward way to investigate students' interpretation abilities is to observe them in situations where the development of a useful interpretation is the thing that is most problematic. Therefore, MEA's are defined to be goal-directed activities in which students need to make significant adaptations to their current interpretations of the situations. Consequently, solutions to MEA's generally involve sequences of modelling cycles in which students iteratively express, test, and revise or reject current ways of thinking. Therefore, solution processes often generate observable and auditable trails of documentation that produce information similar to that which we used to identify processes using clinical interviews or videotape analyses. In fact, the research methodologies that we use to develop MEA's has led to the development of a distinctive form of design research that is proving to be especially powerful for use in the learning sciences. We refer to these research methodologies as multi-tier design studies (Lesh & English, 2005) Kelly, Lesh, & Baec, 2008).Thus, among their distinctive characteristics are that (a) students develop models in response to MEA's, (b) teachers and/or researchers develop models for making sense of students' modelling activities, and (c) researchers develop models of student-teacher and student-student interactions.

Principles for designing MEA's have been described in a number of past publications (Lesh et al., 2000) and these principles have now been used productively by teachers in primary grades through high school (Lesh & English, 2005) – as well as by teachers of college students and professionals in fields ranging from engineering (Zawojewski et al., 2008; Lesh et al., 2007) to teacher development (Zawojewski, Lewis, & Hjalmarson, 2008). A brief summary of these principles follows.

The personal meaningfulness principle. (sometimes called the "Reality Principle"): Could this really happen in a student's "real life" beyond school? No problem is meaningful for all students. Nor is any situation problematic for all students. Nor are students' interpretations of "reality" likely to be the same as those of a given adult. Nonetheless, when students work on a problem, it often is clear that they are using their "school heads" rather than their "real heads" – and that they are not trying to make sense of the situation based on extensions of their own "real life" knowledge and experiences (Verschaffel, Greer, & De Corte, 2000). So, it is these latter kinds of situations that MEA designers need to avoid.

The model construction principle. MEA's are intended to focus on the "big ideas" in a given course and most "big ideas" in mathematics involve the development of a conceptual system that is used to generate purposeful interpretations (descriptions, explanations) of relevant situations. No situation is model-eliciting unless it actually elicits a model for a given student. So, the model-construction principle requires researchers to ask themselves: *What is it that creates the need for a specific type of model (and its underlying concepts or conceptual system)?* In order to optimise the chances that the conceptual tools that students produce will embody the targeted conceptual system, MEA designers need to develop design "specs" for students that are similar to the design "specs" that are given to engineers – or other design scientists who develop artifacts ranging from space shuttles to sustainable ecological systems. The "specs" do not say what the desired artifact is, they say how the designers will know when they've produced one! In some ways these design "specs" are similar to a photographic negative of the conceptual system whose development MEA designers wish to investigate. Using these design "specs", students should be able to make judgments about strengths and weaknesses of alternative products and underlying ways of thinking. So, students should be able to make significant adaptations to their current ways of thinking – without the researchers dictating the direction of these adaptations. To achieve this goal, MEA's need to be situations in which students experience some sort of cognitive conflict, and where they are able to go through a series of iterative cycles in which they repeatedly express→test→revise their own ways of thinking.

With the preceding general goals and assumptions in mind, a brief description follows for each of the following six main design principles for developing MEA's.

The self-evaluation principle. Will students be aware of criteria to judge for themselves when their responses are good enough? And will they be able to assess the strengths and weaknesses of alternative responses? For example, will students be likely to believe that their ideas will be taken seriously or will they believe that the responses they are expected to give should conform to the teacher's (or author's) notion of the (only) "correct" way to think about the problem situation? Beyond school, when mathematical thinking is needed, the mathematical product usually needs to serve some purpose outside of mathematics – such as enabling the problem solver to accomplish some goal or make some decision. Therefore, the "math product" is a tool. To judge its usefulness, it needs to be clear who needs the tool (and when, why, and for what purpose).

Because models involve descriptions or explanations, there nearly always exist several different levels and types of descriptions and explanations that are appropriate for a given situation, and the most effective model-eliciting activities tend to be those that encourage the development of a variety of alternative ways of thinking. Sometimes, MEA designers have elevated this assessment criterion to the status of a seventh principle for designing model-eliciting activities. In these cases, they have tended to call it the "Diversity Principle".

When the products that students produce involve descriptions or explanations, these products usually need to go through several stages of development – similar to first drafts, second drafts, and third drafts that occur for other types of documents. But, these cycles only occur if students themselves are able to assess the quality of trial drafts. So, during the development of model-eliciting activities, if solutions do not involve multiple cycles, then this is a strong indicator that the self-assessment principle has not been satisfied.

The model generalisability principle. Will students be likely to recognise the need for the product to be sharable and reuseable? Mathematical tools, like other complex artifacts, are seldom worthwhile to develop if they are only going to be used a single time, in a single situation, and for a single purpose. So, in order for students to recognise the need for a given kind of tool (and underlying conceptual system), it usually is important for them to see that the tool not only needs to be useful for a specific situation and purpose, but that it also should be sharable (with other people), and reuseable (for other purposes). Consequently, sharability and reuseability provide important criteria for assessing the quality of results that are produced, and characteristics such as adaptability tend to be important.

The model-documentation principle. Will the response require students to explicitly reveal how they are thinking about the situation (givens, goals, possible solution paths)? This principle ensures that problem solvers will externalise their ways of thinking in forms that make self-assessment possible – and such that sharability and reuseability are more likely to occur. More importantly, because MEA's are intended to be used for research and assessment, the model-documentation principle is essential in order for the activities to automatically generate auditable trails of documentation that enable important aspects of students' evolving models to be observed directly.

The simplest prototype principle. Is the situation as simple as possible while still creating the need for a significant model? Will the product that is produced provide a useful prototype (or metaphor) for interpreting a variety of other structurally similar situations? The most effective MEA's tend to be those that are remembered by students many months and even years after they have been completed. For example, we have recorded many instances where students have given impressively detailed accounts describing their past experiences with MEA's – sometimes several semesters after the activities were completed.

The testing and revising principle. Because an activity is only model-eliciting if it elicits a model, every MEA should go through several cycles of field testing, assessment, and revision – to ensure that students recognise the need to develop a model – and responses tend to generate auditable trails of documentation that reveal important information about the nature of students' developing ways of thinking. This outcome only tends to happen if the problem elicits a variety of different ways of thinking – and if it is possible for students themselves to assess the strengths and weaknesses of alternative ways of thinking.

When educators see MEA's, they are often inappropriately interpreted to be: (a) applications – which suggests that students must first learn relevant concepts and processes and then put them together and apply them, (b) difficult – which assumes that they must be reserved for high ability students, (c) open-ended – which often assumes that nearly any response is appropriate, and (d) ill-structured – which assumes that the structuring of the task is mostly done by students. But, in fact, MEA's are none of these things. In general, MEA's have been designed to be used with average and below average students. Yet, they are activities in which students are expected to make significant adaptations to existing ways of thinking. That is, students actually create new (to the student) mathematical understandings. Similarly, instead of learning ideas separately (and in the abstract) and then putting them together or applying them, solution processes tend to emphasise sorting out ideas that are globally and indissociably merged in the thinking of the students. To accomplish these goals, students themselves must be able to make judgments about the strengths and weaknesses of alternative responses. So, it definitely is not the case that anything that is produced is acceptable.

SUMMARY

Our goal in this chapter has been to compare (a) model-eliciting activities, (b) mathematics word problems (c) science inquiry activities, and (d) problem-based learning activities of the type used in fields like engineering, medicine, and business management. As both Table 1 and Figure 2 suggest, it is possible for some activities to simultaneously satisfy the criteria for each of these four types of activities. But, there also can occur activities whose characteristics satisfy only one of these four types of activities. For example, many mathematics word problems have characteristics that do not fit the notions of model-eliciting activities, science inquiry activities, or problem-based learning activities.

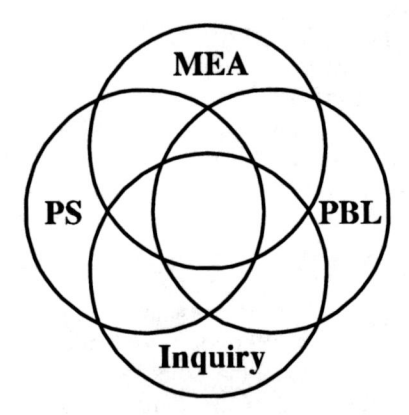

Figure 2. Comparing four types of problem solving activities (MEA = model-eliciting activities, PS = mathematics word problems, Inquiry = science inquiry activities, and PBL = problem-based learning activities)

Table 1. Comparing four types of problem solving activities

	Math Word Problems	Science Inquiry Activities	Problem Based Learning
Model-Eliciting Activities	Many MEA's are presented in written-symbolic forms.	Many MEA's do not involve data gathering; and, the questions are very carefully designed – and are almost never student generated.	Although several levels and types of solutions may be appropriate for MEA's, most are not "open ended" – because students themselves must be able to assess the quality of alternative solution
	Science Inquiry Activities	Problem Based Learning	Model-Eliciting Activities
Math Word Problems	Most mathematics word problems do not involve data gathering, or other characteristics emphasised in science inquiry activities.	Most mathematics word problems only require students to use concepts and procedures that they already have learned. Few are intended to help students develop new understandings.	Very few word problems involve the development of models; and, mathematical "correctness" is the main criteria used to assess the quality of responses – not practical "sensibility" and "usefulness."

(Continued)

	Problem Based Learning	Model-Eliciting Activities	Math Word Problems
Science Inquiry Activities	Many science inquiry activities are contrived situations that would not be likely to occur in students' everyday lives.	Science Inquiry activities tend to provide a great deal of guidance – if students are intended to develop significant new concepts or abilities.	Science inquiry activities tend to focus on process objectives; whereas, most math word problems are intended to provide practice for previously learned skills.
Problem-Based Learning Activities	Model-Eliciting Activities PBL activities seldom ask students to develop sharable and reusable conceptual tools.	Math Word Problems PBL activities often allow students to use additional tools that would be expected to be available in real life situations.	Science Inquiry Activities Most PBL activities are more focused on sorting through existing knowledge to find solutions or explanations – rather than developing new understandings by sorting through patterns or by experimentation.

RECOMMENDATIONS FOR FUTURE WORK IN PROBLEM-SOLVING IN MATH AND SCIENCE

In fields like engineering, or medicine, or business management, we and our colleagues have found that experts consistently emphasise that, as we enter the 21st century, significant changes have been occurring: (a) in the kind of problem-solving situations where some type of mathematical or scientific thinking is needed, and (b) the levels and types of concepts and abilities that are needed in the preceding kinds of situations (Lesh et al., 2007; Zawojewski, Diefes-Dux, & Bowman, 2008). Similarly, in the past quarter of a century, equally significant changes have been occurring is the way learning scientists and cognitive scientists think about learning and problem solving. For example, during recent annual conferences in both cognitive science and learning science, the trends listed below have emerged as common assumptions shared by most leaders in these fields (Bransford, Brown, & Cocking, 1999). Yet, implications of most these trends are scarcely evident in mathematics education.

In fields that are becoming increasingly heavy users of mathematics, science, and technology, there is some evidence that some problem-based learning activities have attempted to reflect modern trends in the levels and types of mathematical thinking that is needed beyond school in the 21st century, and many MEA's have been designed explicitly to focus on new types of learning in problem-solving situations. But, in both mathematics and science education, as well as in fields where mathematical thinking is used, a great deal more research and development will be needed to keep pace with changes that are taking place beyond schools and in modern learning sciences. So, we end this chapter with a list of trends whose implications need to be investigated in research in mathematics and science education.

Mathematical and scientific understanding and abilities should focus on seeing as much as on doing.

- In virtually every area of learning or problem solving where researchers have investigated differences between effective and ineffective learners or problem solvers (e.g., between experts and novices), results have shown that the most effective people not only *do* things differently, but they also *see* (or *interpret*) things differently.
- Even the "process objectives" (and problem-solving strategies) that we develop often are descriptive instead of prescriptive in nature – and are integral parts of the interpretation systems that we develop.

Mathematical and scientific understandings and abilities should focus on situated competencies.

- Knowledge is organised around experience at least as much as it is organised around abstractions.
- Even though models (and underlying conceptual systems) are shaped by the situations in which they are developed, they are like other types of conceptual tools in the sense that they generally are not worth developing unless they are intended to be used more than a single time and in more than a single situation. So, in general, they are not just powerful (in a specific situation) but they also are designed to be sharable (with others) and reuseable (in other situations).

Mathematical and scientific understandings and abilities should focus on socially shared and shaped competencies.

- In the 21st century, where countries have knowledge economies, where companies involve learning organisations, and where learners and problem solvers may consist of teams of diverse specialists, it is naïve to imagine that thinking goes on exclusively within the minds of isolated individuals.
- The nature of knowledge development is influenced by the fruits as well as by the roots of ideas and feelings – and by sociocultural constraints and affordances related to the availability of capability-enhancing tools.

Mathematical and scientific understandings and abilities should focus on inherently connected competencies.

- Realistically complex problem solving situations usually involve more than a single actor – and decisions that involve trade-offs (such as low costs and high quality). So, productive ways of thinking usually need to integrate ideas and abilities drawn from a variety of textbook topic areas.

- Rather than being learned in isolation and then connected, many ideas are learned as parts of models that draw on multiple theories (and textbook topic areas) – and are only later differentiated and sorted out.

Mathematical and scientific understandings and abilities should focus on systemic/ emergent competencies.

- Many of the most important things that need to be understood and explained are complex adaptive systems whose most obvious distinguishing characteristics are that they involve emergent properties of the systems-as-a-whole – which cannot be explained using only a single function (or input-output rule).

Mathematical and scientific understandings and abilities should focus on distributed competencies – which are expressed or embodied using a variety of external media.

- In the 21st century, our abilities to store, retrieve, manipulate, and use information are continually being off-loaded using tools ranging from spell checkers to Internet-based search engines, and the conceptual tools that we develop are shaped as much by our continually evolving purposes as by currently existing artifacts or events.

Mathematical and scientific understandings and abilities should focus on knowledge that is increasingly infrastructural in a technology-based age of information.

- Conceptual tools (and expressive media) that humans develop are not just neutral carriers of thought, nor are they neutral descriptions of experiences. They induce significant changes on thinking that evolves, and they also structure the situations that we need to understand and explain. In other words, they are infrastructural! The same conceptual systems that we develop to understand the world are also used to mould and shape that world. As soon as we understand a situation, we tend to change it and, as soon as a conceptual system is expressed, it changes.

Mathematical and scientific interpretations of situations are not just logical and mathematical in nature.

- When we interpret situations, we don't simply engage models that are purely logical and mathematical in nature. They also involve feelings, values, and a variety of metacognitive capabilities.

Mathematics and science education research should focus more attention on tacit understandings and abilities.

- The conceptual systems that we develop to interpret experiences often are more like windows that we look through than objects that we look at. So, we can think *with* them without necessarily thinking *about* them. In fact, when people need to develop abilities that involve smoothly functioning complex systems, it often is debilitating to think about these systems formally and analytically.

Mathematics and science education research should focus more attention on early understandings and abilities that are piecemeal (both undifferentiated and unintegrated) and unstable.

- Regardless whether the "problem solver" is an isolated individual or a group, solutions to MEA's tend to involve communities of competing conceptual systems, and conceptual evolutions tend to occur best when Darwinian factors such as diversity, selection, propagation, and conservation come into play. Thus, we go beyond emphasising *the mind in society* (and *the mind of society*) to also emphasise *societies of mind.*

Mathematics and science education research should focus more attention on understandings and abilities which are characterised by complex adaptive systems.

- When we develop models of students' modelling abilities, it has become necessary to move beyond machine-based metaphors (hardware), and beyond computer-age metaphors (software), toward metaphors grounded in an age of biotechnologies (wetware) and complex adaptive systems – where "agents" within systems often are living organisms governed by wetware that obeys logics that are distributed, multi-media, and fuzzy (rather than being characterised by simple, linearly combined or concatenated rules or declarative statements). Thus, knowledge development is considered to be less like the construction of a machine or a computer program, and more like the evolution of a community of living, adapting, and continually evolving biological systems.

Mathematics and science education research should focus more attention on understandings and abilities which are continually developing in non-linear ways along a variety of interacting dimensions.

- During MEA's, conceptual systems typically develop along a variety of interacting dimensions: concrete/abstract, intuitions/formalisations, holistic/analytic, external/internal, simple/complex, situated/decontextualised, unstable/stable, and so on. However, the most appropriate model is not necessarily the one that is most abstract, most formal, most complex, most analytic, or most decontextualised and its development seldom occurs along linear paths. Conceptual evolution tends to involve differentiation, integration, adaptation, and elaboration, and final ways of thinking usually can trace their heritage to a variety of conceptual ancestors.

REFERENCES

Albanese, M. A., & Mitchell, S. (1993). Problem-based learning: A review of literature on its outcomes and implementation issues. *Academic Medicine, 68*, 52–81.
American Association for the Advancement of Science. (1990). *Project 2061: Science literacy for all in the 21st century*. New York: Oxford University Press.
American Association for the Advancement of Science. (1993). *Benchmarks for science literacy*. New York: Oxford University Press.
Begle, E. G. (1979). *Critical variables in mathematics education*. Washington, DC: The Mathematics Association of America and the National Council of Teachers of Mathematics.
Bransford, J. D., Brown, A. L., & Cocking, R. R. (1999). *How people learn: Brain, mind, experience, and school*. Washington, DC: National Academy Press.
Bruner, J. (1960). *The process of education*. New York: Vantage Books.
Colliver, J. (2000). Effectiveness of problem based learning curricula. *Academic Medicine, 75*, 259–266.
Deboer, G. E. (1991). *A history of ideas in science education: Implications for practice*. New York: Teachers College Press.
Dewey, J. (1938). *Logic: The theory of inquiry*. New York: Henry Holt.
Hjalmarson, M., & Lesh, R. (2008). Six principles for developing model-eliciting activities. In L. English (Ed.), *International handbook of research in mathematics education* (2nd ed.). Hillsdale, NJ: Erlbaum.
Hamilton, E., Lesh, R., Lester, F., & Yoon, C. (2007). The use of reflective tools in building personal models of problem solving. In R. Lesh, E. Hamilton & J. Kaput (Eds.), *Models & modeling as foundations for the future in mathematics education* (pp. 349–367). Mahwah, NJ: Erlbaum.
Hurd, P. D. H. (1998). Scientific literacy: New minds for a changing world. *Science Education, 82*(3), 407–430.
Kelly, A. E., Lesh, R. A., & Baec, J. Y. (2008). *Handbook of innovative design research in science, technology, engineering, mathematics (STEM) education*. New York: Taylor & Francis.
Kilpatrick, J. (1985). A retrospective account of the past twenty-five years of research on teaching mathematical problem solving. In E. A. Silver (Ed.), *Teaching and learning mathematical problem solving: Multiple research perspectives* (pp. 1–16). Hillsdale, NJ: Erlbaum.
Lederman, N. G., Abd-El-Khalick, F., Bell, R. L., & Schwartz, R. S. (2004). Views of nature of science questionnaire: Toward valid and meaningful assessment of learners' conceptions of nature of science. *Journal of Research in Science Teaching, 39*, 497–512.
Lesh, R. A., & Doerr, H. M. (Eds.). (2003). *Beyond constructivism: Models and modeling perspectives on mathematics problem solving, learning, and teaching*. Mahwah, NJ: Erlbaum.
Lesh, R., & English, L. (2005). Trends in the evolution of models & modeling perspectives on mathematical learning and problem solving. *International Reviews on Mathematical Education (ZDM), 37*(6), 487–489.
Lesh, R. A., Hamilton, E., & Kaput, J. J. (2007). *Foundations for the future in mathematics education*. Mahwah, NJ: Erlbaum.
Lesh, R., Hoover, M., Hole, B., Kelly, E., & Post, T. (2000). Principles for developing thought-revealing activities for students and teachers. In A. Kelly & R. Lesh (Eds.), *Handbook of research design in mathematics and science education*. Mahwah, NJ: Erlbaum.
Lesh, R., & Zawojewski, J. S. (2007). Problem solving and modeling. In F. Lester (Ed.), The second handbook of research on mathematics teaching and learning (pp. 763–804). Reston, VA: National Council of Teachers of Mathematics.
Lester, F. K., & Kehle, P. E. (2003). From problem solving to modeling: The evolution of thinking about research on complex mathematical activity. In R. Lesh & H. Doerr (Eds.), *Beyond constructivism: Models and modeling perspectives on mathematics problem solving, learning and teaching* (pp. 501–518). Mahwah, NJ: Erlbaum.

National Research Council. (1996). *National science education standards*. Washington, DC: National Academy Press.
Pianta, R. C., Belsky, J., Houts, R., & Morrison, F. (2007). Teaching: Opportunities to learn in America's elementary classrooms. *Science, 315*(5820), 1795–1822.
Polya, G. (1957). *How to solve it: A new aspect of mathematical method*. Princeton, NJ: Princeton University Press.
Savery, J. R., & Duffy, T. M. (1995). Problem based learning: An instructional model and its constructivist framework. *Educational Technology, 35*(5), 31.
Schoenfeld, A. H. (1985). *Mathematical problem solving*. New York: Academic Press.
Schoenfeld, A. H. (1992). Learning to think mathematically: Problem solving, metacognition, and sense making in mathematics. In D. Grouws (Ed.), *Handbook of research on mathematics teaching and learning* (pp. 334–370). New York: McMillan.
Schoenfeld (2007). Plenary Address for the Research Presessions for the 2007 annual conference for the National Council of Teachers of Mathematics.
Silver, E. A. (Ed.). (1985). *Teaching and learning mathematical problem solving: Multiple research perspectives*. Hillsdale, NJ: Erlbaum.
Verschaffel, L., Greer, B., & De Corte, E. (2000). *Making sense of word problems*. Lisse, The Netherlands: Swets & Zeitlinger.
Zawojewski, J., Diefes-Dux, H., & Bowman, K. (Eds.). (2008). *Models and modeling in engineering education: Designing experiences for all students*. Rotterdam, The Netherlands: Sense Publishers.
Zawojewski, J., Lewis, K., & Hjalmarson, M. (in press). Design research investigating teacher development. In A. Kelly, R. Lesh, & J. Baec (Eds.), *Design research in mathematics, science & technology education*. Hillsdale, NJ: Erlbaum.

Richard Lesh
School of Education
Indiana University
U.S.A.

Beth Caylor
School of Education
Indiana University
U.S.A.

LYN D. ENGLISH

THE CHANGING REALITIES OF CLASSROOM MATHEMATICAL PROBLEM SOLVING

Discussion of Part V: Changing Classrooms

INTRODUCTION

For many decades, mathematics educators have been calling for more relevance and meaning in students' classroom mathematical activities (e.g., Brownell, 1945; Freudenthal, 1991). Each of the authors in this section makes similar calls. The need to make mathematics and mathematical problem solving relevant to students' lives has never been greater – nor has been the challenge in doing so. The "real world" of today is becoming rapidly different from that of even five years ago. Advances in technological communications, breakthroughs in medical research, meltdowns in the global economy, and the increasing dominance of complex systems in our lives necessitate a very different approach to "real-world" problem solving in the classroom.

Indeed, as numerous researchers and employer groups have been emphasising in recent years, we are not giving adequate attention to the understandings and abilities that are needed for success in the real world beyond school. For example, potential employees most in demand in mathematics/science related fields are those who can (a) interpret and work effectively with complex systems, (b) function efficiently and communicate meaningfully within diverse teams of specialists, (c) plan, monitor, and assess progress within complex, multi-stage projects, and (d) adapt quickly to continually developing technologies (Lesh, 2007).

It is clear that we need to rethink the nature of the problem-solving experiences we present to our students, as the authors in this section emphasise. They raise a number of common concerns regarding mathematical problem solving in many of today's classrooms. These concerns include the limitations of traditional stereotyped word problems, students' difficulties in making sense of a given problem and the solutions they generate, and the apparent ineffectiveness of instructional practices in improving students' problem solving. In this discussion chapter I review these major concerns, offering some suggestions for why they exist and what we might do in addressing them. I then consider some ways in which modelling and problem posing can advance students' mathematical learning.

CONCERNS WITH REAL-WORLD CLASSROOM PROBLEM SOLVING

Limitations of Traditional Stereotyped Word Problems

Bonotto (this volume) maintains that if we are to gain a better interplay between classroom problem solving and every-day life experiences, then traditional stereotyped word problems must be replaced by more realistic situations. Traditional word problems typically focus on the application of operational rules that involve a mapping between the structure of the problem situation and the structure of a symbolic mathematical expression (e.g., the problem, *Suzie has saved $12. Lillian has saved 3 times this amount. How much has Lillian saved?* can be solved by the calculation, 12 x 3 = 36). Oftentimes, solving these word problems is not a problem-solving activity for students; rather, it is an exercise that relies on syntactic cues for solution, such as key words or phrases in the problem (e.g., "times," "less," "fewer"). Furthermore, as Lesh and Caylor indicate, most word problems require only "minimum amounts of mathematisation, interpretation, or verification" (p. 334). While not denying the importance of these types of problems in the curriculum, they do not address adequately the mathematical knowledge, processes, representational fluency, and communication skills that our students need for the 21st century.

As Selter and numerous other researchers have indicated, students who are fed a diet of stereotyped one- or two-step word problems frequently divorce their real-world knowledge from the solution process, that is, they solve the problems without regard for realistic constraints (e.g., Greer, 1997; Greer, Verschaffel, & Mukhopadhyay, 2007; Verschaffel, De Corte, & Borghart, 1997). In standard word problems, questions are presented to which the answer is already known by the one asking them (i.e., the teacher). As Verschaffel et al. (1997) commented, questions are not given so students can obtain information about an authentic problem situation, rather, the questions are designed to give the teacher information about the students. Furthermore, both the students and the teachers are aware of this state of affairs and act accordingly (cf. Brousseau's [1997] notion of "didactical contract"). For example, because students are accustomed to operating on numbers in a word problem to produce an expected numerical answer, they often fail to make sense of the textual representation of the problem and the answer they generate (Selter, this volume).

Difficulties with Sense Making

The importance of problem context in students' interpretation and subsequent solving of a problem is nicely illustrated in Selter's review of his own research and that of others. By embedding problems in more realistic contexts, there is less likelihood that students will interpret and solve them in a stereotyped way. This was evident in DeFranco and Curcio (1997)'s study, for example, where students' performance improved substantially when a variation of the *army bus problem* (Carpenter, Lindquist, Matthews, & Silver, 1983) was presented in an authentic context (the students were asked to make a phone call to order minivans [5 children per van] that should take 32 children to a party). Of the 20 students, 16 gave an appropriate response, in contrast to just two students when the problem was presented as a standard word problem.

Selter makes the important point that we need to look more closely at students' thinking as they interpret and solve word problems, especially those problems that require critical reasoning. It is particularly interesting to read of the responses of third-graders in Selter's (1994) study, who were asked to explain how they arrived at their solutions in working problems such as, *A shepherd owns 19 sheep and 13 goats. How old is the shepherd?* and *There are 13 boys and 15 girls sitting in a classroom. How old is the teacher?* The students displayed quite diverse and creative interpretations of the problems, such as "He bought one animal for each year of his life; so he always knows his age" and "This class is a special one because there are just as many children in it as the teacher is old. The problem would not work in our class." As Selter and other authors in this volume note, students' responses to such problems do not always indicate a "suspension of sense-making," rather, an activity of *diverse* sense-making. Students can be surprisingly creative and divergent in their efforts to solve non-traditional problems. We need to capitalise on their innovative thinking in desiging classroom problem-solving experiences.

Relationships between Word Problems, Problem Solving, Problem Posing, and Modelling

The word "problem" is often ambiguous, but the most usual meaning includes the connotation that it is a task whose solution requires more than the application of a known procedure. From this standpoint, most "word problems", as typically used in school mathematics, are not problems, often amounting to exercises in the four basic arithmetical operations. (However, a task cannot, in itself, be characterised as a problem or not, since this determination will depend on the person or group of people working on the task.) A relevant distinction is the one Hatano (2003, p. xi) draws between adaptive expertise, namely "the ability to apply meaningfully learned procedures flexibly and creatively" and routine expertise, namely "being able to complete school exercises quickly and accurately without understanding."

A central theme of the book by Verschaffel, Greer, and De Corte (2000) is that word problems can be characterised as exercises in mathematical modelling. As such, they have an essential purpose in introducing students to considerations of how the "two faces" of mathematics – as a set of autonomous formal structures, and as a means of describing aspects of the world – relate. Mathematical modelling, by its nature, requires adaptive expertise. Even in the simplest cases, adaptive expertise may be required to decide whether or not the application of an arithmetical operation provides an appropriate model (exact or more or less approximate) or not (Usiskin, 2004).

Many of the examples discussed in the chapter by Lesh and Caylor imply a further type of expertise that could be termed "creative expertise". In contrast to Hatano's adaptive expertise, this form of expertise implies an analysis of a situation and the combination of known mathematical structures or even the invention of new (to the student) structures that capture the essence of that situation, rather than the (albeit flexible) application of a known structure. As pointed out by Lesh and Caylor, such demands stand in stark contrast to those presented by typical word problems, in which most of the structuring has already been done in advance. This distinction is reminiscent of Freudenthal's (1991) comment, in relation to manipulatives such as the Dienes' Logic Blocks, about "the difference between poor and structured on the one hand, and rich and to be structured on the other" (p. 30).

Problem posing is a form of creative activity that operates within such tasks involving to-be-structured rich situations (including situations involving real-life artifacts and human interactions, as discussed by Bonotto). It represents one of the forms of authentic mathematical inquiry, as surveyed in the chapter by Lesh and Caylor, that move well beyond the limitations of word problems, at least as they are typically utilised.

Ineffectiveness of Instructional Practices in Improving Students' Problem Solving

For several decades now, mathematics educators have been recommending the teaching of heuristics and strategies to help students solve non-routine problems. These problems are often pure mathematical examples from areas such as geometry, algebra, and number theory, and require the student to have at least some mathematical content and tools to tackle the problem. The problems are more challenging than traditional word problems as it is usually not immediately apparent how to progress from the given state to the goal state. Polya's (1945) seminal book, *How to Solve It*, was the impetus for instruction that focused on providing students with assistance to solve these problems, namely, "expert" problem-solving tools such as working out a plan, identifying the givens and goals, drawing a picture, working backwards, and looking for a similar problem.

Despite the ground-breaking contribution of Polya's book, it seems that the teaching of heuristics and strategies has not made significant inroads into improving students' problem solving (Lesh & Caylor, this volume; Lesh & Zawojewski, 2007; Schoenfeld, 1992; Silver, 1985). Indeed, it is worth repeating Lesh and Caylor's quote from Begle's (1979) seminal book, *Critical variables in mathematics education*:

> A substantial amount of effort has gone into attempts to find out what strategies students use in attempting to solve mathematical problems... no clear-cut directions for mathematics education are provided... In fact, there are enough indications that problem-solving strategies are both problem- and student-specific often enough to suggest that hopes of finding one (or few) strategies which should be taught to all (or most) students are far too simplistic. (p. 145)

Six years later, Silver's (1985) report was no more encouraging. His assessment of the literature showed that, even in studies where some successful learning had been reported, transfer of learning was unimpressive. Furthermore, improvement in

DISCUSSION PART V

problem solving usually occurred only when expert teachers taught lengthy and complex courses in which the size and complexity of the interventions made it unclear exactly why performance had improved. Silver suggested that these improvements could have resulted simply from the students learning relevant mathematical concepts, rather than from learning problem-solving strategies, heuristics, or processes.

Seven years on, Schoenfeld's (1992) review of problem-solving research also concluded that attempts to teach students to apply Polya-style heuristics and strategies generally had not proven to be successful. Schoenfeld suggested that one reason for this lack of success could be because many of Polya's heuristics appear to be "descriptive rather than prescriptive' (p. 353). That is, as Lesh and Caylor indicate, most are really just names for large categories of processes rather than being well-defined processes in themselves. Therefore, in an effort to move heuristics and strategies beyond basic descriptive tools to prescriptive tools, Schoenfeld recommended that problem-solving research and teaching should: (a) help students develop a larger repertoire of more specific problem-solving strategies that link more clearly to specific classes of problems, (b) foster metacognitive strategies (self-regulation or monitoring and control) so that students learn when to use their problem-solving strategies and content knowledge, and (c) develop ways to improve students' beliefs about the nature of mathematics, problem solving, and their own personal competencies. However, there were some limitations to these recommendations, as Lesh and Caylor explain.

A decade after Schoenfeld's recommendations, Lester and Kehle (2003) drew similar conclusions regarding the impact of problem-solving research on classroom practice. "Teaching students about problem-solving strategies and heuristics and phases of problem solving... does little to improve students' ability to solve general mathematics problems" (p. 508). This is a disconcerting finding and one that needs further investigation. One explanation for the apparent failure of this teaching approach is that heuristics such as "See, Do, Plan, Check" are too general for students to apply and long lists of strategies to choose from can become so numerous that knowing when, where, why, and how to apply them becomes problematic in itself.

Addressing the issues of whether and how we can best teach heuristics and strategies to students and the impacts of this instruction on their problem solving is not sufficient. We need to ask more fundamental questions including: (a) What does it mean to "understand" problem-solving heuristics, strategies, and other tools? (b) How, and in what ways, do these understandings develop and how can we foster this development? and (c) How can we reliably observe, document, and measure such development? (English, Lesh, & Fennewald, 2008). A further issue that needs attention is how we can more effectively integrate core concept development with problem solving. Existing, long-standing perspectives on problem solving have treated it as an isolated topic. Problem-solving abilities are assumed to develop through the initial learning of basic concepts and procedures that are then practised in solving word "story" problems. More opportunities are needed for students to generate their own mathematical learning as they solve thought-provoking, authentic problems. The authors in this section offer some rich examples of such opportunities.

ADVANCING STUDENTS' MATHEMATICAL LEARNING THROUGH MODELLING AND PROBLEM POSING

Drawing upon the authors' work and my own research, I identify some powerful forms of learning that can be fostered by engaging students in mathematical modelling and problem posing, namely, generative learning, critical and reflective thinking, and interdisciplinary learning.

Generative Learning

In contrast to the traditional word and non-routine problems found in textbooks, modelling problems shift attention beyond mathematics as computation towards mathematics as conceptualisation, description, and explanation (Lesh, Yoon, & Zawojewski, 2007). In usual textbook problems the givens, the goal, and the "legal solution steps" are specified clearly; this is in contrast to modelling problems that present students with the added challenge of interpreting both the goal and the given information as well as permissible solution steps. Each of these components might be incomplete, ambiguous, or undefined; there might be too much data, or there might be visual representations that are difficult to interpret. This means that *adaptations* need to be made to existing ways of thinking about the givens, goals, and possible solution steps (Lesh et al., 2007).

Standard textbook problems also constrain problem-solving contexts to those that often artificially house and highlight the relevant concept (Hamilton, 2007). These problems thus preclude students from creating their own mathematical constructs out of necessity. Indeed, as Hamilton notes, there is little evidence to suggest that solving standard textbook problems leads to improved competencies in using mathematics to solve problems beyond the classroom.

In contrast, as the authors here have shown, mathematical modelling and problem-posing activities are couched within authentic interdisciplinary contexts that provide opportunities for students to generate and apply their own mathematical ideas. The use of "experientially real" contexts (such as Bonotto's artefacts) provides a platform for the growth of students' mathematisation skills, thus enabling students to use mathematics as a "generative resource" in life beyond the classroom (Freudenthal, 1973; Stevens, 2000; Streefland, 1993). Furthermore, the mathematics that students experience as they work these activities usually differs from what is taught traditionally in the curriculum for their grade level – because different types of quantities and operations are needed to mathematise realistic situations (e.g., quantities such as accumulations, probabilities, frequencies, ranks, and vectors; and operations such as sorting, organising, selecting, quantifying, weighting, and transforming large data sets (Doerr & English, 2003; English, 2006; Lesh & Zawojewski, 2007).

For students to engage with these different types of quantities and operations, we need to ensure that both the design and implementation of the problem activities facilitate this engagement. Lesh and Caylor provide a number of principles for designing their model-eliciting activities, while Bonotto and Selter offer guidelines for the design and use of artefacts and learning environments respectively. Drawing upon their work and my own, I list below some recommendations that I consider important in promoting generative learning through students' problem-solving activities.

Classroom problem-solving experiences should:
- Enable students to relate to and make sense of the problematic situation confronting them.
- Engage students with the underlying structural characteristics (key ideas and their relationships) of the problematic situation.
- Engage students in making significant adaptations to their current ways of thinking.
- Allow for multiple approaches and call for multifaceted solutions/products.
- Enable different levels of mathematical sophistication, thereby providing all students with access to powerful mathematical ideas embedded in the problematic situation.
- Require students to develop explicit mathematical constructions, descriptions, explanations, and justifications and to externalise these in a variety of ways, including through representational formats such as lists, tables, graphs, diagrams, and drawings.
- Provide sufficient criteria to enable students to determine whether their solutions are effective and adequately meet the demands of the problematic situation.
- Encourage the development of generalisable mathematical constructs and tools.
- Encourage students to test, revise, and refine their mathematical constructs and tools.
- Provide opportunities for students to share, reflect on, and constructively critique their mathematical creations.
- Provide opportunities for students to work collaboratively on challenging problems, thereby fostering effective communication and teamwork skills.

The above recommendations also incorporate opportunities for students to develop reflective and critical thinking.

Reflective and Critical Thinking

Modelling is increasingly recognised as a powerful vehicle for not only promoting students' understanding of a wide range of key mathematical and scientific concepts, but also for helping them appreciate the potential of mathematics as a critical tool for analysing important issues in their lives, communities, and society in general (Greer et al., 2007; Romberg, Carpenter, & Kwako, 2005). For example, in Tate's (1995) study, cited by Greer et al. (2007), students in a predominantly African American urban middle school were asked to pose a problem negatively affecting their community, to research the problem, and to develop and implement strategies to solve it. One particularly interesting problem that was posed addressed the presence of 13 liquor stores within 1000 feet of the students' school. The students devised a plan to move the stores away and carried out their plan through various means including lobbying the state senate. Mathematical modelling was an important tool in solving this real-world problem, as was evident in the students' analysis of the local tax and other codes that led to financial advantages for the liquor stores. The students subsequently reconstructed this incentive system to protect their school community.

The modelling and problem-posing activities addressed in the chapters of this section also foster reflective and critical thinking. These activities are usually designed for small-group work where members of the group act as a "local community of practice" analysing a complex situation (Lesh & Zawojewski, 2007). Numerous questions, issues, conflicts, revisions, and resolutions arise as students develop, assess, and prepare to communicate their products to their peers. Because the products are to be shared with and used by others, they must hold up under the scrutiny of the team and other class members. The use of a critical "reflection tool" (Lesh & Caylor, this volume) can assist students here. For example, such a tool can help students reflect on the adequacy of their own and their peers' models for the problem at hand, provide constructive feedback on how the model could be improved, and identify other problem situations in which the model could be applied.

Furthermore, critical reflective tools serve to promote structured reflection during problem solving (Hamilton, Lesh, Lester, & Yoon, 2007), that is, students are encouraged to focus on the important structural elements of modelling and problem posing. In a similar vein, Selter's focus on students' "intensive reflection and communication about solving word problems" (p. 328) led them to identify important features to consider in posing and solving problems (e.g., the "hints and tricks" of Nikolina).

The development of reflective and critical learning is being recognised increasingly as an essential component of the mathematics curriculum. In reflective classrooms, students develop critical dispositions and ask questions on their own (Elbers, 2003; Prediger, 2005). However, fostering a critical and reflective disposition in the mathematics classroom presents a special challenge to teachers. As Prediger (2005) commented, students should not only be given opportunities to be reflective but also to develop the skills and disposition to do so. Encouraging students to reflect on, describe, and critically evaluate their problem-solving approaches can promote important metacognitive processes as well as enhance future problem solving including dealing with interdisciplinary problems (DaPueto & Parenti, 1999; Hamilton et al., 2007; Lesh & Zawojewski, 2007; Prediger, 2005).

Interdisciplinary Learning

Research suggests that although professionals in mathematics-related fields draw upon their school learning, they do so in a flexible and creative manner, unlike the way in which they experienced mathematics in their school days (Gainsburg, 2006;

Hall, 1999; Hamilton, 2007; Noss, Hoyles, & Pozzi, 2002; Zawojewski & McCarthy, 2007). Furthermore, this research has indicated that such professionals draw upon interdisciplinary knowledge in solving problems and communicating their findings.

Lesh and Caylor further highlight the importance of interdisciplinary knowledge in their discussion on how modelling is fundamental to many fields that are becoming increasingly dependent on developments in mathematics, science, and technology. For example, disciplines such as economics, information systems, social and environmental science, and the arts have contributed in large part to the powerful mathematical models we have in place for dealing with a range of complex problems facing the world today (Lesh & Sriraman, 2005). Unfortunately, our mathematics curricula do not capitalise upon the contributions of other disciplines. A more interdisciplinary and unifying model-based approach to students' mathematics learning could go some way towards alleviating the well-known "one inch deep and one mile wide" problem in many of our curricula (Sabelli, 2006, p. 7; Sriraman & Steinthorsdottir, 2007). There is limited research, however, on ways in which we might incorporate other disciplines within the mathematics curriculum. The authors in this section have provided some examples, including Bonotto's use of real-world artefacts.

In my research on implementing modelling activities in the elementary and middle schools, I have been working with teachers to design interdisciplinary mathematical modelling problems that align themselves with the learning themes being implemented in their classrooms. Such themes have included, among others, natural disasters, the local environment, classroom gardens, early colonisation, the gold-rush days, book reading clubs, class excursions to fun parks, and the Olympic and Commonwealth Games (e.g., English, in press). Such interdisciplinary problems provide a powerful means of forging "strong and explicit connections between mathematical knowledge on the one hand, and the contexts within which that knowledge can be used on the other" (Swan, Turner, Yoon, & Muller, 2007, p. 276).

CONCLUDING POINTS

In this discussion chapter I have attempted to address the changing realities of classroom problem solving – realities with respect to what is happening outside the classroom and what is, and is not, happening inside the classroom. Our great challenge is to bring more of the outside realities into the classroom. As the authors in this section have demonstrated, mathematical modelling and problem posing are powerful ways of addressing this challenge.

These learning activities explicitly draw upon problematic situations from beyond the classroom – situations that are actually occurring in the students' lives. These situations require students to develop different interpretation and representation systems that encourage them to elicit core concepts and utilise diverse reasoning processes and that require "socially shared and shaped competencies" (Lesh & Caylor, p. 346). If we can help students make better connections between their within-class and out-of-class learning, we are well on the way to improving their mathematical learning and problem solving. Assisting students in making better connections requires redesigning outmoded problem activities and restructuring classroom learning environments so that students are intrigued by a problematic situation, feel an urgency to resolve it, are eager to debate their different ideas, and have a desire to communicate and share their creations.

REFERENCES

Begle, E. G. (1979). *Critical variables in mathematics education*. Washington, DC: The Mathematics Association of America and the National Council of Teachers of Mathematics.

Brousseau, G. (1997). *Theory of didactical situations in mathematics*. Dordrecht, The Netherlands: Kluwer.

Brownell, W. A. (1947). The place of meaning in the teaching of arithmetic. *Elementary School Journal, 47*, 256–265.

Carpenter, T. P., Lindquist, M., Matthews, W., & Silver, E. A. (1983). Results of the third NAEP mathematics assessment: Secondary school. *Mathematics Teacher, 76*, 652–659.

DeFranco, T. C., & Curcio, F. R. (1997). A division problem with a remainder across two contexts: Children's solutions in restrictive vs. real-world setting. *Focus on Learning Problems in Mathematics, 19*, 58–72.

DaPueto, C., & Parenti, L. (1999). Contributions and obstacles of contexts in the development of mathematical knowledge. *Educational Studies in Mathematics, 39*, 1–21.

Doerr, H. M., & English, L. D. (2003). A modeling perspective on students' mathematical reasoning about data. *Journal for Research in Mathematics Education, 34*, 110–136.

Elbers, E. (2003). Classroom interaction as reflection: Learning and teaching mathematics in a community of inquiry. *Educational Studies in Mathematics, 54*, 77–99.

English, L. D. (2006). Mathematical modeling in the primary school: Children's construction of a consumer guide. *Educational Studies in Mathematics, 62*, 303–323.

English, L. D. (in press). Modeling with complex data in the primary school. In R. Lesh, P. Galbraith, & W. Blum (Eds.), *Mathematical modeling ICTMA 13: Education and the design sciences*. Kluwer.

English, L. D., Lesh, R. A., & Fennewald, T. (2008). *Future directions and perspectives for problem solving research and curriculum development*. Paper presented for TSG 19 at the International Congress on Mathematical Education, Monterrey, Mexico.

Freudenthal, H. (1973). *Didactical phenomenology of mathematical structures*. Dordrecht, The Netherlands: Kluwer.

Freudenthal, H. (1991). *Revisiting mathematics education. China lectures*. Dordrecht, The Netherlands: Kluwer.

Gainsburg, J. (2006). The mathematical modeling of structural engineers. *Mathematical Thinking and Learning, 8*, 3–36.

Greer, B. (1997). Modeling reality in mathematics classroom: The case of word problems. *Learning and Instruction, 7*, 293–307.

Greer, B., Verschaffel, L., & Mukhopadhyay, S. (2007). Modelling for life: Mathematics and children's experience. In W. Blum, H.-W. Henne, & M. Niss (Eds.), *Applications and modelling in mathematics education* (ICMI Study 14; pp. 89–98). Dordrecht, The Netherlands: Kluwer.

Hall, R. (1999). *Case studies of math at work: Exploring design-oriented mathematical practices in school and work settings* (NSF Rep. No. RED-9553648), Arlington, VA: National Science Foundation.

Hamilton, E. (2007). What changes are needed in the kind of problem solving situations where mathematical thinking is needed beyond school? In R. A. Lesh, E. Hamilton, & J. Kaput (Eds.), *Foundations for the future in mathematics education* (pp. 1–7). Mahwah, NJ: Erlbaum.

Hamilton, E., Lesh, R. A., Lester, F., & Yoon, C. (2007). The use of reflection tools in building personal models of problem solving. In R. A. Lesh, E. Hamilton, & J. Kaput (Eds.), *Foundations for the future in mathematics education* (pp. 349–366). Mahwah, NJ: Erlbaum.

Hatano, G. (2003). Foreword. In A. J. Baroody & A. Dowker (Eds.), *The development of arithmetic concepts and skills* (pp. xi–xiv). Mahwah, NJ: Erlbaum.

Lesh, R. A. (2007). What changes are occurring in the kind of elementary-but-powerful mathematics concepts that provide new foundations for the future? In R. A. Lesh, E. Hamilton & J. Kaput (Eds.), *Foundations for the future in mathematics education* (pp. 155–159). Mahwah, NJ: Erlbaum.

Lesh, R. A., & Sriraman, B. (2005). John Dewey revisited—pragmatism and the models-modeling perspective on mathematical learning. In A. Beckmann, C. Michelsen, & B. Sriraman (Eds.), *Proceedings of the First International Symposium of Mathematics and its Connections to the Arts and Sciences* (pp. 7–31). Schwäbisch Gmund, Germany: The University of Education.

Lesh, R., & Zawojewski, J. S. (2007). Problem solving and modeling. In F. Lester (Ed.), *The second handbook of research on mathematics teaching and learning* (pp. 763–804). Charlotte, NC: Information Age Publishing.

Lesh, R. A., Yoon, C., & Zawokewski (2007). John Dewey revisited—Making mathematics practical VERSUS making practice mathematical. In R. A. Lesh, E. Hamilton & J. Kaput (Eds.), *Foundations for the future in math education* (pp. 315–348). Mahwah, NJ: Erlbaum.

Lester, F. K., & Kehle, P. E. (2003). From problem solving to modeling: The evolution of thinking about research on complex mathematical activity. In R. A. Lesh & H. M. Doerr (Eds.), *Beyond constructivism: Models and modeling perspectives on mathematics problem solving, learning, and teaching* (pp. 501–518). Mahwah, NJ: Erlbaum.

Noss, R., Hoyles, C., & Pozzi, S. (2002). Abstraction in expertise: A study of nurses' conceptions of concentration. *Journal for Research in Mathematics Education, 33*, 204–229.

Polya, G. (1945). *How to solve it.* Princeton, NJ: Princeton University Press.

Prediger, S. (2005). Developing reflectiveness in mathematics classrooms—An aim to be reached in several ways. *ZDM-The International Journal on Mathematics Education, 37*, 250–257.

Romberg, T. A., Carpenter, T. P., & Kwako, J. (2005). Standards-based reform and teaching for understanding. In T. A. Romberg, T. P. Carpenter & F. Dremock (Eds.), *Understanding mathematics and science matters.* Mahwah, NJ: Erlbaum.

Sabelli, N. H. (2006). Complexity, technology, science, and education. *The Journal of the Learning Sciences, 15*(1), 5–9.

Schoenfeld, A. (1992). Learning to think mathematically: Problem solving, metacognition, and sense making in mathematics. In D. A. Grouws (Ed.), *Handbook of research on mathematics teaching and learning: A project of the National Council of Teachers of Mathematics* (pp. 334–370). New York: Macmillan.

Selter, C. (1994). How old is the captain? *Strategies, 5*(1), 34–37.

Silver, E. A. (1985). Research on teaching mathematical problem solving: Some underrepresented themes and needed directions. In E. A. Silver (Ed.), *Teaching and learning mathematical problem solving. Multiple research perspectives* (pp. 247–266). Hillsdale, NJ: Erlbaum.

Sriraman, B., & Steinthorsdottir, O. (2007). Research into practice: Implications of research on mathematics gifted education for the secondary curriculum. In C. Callahan & J. Plucker (Eds.), *Critical issues and practices in gifted education: What the research says* (pp. 395–408). Austin, TX: Prufrock Press.

Stevens, R. (2000). Who counts what as mathematics: Emergent and assigned mathematics problems in a project-based classroom. In J. Boaler (Ed.), *Multiple perspectives on mathematics teaching and learning* (pp. 105–144). Westport, CT: Ablex Publishing.

Streefland, L. (1993). The design of a mathematics course. A theoretical reflection. *Educational Studies in Mathematics, 25*, 109–135.

Swan, M., Turner, R., Yoon, C., & Muller, E. (2007). The roles of modelling in learning mathematics. In W. Blum, P. L. Galbraith, H.-W. Henne, & M. Niss (Eds.), *Modelling and applications in mathematics education* (ICMI Study 14; pp. 275–284). New York: Springer.

Tate, W. F. (1995). Returning to the root: A culturally relevant approach to mathematics pedagogy. *Theory into Practice, 34*, 166–173.

Usiskin, Z. (2004). The arithmetical operations as mathematical models. In H.-W. Henn & W. Blum (Eds.), *Pre-conference volume, ICMI Study 14: Applications and modelling in mathematics education* (pp. 279–284). Dortmund, Germany: University of Dortmund.

ENGLISH

Verschaffel, L., De Corte, E., & Borghart, I. (1997). Pre-service teachers' conceptions and beliefs about the role of real-world knowledge in mathematical modeling of school word problems. *Learning and Instruction, 7*, 339–360.
Verschaffel, L., Greer, B., & De Corte, E. (2000). *Making sense of word problems*. Lisse, The Netherlands: Swets & Zeitlinger.
Zawojewski, J., & McCarthy, L. (2007). Numeracy in practice. *Principal Leadership, 7*, 32–38.

Lyn D. English
School of Mathematics, Science, and Technology Education
Queensland University of Technology
Australia

CPSIA information can be obtained at www.ICGtesting.com
Printed in the USA
BVOW04*1430230914

367606BV00005B/54/P

9 789087 909376